Y0-DOV-685

DATE DUE

GAYLORD			PRINTED IN U.S.A.

NEW HORIZONS IN THE ECONOMICS OF INNOVATION

Series Editor: Christopher Freeman, *Emeritus Professor of Science Policy, SPRU – Science and Technology Policy Research, University of Sussex, UK*

Technical innovation is vital to the competitive performance of firms and of nations and for the sustained growth of the world economy. The economics of innovation is an area that has expanded dramatically in recent years and this major series, edited by one of the most distinguished scholars in the field, contributes to the debate and advances in research in this most important area.

The main emphasis is on the development and application of new ideas. The series provides a forum for original research in technology, innovation systems and management, industrial organization, technological collaboration, knowledge and innovation, research and development, evolutionary theory and industrial strategy. International in its approach, the series includes some of the best theoretical and empirical work from both well-established researchers and the new generation of scholars.

Titles in the series include:

Innovation and Small Enterprises in the Third World
Edited by Meine Pieter van Dijk and Henry Sandee

Innovation, Growth and Social Cohesion
The Danish Model
Bengt-Åke Lundvall

The Economics of Power, Knowledge and Time
Michèle Javary

Innovation in Multinational Corporations in the Information Age
The Experience of the European ICT Industry
Grazia D. Santangelo

Environmental Policy and Technological Innovation
Why Do Firms Adopt or Reject New Technologies?
Carlos Montalvo Corral

Government, Innovation and Technology Policy
An International Comparative Analysis
Sunil Mani

Innovation Networks
Theory and Practice
Edited by Andreas Pyka and Günter Küppers

Systems of Innovation and Development
Evidence from Brazil
Edited by José E. Cassiolato, Helena M.M. Lastres and Maria Lucia Maciel

Innovation, Competence Building and Social Cohesion in Europe
Towards a Learning Society
Edited by Pedro Conceição, Manuel V. Heitor and Bengt-Åke Lundvall

The Dynamics of Innovation Clusters
A Study of the Food Industry
Magnus Lagnevik, Ingegerd Sjöholm, Anders Lareke and Jacob Östberg

Innovation, Competence Building and Social Cohesion in Europe

Towards a Learning Society

Edited by

Pedro Conceição and Manuel V. Heitor

Center for Innovation, Technology and Policy Research, Instituto Superior Técnico, Technical University of Lisbon, Portugal

Bengt-Åke Lundvall

Professor of Economics, Department of Business Studies, Aalborg University, Denmark

NEW HORIZONS IN THE ECONOMICS OF INNOVATION

Edward Elgar
Cheltenham, UK • Northampton, MA, USA

Published by
Edward Elgar Publishing Limited
Glensanda House
Montpellier Parade
Cheltenham
Glos GL50 1UA
UK

Edward Elgar Publishing, Inc.
136 West Street
Suite 202
Northampton
Massachusetts 01060
USA

A catalogue record for this book
is available from the British Library

Library of Congress Cataloguing in Publication Data
Innovation, competence building, and social cohesion in Europe : towards a
    learning society / edited by Pedro Conceiçao and Manuel V. Heitor, Bengt-Åke
    Lundvall.
        p. cm. — (New horizons in the economics of innovation series)
    "Supported by the target Socio-economic Research, TSER, during the 5th
    Framework Programme for RTD of the European Union" —Pref.
    Edited papers prepared following a seminar held at Quinta da Marinha,
    Guincho, Lisbon on May 23-30, 2000, and following the Lisbon Summit in
    March 2002.
    Includes bibliographical references and index.
    1. Information society—European Union countries—Congresses. 2.
    Technological innovations—Social aspects—European Union countries. 3.
    European Union countries—Economic policy—Congresses. 4. European
    Union countries—Social policy—Congresses. 5. Social change—European
    Union countries—Congresses. 6. Organizational learning—European Union
    countries. I. Conceiçao, Pedro. II. Heitor, M. V. (Manuel V.), 1957– III.
    Lundvall, Bengt-Åke, 1941– IV. New horizons in the economics of
    innovation.

    HC240.9.I55157 2003
    303.48'3'094—dc21
                                                                    2003049039

ISBN 1 84064 980 1

Printed and bound in Great Britain by MPG Books Ltd, Bodmin, Cornwall

Contents

Figures

Tables

Contributors

Cristiano Antonelli is the Professor and Chair of Economics at the School of Communication Studies and at the Department of Economics of the University of Torino. He is vice president of the International Schumpeter Society, the managing editor of *Economics of Innovation and New Technology* and an associate editor of *Information Economics and Policy*. He is the co-editor of the Kluwer series on Economics of Science, Technology and Innovation. He has been a Rockefeller Fellow at MIT and a junior economist at the OECD. He has held appointments at the Victoria University of Manchester, and at the Universities of Paris-Dauphine, Nice and Aix-en-Provence. His most recent book is *The Microeconomics of Technological Systems*. (Oxford University Press, in press). Previous books include: *The Economics of Industrial Modernization* (with Pascal Petit and Gabriel Tahar) (Academic Press, 1992), *The Economics of Localized Technological Change and Industrial Dynamics* (Kluwer, 1995), and *The Microdynamics of Technological Change* (Routledge, 1999). He edited *New Information Technology and Industrial Change* (Kluwer, 1988) and *The Economics of Information Networks* (Elsevier, 1992).

Hans-Peter Blossfeld is Professor of Sociology (chair in theory and empirical analysis of social structures and economic systems) at the University of Bielefeld, Germany. He has published 16 books and over a hundred articles on social inequality, youth, family, and educational sociology, labour-market research, demography, social stratification and mobility, the modern methods of quantitative social research, and statistical methods for longitudinal data analysis. He directs the project GLOBALIFE (Life Courses in the Globalisation Process) and since 1990 he has been editor-in-chief of *European Sociological Review*.

Alison Booth is Professor of Economics at the University of Essex, editor-in-chief of *Labour Economics*, and research fellow of the CEPR and IZA. She has published extensively on the economics of training and of the trade union, as well as on employment protection.

João Caraça obtained a D.Phil. in Nuclear Physics at the University of Oxford (1973) and the Aggregation in Physics at the Lisbon Faculty of Sciences (1974). He is the Director of the Science Department of the Calouste Gulbenkian Foundation in Lisbon. He is also Full Professor of Science and Technology Policy at the Instituto Superior de Economia e Gestão of the Technical University de Lisbon, where he coordinates the MSc course in Economics and Management of Science and Technology. João Caraça is Science Adviser to the President of the Portuguese Republic and has published 140 scientific papers. His interests are centred on science and technology policy and on prospective studies. He authored *Do Saber ao Fazer: Porquê Organizar a Ciência* (1993), *Ciência* (1997), *Science et Communication* (1999) and *Entre a Ciência e a Consciência* (2002). He has also co-authored *Limits to Competition* (1995) and co-edited *O Futuro Tecnológico* (1999).

Roberto Carneiro is a former Education Minister (1987–91) and Regional and Local Government Junior Minister (1981–83) of Portugal. He teaches Education Policy at the Catholic University of Portugal and Public Policy Studies at the European Institute of Macau. Roberto Carneiro was a member of the UNESCO International Commission on Education for the 21st Century and is currently President of Grupo Forum, a leading multimedia publishing house. He acts as a senior consultant to several international organisations, namely the OECD, the World Bank, the Council of Europe, the UNESCO and the European Union.

Jesper Lindgaard Christensen graduated with a MA in economics from Aalborg University in 1988. In 1992 he became a PhD with a thesis on the role of finance in technological development. The PhD thesis was funded by the Danish Social Science Research Council. In 1993–94 he was a lecturer and assistant professor. In 1995–97 he was a research fellow with almost solely research obligations. In 1998–2001 he was an assistant professor, and in 2001 he became Professor of Industrial Dynamics in the Department of Business Studies, where he teaches both business administration education and economics education.

Pedro Conceição is Assistant Professor at the Instituto Superior Técnico (IST), Technical University of Lisbon, and a researcher at the Centre for Innovation, Technology and Policy Research at IST. He is also a Deputy Director and Senior Policy Analyst, Office of Development Studies, United Nations Development Programme, New York.

Duncan Gallie is a Fellow of Nuffield College, Oxford, and Professor of Sociology at the University of Oxford. He has carried out research on changes in employment relationships leading to the publication of *In Search of the New Working Class* (1978) and (as co-author) *Restructuring the Employment Relationships* (1998). He also has been actively involved in research on the social consequences of unemployment, co-editing *Social Change and Experience of Unemployment* (1993) and *Welfare Regimes and the Experience of Unemployment* (2000). He was coordinator, with Serge Paugam, of the collaborative Fourth Framework research programme – Employment Precarity, Unemployment and Social Exclusion.

Allan Næs Gjerding is Associate Professor of International Business Economics at the Department for Business Studies, Aalborg University, Denmark. He holds the degrees of Bachelor in Business Administration, Master in Economics, and PhD in Economics. He is associated with the Danish Research Unit for Industrial Dynamics (DRUID) and the International Business Economics Unit at Aalborg University. He is currently on leave from the University, occupying a position as Head of the Department for Regional Policy at the regional government of North Jutland, Denmark. He has been a researcher in the field of innovation economics since 1987 with a special emphasis on the interaction between technical and organisational innovation. Further information and bibliography are available at www.business.auc.dk/.

Manuel V. Heitor is Full Professor at the Instituto Superior Técnico (IST), Technical University of Lisbon, and Director of the IST's Centre for Innovation, Technology and Policy Research, IN+, http://in3.dem.ist.utl.pt. He also coordinates the IST's MSc Programmes on Engineering Policy and Management of Technology and on Engineering Design. Since 1995, he has been Senior Research Fellow of the IC2 Institute, Innovation, Creativity and Capital, the University of Texas at Austin, USA. He is a member of the advisory board of *Technological Forecasting and Social Change* and the *International Journal of Technology, Policy and Management*, where he has served as guest editor for several Special Issues. He chairs the Organising Committee of the series of International Conferences on Technology Policy and Innovation, http://in3.dem.ist.utl.pt/confpolicy/, which have been organised annually since 1997. He his co-editor of *Science, Technology and Innovation Policy: Opportunities and Challenges for the 21st Century* (1999) and *Knowledge for Inclusive Development* (2001), (QUORUM Publishers, http://in3.dem.ist.utl.pt/quorumseries/).

Edward Lorenz is Associate Researcher at the Centre d'Etudes de l'Emploi in Noisy-le-Grand and Professor at the University of Technology of Compiègne. He is also Associate Researcher at the Centre for Business Research, University of Cambridge and Associate Research Fellow at Birkbeck College, London. He has worked on economics of innovation, national systems of innovation and on comparative analysis of labour markets. His recent books include *The Economics of Trust and Learning* (Edward Elgar Publishing, 1998) (with Nathalie Lazaric) and *Knowledge, Learning and Routines*, (Edward Elgar, forthcoming) (with Nathalie Lazaric).

Bengt-Åke Lundvall is Professor of Economics in the Department of Business Studies, Aalborg University. In 1992–95 he was Deputy Director of DSTI, OECD. He has introduced the concepts of the 'innovation system' (together with Chris Freeman) and 'the learning economy' (together with Björn Johnson). His current research is focused on innovation and competence building in the context of the globalising learning economy (see Lundvall, B.-Å., *Innovation, Growth and Social Cohesion – the Danish Model*, 2002).

Lynn K. Mytelka is Director of the United Nations University Institute for New Technologies (UNU/INTECH) at Maastricht, The Netherlands, on leave from her post as Professor in the Faculty of Public Affairs and Management, Carleton University, Ottawa. From 1996 to 1999 she served as Director of the Division on Investment, Technology and Enterprise at the United Nations Conference on Trade and Development (UNCTAD) in Geneva. Professor Mytelka has researched and taught in the fields of technology, innovation and development with particular attention to learning and innovation at the enterprise level; clustering, innovation systems and regional integration; the technology and investment strategies of multinational corporations, and innovation policy. Her recent publications include: *Competition, Innovation and Competitiveness in Developing Countries* (edited) OECD Development Centre, 1999, *Technological Capabilities and Export Success in Asia* (edited with Dieter Ernst and Tom Ganiatsos) Routledge, 1998, 'Local Systems of Innovation in a Globalized World Economy', *Industry and Innovation* (June: 2000), 'Locational Tournaments for FDI: Inward Investment into Europe in a Global World', in Neil Hood and Stephen Young (eds) *The Globalisation of Multinational Enterprise Activity and Economic Development* (St. Martins Press, 1999), 'Strategic Partnerships and the Rise of Knowledge-Based Networked Oligopolies' (with Michel Delapierre), in C. Cutler, V. Haufler and T. Porter (eds) *Private Authority and International Affairs*, Binghamton: (SUNY Press, 1999), and 'Learning, Innovation and Industrial Policy: Some

Lessons from Korea' in M. Storper and L. Tsipouri (eds) *Industrial Policy for Latecomer Industrialization*, (Routledge, 1998).

Hannele Niemi is Professor of Education, and Dean of the Faculty of Education at the University of Helsinki. She has had many memberships of scientific councils, for example the Standing Committee of Social Sciences of the European Science Foundation, the Council for Society and Culture of the Academy of Finland and the Scientific Council of the University of Helsinki. She has been a chair, researcher and author for many national and international evaluation projects for development of quality of learning, teacher education and ICT in education. Her website: http://www.edu.helsinki.fi/ktl/hanneleniemi.htm

Maria João Rodrigues is Professor of Economics at the University of Lisbon – ISCTE and President of the Advisory Group of Social Sciences in the European Framework Programme, EC. She has served as Special Advisor of the Prime Minister of Portugal and has coordinated the Line of Action of the Portuguese Presidency of EU on "Employment, Economic Reforms and Social Cohesion", and of the European Council, that has defined the Lisbon strategy (2000). Among many other publications, Maria João Rodrigues has recently coordinated the *Report of the High Level Group on Industrial Relations and Change in the European Union*, European Commission, Directorate-General for Employment & Social Affairs, 2002, and edited *The New Knowledge Economy in Europe – A Strategy for International Competitiveness and Social Cohesion*, Edward Elgar, 2002.

Chiara Saraceno is Professor of Sociology at the University of Turin, Italy. She has published extensively on gender and the family, on social policies and on poverty and social exclusion. Among her publications are *Sociologia della Famiglia (Sociology of the Family)* (il Mulino 1996); (with Nicola Negri) *Politiche Contro la Povertà in Italia (Policies Against Poverty in Italy)* (il Mulino 1996); (with Marzio Barbagli) *Separarsi in Italia (Ending Marriage in Italy)* (il Mulino, 1998); 'Family Change, Family Policies and the Restructuring of Welfare', in *Family, Market and Community, Social Policy Studies* No. 21 (OECD, 1997), pp. 81–100. She is the Chair of the Commission on Social Exclusion in the Italian Prime Minister' Office.

Keith Smith is Senior Research Fellow at the United Nations University Institute for New Technologies (UNU/INTECH) at Maastricht, The Netherlands. He was trained at the Universities of Cambridge and Sussex. Following nine years as University Lecturer in Economics at the University of Keele, he was appointed as Economic Adviser to the Science Policy Council of Norway in 1988. From 1990 to 2000 he was Research Director of the

STEP Group in Oslo, carrying out a wide range of research on innovation issues for ministries, research councils and the European Commission. His main fields of research are innovation and economic growth, the development of innovation statistics and indicators, regional innovation, innovation in 'low technology' industries, and the economic and social organisation of knowledge production. From 1993 he was Professor at the Norwegian Science and Technology University. Keith Smith has worked extensively as a consultant to policy agencies on innovation policy, both at a national and international level, including the OECD and the EU. He has recently been a member of the expert panel 'Innovation Policies in the Knowledge-Based Society' for the European Commission, and deputy chairman of the Norwegian Government Commission on Tax Incentives for Business-Financed Research and Development.

Hilary Steedman is Senior Research Fellow at the Centre for Economic Performance at the LSE. She worked on international benchmarking of skills for the UK Government's Skills Audit in 1996 and for the Skills Task Force in 1999. She recently coordinated a three-year programme of research on the future of low skilled work in Europe – the NEWSKILLS project – for the European Commission.

James Wickham is Jean Monnet Professor of European Labour Market Studies in the Department of Sociology at Trinity College Dublin. He has researched and published on Irish industrialisation and labour market issues, especially in the electronics industry. Main interests: high technology industry and high skill labour markets, equal opportunities, sustainable development and transport. He is Director of the Employment Research Centre (http://www.tcd.ie/erc)

Preface

Maria João Rodrigues

Innovation, competence building, social cohesion and the learning society in Europe are the key words which led an important research line supported by the Target Socio-Economic Research, TSER, during the Fifth Framework Programme for RTD of the European Union.

This book gathers outstanding papers of this research agenda which also inspired a renewal of the European agenda for economic and social development with a new focus: preparing the transition to a knowledge-based economy and, as the authors highlight, building a learning society.

The implementation of this new European strategy, adopted at the Lisbon Summit (March 2000), is now raising interesting issues for further research, encouraged by the Sixth Framework Programme and the European Research Area. This preface will also be used to suggest some of these key issues for research.

THE RESEARCH AGENDA AS A POINT OF DEPARTURE OF A EUROPEAN STRATEGY

In our preparations for the Lisbon Summit, we faced the following main question: Is it possible to update Europe's development strategy so that we can rise to the new challenges resulting from globalisation, technological change and population ageing, while preserving European values? In the new emerging paradigm, knowledge and innovation are the main sources of both wealth and divergence between nations, companies and individuals. Europe is losing ground to the United States, but this does not mean we have to copy them.

The purpose was to define a European way to evolve to the new innovation- and knowledge-based economy, with distinctive attributes ranging from the preservation of social cohesion and cultural diversity to the technological options themselves. A critical step would be to set up a competitive platform that can sustain the European social model, which should also be renewed.

Answering this question requires institutional innovations, if we want to tap into the potential of this new paradigm while avoiding risks of social division. We need innovation, for example, of norms regulating international trade and competition, of social models, and of education systems. Moreover, in each and every Member State of the European Union, institutional innovation has to internalise the level of integration accomplished through the single market and the single currency. This means that some level of European coordination is required to carry out institutional reforms, while respecting national specificity. A multilevel governance system is needed that enables its various levels (that is, European, national and local) to interact. Our purpose was to ascertain which institutional reforms could change the way in which European societies are currently regulated, so as to pave the way for a new development trajectory towards a knowledge-based economy.

The European economic and social model is being confronted with the new conditions created by globalisation, technological change and ageing trends. A paradigm shift is under way: the transition to a knowledge-based economy with implications for all social institutions. Acknowledging this new horizon, a long term strategy for economic and social modernisation was adopted by the Lisbon European Council in 2000, in order to foster and to shape this transition according to the main values of the European project. The European way can be identified by its main concern with social cohesion, cultural diversity and subsidiarity.

We can illustrate some of the implications of this European strategy for the redesign of public policies (Rodrigues, 2002):

- *information society policy* is focusing on spreading the access to the internet and broadband, fostering knowledge-intensive products and services in health, education and transport and encouraging content industries in different languages;
- *research policy* is being redeployed to create a European research area and to improve coordination among national programmes towards some common priorities, while respecting national diversity;
- *innovation policy* is targeting knowledge management by companies and by networks operating at local and international level, with a special focus on SMEs;
- *education policy* is developing new priorities, such as spreading new competences, building local learning centres open to all social groups, and developing access to different languages and cultures;
- *employment policies* are putting the emphasis on employability and adaptability, underpinned by stronger opportunities for lifelong

learning and more flexible working time management over the life cycle;

- *social inclusion policy* is tackling not only old forms of social exclusion, but also new forms related to the risk of a 'digital divide';
- *macroeconomic policies* are not only controlling public deficit and debt levels, but also improving the quality of public finances, according higher priority to research, education, training and innovation;
- *the goal of sustainable development* encompasses the environmental, economic and social dimensions with implications for the new global agenda which the European Union is trying to formulate in the international fora.

This new strategic focus of policy making is already leading to relevant outcomes, but they are likely to increase with further research on the very nature and the implications of a knowledge-based economy and a learning society.

THE TRANSITION TO A KNOWLEDGE-BASED ECONOMY

Why can we speak about knowledge-based economies? If knowledge has always been present in human societies, what is making the difference? The difference exists because we are entering a new mode of knowledge production, diffusion and utilisation due to three main factors:

- the impact of information and communication technologies;
- the social perception of knowledge as a strategic asset;
- the increasingly sophisticated procedures to codify and to manage knowledge involved in a learning society.

These three factors are gradually transforming:

- knowledge production by researchers, artists, and engineers as well as by the various social communities developing the various forms of life: working life, family life, leisure, public space;
- knowledge diffusion by telecommunication networks, content industries, media, education and training;
- knowledge utilisation by companies, public services, local authorities and the different actors of civil society.

All this is taking place in a globalised and plural world, which is being completely reorganised by the poles, companies, cities, and centres of excellence which are taking a leading role in knowledge production, diffusion and utilisation. The new competitive factors are reorganising the international hierarchies in economy, culture and geo-politics.

Knowledge is becoming the main source of the wealth of nations, companies, and people, but it can also become the main factor of inequality. Therefore, public policies at national, European and international levels, should be more concerned to facilitate access to knowledge and enhance creative and learning capacities. This is why we can also speak about knowledge policies, aiming at competence building in a learning society.

Knowledge policies can be defined as the policies aimed at fostering and shaping this transition to a knowledge-based society.

In terms of knowledge production, these policies support basic research, applied research and development as well as culture industries and they encourage dialogue among different cultures, social groups and generations.

In terms of knowledge diffusion, these policies develop broadband networks, spread access to the internet, promote content industries and their dissemination by different media, and reform education and training towards what we can call a learning society.

In terms of knowledge utilisation, these policies foster innovation in products and process, as well as knowledge management and learning organisations in companies and public services, as well also as local and international partnerships for innovation.

Against this background, we can highlight new roles for the policies which notably concern research, culture, media, innovation, the information society, education and training, and even employment, social inclusion and regional development. Moreover, some implications should also be drawn for macroeconomic policies and their impact on structural change. Budgetary policies should give a stronger priority to knowledge policies and even tax policies should encourage new patterns of behaviour in line with these policies.

Knowledge policies are being reinforced in the general architecture of the European strategy for economic and social development. This trend should be based on more precise scientific elaborations.

A LEARNING SOCIETY

A knowledge-based economy is based on people, their creativity, their initiative but also their ability to learn more systematically. To cope with rapid change and the new conditions created by information technologies, people should be able to return to learning throughout their lives. Well-trained elites are not enough to deal with this pace of change. This is not only a matter of growth potential, competitiveness and employability but it is becoming a matter of basic citizenship and of civilisation. Learning enables people to play a full part in their community, family, neighbourhood, workplace and public space. Learning is important not only to increase economic performance, but also to enhance the capacity to participate in public life and to enjoy sport or art. Moreover, the synergies among these different dimensions of life are increasing.

Without a learning society, this transition to a knowledge-based economy will create new and deep social divides.

Therefore, a knowledge-base economy also means a learning society, with a higher demand for knowledge and more powerful instruments to answer to this increasing demand. The answer must go well beyond a new reform of the traditional education and training systems. Many other forms of supplying knowledge can be developed and combined, more custom-made for each individual:

- multimedia databases are becoming available through the internet and CD-ROMs;
- interactive television and specialised cable channels are addressing more particular demands;
- some libraries are turning into more active knowledge resource centres;
- some schools and training centres are evolving in more open learning centres;
- some companies are developing learning organisations.

All these new instruments are not replacing the more traditional ones, such as the book or the teacher, which remain crucial, but must be reinvented in the context of this wide multimedia learning process.

On the other hand, the increase in knowledge demand depends on many conditions, such as these:

- each individual should be encouraged to develop his/her own personal and professional project, on the basis of a regular assessment of competences as well as effective guidance services;
- a framework of basic competences and of the main occupational profiles should be regularly updated and made widespread;
- companies should focus more systematically on developing their competences tree in order to meet competitive targets;

- collective bargaining and individual labour contracts should incorporate more explicit rights and duties concerning lifelong learning in order to promote competitiveness and employability;
- working time management and child care facilities should create better conditions for lifelong learning;
- the costs of this investment should be shared between public authorities, companies and individuals according to the relative benefits of each initiative.

FOSTERING INNOVATION IN THE EUROPEAN LANDSCAPE

With this approach we are at the very heart of a strategy to speed up the transition to a knowledge-based society. The creation of knowledge by research is central but is not enough to ensure economic growth. Technology transfer and diffusion are not an automatic process. As shown by the more recent growth models which endogenise technical progress, R&D can affect total factors productivity growth since it is coupled with innovation aiming at more added value. And to speed up innovation, the interactions within the innovation systems are crucial. This was a fundamental background to defining the strategy adopted at the Lisbon Summit towards 'a Europe of knowledge and innovation', quoting the expression used at that moment.

Nevertheless, it is not easy to develop a policy for innovation at European level, and this for three main reasons. Firstly, because there is a huge diversity in national systems of innovation. Secondly, because Member States, in spite of important differences, still present many shortcomings and system failures if the aim is to enhance their potential for innovation. Finally, because it is important to clarify what should be done at European level and what should remain at national or even local level.

Building on existing experience, a new framework for innovation policy was adopted in the European Union as requested by the Lisbon Summit, using the open method of coordination and pointing out five priorities to be adapted by each Member State (European Comission, 2001):

- improving the coherence of innovation policies, namely by ensuring coordinating mechanisms between the different departments responsible for matters relevant to innovation, at regional, national and European levels;
- creating a regulatory framework conducive to innovation, namely by adapting the rules for diffusion, exploitation and transfer of research

and by putting in place fiscal incentives to private investment in research and innovation as well as employment of researchers;

- encouraging the creation and growth of innovative enterprises, namely by creating a legal, fiscal and financial environment favourable to the creation of start-ups, by developing support services including incubators and by spreading educational and training schemes in entrepreneurship and innovation;
- improving the key interfaces in the innovation system, namely by stimulating regional initiatives for networking the innovation system, by developing education and training programmes addressing the skill gaps, by encouraging universities to promote the diffusion of knowledge and technologies and by stimulating large public research facilities to improve their partnerships with enterprises;
- promoting a society open to innovation, namely by encouraging comprehensive 'stakeholder' debates on innovation involving scientists, industry, consumers and public authorities and by stimulating public demand for innovation with dynamic purchasing policies.

The innovation policy is at the core of the Lisbon strategy as it is a kind of catalyst to speed up the transition to a knowledge-based economy. More general framework conditions for the success of this innovation policy are pointed out by the overall Lisbon strategy. This is the case, for instance, with the policies for education and training, for the modernisation of the financial markets and for the reorientation of the European research policy. Innovation policy is a very particular policy because it works with the interfaces of the other policies, focusing the key elements of the innovation system, fostering not only technological but social innovation. Therefore, taking into account this specificity, some key issues for further development should be suggested:

- to improve the methods for learning and competence building in education institutions, companies and so on as a basic condition for innovation;
- to improve the different forms of networking and clustering as a basic device for innovation;
- to develop new types of enterprise as the key actors of a knowledge-based economy;
- to develop and to make more sophisticated the most knowledge-intensive services and markets for knowledge as a precondition of innovation;

- to improve the governance of the innovation systems and in particular the coordination of public policies at regional, national and European levels (OECD, 2002).

The present book offers many intellectual resources to address these issues and paves the way for highly very relevant research.

REFERENCES

European Commission, *Communication: Innovation in a Knowledge-Driven Economy*, Ref. COM (2000) 567 final, 20.09.2000.

OECD, (2002), *Dynamising National Innovation Systems*, Paris: OECD.

Rodrigues, Maria João (coord. with the collaboration of Robert Boyer, Manuel Castells, Gøsta Esping-Andersen, Robert Lindley, Bengt-Åke Lundvall, Luc Soete and Mario Telò) (2002), *The New Knowledge Economy in Europe – A Strategy for International Competitiveness and Social Cohesion*, Cheltenham and Northampton, MA: Edward Elgar.

Acknowledgements

This book includes a set of original contributions aimed at capturing new socioeconomic trends and finding policy strategies promoting the learning society in Europe through joint efforts and integrated actions on innovation, competence building and social cohesion. It was prepared and edited following a meeting organised in Guincho, on the coast of Lisbon, during the period 28–30 May 2000, which was conceived in the context of the Portuguese presidency of the EU and following the Lisbon Summit in March 2000, which defined new policy horizons for Europe. Then, the work associated with the preparation of the book was partly integrated in a project promoted by the Portuguese Observatory of Science and Technology (Portuguese Observatory for Sciences and Higher Education, http://www.oces.mces.pt, from the summer 2002) through the Center for Innovation, Technology and Policy Research at Instituto Superior Técnico, Lisbon, http://in3.dem.ist.utl.pt, in order to improve understanding of innovation in Portugal within a diversified European context.

The aim of the Guincho conference (http://in3.dem.ist.utl.pt/learning2000) was to review, discuss and integrate new developments in socioeconomic research on innovation, competence building and social cohesion in Europe, reflecting the Portuguese presidency's priorities for innovation and social cohesion. The conference brought together nearly 250 scientists, engineers, managers, entrepreneurs and policy makers from over 25 different countries and was organised so as to enhance interactions and activities with key representatives from the academic, business and government sectors. The event also aimed at interrelating the EC's Target Socio Economic Research (TSER) three broad research areas (science and technology policy options; education and training; and social exclusion and social integration) with the objectives of the key actions on socioeconomic research.

Thanks are due to many individuals and institutions that helped in various ways to bring this project to fruition. We thank the chapter authors for sharing their insights and perspectives on a range of important topics regarding technology policy and innovation. In addition, the leading contributions of James Galbraith, The University of Texas at Austin, and of Jean-Pierre Contzen, Instituto Superior Técnico, to the Guincho conference are acknowledged. We are grateful to our colleagues members of the Guincho conference's Organising and Programme Committees for planning the conference and for having made possible such a high level forum. A special acknowledgement goes to Virginia Vitorino, and colleagues at the EC's Key Action on Socioeconomic Research programme, who made the Guincho conference possible. The support of Teresa Patrício from the Institute for International Science and Technology Cooperation of the Portuguese Ministry of Science and Technology, and of John Smith from the European Science Foundation, are much appreciated. And we are grateful to those who so effectively managed the event, in particular the staff at the Centre for Innovation, Technology, and Policy Research, Lisbon, Portugal. Finally, we are especially grateful for the dedicated and excellent publication effort of Alexandra Coimeiro, also at the Centre for Innovation, Technology, and Policy Research, at IST, Lisbon.

The Guincho conference and the project of this book were supported by the European Commission's Key Action on Socioeconomic Research, http://www.cordis.lu/improving/, the Portuguese Science and Technology Foundation, http://www.fct.mces.pt/, the Portuguese Observatory of Science and Technology, (Portuguese Observatory for Sciences and Higher Education, http://www.oces.mces.pt, from the summer 2002), the Institute for International Science and Technology Cooperation of the Portuguese Ministry of Science and Technology, (Office for International Relations in Science and Higher Education, http://www.grices.mces.pt/, from the summer 2002), and the Portuguese-American Development Foundation, http://www.flad.pt. Thanks are also due to the Instituto Superior Técnico, http://www.ist.utl.pt/, for co-sponsorship.

Lisbon, January 2003

Pedro Conceição
Manuel V. Heitor
Bengt-Åke Lundvall

INTRODUCTION

1. Towards a learning society

Pedro Conceição, Manuel V. Heitor and Bengt-Åke Lundvall

1.1 COMMONPLACES AND UNCERTAINTIES

We would not be adding much, nor creating controversy, by saying that we live in a context in which knowledge is becoming increasingly important. However, saying that 'knowledge is increasingly important' is obviously ambiguous. It is important for what? What do we mean by 'important'? What does 'increasingly' really mean: does it refer to the last few months, the last couple of years, the last decade? The lack of surprise at, or questioning of, our initial statement is a testimony to the level of agreement around the relevance of concepts associated with the information society or the knowledge economy. It has become a commonplace to say that 'knowledge is increasingly important'. Commonplaces are comfortable, but often sterile, both intellectually and in terms of suggesting actions to private and public decision makers.

In this book, we have taken on the challenge of attempting to probe deeper into the relationships between knowledge and development. Our inspiration comes from the contribution of Lundvall and Johnson (1994), who challenge the commonplace by introducing the simple, but powerful, idea of learning. Lundvall and Johnson speak to us of a 'learning economy', not of a 'knowledge economy'. The fundamental difference is associated with a dynamic perspective. In their view, some knowledge does indeed become more important, but there is also knowledge that becomes *less* important. There is both knowledge creation *and* knowledge destruction. By forcing us to look at the process, rather than the mere accumulation of knowledge, Lundvall and Johnson add a dimension that makes the discussion more complex and more uncertain, but also more interesting and intellectually fertile. The richness associated with the concept of the learning economy is demonstrated in the volume edited by Archibugi and Lundvall (2001).

We attempt to extend the concern associated with the process and with its dynamic character even further. Thus, the subtitle of the book is 'Towards a Learning Society', implying movement, unfinished business, an ongoing process. Also, each part of the book is titled using a verb that suggests actions oriented to contributing to making progress *towards* a learning society. So, the verbs in the titles of the parts should not be regarded in a normative sense (suggesting what should be done) but rather as a way to suggest movement, a dynamic perspective. The contributions are organised in four parts. The first two parts deal with innovation, respectively at the policy and institutional levels. Then, Parts Three and Four deal with competence and social cohesion respectively. This is because we focus on the three lines of thrust that propel us towards the learning society: innovation, competence and social cohesion.

'Innovation' is really the word that best fits with the idea of the knowledge economy understood from a dynamic perspective. Lundvall and Johnson's learning economy is about new knowledge replacing old knowledge. This dynamics is very close to Schumpeter's concept of 'creative destruction', which was his way of describing the innovation process. Innovation is associated with creativity, with the generation of new ideas, but it is also about initiative and risk taking. In fact, invention is a necessary condition for innovation, but it is clearly not sufficient. Innovation entails bringing new ideas to fruition in the marketplace, satisfying demands or creating new needs, in a process that improves overall welfare. This requires at least two distinct levels of analysis, namely: (i) considering policy approaches and their links with theory building; and (ii) taking into account the institutional perspective and inter-firm organisational changes and innovations.

Competence is the foundation based upon which innovation emerges. Competence is equally fuelled by innovation itself. Competence is associated with skills and capacities, both individual and collective. It is important to stress that new skills are part of the competence foundation, but we are not necessarily arguing that technological change is skill-biased. It may often be, but there are also cases in which it is not. When we consider competence we focus on a 'higher order of skills' as Carneiro (Chapter Eight in this volume) asserts. These generic skills include higher levels of education (who can ever be against more education?) but also capacities that are more generic, such as creativity, risk taking, and initiative.

Finally, social cohesion provides the contextual environment that defines how the benefits of innovation and competence are shared. Do the progress and development associated with more innovative and competent societies have to be bought at the cost of the exclusion of some? Is it even compatible to speak about a learning society if large shares of the population are not included in the process? Beyond the more ethical or justice-associated concerns, do we not increase the likelihood of having innovation and better competence if we improve social cohesion?

By choosing the three themes (innovation, competence and social cohesion) that we consider in this volume as contributing to the learning society we move from the space of consensus associated with commonplaces into the realm of uncertainty. Why do we take only these three themes, and do not include others? There are clearly other issues of major importance, especially if we consider the objective of achieving a learning society in Europe, namely those associated with macroeconomic conditions – including the development of the Euro – trade and globalisation, and the environment, to name but a few. The point is that we do not intend to be comprehensive. Our aim is to look for insights through the contributions collected in this volume. We turn now to the presentation of these contributions, in the context chosen by us to organise the conceptual approach to the book.

1.2 THE IMPORTANCE OF PROMOTING INNOVATION POLICIES

It is by now well understood that the early conceptualisations of innovation as a linear process were clearly insufficient to describe the complexity and contingency of the innovative effort of people, firms and countries. Nelson (1993) shows the complexity and diversity across countries of *national innovation systems*. The most often cited reference associated with the interactive – as opposed to linear – understanding of innovation is Kline and Rosenberg (1986). In the interactive model the innovation is depicted as a multi-layer process with multiple feedbacks between different activities and functional units of the firm. Innovation does not flow linearly from R&D and does not result only from knowledge generated within the firm.

The 'European school', in parallel, has equally developed the more sophisticated approaches to innovation like those led by Rosenberg and others across the Atlantic. Freeman and Soete (1997) summarise the main conclusions of this school, and Dosi (1988) provides an integrative review of the main differences between these perspectives and traditional neoclassical approaches in economics. The fundamental difference, at the microeconomic level, is associated with the rejection of the representative production function. Nelson and Winter (1982) attempted to provide an epistemological alternative to microeconomic foundations of neoclassical modelling.

Still, what is surprising is the extent to which the linear perspective still informs much of today's public perceptions about innovation, as well as policy design and implementation. The reliance on simple and direct indicators such as expenditure on R&D by the private sector, and the obsession in some circles associated with improving these types of indicators, reflects the dominance of the linear perspective.

We do not question the importance of these and other indicators; we are merely asserting that they provide an incomplete description of the innovation process and are tied to the linear perspective. A recent example is Guellec and Pottelsberghe (2000). While their paper is methodologically well constructed, it is informed in its conceptual approach (even if only implicitly) by the linear model. The authors' conclusions have clear policy implications, which may very well be right, but they need to be circumscribed by the constraints imposed a priori by the linear approach.

Romer (1993) recognises the importance of what he calls *appreciative theories* of growth and innovation (following the introduction of the term by Nelson and Winter, 1982) in helping more formal approaches to better describe the richness of the innovation process. Somehow, the link has been hard to accomplish, possibly due to insurmountable epistemological differences between scholars in the neoclassical tradition and others of a more appreciative nature.

The link between the complexity of the innovation process and the special economic characteristics of knowledge could be a bridge. In fact, Romer (1990) constructs his theory of endogenous growth drawing on the non-rival nature of ideas. Dasgupta and David (1994) advance new ideas about the economics of science building also on the same principles associated with the special characteristics of knowledge.

Using the economic characteristics of knowledge is useful not only as a modelling tool, allowing the development of new conceptual approaches, but also as a guide for policy. Policy implications in terms of innovation policy were proposed by Nelson and Romer (1996). And, in a series of papers, Conceição and Heitor (1999, 2001) and Conceição, Heitor and Oliveira (1998) have explored the implications of the non-rival character of ideas and the rival character of tacit knowledge to advance policies associated with higher education policy.

Caraça introduces the part of this volume dealing with innovation policy taking into account the non-rival character of ideas and the rival character of tacit knowledge and advances a new approach to the economic significance of knowledge and learning. For Caraça, the essence of knowledge is sharing: after two people communicate an idea they both have it. This reflects the non-rival character of knowledge. But his novel twist is associated with the *process* of communicating, that is to say, with the process of transmitting and apprehending knowledge. This is not an easy process, being, in fact, based on language (a complex construction) and giving rise to possible miscommunication and misapprehension of the message. This creates the equivalent of 'scarcity' in the transaction of tangible goods and services: the constraint that limits, and moulds, the economic transactions of knowledge.

Caraça takes the evolution from the linear to the interactive approach to innovation in a historical context, associated with the evolving perceptions concerning the relative importance of what he calls 'disciplinary knowledge': knowledge that is highly specialised and associated with 'larger and highly developed repositories of meaning'. The creation of this type of knowledge is influenced by social processes, and the interaction between the social aspects and the nature of disciplinary knowledge defines the context that leads to policy formulation. Thus, while the linear perspective leads to policies oriented to the promotion of science – that will somehow trickle down into innovations – the recognition and growing interaction with society have led to policies oriented towards the diffusion of innovations.

The issues raised by Caraça are addressed in detail in the three chapters included in Part One of this volume. Lynn Mytelka and Keith Smith consider the co-evolving process of policy making and theory building, which has been critical to improving our knowledge of innovation patterns. Antonelli brings us back to the conceptual issues, and policy implications, associated with the economics of innovation. Antonelli moves Caraça's discussion of the interactions between innovation and society on to the discussion of the interaction between innovation *studies* (economics of innovation) and other areas of scholarship, claiming that areas ranging from sociology to philosophy have been important influences on the economics of innovation. Finally, Pedro Conceição and Manuel Heitor introduce the need to consider innovation policy formulation in the presence of diversity. They argue that the unified goal of building integrated R&D and innovation policies across the EU requires policies that are designed in an integrated way, but that are implemented with diversified actions. 'Policy integration' should occur across a 'portfolio dimension', since innovation policies require coordination across several areas.

1.3   THE NEED TO STIMULATE ORGANISATIONAL INNOVATION

Enterprise organisation has become central to the policy debate on the sources of European competitiveness, leading to the promotion of many forms of organisational change. As noted by Edward Lorenz in Part Two of this volume, this has derived from the growing recognition that ICT investments alone generally fail to deliver improved enterprise performance, which require adequate human practices among a complex set of other interrelations.

The need for organisational innovation has promoted in recent years a large number of works contesting a traditional, neoclassical understanding of the firm and the economy. The emerging knowledge perspective is concerned with the role of technological change and firm behaviour in economic growth. The foundations of this approach can be found in the work of Joseph Schumpeter (1942), but its main development and application was made by Nelson and Winter in their seminal work on evolutionary economics (Nelson and Winter, 1982). In their approach, the firm is understood essentially as a repository of knowledge, which is translated into routines that guide organisational action. Building on these perspectives and on earlier work in organisational theory that emphasised the mechanisms for the growth of firms (Penrose, 1959), a knowledge-based vision of the firm has been under development in the last decade, offering new insights for strategy and management theory (Teece and Pisano, 1997). It includes natural systems and institutional theory while embracing global perspectives. Also, it encourages multidisciplinary perspectives to better explore the meaning of competitive advantage in developing, acquiring, and using knowledge for enhanced products and processes and in better understanding the interaction between organisations and the economy in which they are embedded.

In Part Two of this volume, we include various results that go beyond a perspective of theory building and include empirical results related to critical aspects of organisational innovation. Lorenz introduces this part of the volume, calling our attention to a diversified range of aspects influencing enterprise performance, which certainly represent barriers to the learning society in Europe. These include differences in the penetration rates of participatory work practices across European nations and in the speed of promoting flexibility at the workplace; the performance effects of the diffusion of high involvement work practices; the impact of new organisational practices on worker outcomes, and the impact of organisational change on employment and the demand for skills. The empirical studies in Part Two help elucidate these various aspects and improve understanding of the complex relation between organisational changes, economic performance and worker outcomes, leading to a learning society.

1.4   THE RELEVANCE OF COMPETENCE BUILDING

Competence is the foundation upon which innovation is generated and diffused. Competence is associated with individual skills, but also with collective capacities. It is also on competence that a learning society can be constructed and sustained. One 'commonplace' is to assume that technological change is (or has become) skill-biased, in the sense that it requires people with high skills. Specifically, digital computers and, more generically, information technologies, are considered the 'trend breaking technology' that is responsible for the inequality increases (Autor, Katz, and Krueger, 1997).

Empirical work supporting the skill-biased technological change conjecture includes studies such as Krueger (1993) on the direct implications of computers for the labour market. Still, the skill-biased technological change hypothesis is far from being uncontroversial. Criticisms have unfolded both on conceptual and empirical grounds. From a conceptual point of view, critics note that the treatment of technological change rarely goes beyond asserting that new technologies, and especially computers, are responsible for a steady increase in the demand for skills. Technology is conceptualised as an exogenous flow of innovations and as a purely public good, freely and universally available, as in the linear models of innovation described above. This simplified treatment of technology comes at a time when there is growing vitality in the study of technology and its micro and macroeconomic context, with attempts to formalise and to explore more sophisticated treatments of technology.

Criticisms based on empirical analysis include the outright refutation, namely by Di Nardo and Pishke (1997), of the association between computer usage and wage level proposed by, among others, the Krueger (1993) study. Other empirical problems include the mismatch in the timing of the increase in inequality and the spread in the diffusion of computers, and the fact that the increased adoption of information technology has not noticeably contributed to increased productivity (Galbraith, 1998, has a comprehensive review).

Alternatives to the skill-biased technological change hypothesis include the perspective advanced by Bresnahan (1999), who rejects (based both on what he regards as an inadequate treatment of technology as a residual and on the empirical difficulties mentioned in the last paragraph) the complementarity between computers and the human capital (or skills) of individual computer users. Instead, Bresnahan proposes an organisational complementarity between information technologies and telecommunications (ICTs) and highly skilled workers. In Bresnahan's model, ICTs, instead of improving the productivity of individual workers change the organisational structure of firms, reducing the need for back-office workers, and increasing the demand for front-office workers and managers.

Thus, skill-biased technological change has been advanced as an explanation for rising levels of income inequality. This explanation is grounded on the assumption that wages are the result of market clearing via the competitive pricing of the capabilities of people. Different capabilities are associated with different levels of skill, education, and seniority in the workforce. High skill/education/experience are associated with a higher marginal product of labour and command higher wages than low skill/education/experience. The evolution of the difference between the prices of skill, the relevant issue in studying changes in inequality, depends on the interaction between shifts in the relative demand for more skilled labour over less skilled workers and changes the relative supply of skilled labour.

There is, however, a second class of explanations, not necessarily excluding the labour market perspective outlined above, which puts much more emphasis on the role of institutions. Specifically, changes in the institutions that constrain the definition of wages override competitive forces in the dynamic evolution of income associated with rising inequality. These institutional changes include the weakening of unions – which erodes the bargaining power of low paid workers – changes in pay norms (more contingent employment and pay), and the decline in the real value of the minimum wage, which, as Freeman (1996) argues, can constitute an important redistributive tool.

A standard division of OECD countries according to these two classes of explanations places the US, and also the UK in the 1980s, in the realm of the labour market category, and the remaining OECD countries in the wage setting institutions class (Blau and Kahn, 1996). The reason, it is argued, is that the labour market in the US and the UK after the 1980s is much more free from the strength of collective, centralised bargaining than the remaining OECD countries. However, even for the OECD countries other than the US and the UK, the skill supply and demand hypothesis has been gaining momentum,[1] and thus we will spend some more time analysing this hypothesis.

There are two dimensions to the skill supply and demand story. The first concerns the validity of the assumption that labour market mechanisms are dominant in driving the dynamics of inequality. Assuming that the labour market provides a good framework for analysis, the second dimension relates to the ultimate causes that originate the labour market responses that generate inequality. At a very fundamental level, some scholars totally reject the validity of considering the existence of a labour market rewarding skill and human capital. Some of the critiques of the human capital theory and the returns to education occur even at the epistemological level. In fact, many sociologists oppose the mainstream economic theory of human capital, arguing that cultural and institutional factors are much more important in determining wages. Some authors have also argued that sociological and psychological factors, rather than economic factors associated with supply and demand for qualified labour, are dominant in setting wages.

Thus Dore (1976) differentiates 'education' from 'schooling', which refers to 'mere qualification-earning', leading to an 'educational inflation' spiral. Bourdieu and Passeron (1970), Jencks (1972), Boudon (1973) and

Bowles and Gintis (1976) are similarly skeptical about a direct relationship between increases in the level of education and economic performance. The differences between the economists of human capital and these other authors, who come primarily from sociology, remain up to the present day. In fact, some of the critiques have important parallels with economic perspectives, such as Bourdieu and Passeron's theory of the social filter, whereby schools work as filters to preserve and maintain social and educational differences, and the 'inheritance of inequality' perspective of Meade (1964).

However, if one is ready to accept the existence of a labour market where wages reward, at least partially, productivity and skill, Katz and Murphy (1992) provide strong evidence that supply and demand go a long way in explaining the patterns in the evolution of inequality. Most of the recent studies on inequality that focus on a single country longitudinal analysis of the evolution of the dispersion of income, follow Katz and Murphy (1992). Examples of the same methodology applied to other single country studies include Schmitt (1995) for the UK, and Edin and Holmlund (1995) for Sweden. Blau and Kahn (1996) apply a similar procedure to a cross-section of OECD countries for a single year.

This discussion clearly highlights the link between competence (skills, education), innovation (technological change) and social cohesion (economic inequality). The connection between education, skills and competence, on the one hand, and the learning society, on the other, is clearly discussed in Part Three of this volume. The various chapters in this part of the volume take the manifold interconnections between competence and the learning society and link them with the broader context of the anxieties and concerns, hopes and expectations that we live with today.

1.5   THE NEED FOR SOCIAL INCLUSION

When Henry Ford, at the outset of his industrial endeavours, was asked to whom he would sell his cars – then considered luxury objects especially in Europe – he allegedly replied that he would sell the cars, if things came to the worst, to his own employees. But Ford knew better; in fact, he knew that, in his own words, he was capable of building a car 'for the great multitude, constructed with the best materials after the simplest designs that modern engineering can devise, so low in price that no man making a good salary will be unable to own one'.[2] Clearly, two things were crucial to Ford's success. First, he had to be able to make good on his promise to use the best materials and designs, and the best engineering available. This is, in a sense, the technical challenge. But Ford also faced a second challenge: he needed a large enough number of Americans 'making a good salary' for his commercial enterprise to be successful.

The first challenge was met through a series of technological and organisational innovations. However, the second challenge related more to the economic and social conditions of America than to whatever Ford himself could do – beyond adding his own employees to the 'great multitude' he was aiming his cars at. Luckily for Ford, America at the time had a large enough number of people making a good salary for his commercial enterprise to be successful.

The previous paragraph's anecdote illustrates the importance of demand conditions to allow for technological diffusion. It is through the diffusion process that technological innovations are translated into wide economic impact, as more and more people and firms consume and use the new products or processes. And if we accept that this increasingly generalised usage of technological innovations fuels, not only increases in wellbeing, but also the conditions to generate further innovations, one cannot escape the importance of demand conditions for economic and technological prosperity. In fact, historians of economic evolution have shown that demand conditions were crucial in the process of early industrialisation in the US.

Rosenberg (1994) describes the demand conditions that were conducive to the earliest stages of industrialisation in the 19th century. In an economy that was primarily agricultural (in 1810, 80 per cent of active Americans were in agriculture), the most important resource was arable land, which was plentiful. This was, indeed, the most important source of wealth for economically active Americans, and the availability of land ensured a fairly equal distribution of this resource. This, in turn, meant that food prices were relatively low, allowing, for the same level of income, a higher margin left to buy non-food products.

This scenario is in stark contrast with the situation in Europe, where poor peasants and farm labourers had virtually no income beyond that needed for subsistence needs. The American conditions fuelled also a rise in fertility that was translated into a large population growth that could go and occupy even more of the still available fertile land, in a virtuous cycle of development. Therefore, the low level of economic inequality, coupled with a relatively high level of income per capita, generated the conditions that allowed for a demand of mass-manufactured goods.

The connection with Ford's history is provided by Rosenberg (1994: 115):

> Thus, out of the social and geographic conditions of land-abundant America emerged a set of tastes and preferences highly congenial to a technology capable of producing large quantities of standardized, low-priced goods. These circumstances even left their indelible imprint on the American automobile in the

early years of the twentieth century. The Ford Model T was designed in a manner which strongly resembled the horse and buggy, and the primary buyers were farmers for whom a cheap car offered a unique opportunity for overcoming rural isolation.

Therefore, demand conditions were important determinants in the diffusion of new technologies. In fact, in Rosenberg's argument, they were crucial to creating a new industrial system out of an agricultural society. Important components of the demand conditions were a relatively high level of income per capita and, equally crucial, a relatively egalitarian distribution of the marginal income available beyond that needed for subsistence. Inspired by this analysis of the interaction between inequality and technology, we are interested in understanding whether, with the current wave of technological innovations, there is also a relationship between levels of inequality at the country level and the rates of diffusion of technology.

The argument we are advancing here is that social cohesion, beyond the issues associated with ethical judgement and justice, can be of importance to efficiency as well. Galbraith (2000) proposes an interpretation of the economic success of the US over the 1990s that is associated, precisely, with this view.

For Galbraith, the reasons for the success of the American economy can be associated with the creation of a more equitable society, in which access to education is more generalised and where income is more equitably distributed than in Europe. The comparison between the distribution of income across Europe and across the US is based on taking Europe as a whole. That is, instead of comparing the US with individual European countries, Galbraith takes into account the large differences that exist across European countries (see also Galbraith, Conceição, and Ferreira, 1999).

In Galbraith's view, the US has made a large effort over time to create a more equitable country through the reinforcing of the role and services provided by the federal government, as the state governments become less and less relevant, especially in the determination of macroeconomic policies. In particular, the role played by the federal government in terms of social policy as been crucial in reducing geographic inequities. Additionally, an impetus should be given to the creation of large, publicly funded European universities in the less developed zones of Europe, mimicking the land grant act of the US in the mid 19th century, which led to the creation of focal points of development, especially in terms of innovation, dispersed around the US.

The major threat to social cohesion in Europe, according to Galbraith, is the relatively high level of unemployment and this is particularly discussed in Part Four of this volume. Gallie tackles the problem of unemployment from the perspective of the policies and institutions generating or mediating unemployment, finding, among other important things, that poverty is, indeed, often associated with unemployment. Then, Sarraceno takes the analysis of social cohesion from the perspective of 'local' communities or societies. The spatial patterns of social cohesion are clear and, according to several studies and Sarraceno's own perspective, largely self-reinforcing. Finally, Blossfeld considers the country level, arguing that country-specific institutions mould the way in which the impact of globalisation is felt across countries and, since institutions evolve and change, there are also dynamic implications for social cohesion.

More than answers, we are left with questions. But, again, the objective of this book is precisely to force us to think beyond commonplaces, which can be done quite effectively by raising questions. This is certainly more fertile than adding a voice to the chorus of commonplaces.

NOTES

1. Leuven, Oosterbeek and Ophem (1998) directly criticise Blau and Kahn (1996), and defend the claim that the skill supply and demand story is applicable also to a set of European OECD countries.
2. As cited in The Economist, Millennium Issue: 'Putting America on Wheels', (Dec. 23rd, 1999: 82).

REFERENCES

Archibugi, D. and Lundvall, B.A. (eds), (2001). *The Globalizing Learning Economy*, Oxford and New York: Oxford University Press.

Autor, D., Katz, L. and Krueger, A. (1997). *Computing Inequality: Have Computers Changed the Labor Market?*, NBER Working Paper 5956.

Blau, F. and Kahn, L. (1996). 'International Differences in Male Wage Inequality: Institutions versus Market Forces', *Journal of Political Economy* 104(4): 791–837.

Boudon, R. (1973). *L'Inegalité des Chances*, Paris: Libraire Armand Collin.

Bourdieu P., Passeron J.-C. (1970). *La Réproduction: Éléments pour une Théorie du Système d'Ensignement*, Paris: Éditions du Minuit.

Bowles, B. and Gintis, H. (1976). *Schooling in Capitalist America*, London: Routledge.

Bresnahan, T. (1999). 'Computerisation and Wage Dispersion: An Analytical Reinterpretation', *Economic Journal* 109(456): 390–415.

Conceição, P. and Heitor, M.V. (1999). 'On the Role of the University in the Knowledge Economy', *Science and Public Policy* 26(1): 37–51.

Conceição, P. and Heitor, M.V. (2001). 'Universities in the Learning Economy: Balancing Institutional Integrity with Organizational Diversity', in D. Archibugi and B. Lundvall (eds), *The Globalizing Learning Economy*, Oxford and New York: Oxford University Press, pp. 83–107.

Conceição, P., Heitor, M.V. and Oliveira, P. (1998) 'Expectations for the University in the Knowledge Based Economy', *Technological Forecasting and Social Change:* 58(3): 203–14.

Dasgupta, P. and David, P. (1994). 'Toward a New Economics of Science', *Research Policy* 23: 487–521.

DiNardo, J. and Pischke, J. (1997). 'The Returns to Computer Use Revisited: Have Pencils Changed the Wage Structure Too?', *Quarterly Journal of Economics* 112(1): 291–303.

Dore, R. (1976). *The Diploma Disease: Education, Qualification, and Development*, Berkeley, CA: University of California Press.

Dosi, G. (1988). 'Sources, Procedures and Microeconomic Effects of Innovation', *Journal of Economic Literature* 26(3): 1120–71.

Edin, P. and Holmlund, B. (1995). 'The Swedish Wage Structure: The Rise and Fall of Solidarity Wage Policy?', in Freeman, R. and Katz, L. (eds), *Differences and Changes in Wage Structures*, Chicago: Chicago University Press.

Freeman, C. (1996). *The Long Wave in the World Economy,* International Library of Critical Writings in Economics, Aldershot, Elgar.

Freeman, C. and Soete, L. (1997). *The Economics of Industrial Innovation,* third edition, Cambridge, MA: MIT Press.

Galbraith, J.K. (1998). *Created Unequal*, New York and London: Free Press.

Galbraith, J.K. (2000). 'Technology, Inequality and Unemployment in Europe and America' in *Towards a Learning Society - Innovation and Competence Building with Social Cohesion for Europe*, Guincho, Lisbon, 28–30 May 2000; http://in3.dem.ist.utl.pt/learning2000/pro.html

Galbraith, J.K., Conceição, P. and Ferreira, P. (1999), 'Inequality and Unemployment in Europe: The American Cure', *New Left Review* 237(September/October): 28–51.

Guellec, D. and Pottelsberghe, B. V. (2000). *The Impact of Public R&D Expenditure On Business R&D*, STI Working Paper 2000/4, Paris: OECD.

Jencks, C. (1972). *Inequality*, New York: Basic Books.

Katz, L. and Murphy, K. (1992). 'Changes in Relative Wages, 1963-1987: Supply and Demand Factors', *Quarterly Journal of Economics* 107(1): 35–78.

Kline, S.J. and Rosenberg, N. (1986). 'An Overview of Innovation', in Landau, R. and Rosenberg, N. (eds), *The Positive Sum Strategy: Harnessing Technology for Economic Growth*, Washington, DC: National Academy Press.

Krueger, A. (1993) 'How Have Computers Changed the Wage Structure? Evidence from Micro Data', *Quarterly Journal of Economics* 108(1): 33–60.

Leuven, E., Oosterbeek, H. and Ophem, H. (1998). 'Explaining Differences in Male Wage Inequality by Differences in Demand and Supply of Skill' Centre for Economic Performance Discussion Paper 392, London: London School of Economics.

Lundvall, B.A. and Johnson, B. (1994). 'The Learning Economy', *Journal of Industry Studies* 1/2: 23–42.

Meade, J.E. (1964). *Efficiency, Equality and the Ownership of Property*, London: Allen and Unwin.

Nelson, R.R. (1993). *National Innovation Systems: A Comparative Analysis*, New York and Oxford: Oxford University Press.

Nelson, R. R. and Romer, P. (1996). 'Science, Economic Growth, and Public Policy', in Smith, B.L.R. and Barfield, C.E. (eds), *Technology, R&D, and the Economy*, Washington, DC: Brookings.

Nelson, R.R. and Winter, S.G. (1982). *An Evolutionary Theory of Economic Change*, Cambridge MA: The Belknap Press of Harvard University Press.

Penrose, E. (1959). *The Theory of the Growth of the Firm*. Oxford: Basil Blackwell.

Romer, P. (1990). 'Endogenous Technological Growth', *Journal of Political Economy* 98(5): s71–s102.

Romer, P. (1993). 'Idea Gaps and Object Gaps in Economic Development', *Journal of Monetary Economics* 32: 543–73.

Rosenberg, N. (1994). *Exploring the Black Box: Technology, Economics and History*, Cambridge and New York: Cambridge University Press.

Schmitt, J. (1995). 'The Changing Structure of Male Earnings in Britain 1974–1988', in Freeman, R. and Katz, L. (eds), *Differences and Changes in Wage Structures*, Chicago: Chicago University Press.

Schumpeter, J. (1942). *Capitalism, Socialism and Democracy*. New York: Harper.

Teece, D.J. and Pisano, G. (1997). 'Dynamic Capabilities and Strategic Management', Strategic Management Journal 18(7): 509–22.

PART ONE

Fostering innovation

Introductory note: Novelty, knowledge and learning

João Caraça

The rate of change and the volume of communication in today's life have no parallel in any period in the history of mankind. The growing development of industries based on information technologies, and the increasing weight of intangible or immaterial investment (R&D, software, education and training, organisation, marketing, design) make clear that the nature of the regulating processes of economic activity are being profoundly altered. We therefore need to rethink the economic analysis of human societies and their organisations, to introduce a new perspective that fully encompasses the intangible elements and their implications. The basic regulators of information activities are not exchange ('exchange' used in a narrow economist's perspective: the exchange of tangible goods or the rendering of tangible services) and scarcity, but rather 'sharing' and its limiting factor, 'misunderstanding'. Following an 'information transaction', both partners retain the information which was the object of such transaction (if, of course, the recipient was sufficiently capable of understanding it).

The increasing importance of sharing transactions reveals that the restrictions on the performance of modern economies inhere essentially in the capacities of the operators themselves. Thus, endogenous (or accessible) knowledge potential, its form of organisation, and the ability to exploit it, are crucial elements for success and survival in the new economic environment. The main limiting problem faced in this kind of transaction is not that of (material) scarcity, but rather that of a new type of 'scarcity' – the effect of misunderstanding, that is of the non-apprehension of communicated knowledge and information, which prompts the inability to generate relevant meanings at the receptor's level.

The economic impact of knowledge, arising from the globalisation of the economy, forces us to reconsider the dynamics and the strategies of knowledge. We thus have to understand what knowledge is and where it is embodied. It is striking to see how loosely knowledge is being treated today in the economic sciences. Knowledge can no longer be envisaged as a mysterious fluid, flowing in and out of countries and walls, sometimes embedded in machines, sometimes encoded in documents, sometimes even broadcast electronically. Knowledge resides in human bodies, like physical human strength, and the whole issue is about capacities of human bodies, organised in teams, firms, societies or nations.

Unlike physical strength, however, knowledge is not simply cumulative. Knowledge is communicated through the articulation of languages. But the role of language is not only that of a repository of meanings – representing the capacity of a human being to direct the interaction with the world around them, and thus their ability to survive – but also that of a medium to communicate with their fellow human beings, building up the sense of community.

The purpose of organisations, of institutions, is to enable (through communication) the creation of higher, more complex languages, and the 'election' to command of persons who generate and manage higher repositories of knowledge. It has been pointed out (Caraça and Carrilho, 1994) that sharing regulates the relationship of humanity with the world, according to three modalities, which correspond to increasing degrees of complexity.

First, tacit knowledge, governing the relationship of the human being with the world as a whole (the outside world and their own group) experienced particularly as the confrontation of two orders, the 'objective' and the 'subjective'. It is the level of knowledge which corresponds to what can be defined as 'common knowledge', the type of knowledge which is not taught explicitly to us (Polanyi, 1967), but which we learn by 'exposure' in society or in our own groups. This level has evolved with historical time, but not in a simple linear progression. This level corresponds to that of the unskilled worker.

Second, there is a level of explicit knowledge in which language emerges as its definite operator, through the creation of 'specialised languages' leading to the affirmation of the identity and the diversity of groups within a community, and corresponding to a growing level of complexity in the interaction between human beings and their world: that of 'intersubjectivity'. Explicit knowledge is associated with the regime of specialised information. This is the level of enterprises.

Third, emerging from the level of explicit knowledge through a permanent process of increasing complexity in the relationship between human beings and their world, the densification and intensification of communication processes lead intersubjectivity to be replaced by an enlarged 'interactivity', which in turn correspond to languages of higher precision. This is the level of disciplinary knowledge, the context in which disciplines, (that is sciences, philosophy, ethics, aesthetics) appear. Disciplines are associated with larger and highly developed repositories of meanings (Caraça and Carrilho, 1996). This level is important for understanding the emergence of high technology or science-based sectors in the economy.

It is in this light that we must treat the effect of knowledge and communication in any area. For instance, if we are dealing with economic activity, we have to understand what are the intellectual levels of the various segments of the population, how the diverse institutions are organised, and which rules of overall coordination and operation of the economic system are being used. High level repositories of knowledge are effective only if proper institutions are created, or are at work, which make full use of their specific meanings, values and perceptions.

Science is about understanding and coping with change in the natural world. In the 1960s a universal model of science and technology was accepted that corresponded to an instrumental concept of scientific practice with respect to social and economic development. More investment in science was supposed to bring about a greater capacity to generate new wealth. More effort in the diffusion of scientific concepts was assumed to bring about generalised public acceptance of new technological projects.

Nowadays, however, we know that it is not possible to isolate research activities from the social context in which they are conducted; this is reflected in the growing scientific basis of the culture of contemporary societies, as well as by the increasing societal involvement of scientists and researchers and their organisations. A new need has been created: the need to ensure that public funds spent on science are used in a way beneficial to society – with evaluation performing the primary role of mediator in this process. This is why the nature of science policies at the national level has changed from a mission-oriented character (from the launching of strategic sectors to the emphasis on the generation of technological innovations and the support of national 'champions') to a more diffusion-oriented one, through enhancing the mechanisms of knowledge circulation and learning, technology transfer and assimilation, awareness and exploitation of research results.

But the role of governments in modern economies is incompatible with the conduct of operations too close to the market. So, what is being left to government policy and action is the building up of infrastructure (including the development of human resources – the notion of human capital); the support of networking activities (and hence the concept of human mobility); the financing of research programmes in basic 'pervasive' technologies (prompting the notion of generic technologies); and the provision of scientific services, education and training at the national level (leading to the concepts of public understanding of science and of scientific literacy).

This is clearly too reactive, and also inadequate, in terms of public policy for science in this era of emerging new ways to behave and relate to other humans and to the environment. Knowledge and learning are the central resources and mechanisms of the new nations, communities, and organisations. Science and technology policy will have to be closely linked to policies in all other fields of knowledge, from the arts and humanities to the cognitive and social sciences. Further, implications of the free circulation of knowledge will have to be recognised and fostered: disciplinary knowledge can only evolve in the context of a strong communicative framework which will enable the attitude of sharing meanings and values to realise its full potential. And the relations of science with the bodies of explicit knowledge, such as technologies, specialised crafts, laws and regulations, business management, and fine arts, will need special attention in terms of the diffusion of new learning abilities throughout civil society, leading to the build-up of more adequate competences.

Thus, a crucial historical role is to be played by the social sciences in the 21st century, by reinventing and redefining the 19th century framework that was the basic for the construction of nation states. Learning is necessary for understanding and coping with change in society.

This forces us to introduce complexity and self-organisation, or self-regulation, as main concepts of the new societal framework. New collective behaviour, or innovations (novelty in the economy) therefore appear as emergent properties of socioeconomic structures, in their unfolding through time. And policies are prompted as powerful social adaptation mechanisms, implying a permanent awareness of change, and a capacity for social adjustment to change, in other words, of learning to perform under new conditions. The times of learning set the pace of innovation and development.

The three chapters of Part One directly address these issues. Lynn Mytelka and Keith Smith argue in Chapter Two that the theory-policy link has been central to the intellectual development of the field of innovation, which would have been impossible within the constraints of existing disciplinary structures and university funding systems. On the other hand, the analytical achievements have permitted a wide expansion in the conceptualisation of policy targets and in the design of instruments available to policy makers: the authors consider this as an example of an interactive and co-evolving process.

In Chapter Three, Cristiano Antonelli discusses the interactions between economics of innovation and other areas of disciplinary knowledge, ranging from sociology to philosophy. The author acknowledges the contribution of innovation studies to a better understanding of the more general process of formation of new ideas in an advanced society. He envisages a problematic core of remaining open questions, ranging from how innovations come to the marketplace to how and why total factor productivity growth increases.

Finally, Pedro Conceição and Manuel Heitor review in Chapter Four the Portuguese path in the evolution of its scientific and innovative activities, in order to identify the ongoing process aimed at stimulating the reorganisation, reorientation and redefinition of research units in the less favoured regions of Europe, in a climate of intensified international competitiveness. Their analysis implies that the goal of building integrated R&D and innovation policies across the EU needs decentralised capacities together with international criteria to be considered, in order to identify poles of research competences and to support networks of excellence, as enablers of new competences and excellence in the coming decades.

In the three followings chapters, the full circle of novelty and innovation is repeatedly redrawn, from knowledge to learning, from learning to knowledge.

REFERENCES

Caraça, J.M.G. and Carrilho, M.M. (1994). 'A New Paradigm in the Organization of Knowledge', *Futures* 26 (7): 781.
Caraça, J.M.G. and Carrilho, M.M. (1996). 'The Role of Sharing in the Circulation of Knowledge', *Futures* 28 (8): 771.
Polanyi, M. (1967). *The Tacit Dimension*, London: Routledge & Kegan Paul.

2. Interactions between policy learning and innovation theory

Lynn K. Mytelka and Keith Smith

This chapter explores links between the development of innovation theory since the late 1970s, and the evolution of innovation policy ideas, primarily in the 1990s. The argument is that there is a close connection between theory and policy, so that theory and policy learning can be seen as an integrated, co-evolving and interactive process. We analyse the theory-policy learning link in terms of two phases. We suggest that the complex economic crisis of the 1970s created an opening for rival analyses of events. During the 1980s, the development of evolutionary theories (pioneered by Richard Nelson and Sidney Winter) and of empirically-based theories of the innovation process (pioneered by Nathan Rosenberg) created a framework in which policy agencies could consider heterodox ideas concerning objectives and instruments of public policy. By the early 1990s policy makers, particularly in Europe, came to see RTD and innovation policies not just as important arenas of action in themselves, but as instruments towards more wide ranging policy objectives. The policy agencies involved, though hierarchical, were characterised by relatively open structures that permitted a degree of intellectual diversity: so organisations like the OECD and the European Commission played a central role, whereas the World Bank, for example, did not. Increasing policy interest stimulated a second phase of research in the 1990s, sponsored both nationally and by various EU programmes, in which expanding the innovation-oriented knowledge base became a significant objective for policy makers. The chapter argues that the theory-policy link has been central to the intellectual development of this field, which would have been impossible within the constraints of existing disciplinary structures and university funding systems. At the same time the analytical achievements have permitted a wide expansion in the conceptualisation of policy targets and in the design of instruments available to policy makers. In a sense, this is itself an evolutionary story: of a crisis and a conjunctural niche that permitted

24

the creation and (so far) survival of a set of diverse and certainly non-conventional ideas.

2.1. INTRODUCTION

The development of innovation theory over the past 20 years has involved a major reformulation, with innovation no longer seen primarily as a process of discovery (that is, of new scientific or technological principles) but rather as a non-linear process of learning. This revision has been powerfully influenced by the work of Richard Nelson and Sidney Winter, whose *An Evolutionary Theory of Economic Change* (1982) proposed the idea that innovation is shaped by crisis-driven search programmes by firms. As existing procedures falter in the face of shifting economic or technological conditions, firms began the search for alternatives, in experimental learning processes. A major theme in innovation research subsequently has been exploration of the nature and characteristics of such learning, across firms, sectors, regions and national systems.

A related theoretical development was the idea that learning occurs in specific institutional contexts: that is, in systemic environments shaped inter alia by regulation, law, political cultures, and the 'rules of the game' of economic institutions. These environments of course include policy institutions and actions. But policy structures are not developed once and for all. Although they exhibit inertia, they also have dynamic aspects, and this dynamism often results from learning – from improved understanding of the agents, interactions and patterns that are the objects of policy. A central component of understanding the dynamics of innovation as a whole should therefore include the nature and effects of learning within policy systems.

There can be little doubt that there has been significant change within innovation-related policy arenas during the last 20 years. This has been a matter both of the objectives and instruments of policy and it has been most pronounced within the Organisation for Economic Cooperation and Development (OECD) and the European Union (EU). In terms of objectives, innovation policy has come to be seen as a central instrument for achieving outcomes that lie well beyond the field of RTD or innovation alone. The concepts and instruments of policy have also shifted, with non-linear models of innovation and the 'innovation system' concept playing a central role in policy discourse, and with a wide range of new policy instruments directed at networking, clustering, and personnel mobility. We argue that this complex process of change can best be understood as policy learning.

Why did these particular institutions become the location of policy innovation? We suggest that in contrast to more hierarchical organisations such as the IMF and the World Bank, access to policy making circles and opportunities for influence have been far greater in these ostensibly weaker siblings over the same period. While in both sets of international organisations, problems growing out of the twin processes of globalisation and rapid technological change were being placed squarely on the agenda from the 1970s onward, more hierarchical organisations retained the macroeconomic perspective and broadly neoclassical conceptual approaches with which they were most familiar.[1] By contrast, faced with the paradoxes of productivity growth in the 1970s, the challenge of competitiveness in the 1980s and the problem of equity in the 1990s, other – perhaps more internally differentiated or consensual – organisations contained niches in which conceptual diversity was possible. The OECD and the European Community contained both staff and national delegates who were receptive to new approaches. Although such diversity was often the object of internal conflict, nevertheless these were organisations that could tolerate a degree of intellectual variety. It was into this breach that evolutionary economists, regional geographers and other students of innovation stepped.

In this chapter we chart the shift towards innovation theory-based policy through a brief examination of the concepts and theoretical approaches introduced into academic debates and echoed in working documents and publications of the OECD and EC a few years later. The questions we address concern the drivers and mechanisms of such learning. The argument in this chapter is that the process of policy learning cannot be separated from the development of the field of innovation research itself. The scale and scope of such research have expanded greatly during the past two decades. Theory and policy are best seen as co-evolving: so this is a process of interactive learning, in which a social science field, and a policy arena, have been jointly and interactively shaped. A primary driver of this has been the long-term impact of the economic crisis of the 1970s.

2.2.   GROWTH, COMPETITIVENESS AND INNOVATION: THE REFOCUSING OF A DEBATE

During the 1950s and 1960s, a set of social conventions and economic mechanisms were put in place across Europe and North America that ensured the mutual adjustment of mass consumption and mass production and provided a quasi constancy in profit share with respect to value added. In this way investment was stimulated, but only so long as demand was buoyant. By the 1970s, a crisis was in the making when productivity increases became more difficult to achieve and the growth of demand faltered.

We are still far from a full understanding of the factors that combined to produce this slowdown in productivity growth from the early 1970s. On the one hand, there were a number of major system shocks: the collapse of the Bretton Woods system (itself stemming from a complex financial crisis); the two OPEC oil price shocks of 1973/4 and 1978; and general political instability (including the effects of prolonged war). On the other hand, there were economic and technological factors that attracted little attention at the time, though increasing attention in subsequent decades (Aglietta, 1976; Piore and Sabel, 1984; Boyer, 1988; Freeman and Perez, 1988). The argument there was that on the production side, imbalances in capacity utilisation between highly specialised mass-production machinery, rigidities in supplier-client relationships and management structures, as well as labour problems, all played a role in slowing down the diffusion of productivity enhancing techniques, both material and immaterial. On the consumption side, the crisis of the 1970s led to slower growth in domestic purchasing power and a segmentation of markets into income and product categories within which price and income elasticities of demand differed. Market saturation in many of the consumer durables that had been the staple fare of large corporations also occurred and was exacerbated by rising imports of standardised, mass-produced products from low-wage countries (Mytelka, 1987).

Although the responses by economists to this crisis were primarily macroeconomic in character, the crisis of the 1970s also led to serious questioning of earlier approaches to the analysis of growth. In a 1981 symposium on the consequences of new technologies for economic growth, structural change and employment, Christopher Freeman (1982, p. 1) pointed to the importance that economic theorists such as Adam Smith, Karl Marx and Joseph Schumpeter attached to innovation as an engine of economic growth. But these insights were not part of mainstream growth theory at that time – from the 1950s, the broad conception of innovation as a process of technological and organisational change that these theorists shared had been supplanted by a narrower approach to technological change within a series of macroeconomic growth models. As Richard Nelson cogently argued, the models of the 1950s and 1960s clearly showed their limitations in dealing with the paradox of productivity growth that became apparent in the 1970s (Nelson, 1981) and the challenge of competitiveness in the 1980s. This was partly because of the static, allocative assumptions upon which these models were based. But it was also the result of a dual view of 'technology', seen either as knowledge embodied in capital and intermediate goods, or as exogenous knowledge creation, with knowledge itself seen as akin to information, and therefore a public good.

This simplification allowed technology to be assimilated to any other good or service that could be bought and sold in a market. Information, on the other hand, was regarded as freely accessible and non-rival, in the sense that many people could use that information at the same time without diminishing it. As a public good, its transfer was believed to be costless. On the one hand, this provided a rationale for public provision or subsidy of research, since the public good characteristics of technological information implied a market failure.[2] On the other hand, in growth accounting, knowledge, too intangible to be measured, formed part of the residual (Abramowitz, 1971).[3] Its acquisition was assumed to result from a quasi automatic process of learning-by-doing. Over the next several decades, statistical efforts focused unsuccessfully on reducing the residual by rendering knowledge more tangible. Labour was thus differentiated by skill level and industries classified by research and development (R&D) intensity.[4] But the underlying assumptions – concerning knowledge as a public good and innovation as a process that involved a direct and automatic link between research and development expenditures, innovation, productivity gains and commercial success – remained unchallenged. Empirical research, however, began to cast serious doubt on both the theoretical and practical usefulness of these linear 'research to competitiveness in the market' models.

At its simplest, the development of innovation studies as a field rests on a rejection of the neoclassical growth model, a rejection of implicit neoclassical ideas concerning knowledge, and a rejection of the linear model of innovation. Something that has attracted far less attention is the fact that much empirical innovation research has also challenged the innovation ideas of Schumpeter. The development of the field could be argued to result primarily from two bodies of work. During the late 1970s and early 1980s, there emerged a well articulated evolutionary critique of neoclassicism, in the shape of Nelson and Winter's *An Evolutionary Theory of Economic Change* (1982). This provided a coherent micro-based alternative to the dominant neoclassical paradigm.

Of equal importance, and over roughly the same time period, were a series of chapters and books by Nathan Rosenberg, that significantly shifted the ground in the understanding of innovation, and that have had a powerful albeit indirect effect on policy thinking across countries. In *Perspectives on Technology* (1976) and *Inside the Black Box: Technology and Economics* (1982), Rosenberg addressed an astonishingly wide range of issues to do with innovation. These included a critique of neoclassical concepts of technology; a sustained critique of Schumpeter's invention-innovation-diffusion schema; a broad set of industry studies (woodworking, machine tools, aircraft, electronics, chemicals); important work on the economic role of science (and its relation to technology); and some more or less unique work on factors shaping the direction of specific lines of technical advance. A connecting theme in this work is the rejection of both neoclassical and Schumpeterian notions of linearity. For example, Rosenberg stresses the importance of the fact that innovations, when introduced to the market, invariably require major post-innovation improvements, and it is these that shape adoption. This undermines the distinction between innovation and diffusion, while positively emphasising the need for learning feedbacks between marketing, production and development as a basis for the wider process of innovation. This sustained research programme deserves specific mention because it gave rise to a deceptively simple model of the innovation process that has had a powerful impact on policy makers – the so called 'chain link' model (Kline and Rosenberg, 1986). Some of its applications of this model will be mentioned below.

These pioneering contributions have been followed by a very substantial research programme and literature during the past 20 years. At the risk of oversimplifying considerably, we could sum up some of the results of this literature, and its policy conclusions, around its robust and generally accepted conclusions concerning innovation and its effects. Framed by an evolutionary economics perspective, rejecting all notions of optimal decision making and hence optimality properties in the economic system, non-linear models of the innovation process were developed. Based on the interactive effect between variables as opposed to the impact that any single variable might have in explaining the process of innovation and diffusion, they involve feedback loops between: (i) research; (ii) the existing body of scientific and technological knowledge; (iii) the potential market; (iv) invention; and (v) the various steps in the production process (Kline and Rosenberg, 1986; OECD, 1992b). These models emphasised the uncertainties and unpredictable nature of the innovation process (Rosenberg, 1976, 1982) and stressed the dynamic impact of innovation clusters as opposed to single innovations (Freeman and Perez, 1988). Within these approaches, the firm was reconceptualised as a learning organisation embedded within a broader institutional context (Lundvall, 1988). By focusing on the knowledge, learning and interactivity among actors that gives rise to 'systems of innovation' (Freeman, 1988; Lundvall, 1992, 1995), the new innovation paradigm drew attention to the 'national or local environments where organisational and institutional developments have produced conditions conducive to the growth of interactive mechanisms on which innovation and the diffusion of technology are based' (OECD, 1992b, p.238). The process of innovation thus came to be seen as both path dependent, locationally specific and institutionally shaped.[5]

Among these diverse concepts, and from a policy perspective, the notion of the 'national system of innovation' has had by far the greatest impact, indeed an astonishing take-up. Despite the fact that the notion of system had in fact been widely present in the work of innovation theorists such as Rosenberg, technology historians such as Thomas Hughes, that of the regulation school in France, and in technology systems analysis (Carlsson, 1995), the decisive 'systems' impact on policy thinking came via the work of Bengt-Åke Lundvall (1992) and Richard Nelson (1993). The difference between these volumes can probably best be summed up in terms of two approaches to national systems, described by Lundvall himself. According to

Lundvall a distinction can be made between a narrow and a broad definition of an innovation system respectively:

> The narrow definition would include organisations and institutions involved in searching and exploring – such as R&D departments, technological institutes and universities. The broad definition ... includes all parts and aspects of the economic structure and the institutional set-up affecting learning as well as searching and exploring – the production system, the marketing system and the system of finance present themselves as subsystems in which learning takes place.[6]

Nelson's *National Innovation Systems* essentially followed the narrow definition. In *National Systems of Innovation*, Lundvall and his collaborators focused much more on a conceptual account of the characteristics and effects of learning. Their definition of a system was as follows:

> ... a system of innovation is constituted by elements and relationships which interact in the production, diffusion and use of new and economically useful, knowledge ... a national system encompasses elements and relationships, either located within or rooted inside the borders of a national state.[7]

In the Lundvall framework innovation is conceptualised as learning, since innovation is – by definition – novelty in the capabilities and knowledges which make up technology. It sought to understand the nature and dynamics of learning via three basic concepts: the organised market, interactive learning, and the institutional framework. What this approach essentially did was to place the empirical work on innovation within a conceptual framework that enabled sympathetic policy makers to challenge (or simply ignore) the neoclassical approach to economic and policy analysis.

This is not to say that the economic mainstream was not changing. This period also saw the emergence of the 'new growth theory' and the 'new industrial economics'. New growth theories have attempted to move away from the earlier linear perspective, to endogenise the knowledge creation process and to relax neoclassical assumptions of perfect competition, perfect information and identical levels of technology (Verspagen; 1992, Romer, 1994). But a fundamental problem is that the conception of technology within these models remains very thin and stylised (Mytelka, 1999, pp. 16–17). Such models did not deal well with the uncertainties and dynamics that characterised changes in production and competition then underway; notably, the increasing knowledge-intensity of production and the diffusion of innovation-based competition as markets liberalised around the globe. They proved unable to incorporate, as the NSI notions did, a variety of ways of understanding the innovation process itself. But while the new growth theories have yet to generate useful guidelines for policy, they have made important contributions to academic debates about the role of innovation in the competitiveness of firms and of countries that emerged in the 1980s. Somewhat similar problems were associated with the new approaches to industrial economics. These approaches introduced far richer concepts of technology, and of the strategic environments of firm decision making. But they retained the notion of optimal decision making by modelling within a game-theoretic context that replaced optimal choice within well defined choice sets with selection of optimal strategies. Some of the key elements that had emerged from empirical innovation research, such as radical uncertainty, interactivity, and clustering issues, never made an appearance.

2.3   LINKING INNOVATION THEORY AND INNOVATION POLICY: THE EMERGENCE OF NEW CONCEPTUAL APPROACHES TO POLICY

During the 1980s and 1990s, the OECD, the EC and UN agencies such as UNCTAD and ECLA took the new innovation paradigm increasingly on board. In part, this involved such organisations taking a wider perspective on the role of innovation policy, and in part it involved changed conceptualisations of the nature of innovation and of appropriate policy instruments.

These changed emphases had their roots in the 1970s. The rather conventional views of the Brooks report on *Science, Growth and Society* (OECD, 1971) began to be supplanted by a new conceptualisation of the innovation process. A key document was *Technical Change and Economic Policy* (OECD, 1980), which was probably the first major policy document to challenge the macroeconomic interpretations of the 1970s crisis, and to emphasise the role of technological factors in potential solutions to the crisis. The group that produced this report was a high powered one, and included a number of figures who were already central to the emerging field of innovation studies, including Richard Nelson, Christopher Freeman and Keith Pavitt. The report looked well beyond the specifics of the energy crisis of the 70s, developing a critique of conventional growth theory. It looked to the impacts of new technologies in ways that have themselves become part of the conventional wisdom in subsequent decades:

> ... electronics is the major research-based sector which has maintained, and even increased its innovative vitality. The principal feature has been innovation in the manufacture and design of electronic components. The years from 1975/76 on have seen what has come to be known as a 'microelectronic revolution'. ... such radical innovations are bound to have pervasive effects in many sectors where improved methods of calculation, communication, control and the storage and

manipulation of information are necessary or possible. The diffusion of electronics throughout other manufacturing and service industries will result in an economy in which one technology influences innovation almost everywhere. (OECD 1980, p. 48)

This process of analytical change led on to the Sundquist Report (OECD, 1988) which took the need for an integrated overall approach to technological, economic and social issues as its conclusion and stressed that technological change is a 'social process, not an event, and should be viewed not in static, but in dynamic terms' (op. cit., p. 11). Such developments occurred within the Directorate for Science, Technology and Industry (DSTI) of the OECD. DSTI had been established in the early 1960s, and had had considerable success in promoting technology issues (for example, around the concept of the 'technology gap'), and in fostering the systematic collection of R&D data (in the late 1960s, producing the 'Frascati Manual' that became the basic standard for R&D data collection within OECD countries). While the OECD's Economics Department tended to be rather orthodox in its views, DSTI had a place for the heterodox, and such important figures in innovation studies as Christopher Freeman and Keith Pavitt worked within it.

This background within DSTI ultimately formed the basis for a three year work programme known as TEP (the Technology-Economy Programme) which ran from 1989 to 1992. The TEP programme was a loosely coordinated set of conferences, workshops, and data development exercises, accompanied by a rather vigorous process of report production. These had the effect of importing, for the first time, the new ideas circulating in the innovation studies environment, into OECD documents and publications. For example, the major conference report *Technology and Productivity* (OECD 1991) combined extensive econometric and other quantitative analysis of the productivity slowdown with chapters on technology and growth, radical innovations and paradigm shifts in the growth process, networks and innovation, system effects and diffusion. Extensive indicator work within TEP included the *Oslo Manual*, which was explicitly based on the Kline-Rosenberg model of innovation as its conceptual core, and which attempted to expand the direct measure of innovation and of non-R&D innovation inputs (OECD 1992a, 1997).

By far the clearest statement of the new approaches came, however, in the final report from TEP, *Technology and the Economy: The Key Relationships* (OECD, 1992b), a document piloted through OECD by Robert Chabbal, François Chesnais, Bengt-Åke Lundvall, Paul David, Luc Soete and other economists in the evolutionary and institutional economics mode. This document also opened up with the Kline-Rosenberg model as its analytical framework (op. cit. 1992b, p. 25). But it introduced into the policy discussion a wide range of other concepts from innovation studies – networking and clustering, strategic partnering, spillovers, the importance of tacit knowledge. Less tangible in the report, but of greater long term significance in policy discussions, was the concept of national innovation systems, derived from the recently published books by Lundvall and Nelson on this topic. 'When the outcome of this programme was summed up in Montreal in 1991, the concept, national systems of innovation, was given a prominent place in the conclusions' (Lundvall, 1992, p. 5). The dramatic breakthrough represented by the TEP report in the consideration it gives to linkages within national innovation systems (OECD, 1992) was carried through in subsequent OECD policy studies such as the 1994 Jobs Study and the policy recommendations related to learning in the knowledge-based economy contained in its sequels, the 1996 *Technology, Productivity and Job Creation* report, and the 1998 *Technology, Productivity and Job Creation: Best Policy Practices*. It has in fact become a core concept within policy discussion related to innovation, both at OECD, in the EU and to a lesser extent in development studies at UNCTAD and ECLA.

By the last of the OECD studies mentioned above, the transition away from a linear approach to growth and competitiveness based on the stimulation of research and development and its transfer to the productive sector was conceptually complete. The problem itself had been reformulation to include the distributional issues resulting from a process of innovation and technological change and the nature of the solution was conceptually more holistic:

> Today's rapid technological change coupled with the restructuring underway in OECD economies leads some to associate technology with unemployment and social distress. However technology per se is not the culprit. Its economy-wide employment impact is likely to be positive provided that the mechanisms for translating technology into jobs are not impaired by deficiencies in training and innovation systems and rigidities in product, labour and financial markets … wide-ranging and coherent policy reforms [will be needed] … to enhance the contribution of technology to growth, productivity and jobs … innovation and technology diffusion policies themselves continue to be too piecemeal, with insufficient consideration of the linkages within national innovation systems. (OECD, 1998, p. 7)

Directly operational studies such as the OECD Science Policy Reviews, however, failed to make the transition to an innovation focus. Designed 'to produce a friendly but independent and critical assessment of each country's performance against an international comparative yardstick, [in practice they] concentrated mainly on the formal R&D system and technical education'

(Freeman, 1995, p. 30). But their legacy provided a learning experience for UNCTAD in the design of its Science, Technology and Innovation Policy (STIP) Reviews (UNCTAD, 1999a, 1999b). These latter studies were explicitly organised around the national innovation systems concept.

2.4 POLICY DEVELOPMENTS IN THE EUROPEAN COMMISSION

A similar, if slower, process of conceptual change took place within the European Union. Neither industrial policy nor research and development policy were among the areas covered in the 1967 Treaty of Rome. By the early 1980s, however, both had found a place among the European Commission's directorates (Guzzetti, 1995, pp. 1971–83). Cumbersome rule making procedures within the EU were responsible, in part, for this slowness. But it is also important to remember that the first research and technology development (RTD) programmes were designed and implemented in the early 1980s when seminal works in innovation theory were only beginning to appear (Nelson and Winter, 1982; Dosi et al., 1988). With the information technology revolution already underway and evidence of Europe's declining market share accumulating, RTD programmes under the First and Second Framework Programmes were thus designed more for competitiveness than for innovation. This included well known programmes such as the European Strategic Programme for Research and Development on Information Technologies (ESPRIT) whose main goals were: (i) to promote intra-European industrial cooperation through precompetitive R&D; (ii) to thereby furnish European industry with the basic technologies that it needed to bolster its competitiveness through the 1990s; and (iii) to develop European standards (Cadiou, 1996; Commission of the European Communities 1987) and the Basic Research in Industrial Technologies (BRITE) programme, also aimed at enhancing competitiveness.

During the 1980s and well into the 1990s, EU policy makers were hard put to deal with the complex reality that innovation processes represent and tended to fall back upon a simpler 'linear research to competitiveness in the market' model in designing RTD policies whether these were intended to stimulate a process of catching up, keeping up or getting ahead. Thus, as large, diversified Japanese information technology firms accelerated their investment in product and process development in the 1970s and began to move from technological catch-up towards the frontier through collaborative R&D projects, their relatively smaller European rivals, cloistered within national markets, lacking economies of scale and slow to move towards economies of scope, steadily lost competitiveness. In response to this deteriorating situation, the European Communities launched ESPRIT with a pilot year in 1983.

ESPRIT was followed in 1985 by the Programme for R&D in Advanced Communications Technologies in Europe (RACE),[8] the Basic Research in Industrial Technologies (BRITE) programme, 'designed to help the European manufacturing industry to become more competitive'[9] by collaborating in basic research and in the implementation of new technologies by users, and the Biotechnology Action Programme (BAP). Subsequently, BRITE was merged with the European Advanced Materials programme (EURAM) and the range of activities covered by BAP was extended under the Biotechnological Research for Innovation, Development and Growth in Europe (BRIDGE) programme. Up to 1989, all Community RTD programmes, including training programmes such as the Community Programme in Education and Training for Technology (COMETT), aimed at achieving competitiveness by pumping up the supply of RTD and technological skills and somewhat belatedly by stimulating demand for these outputs.

Prior to 1989 all major European Community RTD policies were thus supply side-oriented, dealing with the 'upstream' knowledge inputs provided by research, development and training. Many of the RTD programmes of the early 1990s, such as the SPRINT Specific Projects Action Line (SPAL) which promoted technology transfer across sectors and regions, and the Value programme, set up to diffuse the results of European RTD projects were also supply side-oriented. They recreated linearity by emphasising the outputs of upstream activities such as research and development or end-of-the-pipe products, patents or products, for example, as opposed to the intangible, continuous and interactive processes of 'learning to learn' and knowledge diffusion and absorption which are the bases for innovative behaviour.[10] In what follows we look briefly at an experimental programme of the 1990s, the SPRINT-SPAL from the innovation perspective.

In the innovation literature, interactivity, bottlenecks in production, challenges from other firms in a competitive environment or simply by the availability of new technology are believed to stimulate innovation (Rosenberg: 1976, Lundvall: 1988). But if the firm does not have an experience of innovating and has not built up a culture of innovation or to paraphrase Stiglitz, has not 'learned to learn', there is no guarantee that it will respond positively to such bottlenecks, challenges or opportunities. Small and medium sized enterprises, for example, may not perceive either their own problems or the opportunities that new technology opens up for them. Interviews with firms participating in the SPRINT Specific Projects Action Line, a programme dedicated to technology transfer, revealed precisely this kind of orientation among end users, many of whom were initially either 'unable' or 'reluctant' to appreciate (the) benefits of a technology transfer project (Technopolis, 1994: 27) and were thus uncommitted and reluctant to be involved in demonstrators (Technopolis, 1994: 54). Under such conditions, simply adding end users over the lifetime of a project neither widens nor accelerates the diffusion process.

Firms that are risk adverse, moreover, may be unwilling to take a leap into the unknown without considerable support. For these firms, a minimalist solution of sticking to what is known will be preferred to a maximalist one in which the firm engages in a process of innovation in cognitive frames, work arrangements and cultures. Taking the minimalist approach, however, does not guarantee that the recipient firm has been set on a dynamic path for the future. Yet technology transfer projects are rarely designed to break the non-innovative habits and practices of recipient firms. Rather, to a large extent, by focusing on existing technology, they give the appearance of linearity and certainty. Since the points of both departure and arrival are known, there is a tendency to miss all of the steps in between. Technology transfer thus comes to be viewed as a one time means to upgrade the technological level of a firm by transferring the hardware and software required for a particular production process from one producer to another or between a producer and a user. Conceptualised in this way, innovation is reduced to the introduction of a new product or process into a new setting and technology transfer becomes a vehicle for the promotion of innovation only to the extent that it enables a recipient to learn how to use a new process or to produce a new product. It is grafted upon existing routines rather than entailing any real break with them.

Innovation, however, is much more than this. It involves producers and users in a continuous, non-linear, interactive process of change that leads to new ways both of thinking about and of doing things. This goes well beyond the introduction of new production processes and products to include the development of management routines that are better attuned to problem sensing and problem identification; the revamping of communications channels between production, marketing and R&D; and changes in the organisation of production so as to enhance quality, speed throughput and improve the longer term adaptive potential of the firm. Only a continuous process of innovation enables the firm to deal positively with challenges to its competitiveness as these arise. This is why 'learning to learn' must become a component of technology transfer projects if they are to contribute positively to innovation in the longer term.

Although Commission documents at that time began to reflect the conceptual shift to innovation policy, the design of RTD programmes remained influenced by the earlier supply side orientation throughout much of the 1990s. The SPRINT case study underscored the need to refocus such programmes on the process of innovation and thus upon the habits and practices of the actors whose behaviour policy was intended to influence. It also pointed to the need to replace existing hierarchical models of performance appraisal by more collaborative approaches that stimulated interaction among partners, providing the kind of continuous feedback between partners and monitors that alters not only the goals of a project but the means and routines that govern activity between and within participants.

But despite these limitations at the conceptual and implementation levels, it was precisely within somewhat 'linear' programmes such as these that new approaches to conceptualising innovation and hence re-conceptualising policy approaches emerged.   SPRINT was aimed at innovation and technology transfer, but it also incorporated an analysis programme, the 'European Innovation Monitoring System' (EIMS), which became a focus for innovation studies across a wide field of applications. EIMS also became the initiator, together with Eurostat, of the 'Community Innovation Survey', which was based on the conceptual and statistical work initiated by the OECD's TEP programme – so there was a also a general interplay between some of the agencies that were open to the ideas of the new innovation theory. This programme is a good example of a niche area in which heterodox approaches took root, supported and encouraged by small numbers of policy makers and administrators seeking new approaches and tolerant of the complexities and messiness of empirical innovation research.

These EU programmes – and earlier initiatives such as the late 1980s-early 1990s programmes MONITOR (on evaluation) and FAST (on forecasting and technology assessment) provided both research support and a meeting place for European innovation researchers. As such, they played an important role in the evolution of the field, giving it both intellectual credibility and financial support that were crucial to some research institutions. This process can arguably be seen as an example of precisely the type of interactive and feedback-based learning modelled within innovation theory itself. On the one hand there was a supply of new ideas emanating from a vibrant but very small intellectual community. On the other there was a demand for policy solutions to growth and equity issues at regional, national and European levels. But most importantly, there were continuous feedback loops in the form of monitoring and evaluation projects, analysis and development of the results of innovation survey data, and a continuous dialogue between research and policy makers in regional authorities and relevant EU agencies. Continuous interaction and feedback had an important impact on both innovation theory and the world of policy ideas.

But it was not until the focus shifted to regional development policies that the kind of interactions that theory suggested were critical for innovation became more fully integrated into EU programmes. This was reflected in the participatory methodologies used to capture inputs from the demand side adopted in the new regional policies, particularly the set of regional innovation and technology transfer initiatives called RTP, RITTS and RIS. These actions differed significantly from the more traditional RTD policies, from efforts to transfer technology to smaller firms and less favoured regions and from earlier uses to which structural funds were put. To some extent, therefore, the equity issue played the role of a demand side factor in pulling forward conceptual change. Over time, and in parallel with the OECD, the problem was reformulated from competitiveness to innovation and equity, the inter relatedness of policies was given greater consideration and the process itself became more interactive. Social scientists played a major role in this transformation both at the design stage and in undertaking the monitoring and evaluation that provided feedback into the policy process. This kind of interactivity in a sense reflects the interactivity of the chain link model, with feedbacks providing a key dynamics to the overall process; once again, this would suggest that innovative learning and policy learning have fruitful analogies, and cannot be fully separated from one another.

Such processes began to emerge onto a wider stage over the 1990s. In the early 1990s, RTD issues began to play a more significant role both in policy pronouncements, and in the organisation of policy-related research in the EC. The Maastricht Treaty, for example, specifically mentioned the role of R&D policy in industrial change, and regional cohesion; and this theme was repeated in the EU *White Paper on Unemployment*. The OECD programme on unemployment (the 'Jobs Study') in the mid-1990s focused very much on technological change issues. Country-level reviews in the OECD and UNCTAD, statistical indicators collected by the OECD and the EU and the research and technology development (RTD) programmes of the European Union were slowly developed or redesigned to give effect to the insights flowing from innovation theory.

The increasing policy emphasis on the role of RTD was reflected in action. In the EU, the budget of the Framework programmes, the overall R&D programme budget within which 'packages' dealing with the major European-level scientific and technological RTD effort were organised, became one of the few growing areas. The Framework programmes were coordinated and to some extent implemented by DG-XII (now DG-Research). They incorporated a fluctuating array of mainly supply side technology-push programmes dealing with electronics, telecommunications, pharmaceuticals, and industrial technologies.

The really major impulse to the development of innovation research in support of policy came with the 'Targeted Socio-Economic Research' (TSER) programme in the Fourth Framework programme (1995–99), and the follow-up 'Improving Human Potential' programme in the Fifth Framework programme. Here the initiatives lay with policy makers and administrators. TSER was large, carefully designed and rather well prepared by Commission staff who, in general, were well informed and rather widely read within the field. In effect, they took on board the new innovation theories, identified the gaps and weaknesses, and sought to research some of the key unresolved problems. Projects emerged on a wide range of topics: these were usually multi-year projects, with a wide range of partners across Europe, and were well funded (for an overview of some key first round projects, see Archibugi and Lundvall, 2001). TSER contained no less than 64 projects, mostly large scale, and IHP and smaller number of large scale projects (European Commission 2000, 2001). They included such topics as:

- innovation in service industries
- innovation systems and European integration
- new innovation statistics and data
- S&T policies in transition countries
- institutional restructuring in transition countries
- public participation in environmental policy
- modelling sustainable growth in Europe
- universities and technology transfer on the periphery of Europe
- economic analysis of technology, economic integration and employment
- strategic analysis: policy intelligence and foresight
- regional innovation systems and policy
- multimedia and social learning
- financial systems and corporate governance (focusing on its effects on innovation)

This kind of wide ranging support has continued, and has produced a very substantial change in the character of innovation research in Europe (Bartzokas, 2001). Every significant institution working in the innovation field in Europe has participated, and virtually every significant researcher. The level of networking and contact between researchers has multiplied dramatically, as have the number of journals and the volume of publication. So these EU-backed projects have provided a major dynamic impetus to innovation studies, as well as providing a practical level of support without which some key institutions in the area might not have survived. This ought to be seen as a reciprocal movement out of the impact that innovation theorists had on policy in the 1980s and early 1990s; the EU programmes really represent an interactive mix of concepts and policy approaches.

2.5 CO-EVOLUTION OF THEORY AND POLICY – THE GAPS THAT REMAIN

Innovation theories emerged in a period of dramatic change. Expectations were diminishing after a sustained period of post war growth. Technological ruptures were underway but their impact on productivity was far from being felt. Imports from low wage countries were increasing and, coupled with new patterns of investment and organisational change, created further economic dislocation as regions declined and unemployment rose. Existing theory could not deal with these changes and the paradoxes to which they gave rise. While national governments in the developed world initially fell back upon neoprotectionist solutions and then embraced liberalisation, a small number of international organisations such as the OECD and the EC, became the locus for exploratory thinking around the issue of technological change. Dissenting theorists slowly reformulated the problem as one of learning and innovation and contextualised it in terms of innovation systems and institutions. Passage through international organisations then served to legitimise these concepts and to promote them as focusing devices in national policy making.

In this process, and despite their 'outsider' status, social scientists working within the new innovation paradigm have been extraordinarily successful in building a constituency for innovation systems approaches and in the design and redesign of innovation policies. By emphasising the contextually specific nature of innovation processes, they have brought theory closer to policy, but have not entirely bridged the gap. Nor has the emphasis on a holistic and differentiated approach implicit in the innovation system literature made the task of its use in the development of policy *instruments* any easier. Evolutionary theory, for example, 'would predict that different actors would do different things. They would see opportunities differently. They would rank differently those that all saw' (Nelson, 1996, p. 125). We would thus expect national governments to tailor new policy instruments to the particular habits and practices of actors whose behaviour policy is designed to influence. Only where stakeholders at the regional level have been able to shape policies directly through participatory processes are there small signs of movement in this direction. For the most part, policy makers have been hard pressed to deal with the complex reality that innovation systems approaches represent.

The absence of a unified theory that relates innovation to growth and distribution and links macro approaches to the micro level has slowed the application of innovation theory to policy areas beyond the narrow confines of education or research and technology development policy. Similarly, the lack of new measurement tools has limited the translation of innovation theory into effective policy instruments. This contrasts with the impact of Keynes' theory which was reinforced by the concurrent development of national accounting statistics that made it possible to quantify the analytical categories of his *General Theory*, to estimate empirically the functional relationships between them and to apply the theory to the resolution of policy problems (Patinkin, 1976). Concurrent developments to measure innovation have been undertaken in the 1990s. Paul David, Richard Nelson, Bengt- Åke Lundvall (who in fact made the transition from researcher to deputy director of DSTI in OECD between 1993 and 1995) and Luc Soete were among those who played a role in efforts at the OECD and in the EU to build an empirical base for the analysis of innovation. But these efforts have yet to provide the tools, for example, to test the OECD's conceptually interesting hypothesis that a system's innovative capacity is related to the extensiveness and efficiency with which it distributes and absorbs knowledge (David and Foray 1995).[11] As this chapter has shown, although innovation theory has made considerable conceptual inroads, there is still a way to go before the links between innovation and other policies are well established and the ability to measure the results becomes a reality.

The story we have sought to tell here is itself an evolutionary one. Learning in this field has been interactive, with a strong co-evolution of policy ideas and theoretical and empirical studies of a new field. As with other processes of economic evolution, this has been problem-driven, indeed crisis-driven. Despite the now dissipated euphoria associated with the 'new economy' of recent years, the past three decades have been a time of economic turbulence, with sustained problems of unemployment and productivity growth. This has created a niche for new ideas, and the interaction of policy needs and intellectual endeavour has created a space in which the new field could grow. Simultaneously, and probably for similar reasons, the mainstream of economics has declined, and that discipline now faces its own crisis of declining student numbers and diminished policy credibility. It is of course impossible to say how this situation will pan out. In our view, much will depend on the ability of innovation studies to remain an area of intellectual vitality and advance, something which will require a clear recognition of existing limits and weaknesses, and a clear willingness to seek to overcome those limits.

NOTES

1. Despite extensive criticisms of the IMF/World Bank structural adjustment programmes, the IMF response to the Asian financial crisis, for example, carried forward its traditional approach. Even the presence of an 'outsider', Joseph Stiglitz, as chief economist of the World Bank brought little by way of change in conceptual frameworks or policy approaches in this institution and virtually no ability to influence practices in the World Bank's sister institution, the IMF.
2. The classic statement of this point was Arrow (1962).
3. Abramowitz (1956) found that barely half of the actual growth in output could be explained by the growth of inputs in terms of capital and labour. The residual was classified as unexplained total factor productivity.
4. For an excellent review of the earlier economic literature flowing from the initial work of Moses Abramowitz, see Nelson (1996). In a more recent article Nelson has carried forward his critiques to deal with the 'new' growth theorists (Nelson, 1998).

5.   Although as Saxenian (1994) and Storper (1999) have argued, these localities are not restricted to national spaces.
6.   Lundvall op. cit., p.12.
7.   Lundvall, op. cit., p.2.
8.   RACE began with a definitional phase in 1985–87 and a main programme from 1988–92. Under the Fourth Framework programme for research and technology covering the years 1994–98, RACE because the Advanced Communications Specific Programme whose aim is 'to consolidate European technology leadership in digital broad band communications' (I&T Magazine, DGIII & DGXIII, Spring, 1994, p. 4).
9.   *Innovation and Technology Transfer Newsletter* (Commission, DGXIIID-2): Vol. 14/1 (3/93), p. 12.
10.   Only the Telematics program, the Sprint MINT program which helped small and medium sized enterprises (SMEs) absorb new technology and some of the newer BRITE/EURAM projects in this period, seemed to reflect primarily a demand side orientation. They were not, however, truly 'interactive'.
11.   The tendency, therefore, has been to recreate linearity in formal models and to rely on the indicators used by more conventional approaches. Thus, attempts to operationalise the distribution power of innovation systems, that is, 'the proportion of knowledge "ready for distribution"', use output measures such as publications and patents, common to other approaches and measure the absorptive capacities of firms, as elsewhere, by quantitative indicators such as the amount of in-house R&D (in value or numbers of scientific and technical employment) and the cost of technology licensing.

REFERENCES

Abramowitz, M. (1956). 'Resources and Output Trends in the United States Since 1870', *American Economic Review* 46: 5–23.
Abramowitz, M. (1971). 'Resources and Output Trends in the United States Since 1870', in N. Rosenberg (ed.), *The Economics of Technological Change*, Harmondsworth: Pelican, pp. 320–43.
Aglietta, M. (1976). *Régulation et Crise du Capitalisme*, Paris: Calmann Lévy.
Archibugi, D. and Lundvall, B.-Å. (2001). *The Globalising Learning Economy*, Oxford: OUP.
Arrow, K.J., (1962). 'Economic Welfare and the Allocation of Resources for Invention', in R. Nelson (ed.), *The Rate and Direction of Inventive Activity*, Princeton, NJ: Princeton University Press, pp. 609–25; republished in N. Rosenberg (ed.), *The Economics of Technological Change,* Harmondsworth: Pelican, 1974, pp.164–81.
Bartzokas, A. (2001). 'Policy Relevance and Theory Development in Innovation Studies', *Enterprise and Innovation Management Studies* 2 (1): 1–18.
Boyer, R. (1988). 'Technical Change and the Theory of Regulation', in G. Dosi et al. (eds), *Technical Change and Economic Theory*, London: Pinter, pp. 67–94.
Cadiou, J.M. (1996). 'ESPRIT, un Premier Bilan', *Bulletin de Liaison de la Recherche en Informatique et Automatique*, 105: 127–48.

Carlsson, B. (ed.) (1995). *Technological Systems and Economic Performance: the Case of Factory Automation,* Dordrecht: Kluwer.

Commission of the European Communities (1987). *ESPRIT: the First Phase, Progress and Results,* Brussels: The Commission.

David, P. and Foray, D. (1995). 'Accessing and Expanding the Science and Technology Knowledge Base', *STI Review* 16: 93–119.

Dosi, G., Freeman, C., Nelson R., Silverberg G. and Soete L. (1988). *Technical Change and Economic Theory,* London: Pinter.

European Commission (2000). *Targeted Socio-Economic Research: Project Synopses 1994–1998.* Brussels: The Commission, EUR 18844.

European Commission (2001). *Improving the Socio-Economic Knowledge Base: Project Synopses 1999–2002,* Brussels: The Commission, RTD-2001-00209.

Freeman, C. (1982). 'Innovation as an Engine of Economic Growth', in Giersch, H. (ed.) *Emerging Technologies: Consequences for Economic Growth, Structural Change and Employment,* J.C.B. Bohr: Tubinen, pp. 1–27.

Freeman, C. (1988). 'Japan: A New National System of Innovation?', in G. Dosi et al. (eds), *Technical Change and Economic Theory,* London Pinter, pp. 330–48.

Freeman, C. and Perez, C. (1988). 'Structural Crises of Adjustment: Business Cycles and Investment Behaviour', in G. Dosi et. al. (eds), *Technical Change and Economic Theory,* London Pinter, pp. 38–66.

Guzzetti, L. (1995). *A Brief History of European Union Research Policy,* Science Research Development, Studies 5, Brussels, European Commission: October.

Hall, P. (1989). 'Conclusion: The Politics of Keynesian Ideas', in P. Hall (ed.), *The Political Power of Economic Ideas: Keynesianism Across Nations,* Princeton, NJ: Princeton University Press, pp. 361–92.

Kline, S., and Rosenberg, N. (1986). 'An Overview of Innovation' in R. Landau (ed.). *The Positive Sum Strategy Harnessing Technology for Economic Growth,* 1986, Washington DC: National Academy Press, pp. 275–306.

Lundvall, B.-Å. (1988). 'Innovation as an Interactive Process: From User-Producer Interaction to the National System of Innovation', in G. Dosi et al. (eds), *Technical Change and Economic Theory,* London: Pinter, pp. 349–69.

Lundvall, B.-Å. (ed.) (1992), *National Systems of Innovation: Towards a Theory of Innovation and Interactive Learning,* London: Pinter.

Lundvall, B.-Å. (1995). 'The Social Dimension of the Learning Economy', Danish Research Unit for Industrial Dynamics Working Paper No. 96-1, Aalborg University, Denmark.

Mytelka, L.K. (1987). 'The Evolution of Knowledge Production Strategies Within Multinational Firms', in J. Caporaso (ed.), *A Changing International Division of Labour, Vol. 1*: International Political Economy Yearbook, Boulder, CO: Lynne Reiner, pp. 43–70.

Mytelka, L.K. (ed.) (1999). 'Competition, Innovation and Competitiveness: a Framework for Analysis' in *Competition, Innovation and Competitiveness in Developing Countries,* Paris: OECD Development Centre, pp. 15–27.

Nelson, Richard (1981). 'Research on Productivity Growth and Productivity Differences: Dead Ends and New Departures', in Nelson (1996).

Nelson, Richard (1996). *The Sources of Economic Growth,* Cambridge, MA: Harvard University Press.

Nelson, Richard (1998). 'The Agenda for Growth Theory: A Different Point of View', Cambridge Journal of Economics, 22: 497–522.

Nelson, Richard (ed.) (1993). *National Innovation Systems: A Comparative Analysis*, New York: Oxford University Press.

Nelson, R. and Winter, S. (1982). *An Evolutionary Theory of Economic Change*, Cambridge, MA: Harvard University Press.

OECD (1971). *Science, Growth and Society* (Brooks Report), Paris: OECD.

OECD (1980). *Technical Change and Economic Policy*, Paris: OECD.

OECD (1988). *New Technologies in the 1990s: A Socio-Economic Strategy* (Sundqvist Report), Paris: OECD.

OECD (1991). *Technology and Productivity: The Challenges for Economic Policy*, Paris: OECD.

OECD (1992a). *Proposed Guidelines for Collecting and Interpreting Innovation Data* ('Oslo Manual'), Paris: OECD.

OECD (1992b). *Technology and the Economy: The Key Relationships*, Paris: OECD.

OECD (1994). *The OECD Jobs Study: Facts, Analysis, Strategies*, Paris: OECD.

OECD (1996). *Technology, Productivity and Job Creation*, Paris: OECD.

OECD (1997). *Innovation Manual (Oslo Manual)*, OECD: Paris.

OECD (1998). *Technology, Productivity and Job Creation: Best Policy Practices*, Paris: OECD.

Patinkin, D. (1976). 'Keynes and Econometrics: On the Interaction Between the Macroeconomic Revolutions of the Inter-War Period', *Econometrica*, 44 (November): 1091–123.

Piore, M.J. and Sabel C. (1984). *The Second Industrial Divide*, New York: Basic Books.

Romer, P.M. (1994). 'The Origins of Endogenous Growth', *Journal of Economic Perspectives* 8 (1): 3–22.

Rosenberg, N. (1976). *Perspectives On Technology*, Cambridge: Cambridge University Press, pp. 108–25..

Rosenberg, N. (1982). *Inside the Black Box: Technology and Economics*, Cambridge: Cambridge University Press.

Saxenian, AnnaLee (1994). *Regional Advantage, Culture and Competition in Silicon Valley and Route 128*, Cambridge, MA: Harvard University Press.

Storper, Michael (1999). *The Regional World: Territorial Development in a Global Economy*, New York: The Guilford Press.

Technopolis (1994). *Evaluation of SPRINT Specific Projects Action Line*, Brighton: Technopolis.

UNCTAD (1999a). *The Science, Technology and Innovation Policy Review*, Columbia: UNCTAD, New York and Geneva.

UNCTAD (1999b). *The Science, Technology and Innovation Policy Review*, Jamaica: UNCTAD, New York and Geneva.

Verspagen, B. (1992). 'Endogenous Innovation in Neo-Classical Growth Models: a Survey', *Journal of Macroeconomics* 14: 631–62.

3. Manna trajectories and networks: shifting heuristics in the economics of innovation and new technologies[1]

Cristiano Antonelli

3.1 INTRODUCTION

Economics of innovation and new technologies is a recent fruitful area of specialisation in economic theory. The earliest definition can be traced back to the 50s with the introduction of the concept of residual. Thanks to the contributions of Moses Abramovitz (1956) and Bob Solow (1957) economics of innovation and new technologies concentrates on the problem of explaining the processes of growth which could not be easily identified in an increase in productive factors.

The divide between increasing returns and unexplained growth has been in many ways a useful device. With increasing returns to scale output grows more than inputs and it is difficult to identify the specific contribution of technological change to economic growth. With constant returns to scale all increase in output which cannot be explained by means of appropriate changes in production factors can be considered as the result of the introduction of innovations in processes, products, and in organisations.

Total factor productivity growth is a real puzzle for economics. The introduction of innovations cannot be considered as the outcome of the standard rational behaviour where marginal costs equal marginal revenues. When the costs of introducing an innovation match the revenue, measured either in terms of an increase in sales or a reduction in costs, no total factor productivity growth would take place. This is the real problem economics of innovation and new technologies faces (Griliches, 1979, 1997).

More generally innovation and total factor productivity growth raise a serious problem for economics at large. The results of Solow (1957) in fact show that more than 50 per cent of the growth of the US economy were determined by a factor which cannot be fully understood and analysed with the traditional categories of standard economics.

The birth of economics of innovation as a specific area of enquiry and investigation in the broader context of the increasing specialisation of economics can be considered the ultimate result of the analysis of growth as if increasing returns do not take place.

From this viewpoint, economics of innovation and new technologies is more than a new attempt by economics to extend its methodology into social science, as is the case with the economics of education, health or risk, just to name a few new areas of specialisation of economics. Economics of innovation and new technologies is also and mainly an interface with other social sciences able to consider the role of unexpected events in economic life.

In this context the interaction with sociology and philosophy has been a constant source of inspiration for economics of innovation and new technologies. Sociology and philosophy have in fact provided new heuristic metaphors to apply in the context of the economic analysis of the advent of new knowledge and new technologies.[2]

During the last few years three such wide-ranging heuristic metaphors have been proposed: the manna metaphor, the trajectory metaphor, and the systematic network metaphor. Each of them has made important analytical contributions, which have enabled stylised facts, analytical prospects and sometimes theoretical revelations to be elaborated. These are approaches which today are fighting to make this discipline a particularly fertile and creative area of economic theory.

3.2   MANNA AND TECHNOLOGICAL OPPORTUNITIES

The manna metaphor draws mainly on the path breaking contributions of Kenneth Arrow (1962a, 1962b, 1969). Already at the beginning of the 60s the hypothesis that technical progress was intrinsically exogenous was put forward as a methodological device to better understand its effects on the economic system. The assumptions about full exogeneity had the advantage of making it possible to disentangle the analysis of technological change from the complex web of dynamic forces and their interplay.

Specifically, in the manna tradition of analysis a linear sequence between scientific discoveries and technological innovations is introduced. Scientists deliver inventions and new scientific knowledge. Scientific knowledge eventually translates into technological knowledge which in turn feeds the introduction of technological innovations.

From its first introduction the manna metaphor relied heavily, as an external reference, on the first sociology of innovation. Sociology of innovation drew mainly on the early contributions of Robert Merton (1973), in turn based upon the Weberian tradition, in the attempt to identify the objectives and incentives of the scientific undertaking. Scientists, mainly academics, generate new scientific knowledge in an appropriate institutional context, one where incentives are not defined in strict economic terms. Scientists generate scientific discoveries in the form of public science in order to achieve peer reputation. Publications increase the stock of knowledge available on the shelf and ready to be used, for economic purposes, by firms.

Attributing the characteristics of a public good to scientific knowledge and therefore assuming indivisibility, non-exclusiveness and non-appropriateness, sanctioned a division of labour between firms and universities. The latter were of course responsible for the production and distribution of this public good. Firms had to be able to pick up the stimulus which was set off by new scientific discoveries. The state's role in this situation was that of an indispensable intermediary, which collected the taxes necessary to finance university research. Scientific inventions perfected and improved in an academic ambience, and therefore, in the realm of meta-economics, produced effects in terms of technological opportunities. Firms took these opportunities and introduced the innovations, thanks to which the total factor productivity increased and with it the amount of the income produced but not directly 'explained' by the increase in input.

In order to increase the incentives for innovators, the low levels of natural appropriability of technological innovations could be enhanced by means of intellectual property rights such as patents. Once more a dichotomy takes place. Science is public, while technology is private. Scientific knowledge is the primary source of technological knowledge. The former should remain in the public domain while the latter can be privatised in order to increase the rates of introduction of technological innovations.

The analysis of technological change as the result of an exogenous process provides the framework to study the effects of the introduction of new technologies. New technologies can affect the marginal productivity of production factors and hence the derived demand for inputs when they are non-neutral and exhibit either capital saving or labour saving effects. The direction of technological change has important consequences for the equilibrium levels of the market price for inputs.

Entrepreneurship in this context supplies new evidence on the key role of meta-economic factors in assessing the rate and direction of technological change. Following Schumpeter Mark 1 – as Freeman, Clark and Soete (1982) term the literature inspired by *The Theory of Economic Development* 1936 – the supply of entrepreneurs able to spot new technological opportunities and to understand the possible technological and economic applications of new scientific breakthroughs is considered an important factor in understanding the pace of introduction of new technologies and their specific economic and technological characteristics. The analysis of the institutional and economic conditions which favour entrepreneurship and the entry of new innovative firms into the marketplace at large, becomes an important area of investigation. The linkages and the interfaces between universities and new firms, the role of financial markets in the provision of funds for the innovations introduced by newcomers and the role of spatial proximity in fostering the birth of new high-tech firms, become objects of systematic investigation.

In this context the analysis of the effects of technological change at the firm level are also relevant. New innovative firms enter the marketplace and destroy barriers to entry and monopolistic rents with the reduction of concentration. New technologies can be either centripetal or centrifugal according to their impact on regional and industrial concentration. In the latter case new technologies, such as electric power and lately advanced telecommunications, favour the even distribution of firms and plants in regional space and the reduction in their minimum efficient size. In the latter, new technologies, such as chemistry and assembly lines, may favour concentration when they lead to relevant economies of scale and scope.

A second relevant basket of important research programmes favoured by the manna metaphor is the analysis of the delays in the adoption of given technological innovations. The economics of the diffusion of new technologies is conceived as the study of the factors which account for the distribution over time of the adoption of identifiable successful innovations (Griliches, 1956). A new technology is introduced after a scientific breakthrough and yet it takes time for all prospective users to adopt it. The successful application of the epidemic methodology emerges in this context. Diffusion like contagion takes place in a population of heterogeneous agents which differ mainly in terms of information costs.

Scientific breakthrough and as a consequence technological innovations do fall from heaven, but they do have asymmetric effects. Some firms innovate faster than others. Other firms adopt faster than others.

In this context a first shift takes place as a result of the neoSchumpeterian literature on the relationship between innovation and the size of firms and the concentration within industries. The so-called Schumpeterian hypothesis – or Schumpeter Mark 2 which builds upon *Capitalism Socialism and Democracy* (1942) – according to which large business in concentrated industries is more conducive to fostering the rates of introduction of innovations rather than small firms in fragmented industries, is elaborated and receives great empirical attention. Although the evidence does not provide clear cut answers, this debate provides evidence of the strong albeit non-univocal relationship between types of competition and especially forms of industrial organisation and the rate and direction of technological change (Scherer, 1984, 1999).

In this context, the notion of technological opportunities emerges as an important contribution. Firms and industries, both large and small, with high and low concentration rates are more productive in terms of rates of introduction of technological innovations when technological opportunities are available. Technological opportunities are defined in terms of technical and economic proximity of new technologies and firms to scientific discoveries (Rosenberg, 1976).

The strong evidence on the relevant asymmetries induced by technological change contrasts with the assumption of full exogeneity of scientific breakthrough and technological innovations portrayed in the metaphor of manna. The classical hypothesis about the inducement of technological change by changes in factor prices receives new attention. Technological change is viewed as an augmented substitution. Firms are induced to change both techniques and technology by changes in the prices of production factors which alter significantly the basic characteristics of the production process. Technological change is now viewed as the endogenous outcome of the vertical relations among industries and firms in intermediary markets. All changes in the mix of production factors as determined by relevant shifts in their prices may induce the introduction of new technologies (Binswanger and Ruttan, 1978).

On a parallel ground an important contribution favouring a more complete endogenous presentation of technological change comes from macroeconomic studies which draw on Nicholas Kaldor and the post-Kaldorian literature. There is a strong awareness of the flows of innovation in sectors in which the growth of demand is higher. Again it is possible to highlight how the system is intrinsically able to condition, also through the mechanism of expectations, scientific activity and favour its application in technological fields and industrial sectors where the expectations of profit are highest (Schmookler, 1966).

Even though the generation of new knowledge remains an exogenous factor, its effective application assumes strong endogenous connotations.

Even if technological change is partly induced by market forces – with given and exogenous technological opportunities – the basic puzzle raised by total factor productivity growth cannot be solved. In a world of Olympian rationality non-myopic agents should be fully aware of the possible effects of new technologies and search for them even without any pressure exerted by changes in factor prices or demand pull.

3.3   TRAJECTORIES AND TECHNOLOGICAL PATHS

Two important philosophical contributions characterise the new emerging research agenda: the distinction introduced by Michael Polanyi (1958) between tacit and codified knowledge and the analyses on the limits to Olympian rationality articulated by Herbert Simon (1982).

According to the path breaking analysis of Michael Polanyi (economic) agents often know more than they are able to spell out in a codified and explicit way. Tacit knowledge is the result of lengthy learning processes and is embedded in the idiosyncratic procedures and habits elaborated by each agent. It can be translated into a fully codified knowledge only by means of systematic and explicit efforts.

New technologies may arise from such learning processes and especially from the efforts to convert tacit knowledge into new procedures which can be shared and transferred. A bottom-up understanding of the discovery process which complements the traditional top-down approach to the origin of technological innovations is now acquired (Hayek, 1945).

On a complementary ground Herbert Simon elaborates on the distinction between substantive and procedural rationality. Agents cannot achieve substantive rationality due to the burden of the wide range of activities necessary to gathering and processing all the relevant information. Agents can elaborate procedures to evaluate at each point in time and space the possible outcomes of their behaviour, but within the boundaries of a limited knowledge. Agents can elaborates routines which make it possible to save on information costs.

From the beginning of the 80s, the manna metaphor was contrasted with the new metaphor of trajectories drawn from the well-know contribution in the philosophy of science by Kuhn (1962). The trajectory metaphor is first elaborated and introduced into economics by Dick Nelson and Sid Winter (1982).

It assumes, firstly, the separation of technological knowledge from scientific knowledge and emphasises the different rhythms of evolution of the two kinds of knowledge. The trajectory metaphor, secondly, emphasises which elements contribute to continuity and accumulation in the process of accumulating technological knowledge along both technical and behavioural axes of evolution. Demand pull and technology push are the driving engines which feed each other along such well defined sequences of technological innovations. Finally and most important, building upon Simon and Polanyi, Nelson and Winter elaborate the notion of local search: firms search for new technologies in a technical space defined in terms of proximity with the techniques in use.

The notion of technological trajectory makes possible a source of cumulative research in the discipline. A variety of parallel notions and specifications of the relations among technologies converge. The analysis of the complementarity between product and process innovations articulated by James Utterback (1994) contributes on a more technical ground the notion of trajectory. Nathan Rosenberg contributes to the analysis of technological change with the notion of technological convergence, which stresses the dynamic blending of technologies and their generative relations. The introduction of key technologies can activate an array of derivative innovations, based upon incremental technological changes (Rosenberg, 1976, 1982). The intrinsic cumulability of technological change along the trajectories is itself a major acquisition (Dosi et al., 1988). Innovators can take advantage of previous innovations in many ways: early competitive advantage makes it possible to fund new research; competence and technological knowledge acquired are useful inputs for further innovations; barriers to entry based upon market shares and size delay imitation; technological advance feeds diversification and entry into new industries.

An important reference point in the trajectory metaphor is certainly Kuhn's contribution with his distinction between normal science and paradigm shift. The trajectories then appear as a translation and application of the notion of normal science which moves along predetermined routes until its heuristic ability has run out. In such circumstances there are conditions for a solution of defined continuity, that is to say, paradigm shift. Radical changes in the marketplace and in technology may induce firms to change their routines and introduce radical technological changes. Dosi (1982, 1988) contributes to the analysis of trajectories with the notion of paradigm shift.

Paradigm crises arise as factors of discontinuity. New trajectories are generated and old ones decline. The origin of such changes in technological paradigms however remains unclear but for the implicit reference to the notion of technological opportunities and their eventual exhaustion. The ultimate origin of technological change remains exogenous and a strong deterministic character is now added.

In this context however important contributions come from the analysis of the effects of the cumulability and tacitness of technological change. Trajectories are applied both to understand the dynamics of innovation with respect to the sequence of well defined technologies and to the sequence of innovations introduced by well identified firms and eventually economic systems, such as regions, industries and even countries.

The analysis of trajectories appears especially promising at the firm level and in the analysis of the competitive process. First-comers can now reap substantial competitive advantages and build barriers to entry based on their technological knowledge. An important implication of the distinction between tacit and codified knowledge consists in fact in the increase in the 'natural' appropriability of technological knowledge.

Technological knowledge is now viewed as a quasi public good: it can be partly appropriated by innovators and it spills less easily into the atmosphere because of the bounded rationality of imitators and the important role of tacit knowledge embedded in the organisation of innovators.

The trajectory metaphor appears to be a particularly fertile field of study of the behaviour of large firms which are protagonists in growth and innovation strategies of an incremental kind in markets characterised by oligopolistic rivalries and high levels of product differentiation. In this literature, the large firm takes on a central role and appears, first if not exclusively, as the locus of accumulation of sticky technical knowledge and hence technological progress.

The wealth of definitions in the analysis of the innovative process, the effort to integrate the analysis of innovative strategies with the study of the behaviour of the firms in oligopolistic markets and especially the emphasis placed on learning processes and on accumulation, remain important acquisitions and perhaps indispensable to the economics of innovation and new technologies.

On a parallel ground the analysis of diffusion faces significant changes. Stan Metcalfe, as early as 1981, provides a path breaking context of analysis of diffusion where both demand and supply account for the distribution over time of adoptions. Metcalfe reintroduces the basic laws of standard economics into the epidemic framework and shows the relevance of their dynamic interplay.

Agreement on the trajectory metaphor however disappears quite rapidly when its strong deterministic bent is fully revealed. This trajectory metaphor revives the old temptation to use technological determinism to explain the social and economic changes as a process of alignment of changes dictated by technology (Misa, 1995).

In this context, characterised by the decline of the heuristic power of the notion of trajectory, increasing attention is paid to the role of localised learning, technological irreversibility and local externalities. The notions of localised technological change, introduced as early as in 1969 by Anthony Atkinson and Joe Stiglitz, and of path-dependence, introduced by Paul David (1975, 1985) receive new attention. Technological change is introduced locally by firms able to learn about the specific techniques in place and hence to improve them. Technological paths emerge as corridors into which firms are able to innovate, and increase total factor productivity in a limited technical space so as to retain the original production mix. The notion of technological path replaces the trajectory as the new heuristic metaphor and paves the way for an array of applications (Antonelli, 1995, 1999, 2001, 2003).

At the microeconomic level the rate and direction of technological change can be viewed as the endogenous outcome of the innovative sequential reaction of firms induced by the interplay between irreversibility of their capital stock and economic entropy. Irreversible and clay capital stock can be thought to be constituted by both fixed physical capital and competence and technological knowledge in well defined and circumscribed technical fields.

Firms induced to innovate by irreversibility and economic entropy search locally for new technologies. The direction of technological change is influenced by the search for new technologies that are complementary with the existing ones. The rate of technological change in turn is influenced by the relative efficiency of the search for new technologies. This dynamics leads firms to remain in a region of techniques which are close to the original one and continue to improve the technology in use. This is all the more plausible when the introduction of technological changes is made possible by the accumulation of competence and localised knowledge within the firm.

3.4   COLLECTIVE KNOWLEDGE AND NETWORKS

During the 90s the spread of constructivism in the history and in the sociology of science parallels the discovery of new prospects in the field of innovation economics (Bijker et al., 1987; Latour, 1987; Callon, 1989; Smith and Marx, 1995; Kline and Rosenberg, 1986).

The generation and introduction of technological innovations are now viewed as the result of complex alliances and compromises among heterogeneous groups of agents. Agents are diverse because of the variety of competences and localised knowledge they build upon. Alliances are based upon the valorisation of weak knowledge indivisibilities and local complementarities among technological types of knowledge. The convergence of the efforts of a variety of innovators, each of which has a specific and yet complementary technological base, can lead to the successful generation of a new technology (Freeman, 1991; Nelson, 1993).

In this approach the distinction between innovation and diffusion is blurred and on the opposite side each adoption is viewed as the result of a complementary effort that makes a new technology useful and specifically reliable, increasing its scope of application. Adopters are no longer viewed as passive and reluctant prospective users, but rather as ingenious screeners that assess the scope for complementarity and cumulability of each new technology in the light of their own specific needs and contexts of action. Profitability of adoption is the result of a process rather than a given fact.

A technology diffuses when it applies to a variety of diverse conditions of use. The intrinsic heterogeneity of agents applies in fact not only to their own technological base but also to the product and factor markets in which they operate. The vintage structure of their fixed costs and both tangible and intangible capital can be portrayed as major factors of differentiation and identification of the specific context of action both with respect to technological change and market strategy. New ideas can be implemented and incrementally enriched, so as to become eventually profitable innovations, only when appropriate coalitions of heterogeneous firms are formed.

The diffusion of a new technology is no longer seen as the outcome of the adaptive adoption of a new single technology, but rather of the choice of one new technology among many. Diffusion is the result of the selection of a dominant design out of an original variety of different technological options. Interdependence among users leads to increasing returns in adoption so that technologies that have been adopted by a large share of prospective users have grater chances to win out in the selection process and spread to the rest of the system (Arthur, 1989, 1994).

The analysis of industrial dynamics supplies the arena in which the market construction of new technologies can be observed. A variety of firms can be analysed in the course of their competitive strategies where technological change plays a major role. Each firm is characterised by a specific competence upon which localised knowledge has been implemented. Each firm is also characterised by a specific endowment of fixed capital, and specific contexts of conduct in both factor and product markets. The changing market conditions induce firms to innovate both in market strategies and in technologies.

An important contribution in this context is provided by the systematic application of the replicator elaborated by Stan Metcalfe (1997). Metcalfe has shown the fertility of the replicator, a methodology originally conceived in biology to analyse the dynamics of species, in understanding the competitive process. Metcalfe applies the replicator analysis to show how innovators can earn extra profits, fund their growth and acquire larger market shares. The analysis of the diffusion of innovation is intertwined with the study of the selection mechanism in the marketplace. Firms that have been able to introduce new technologies are also able to increase their growth and their market shares.

Technological choices concerning the introduction of product and process innovations, the adoption of new technologies provided by suppliers and the imitation of competitors are mingled with market strategies such as specialisation, outsourcing, diversification, entry and exit, merger and acquisitions and internal growth. In a continual trial in the marketplace firms experiment with their changing mix of technological and market conduct. At the aggregate level the result is the market selection of new and better technologies, often characterised by strong systemic complementarities.

The changing coalitions between different groups of players in overlapping and yet specific technological arenas shape the rate and direction of technological change at large.

The production of knowledge, both scientific and technological, now appears to be strongly conditioned by the social, institutional and economic conditions in which it takes place (Gibbons et al., 1994). Interaction and communication, among a variety of innovative agents and in the field of scientific production among scientists, plays a central role in the interpretation of the factors which are at the origin of the rates of production of new knowledge and of its specific direction, intended as specific fields of application. The analyses of Bengt-Åke Lundvall (1985) and of Eric Von Hippel (1988) on the key role of user-producer interactions as basic engines for the introduction of new technologies play a key role at this stage. The production of knowledge in fact, becomes a central condition for the subsequent perfection and improvement of technological innovation.

The collective character of technological knowledge and the complementarity of limited areas of knowledge put at the service of each actor are emphasised here. On the specific level of economic analysis the cooperative way in which innovations are perfected and improved is highlighted. It is seen as a process which also involves rival firms and firms situated in the same technological districts. Innovation is set off in such situations by the cross-fertilisation of specific knowledge and its continuous development. The range and the variety of actors involved in these exchanges appear to be determinant factors. The increasing number of the channels of communication among heterogeneous subjects, thus bringing diverse knowledge, but no less susceptible to being taken up, is key to activating new complementarities which call for the participation and the verbalisation of experiences. The parallel development of new technologies of information and communication highlights this approach and emphasises the fundamental role that interaction and communication play as factors of production of new knowledge through processes of formation and contamination (Antonelli, 1999, 2001).

Much advance in this context is provided by the new understanding of the dynamics of network externalities. Network externalities apply not only to the demand side when the utility of a given product is influenced by the number of users, but also on the supply side when the productivity of a capital good is influenced by the number of users. Moreover network externalities apply also to the generation of new knowledge and the introduction of new technological systems when the positive effects of the increasing number of complementary types of knowledge and related technologies are considered. The adoption of innovation, once introduced, is also affected by the number of early adopters (Katz and Shapiro, 1985; Antonelli, 1992).

The dynamics of economies of scope becomes central in this context. Economies of scope cannot be considered to be a windfall or as exogenous (manna), but rather the actual result of the introduction of new technologies that are complementary with the existing ones.

The direction of technological change pursued by each firm leads to the search for and eventual introduction of new technologies that make use of existing portions of the capital stock and rely upon the competence acquired in using the existing technologies. Technological innovations insisting on diverse sets of complementary inputs and valorising diverse combinations of inputs and hence dynamic economics of scope face the test of market selection.

The revival of the Marshallian analysis of externalities, of various shades, and of the Marshallian competitive process offers numerous interpretative points and brings into the centre of the discussion the question of complementarity and interdependence among the subjects in both the accumulation of new technological knowledge and subsequently in the introduction and adoption of new technologies. Metcalfe provides new ground for the notion of technological systems and highlights the role of supply and demand interactions in assessing the rate of technological change (Metcalfe, 1995, 1997).

3.5   CONCLUSIONS

About 50 years after its inception economics of innovation and new technologies is now sufficiently mature to fully acknowledge the contribution made by other social sciences in the definition of its basic categories and heuristic metaphors. At the same time, enriched by significant methodological extensions and unusually intense methodological and analytical discussions, the discipline can contribute to the study of the more general process of formation of new ideas in an advanced society.

The basic puzzle remains a problematic core for this interdisciplinary area of specialisation. How innovations come to the marketplace, how novelty takes place in our understanding of the economic and technological interplay, how and why total factor productivity growth increases, are still open questions.

The basic assumptions about growth with constant returns to scale which made it possible to articulate the very notion of residual and hence total factor productivity growth remain at the core of the problem. The revival of increasing returns, properly blended with the results of the economics of innovation and new technologies, seems a promising direction for future research (Romer, 1986).

In this context technological change can be viewed as a special form of dynamic increasing returns with strong stochastic, localised and contextual features. Increasing returns take place when technological change is introduced into a system. In turn technological change takes place when a number of highly qualified necessary conditions apply.

The successful introduction of technological change can be seen as the fragile result of a complex set of necessary and complementary conditions.

Changes in technology may take place and they may lead to the increase of output, with a given level of inputs, but only when a general process of economic change and industrial dynamics with well defined necessary conditions is actually in place. In this context a large number of complementary and necessary conditions, technological as well as institutional, competitive and macroeconomic, play a central role for a fast rate of introduction of new technologies to take place.

Cumulative technological change can take place when firms are able to react to irreversibility traps with appropriate levels of technological creativity; when, because of effective communication systems, local externalities can turn into collective knowledge; when high levels of investments can help the introduction of new technologies; when industrial dynamics in product and input markets can induce localised technological changes which in turn affect the competitive conditions of firms; when stochastic processes help the creative interaction of complementary bundles of new localised knowledge and new localised technologies to form new and effective technological systems; when the dynamics of positive feedback can actually implement the sequences of learning along technological paths, as well as the interactions between innovation and diffusion. In these circumstances the generation of new technological knowledge and the introduction of new technologies can be viewed as the cause and the consequence of economic growth and increasing returns (Arrow, 2000).

The successful accumulation of new technological knowledge, the eventual introduction of new and more productive technologies and their fast diffusion are in fact likely to take place in a self-propelling and spiralling process and at a faster pace within economic systems characterised by fast rates of growth where interaction, feedback and communication are swifter.

NOTES

1.   The comments of the editors of the volume, an anonymous referee, Martin Fransman and Morris Teubal are acknowledged. The work has been carried out

within the context of the European Union project 'Technological Knowledge and Localised Learning: What Perspectives for a European Policy?' Contract No. HPSE-CT2001- 00051. A broader analysis along these lines can be found in Antonelli (2003).

2. In a broader perspective, economics of innovation has also drawn from natural sciences with major biological grafts such as the epidemic approach to the study of diffusion, the life cycle analysis of the evolution of new technologies, and especially the pervasive applications of the Darwinistic selection process (see Antonelli, 2003).

REFERENCES

Abramovitz, M. (1956). 'Resources and Output Trends in the United States Since 1870', *American Economic Review* 46: 5–23.

Antonelli, C. (ed.) (1992). *The Economics of Information Networks*, Amsterdam: Elsevier.

Antonelli, C. (1995). *The Economics of Localized Technological Change and Industrial Dynamics*, Boston, MA: Kluwer Academic Publishers.

Antonelli, C. (1999). *The Microdynamics of Technological Change*, London: Routledge.

Antonelli, C. (2001). *The Microeconomics of Technological Systems*, Oxford: Oxford University Press.

Antonelli, C. (forthcoming 2003). *Innovation New Technologies and Structural Change*, London: Routledge.

Arrow, K. J. (1962a). 'The Economic Implications of Learning by Doing', *Review of Economic Studies*, 29: 155–73.

Arrow, K.J. (1962b). 'Economic Welfare and the Allocation of Resources for Invention, in R.R. Nelson, (ed.) *The Rate and Direction of Inventive Activity: Economic and Social Factors*, Princeton NJ: Princeton University Press for NBER.

Arrow, K.J. (1969). 'Classificatory Notes on the Production and Transmission of Technical Knowledge', *American Economic Review* 59: 29–35.

Arrow, K.J. (2000). Increasing Returns: Historiographic Issues and Path Dependence', *European Journal of History of Economic Thought* 7: 171–80.

Arthur, B. (1989). 'Competing Technologies, Increasing Returns and Lock-In by Small Historical Events', *Economic Journal* 99: 116–31.

Arthur, B. (1994). *Increasing Returns and Path Dependence in the Economy*, Ann Arbor, MI: University of Michigan Press.

Atkinson, A.B. and Stiglitz, J.E. (1969). 'A New View of Technological Change', *Economic Journal* 79: 573–8.

Bijker, W.E., Hughes, T.P. and Pinch, T. (eds.) (1987). *The Social Construction of Technological Systems*, Cambridge, MA: MIT Press.

Binswanger, H.P. and Rutan, V.W. (1978). *Induced Innovation*, Baltimore, MD: Johns Hopkins University Press.

Callon, M. (1989). *La Science et Ses Reseaux: Genèse et Circulation des Faits Scientifiques*, Paris: La Decouverte.

David, P.A. (1975). *Technical Choice, Innovation and Economic Growth*, Cambridge: Cambridge University Press.

David, P.A. (1985). 'Clio and the Economics of QWERTY', *American Economic Review* 75: 332–7.

Dosi, G. (1982). 'Technological Paradigms and Technological Trajectories: A Suggested Interpretation of the Determinants and Directions of Technological Change', *Research Policy* 11: 147–62.

Dosi, G. (1988). 'Sources, Procedures and Microeconomic Effects of Innovation', *Journal of Economic Literature* 26: 1120–71.

Dosi, G., Freeman, C., Nelson, R.R., Silverberg G. and Soete, L. (1988). *Technical Change and Economic Theory*, London: Pinter.

Freeman, C. (1991). 'Networks of Innovators: A Synthesis of Research Issues', *Research Policy* 20: 499–514.

Freeman, C., Clark, J. and Soete, L. (1982). *Unemployment and Technical Innovation: A Study of Long Waves and Economic Development*, London: Pinter.

Gibbons, M., Limoges, C., Nowotny, H., Schwarzman, S., Scott, P. and Trow, M. (1994), *The New Production of Knowledge: The Dynamics of Research in Contemporary Societies*, London: Sage.

Griliches, Z. (1956). 'Hybrid Corn: An Exploration in the Economics of Technical Change', *Econometrica* 25: 501–522.

Griliches, Z. (1979). 'Issues in Assessing the Contribution of Research and Development to Productivity Growth', *Bell Journal of Economics* 10: 92–116.

Griliches, Z. (1997). 'The Discovery of the Residual', *Journal of Economic Literature* 34: 1324–30.

Hayek, F.A. (1945). 'The Use of Knowledge in Society', *American Economic Review* 35: 519–30.

Katz, M. and Shapiro, C. (1985). 'Network Externalities, Competition and Compatibility', *American Economic Review* 75: 424–40.

Kline, S.J. and Rosenberg, N. (1986). 'An Overview of Innovation', in R. Landau and N. Rosenberg (eds), *The Positive Sum Strategy*, Washington, DC: National Academy Press.

Kuhn, T. (1962). *The Structure of Scientific Revolutions*, Chicago: University of Chicago Press.

Latour, B. (1987). *Science In Action. How to Follow Scientists and Engineers in Society*, Cambridge, MA: Harvard University Press.

Lundvall, B.-Å. (1985). *Product Innovation and User-Producer Interaction*, Aalborg: Aalborg University Press.

Merton, R. (1973). *The Sociology of Science: Theoretical and Empirical Investigations*, Chicago: University of Chicago Press.

Metcalfe, J.S. (1981). 'Impulse and Diffusion in the Study of Technical Change', *Futures* 13: 347–59.

Metcalfe, J.S. (1995), Technology systems and technology policy in historical perspective, *Cambridge Journal of Economics* 19: 25-47.

Metcalfe, J. S. (1997), *Evolutionary Economics and Creative Destruction*, London: Routledge.

Misa, T.J. (1995). 'Retrieving Sociotechnical Change from Technological Determinism', in M.R. Smith and L. Marx (eds), *Does Technology Drive History? The Dilemma of Technological Determinism*, Cambridge, MA: MIT Press.

Nelson, R.R. and Winter, S.G. (1982). *An Evolutionary Theory of Economic Change*, Cambridge, MA: Harvard University Press.

Nelson, R.R. (ed.) (1993). *National Systems of Innovation*, Oxford: Oxford University Press.

Polanyi, M. (1958). *Personal Knowledge: Towards a Post-Critical Philosophy*, London: Routledge & Kegan Paul.

Romer, P. (1986). 'Increasing Returns and Long-Run Growth', *Journal of Political Economy* 94: 1002–37.

Rosenberg, N. (1976). *Perspectives On Technology*, Cambridge: Cambridge University Press.

Rosenberg, N. (1982). *Inside the Black Box: Technology and Economics*, Cambridge: Cambridge University Press.

Scherer, F.M. (1984). *Innovation and Growth: Schumpeterian Perspectives*, Cambridge: MIT Press.

Scherer, F.M. (1999). *New Perspectives on Economic Growth and Technological Innovation*, Washington, DC: Brookings Institution.

Schmookler J. (1966). *Invention and Economic Growth*. Cambridge, MA: Harvard University Press.

Schumpeter, J.A. (1936). *The Theory of Economic Development*, Cambridge, MA: Harvard University Press.

Schumpeter, J.A. (1942). *Capitalism, Socialism and Democracy*, London: Unwin.

Simon, H.A. (1982). *Metaphors of Bounded Rationality: Behavioral Economics and Business Organization*, Cambridge, MA: MIT Press.

Smith, M.R. and Marx, L. (eds) (1995). *Does Technology Drive History? The Dilemma of Technological Determinism*, Cambridge, MA: MIT Press.

Solow, R.M. (1957). Technical Change and the Aggregate Production Function', *Review of Economics and Statistics* 39: 312–20.

Utterback, J.M. (1994). *Mastering the Dynamics of Innovation*, Boston, MA: Harvard Business School Press.

Von Hippel, E. (1988). *The Sources of Innovation*, Oxford: Oxford University Press.

4. Policy integration and action diversification: learning from the Portuguese path

Pedro Conceição and Manuel V. Heitor

4.1   INTRODUCTION

We argue in this chapter that a unified goal of R&D and innovation policy integration across EU requires policies that are designed in an integrated way, but that are implemented with diversified actions. 'Policy integration' should occur across a 'portfolio dimension', since innovation policies require coordination across several areas: science and education policies; social and health policies; environmental and industrial policies; employment and market regulation policies. However, the implementation of policies designed in an integrated way needs, in a multi-country and multicultural context, to consider differences across countries, regions and cultures, thus requiring action diversification.

While pointing out the need for policy integration is hardly questioned – given the growing consensus around the idea that innovation is an interactive, multi-institution, path dependent process – it is not always clear why there should be action diversification. In fact, balancing action diversification with policy integration involves significant problems that extend into the very nature of the relationships between national governments and the role and mission of multi-national political institutions, apart from specific regional and local contexts. Often the argument for action diversification is invoked by countries looking for a way to gain some sort of differentiated treatment in turn invoking the specificity of their context. This is what we would call the 'exception to the rule' argument, which threatens the process of integrated policy design, if not the deepening of transnational political institutions.

The point we make is not so much that the 'exception to the rule' argument should not be invoked, since action diversification does mean that the same policies may have to be implemented differently in different countries. Rather, we believe that the 'exception to the rule' argument, or the specificity of each country, should be considered in the context of the differences between countries taking into account their path of evolution (see for example Smith, 2001) towards their full integration and participation in a 'European innovation area'. This clearly supports the idea of national systems of innovation and competence building, but requires new insights into the process of building and sustaining social cohesion.

To achieve these objectives, we propose a specific conceptual framework based on how countries stand concerning their 'collective capacity for learning' – as suggested by Wright (1999) in the context of the US. The collective capacity of a country to learn depends not only on individual or even aggregated human capital (see for example Cohen and Levinthal, 1990), but also on social capital. The importance of social capital, while still controversial, is increasingly being seen as a significant determinant of economic performance and, especially, of innovation and creativity. Temple (2000) discusses the impact of education and social capital together as determinants of growth. Although noting that evidence is still thin, Temple argues that there is a growing number of works suggesting that social capital is at least as important as education as a driver of economic growth. The related implication for innovation policy strengthens the main argument of this book, in that it requires considering systems of innovation and competence building with social cohesion.

The relationship between social capital and the economic performance of nations was recognised by Olson (1982) and North (1990), in broad descriptions of the process of development, and was framed explicitly in terms of social capital by Putman (1993). Bruton (1998: 904) writes: 'There is increasing doubt that growth is as simple as it appears in [simple] arguments, and renewed emphasis is being placed on more basic characteristics of an economy, especially entrepreneurship, institutions, and knowledge accumulation and application'.

The idea of social capital is – given the understanding of this still controversial concept outlined above – the key instrumental variable that we use to differentiate countries concerning their ability to innovate and to jointly participate in a European innovation area. The importance of *social* capital, as opposed to physical and human capital, is that beyond the aggregation of individual capabilities, it considers collective capacities (Glaeser, 2000). Thus, a country does not necessarily have a high level of social capital with a few brilliant individuals or some outstanding laboratories or one or two stellar universities. It is the integrated logic of the social and economic system as a whole that defines the social capital level and, in our understanding, the ability of the country to fully participate in a transactional innovation area. Moreover, following Smith (2000), knowledge in relation to many key activities is distributed among agents, institutions and knowledge fields, so that learning societies will increasingly rely on 'distributed knowledge bases', as a systematically coherent set of knowledges, maintained across an economically and/or socially integrated set of agents and institutions.

We focus this chapter on the reality of the Portuguese situation, as a specific case study within the EU, and on analysing the ability of Portugal to fully participate in a process of integrated EU policies. Clearly, Portugal has significant quantitative shortcomings, some of which we will review in the next section (4.2). But the country has been exhibiting a catching-up dynamics as we will also illustrate. With these illustrations, we start highlighting the fundamental argument of our understanding of the Portuguese context: we are in the presence of a dual country, with the coexistence of a dynamic, well educated, innovative, cohesive sector, with a lowly educated, non-innovative and highly non-cooperative sector. This clearly contrasts with many other European patterns and, for example, if considered together with the high income and high cohesiveness of Denmark (as recently reported by Lundvall, 2000, 2001), it promotes the need for diversified actions throughout Europe when considering the European innovation area.

After presenting the main figures on important static and dynamic indicators of the Portuguese situation, we move to a detailed analysis of the Portuguese situation in terms of research (Section 4.3). We focus on the evaluation exercise of Portuguese science units, and show the existence of several poles of scientific excellence, which are critical for the establishment of a national science base. In Section 4.4 we outline some implications of the Portuguese context in terms of scientific excellence for the integration of policies. In Section 4.5 we move to the characterisation of the Portuguese situation in terms of innovation, in order to go beyond R&D data and to address other activities central to innovation. To achieve these objectives, we look at results from the Second Community Innovation Survey. The main result of Sections 4.3, 4.4 and 4.5, as in Section 4.2, is that of the duality of Portuguese society: high performance coexisting with low performance. A clear manifestation of this duality is observed through the considerably low level of industry-science relationships (Section 4.6), which reflect systemic failures but also an overall low capacity for building social capital and for making use of distributed knowledge bases. In the concluding remarks (Section 4.7) we note the limitations of current excellence mapping exercises in Europe and derive implications of the case of Portugal for the process of designing integrated policies, arguing for the need to implement these policies in a diversified way.

4.2   AWAY BUT FAST: A SHORT SURVEY OF PORTUGUESE PERFORMANCE IN EDUCATION, SCIENCE AND TECHNOLOGY

According to the OECD (1998), Portugal has, after Turkey, the lowest share of the population aged 25–64 with at least an upper secondary education level. This share is about 20 per cent for Portugal, while the OECD average is three times larger, at 60 per cent. In the United States it is 76 per cent, in Finland it 67 per cent and in Ireland it is 50 per cent. In the Czech Republic almost three quarters of the population aged 25–64 have at least an upper secondary education level. It is important to note that the deficiency is not so great in university or tertiary education.

However, while the share of the Portuguese population with university education is also low (about seven per cent), it is only about half of the OECD average, and is comparable to that of countries such as Italy and Austria. This points to the duality of Portuguese society that looking at average and aggregate numbers may obscure.

Considering some results from the latest literacy survey led by the OECD, Figure 4.1 shows that, for the entire population surveyed, Portugal exhibited the lowest score, excluding Chile. Certainly, the Portuguese population has the lowest literacy score of all the included EU countries, and even of other countries that are likely to become members in the coming years.

Low levels of literacy seem not to be dramatically punished by the Portuguese economy. In fact, Figure 4.2 shows that Portugal has one of the highest levels of labour participation for those people with the lowest level of literacy. This is partially explained by the overall high rate of labour participation in Portugal (note the high figure for the US and Switzerland as well), but the low unemployment rate is not the only explanation (look at the Netherlands and Ireland). Part of the reason may be associated with the demands of large sectors of the economy, which still do not require advanced skills, nor even literacy (see also the discussion by Carneiro and Conceição, 2002).

However, the duality clearly emerges after segmenting the overall population into finer segments. As an example, consider only young people that are relatively educated (20 to 25 years of age with upper secondary education). For this segment of the population, Portugal ranks high, along with the Netherlands, Germany and Norway (see Figure 4.3).

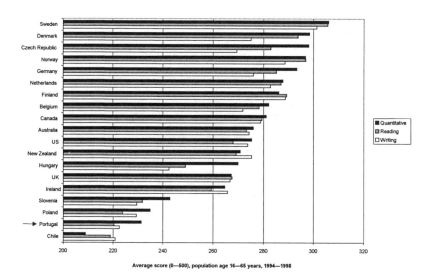

Average score (0—500), population age 16—65 years, 1994—1998

Source: OECD (1998)

Figure 4.1   Average literacy survey results

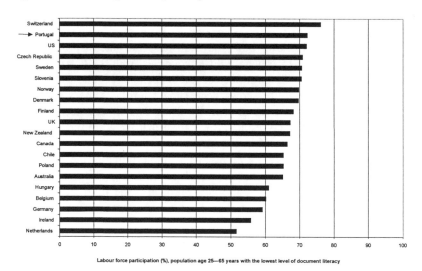

Labour force participation (%), population age 25—65 years with the lowest level of document literacy

Source: OECD (1998)

Figure 4.2   Labour force participation of the population segment with the lowest level of literacy

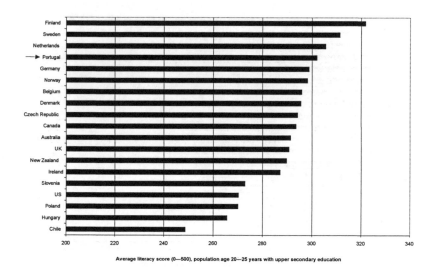

Average literacy score (0—500), population age 20—25 years with upper secondary education

Source: OECD (1998)

Figure 4.3   Literacy scores of people aged 20–25 years and with upper secondary education

The duality is also present when one looks at science and technology statistics. Figure 4.4 shows both the scale and the intensity of national expenditures on R&D for several OECD countries, with the horizontal axis representing the logarithmic scale of the expenditure. The relationship between scale and intensity shows decreasing returns: as the scale of the investment grows, the increase in intensity also grows but at a decreasing (in fact, logarithmic) rate. The results also suggest that there are three different 'paths' in which this relationship is expressed.

The thick line in Figure 4.4 represents a simple fitting of the position of most countries. Nordic countries have a path of their own, with a much higher responsive intensity to increases in scale. Portugal is shown in the lower left hand corner of the figure, part of a line that includes other Southern European countries.

The duality is manifest when one looks not at static comparisons of levels, but at dynamic comparisons of rates of change. Portugal showed one of the largest increases in R&D gross domestic expenditure of all OECD countries from 1995 to 2000. During this five year period, R&D expenditure grew at an annual rate of ten per cent in Portugal, while in the European Union as a whole it grew at three per cent. This growth represented a recovery from the slowdown of 1991–95, when the Portuguese R&D expenditure grew only 3.8 per cent; from 1985 to 1990 it had grown 14 per cent.

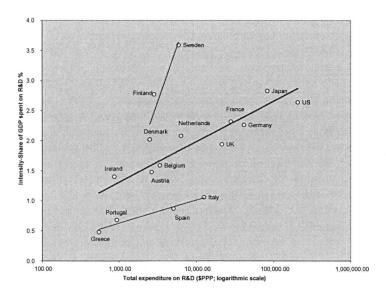

Source: OECD (1999)

Figure 4.4   Intensity and scale of R&D expenditure in the OECD

The same duality is present if one looks at other features. For example, Portugal has one of the lowest shares of new science and technology PhDs per thousand of population aged 25–34 years (only 0.23 per cent, compared with 0.55 per cent in the EU; figures are for 2000). However, it has by far the largest growth rate: 12 per cent growth from 1998 to 1999, compared with no growth at all at the EU level. In terms of publications, Portugal, in 1999, had 248 scientific publications per million population. However, the average annual growth rate from 1995 to 2000 was almost 16 per cent, while for Greece (the second ranking country) it was seven per cent, and in the EU below three per cent.[1]

4.3   EXCELLENCE OF RESEARCH IN PORTUGAL

To identify the locus of research excellence is not easy, nor uncontroversial. In this section, we briefly discuss the implementation of an assessment system in Portugal based on international peer review and on international evaluation criteria. This assessment programme has been used by the Portuguese government to affect public resources to R&D activities, depending on the results that the research units get in the exercise. Thus, this assessment system is of consequence, mobilising considerable resources from the government and the commitment of the research units to cooperate in the process.

The objective of the analysis presented in this section is to identify the existence of research excellence in Portugal and, in conjunction with the assessment made above regarding poor Portuguese performance in terms of level indicators of science and technology, we have further evidence supporting the hypothesis that there is a duality in Portuguese society.

We start with a brief description of the assessment exercise. The main objective of the assessment process is to critically review the research units and activities, encouraging the strategic optimisation of activities in progress and the reorganisation of research units, based on recommendations from external experts with experience in scientific assessment. As well as enabling the implementation of a stable funding model, both for multi-year base funding and specific programme funds for research units, the assessment process has led to the adoption of assessment and monitoring practices in Portugal designed to encourage a 'culture of rigour and quality' in the context of increasingly demanding internationalisation (Heitor, 2000).

The implementation of a new model for funding and assessment of R&D units started in 1996, with the assessment of 270 units. Following the assessment exercise, funding for units classified as Poor was discontinued. The remaining units (257) then received base funding arising from the assessment with total funding proportional to the number of PhDs. Following consideration of appeals submitted by some units, distribution of the classifications Excellent, Very Good, Good and Fair among the units receiving funding was 17 per cent, 31 per cent, 32 per cent and 19 per cent respectively.

The assessment of 1999 included the units assessed in 1996 and funded under the multi-year funding programme for R&D units, covering a total of 263 units and 4068 PhDs, and including new units that had become autonomous or were the result of a merger of units assessed in 1996. Units assessed in an interim assessment in 1997–98 were not included in the 1999 assessment. Around 160 foreign scientists, organised in 21 separate panels, took part in the 1999 assessment, which included the analysis of reports and activity plans as well as visits by the assessment panels to the research units.

The results of the assessment are reported in detail by Heitor (2000), but there are a number of general observations clearly expressed during the evaluation that are of particular interest. In general, the considerable potential for scientific development in Portugal was stressed, related to the marked increase in numbers of PhDs working in research units (namely, from a total of 3465 in 1996 to 4068 in 1999, based on December 1998 figures) and to improved structuring of activities in progress. Several research units include specialists of international renown, as reflected in the number and quality of publications, the high degree of involvement in European consortia, and the significant number of international conferences and other events held in Portugal.

In many areas, the assessment panels noted considerable progress in the way research units define their strategic goals and present their activities. In particular, several assessment panels found a dynamic for change and considerable enthusiasm, the result no doubt of the high proportion of young postdoctoral and doctoral students, as well as an increase in international links. In the opinion of the assessors, these points have contributed to increasing the international profile of Portuguese research units.

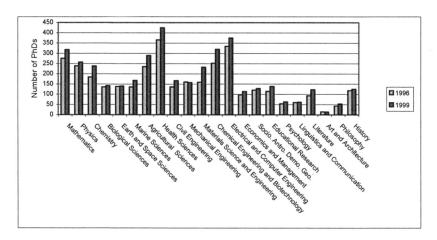

Source: Heitor (2000); Available through http://www.fct.mct.pt

Figure 4.5   *Number of PhD students in units for each scientific area in 1996 and 1999*

The continued increase in the number of PhDs working in research units represents an average annual growth rate of around 5.5 per cent, with Materials Science and Engineering and Art and Architecture reaching the highest figure of around 14 per cent (see Figure 4.5). In general terms, the increase in postdoctoral researchers has been seen mainly in the areas of Engineering Sciences and Technologies and in Arts and Humanities (six per cent average annual growth rate), but also in Exact Sciences, Natural Sciences and Health Sciences (five per cent), being slightly lower in Social Sciences (four per cent). This significant increase, especially when seen in European and international terms, was consistently cited by the majority of assessment panels as a decisive factor in reaching the critical mass essential to scientific development. This is despite the fact that the overall values for Portugal in

1997 in terms of number of researchers as a proportion of the workforce were around half the European average (2.9 and 4.9 per thousand inhabitants respectively).

The comments made by the various assessment panels regarding the increase in the number of researchers in Portugal should also be considered in relation to the increase in the size of units, there having been a relative reduction in the number of units with less than ten PhDs, the typical size now being between ten and fifteen PhDs. Indeed, many assessors noted acquiring a minimum level of staff in order to operate effectively as a unit as a crucial factor in developing the national scientific base. Examples of areas for which observations of this nature were clearly expressed include History, Educational Research, Sociology, Agricultural Sciences, and Mechanical Engineering, in which there are units that are seen as academic structures in administrative terms, but which in reality are no more than groups of micro units in scientific terms, with little contact between them.

This situation obviously requires a new approach to institutional development, a point that was consistently made by the assessors, with particular emphasis on the need to foster institutional cooperation at various national and international levels, especially as a way of encouraging scientific activity in networks that promote institutional interrelations. Besides helping to combat the effects of the limited size of some units, developing such science-based networks will certainly encourage the creation and dissemination of new knowledge and stimulate scientific development in a climate of constant change and growing internationalisation of the scientific base.

The assessors' comments on the need to promote inter-institutional cooperation were particularly relevant to the area of Social Sciences, especially cooperation between units located in the same geographical area to encourage scientific networks. However, these comments are clearly also applicable to the areas of Sociology, Psychology, Linguistics and Communication, Literature, Philosophy and History, in relation to which particular mention was made of the imbalance between the high level of personal internationalisation of the more qualified researchers and the limited degree of institutional internationalisation of the units themselves.

Despite the considerable development of research in Portugal in these areas over the last years, the various panels stressed the need to promote internationalisation of activities in progress in a way that will give a higher profile to the national community and the specific nature of Portuguese culture.

However, for the purposes of international comparison, the performance of the system should be analysed from the standpoint of existing resources and structures, which are dominated by a *rigid* university system, requiring considerable structural changes, as extensively discussed by Santos, Heitor and Caraça (1998), Conceição and Heitor (1999) and Caraça, Conceição and Heitor (2000). As pointed out by the Mathematics panel, 'it is not the education mission that is being challenged or questioned, but the lack of flexibility in recruitment and in the management of teaching duties of each faculty member'. In general, many of these comments confirm observations already made in the various reports produced during the 1996 and 1997/1998 assessments, in which particular reference was made to the need to promote links between university schools and society, especially with companies, as a structural way of developing the potential for scientific activities of a high international standard. While these comments are particularly applicable to the areas of Exact Sciences, Engineering Sciences and Technologies, Natural Sciences and Health Sciences, all the panels consistently pointed to the need to promote science-based cooperation and mobility within Portugal and abroad, particularly in Europe, as one way of overcoming the difficulties arising from the type of relationship with host institutions, in particular universities.

Still in the realm of the relationship between the units and their host university institutions, several assessment panels made specific reference to the need to promote mobility of researchers and teachers through limiting the practice of universities of employing their own postgraduate students (so-called 'inbreeding'), which in turn led to various comments on the need to rethink the structure of doctoral programmes, and postgraduate studies in general, in Portugal. Indeed, the need to expand the recruitment base and to encourage placements and postgraduate and postdoctoral programmes abroad, and in general to promote an effective internationalisation of the scientific community, were consistently stressed by the assessors, including as regards those areas still undergoing rapid growth such as Mathematics.

The overall assessments of units in 1999 are shown schematically, by scientific area, in Figure 4.6 in terms of the number of units and the number of PhDs respectively, covering those units assessed in 1999 (thus excluding those units assessed as Poor in 1996 and which ceased to be funded under the FCT multi-year Funding Program). The results are presented based on the five levels of classification used in the assessments, and show considerable variation between scientific areas, as had also been observed in 1996. However, any comparative analysis between scientific areas should be treated with caution and put into context, given the specific nature of the areas studied, possible variations in the criteria used by different assessment panels, and above all, differences in the average size of units in the various areas. Nevertheless, an analysis of variations in classifications between 1996 and 1999 clearly shows the previously mentioned trend towards a developing culture of high scientific standards, as quantified by significant improvement in classifications.

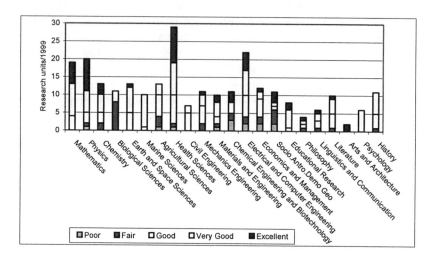

Source: Heitor (2000); Available through http://www.fct.mct.pt

Figure 4.6   Classification of research units in each scientific area in the 1999 evaluation

The distribution of units assessed up to February 2000, by level of classification of overall quality – Excellent, Very Good, Good, Fair and Poor – was 19, 38, 27, 12, and four per cent respectively, while the corresponding percentages for the 270 units assessed in 1996 were 16, 28, 31, 19 and six per cent. The percentages for the 84 units assessed in 1997–98 were 15, 30, 36, 13 and six per cent. Thus, the results clearly show that the most common classification for research units went from Good in 1996 to Very Good in 1999. In fact, while 44 per cent of the 270 units were classified in 1996 as Excellent or Very Good, 57 per cent of the 248 units assessed by February 2000 received these two classifications. Similarly, the percentage of postdoctoral researchers working in units with the two highest classifications went from 56 per cent in 1996 to 65 per cent in 1999. Of all the units assessed by February 2000, ten units were classified as Poor, their size varying between five and 17 postdoctoral researchers, involving a total of 87 post-doctoral researchers (in other words around two per cent).

The present assessment exercise was one more stage in an ongoing process that aims to stimulate development of the scientific and technological system in Portugal, but also in Europe. This process, based on independent assessments by international experts, has stimulated critical debate on research activities and their strategic importance for national development and progress, as well as the reorganisation and reorientation of research units in a climate of growing international competitiveness.

In general terms, the reports from the various panels show that the impact of these activities of excellence is naturally affected by the still limited dimension of the science and technology system, despite the considerable increase in numbers of PhDs over recent years.

However, the international reputation of certain research groups could be used to greater advantage in promoting the quality of research in the country as a whole. This is an important point that led many of the assessment panels to suggest the development of cooperation networks at the national level. Furthermore, attention was drawn to the need for units to further develop existing international links, particularly through granting sabbatical leave to researchers and university teachers, together with efforts to attract foreign researchers, especially at the postdoctoral level. In this context, it should be stressed that the majority of panels repeatedly referred to the need to encourage national and international mobility for researchers, particularly within Europe.

4.4 IMPLICATIONS OF THE PORTUGUESE EVALUATION EXERCISE

The paragraphs above describe main features of the current Portuguese system of evaluating research centres and, in general, of mapping research excellence. The results provide the necessary evidence of existing excellence in many scientific areas, despite the weakness of the Portuguese S&T system if simple statistical indicators are used. We now turn to the overall European context, and discuss current needs to think research excellence in Europe within a broader context of promoting social cohesion and a European research area, (European Commission, 2000a), an example of the concern for the policy integration.

Three main ideas are presented: (i) the need to consider the European research area as a way to promote the inclusive development of the European science base; (ii) the need to promote benchmark exercises as forms of learning by comparing S&T excellence; and (iii) the requirements for centres of excellence with a European dimension, which in itself will allow us to enlarge the European science base through inclusion of the more peripheral and poorer parts of the EU.

The creation of a European science base can be used as a mobilising task to nurture new European talent in science and technology, to attract leading scientists and engineers to Europe, and to stimulate strong national investments in R&D, higher education, and digital technologies. A fundamental concern of the construction of a European research area must be the inclusion of the more peripheral and poorer parts of the EU. In fact, the difference between Europe and the US has not been found at the top levels of scientific performance, but rather on the average level of science, as clearly expressed by Nobel prizewinners in *Pathways for European Research* (European Commission 2000b). In other words, the *scale* and *diversity* of the US science and technological enterprise are not matched in Europe.

Excellence in science and technology depends, more than anything else, on people. Extending the pool of available potential researchers and engineers in Europe needs to consider reaching into those peripheral areas. Europe cannot concentrate all its efforts on a single country or region, but has to include the potential of all countries, including those that are likely to be EU members in the near future.

It is also clear that much has been written during the last years about the European difficulty in transforming scientific knowledge into innovation and wealth, especially in comparison with the American reality. In this context, it would be interesting to frame the problem of European innovation patterns in terms of the necessity to create and sustain conditions for regional and national learning (see for example Lundvall, 2001). This is because, as noted before, social capital has become a critical factor for innovation, and because networks and institutions are the elements out of which social capital is born. Different types of networks and institutions can be effective as long as they enable collective learning and collective innovation. As in every situation where networks are important, history matters. Path dependence and increasing returns lead to self-reinforcing cycles, whereby events, often sporadic and serendipitous, define current patterns of development. But the good news is that if we understand the dynamics of institutional change and evolution, we can also create conditions for future development. Thus, analysis should be promoted to discuss emerging topics in science and technology policy, including:

- the importance of balancing innovation and diffusion;
- the relevance of the conceptual framework established through the interactive model of innovation; and
- the need to promote 'inclusive development' in a learning society.

Regarding the issue of the need to promote 'inclusive development' (for details, see Conceição et al. 2001), that is, of the need for a process of development that includes every citizen in any country looking at local roots, as a problem that goes beyond the creation of conditions to generate knowledge, the most important question concerns the sharing and diffusion of knowledge. The mere fact that in the economics literature this 'diffusion' process has largely been explained in terms of externalities and spillovers, shows that the sharing process is largely an unintended consequence and, in fact, a disincentive for private agents to invest in knowledge creation. Thus the logic of government intervention, that is, in terms of science and technology policies that tackle these market deficiencies, has been to provide incentives to enhance knowledge generation (Pavitt, 1998).

In our opinion, if the issue of inclusive development is indeed to be acknowledged as important, efforts should be channelled towards the understanding of the conditions for globally integrated learning processes. Learning, in this context, reflects the idea of sustainable knowledge creation and diffusion, and we contend that the challenge is to make this a feature not exclusive to a few regions and countries but instead of the entire global economy.

Development results from a combination of all these learning processes, at all levels: individual, organisational, and national. Thus the issue is to try to understand why and how some people, firms, and countries learn, while others do not. Diversity and heterogeneity across individuals and countries will always surely entail some level of inequality in learning performance. In fact, as some have argued, inequality can even be considered positive, since it provides incentives to get ahead and a context where there are many aspirations to achieve. Still, the dimension of the gaps and the size of the world inequalities warrant a search for the reasons why some do learn so well, while others seem to lag, even acknowledging the idiosyncrasies that will always lead to some differentiation across individuals, organisations, and countries.

The challenges for science and technology policy in order to move towards inclusive development are really twofold. First, what can be done at the regional and national level to start and sustain learning networks and trajectories that can lead to development? Second, how can the overall learning processes be made more inclusive, so that fewer regions are excluded, extending the reach of the learning networks at a European level?

In these terms, current evolutionary economics has shown the importance of path dependence of economic processes, in that it is at the core of selection mechanisms between competitive firms and technologies. Competition is therefore the result of the rate of change of market share, apart from being dependent on differences in the rates of growth of individual firms. The result is a fully endogenous process, which, in the presence of increasing returns, gives rise to a strong interdependence between *specialisation* and *diversification*. The direct implication for innovation policies is the important but limited role of demand at the firm level in assessing the amount of incentives for firms to introduce technological innovations. In more general terms, the analysis calls for the need to feed all the processes of learning ('formal' and 'informal'), implement technological cooperation among firms and between firms and research institutions, and the process of on-the-job-training of the workforce. Technological centres specifically designed to sustain localised processes of technological change might play an important role in this context.

If any conclusion can be drawn with direct application to the need to promote the European research area through the 'inclusive development' of peripheral zones in Europe, which are characterised by late industrialised countries, it is that allocation of resources between broad fields of science should increase, and that inadequacies in the rate of technological change should not negatively influence academic research (see for example Pavitt, 2000). However, important questions remain to be resolved, mainly in terms of the way academic governance influences the performance of basic research activities, and the linkages between basic and applied disciplines. Also, the way the demands for knowledge influence research policies remain to be examined.

Turning to our second idea about the need to promote benchmark exercises as forms of learning by comparing S&T excellence, it is clear that this comprises a very important and critical exercise for Europe, namely if considered as 'a collective process leading to mutual learning'. The question is how to achieve this objective, in particular in comparing the performance of quite diverse regions and nations, with structurally different trajectories and 'learning patterns'.

At present various indicators are used to illustrate the structure and the changes of the science and technology system and its impact on the economy and society (OECD, 1999; European Commission, 2001). Beside all the questions associated with the type of indicators, these data have been critically important to designing science, technology and innovation policies worldwide. For example, the measurement of the differences between the private and social returns of private investment in R&D has been pursued by several scholars. Analysis resulting largely from spillovers to the entire society of private R&D efforts, or, in other words, positive externalities, has established the conviction that there is a systematic market failure justifying the intervention of government. However, if any information can really be taken from the broad spectrum of values given for OECD countries, it is that the design of science and technology policies must encompass the careful analysis of specific conditions, following the trajectory of each country. This requires an increased accountability and observational effort, which has clearly not been equally considered by every country.

Beside the need to improve and systematise the collection and use of conventional science and technology indicators, the analysis of intangible investment and innovation surveys shows that knowledge is deeply socially embedded in institutions and in the socioeconomic environment in which they operate. The knowledge content of products and production processes is becoming more and more important, and investment is rapidly evolving towards the acquisition of services and the carrying out of activities that pay off over a long period of time. Intangible investment includes a series of items beyond R&D, such as: training of personnel, software, marketing, as well as goodwill, mineral exploration, development of organisations, and rights or concessions to use intellectual property.

Taking the experience of Finland and the Netherlands, four components – research and development, education and training, software, and marketing – make up about 80 per cent of the total intangible investment which, in turn, represents between 20 and 50 per cent of tangible investment. In Austria it has been calculated that intangible investment is 43 per cent of all business investment.

Innovation surveys conducted in some thirty countries tell a similar story: half of the innovation expenditure of manufacturing firms is linked to the generation and acquisition of new knowledge through design, R&D, trial production, acquisition of know-how, training, and marketing, the other half being spent on new machinery and equipment. Looking at the activities that are most often carried out for introducing new products and processes in service firms, the most frequent ones are R&D, development or acquisition of software, investment in machinery and training of personnel. The data from innovation surveys show also that innovation in firms is a quite diffused phenomenon, with about one third of firms introducing innovations over a three year period.

In this context, the metrics for knowledge (in a learning society) has to face at least three challenges. Firstly, it requires a comprehensive view encompassing many areas such as science, technology, economic growth, inequality, employment, the environment, firm and social organisation, education, and institutional development. While no single model can as yet cover such a vast territory, certainly a new cross-disciplinary understanding can create a new way of looking at indicators and innovation systems. Secondly, we have learnt that national and local institutions and institutional cultures do matter and therefore indicators of these 'intangible' aspects need to be devised. Thirdly, we need to be able to capture the dimensions of knowledge (tacit and codified) as well as how the diffusion process takes place in competitive environments (markets) and in non-competitive settings (education, the health sector in countries where it is mostly publicly funded). This has led Smith (2000) to argue for the need to go beyond direct indicators of knowledge intensity in production and to discuss 'distributed knowledge bases' that have a more systemic and institutionally diffuse location.

Finally, we come to our third idea, that of centres of excellence with a European dimension, which in themselves will allow us to enlarge the European science base through inclusion of the more peripheral and poorer parts of the EU. Although the interest of promoting centres of excellence and research infrastructures in Europe is recognised, it is important to discuss here the critical role these centres and infrastructures should have in promoting a truly European research area. We argue that it requires extending European research excellence to peripheral and less favoured zones, and promoting the movement of scientists and engineers from all over the world as a fundamental part of their mission.

In fact, when it is noted that the great difference between European and the US scientific performance is not to be found at the top (since there is comparable excellent research on both sides of the Atlantic) but in average science, this further strengthens the argument for a need to create infrastructures and centres of excellence beyond those areas traditionally endowed with well funded and well staffed projects. This raises also the issue of *scale*. If there is a need to increase the scale of European research, this can be more easily accomplished in peripheral and poorer areas, with a weaker current scientific base, rather than in those where the natural dynamics of agglomeration reinforces already excellent centres and infrastructures.

At a more conceptual level, the rationale for this discussion is based on the fact that it is crucial not only to make available financial resources (namely public resources) and infrastructures, but to do so in a way that provides the right incentives for S&T organisations to hook up in learning networks that can generate localised social capital and endogenous growth dynamics. That way is definitely not unique and depends on local conditions, roots and trajectories, which raise the question of inclusive development. It should be noted that analysis has shown that the main practical benefits of scientific, and academic-based, research are not 'easily transmissible information', but involve the transmission of tacit and non-codifiable (or not yet codified) knowledge, with a tendency to geographically localised benefits. Furthermore, countries and firms benefit academically and economically from R&D performed elsewhere only if they belong to the international professional networks that exchange knowledge. This requires high quality research training and a strong presence in basic research, mainly because academic research is certainly not a 'free good', although it has some attributes of a 'public good'.

The challenges for policy are twofold. First, what can be done at the various regional and national levels to start and sustain learning networks with centres of excellence and research infrastructures in Europe that can lead to development? Second, how can the location and the selection of centres of excellence and research infrastructures in Europe be made more inclusive, so that fewer countries and regions are excluded, extending the reach of the learning networks globally?

Two main aspects may be considered, as follows:

(i) The definition of a centre of excellence and the related typologies must necessarily encompass the impact on the promotion of a true European research area in terms of a European-wide impact. In practice, analysis must include not only the diversity of research personnel and visiting scientists, but the related impact on the home institutions of those scientists and, more generally, on institutional development outside the boundaries of the centres of excellence, with emphasis for institutions in less favoured zones.

(ii) The need for action in Europe should be considered in terms of the impact centres of excellence and research infrastructures may have in promoting a European research area, taking into account the need for balancing innovation and diffusion. In fact too much emphasis may be given to innovation (namely through establishing intellectual property rights, yielding to private incentives to production) at the expense of diffusion, which can slow the overall rate of technological change, or knowledge diffusion and adoption.

4.5 CHARACTERISTICS OF INNOVATION IN PORTUGAL

The analysis of Section 4.3 is based on traditional S&T indicators, which are important indicators of the commitment and resources a country devotes to knowledge production and diffusion, but the growing importance of knowledge extends beyond those activities traditionally associated with creativity and learning. Following Smith (2000), R&D data tend to rest on a view of innovation that overemphasizes the discovery of new scientific or technical principles as the point of departure of an innovation process (in other words, the so called 'linear model of innovation'), while modern innovation theory considers knowledge creation in a much more diffuse way, with learning being central to innovation. It is also clear that the measurement of the innovative performance of an entire country, specifically in a way comparable across the diverse realities of many countries, is a demanding challenge, which has been addressed by a joint effort of the OECD and the Eurostat, through the development of innovation surveys at the country level according to a set of criteria that values cross-country comparability of results. Portugal has been an integral part of this effort, for which there are results for several European countries. This European effort is designated by Community Innovation Surveys (CIS), and its framework of enquiry has been adopted both in official and autonomous research surveys in many countries, from Eastern European countries to Latin America.

By attaching more importance to cross country comparability, the CIS loses something of its potential ability to probe into the dynamics of innovation within each country, since it only asks broad and generic questions, which can be accepted as having similar meanings in different economies. However, it provides a reliable way to compare national innovation performance across countries.

Figure 4.7 shows the overall innovation performance of countries in Europe measured by the shares of firms that have introduced innovations over a two year period. The horizontal axis indicates innovative performance in manufacturing, and the vertical axis in services. The results show a generally close relationship between innovation in services and in manufacturing, since countries are located across a 45 degree diagonal. In general, innovation rates are lower in services than in manufacturing.

Portugal appears towards the bottom of performance, being the least innovative country in manufacturing. However, in services Portugal innovates more than Belgium, Finland and Norway. Slightly more than a quarter of Portuguese manufacturing firms are innovative, while almost 30 per cent of service firms are innovative, again an indication of the duality: unlike other countries, services in Portugal – which have grown as a share of the economy at rates higher than the EU average – are more innovative than manufacturing firms, which are still largely dominated by the traditional sectors of the Portuguese economy.

Knowledge of the process of innovation in Portugal, and of the way in which it contrasts with the innovation process in Europe can be gathered from other aspects of CIS. For example Figure 4.8 shows that Portuguese firms rely much more on resources external to the firm as information sources for the innovation process than European firms (on average).

Figure 4.9, on the other hand, shows that issues related to high costs and difficulties in funding are much more prominent in Portugal than on average in Europe.

Even though there is a large consensus across Europe that the lack of qualified personnel is the most important factor hampering innovation (Figure 4.10), still this factor pales behind high innovation costs and lack of financing as a deterrent to innovation in Portugal.

However, it is important to look at the diversity that exists within Portugal. We concentrate on manufacturing only. Even within manufacturing, though, there are substantial differences across sectors (Figure 4.11). The machinery, electrical and optical equipment sector exhibits almost 50 per cent of innovative firms (the rate of innovation in this sector is comparable to the average rate in countries such as Italy and Norway).

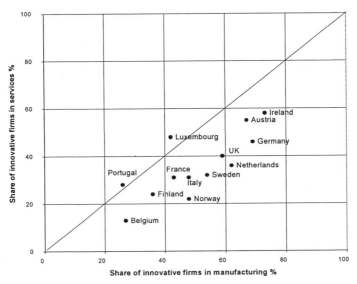

Source: Conceição and Ávila (2001)

Figure 4.7   Innovative performance of EU countries

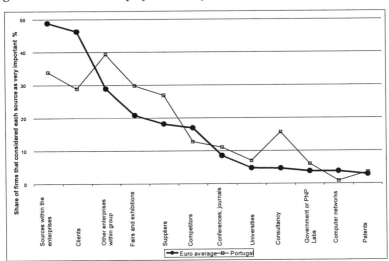

Source: Conceição and Ávila (2001)

Figure 4.8   Sources of information for innovation

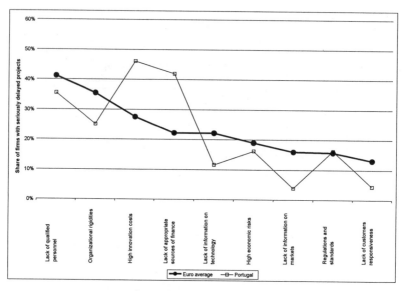

Source: Conceição and Ávila (2001)

Figure 4.9   Factors hampering innovation

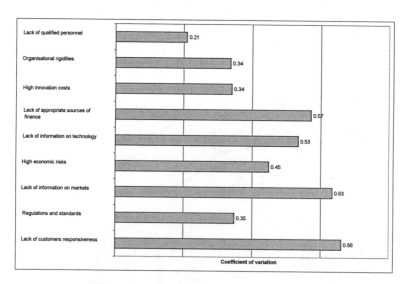

Source: Conceição and Ávila (2001)

Figure 4.10   Degree of consensus across Europe on the hampering factors

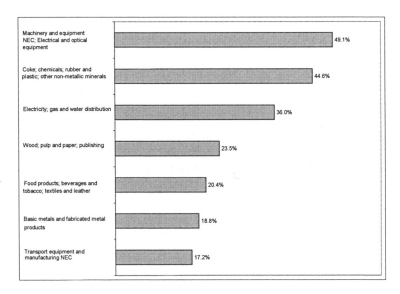

Source: Conceição and Ávila (2000)

Figure 4.11 Innovation rates (% of innovative firms) in the Portuguese manufacturing sector

Innovation in Portugal seems to be associated with a number of characteristics of firms in a way that conforms both with theory, and with results in other countries. A descriptive analysis of the results of CIS shows that size classes composed of large firms have a higher share of innovative firms than size classes composed of small firms. A descriptive analysis also shows that firms that are part of a group of companies show higher rates of innovation. Combining these two variables in a multivariate model, with the dependent variable being dichotomous (1 if the firm has innovated, 0 otherwise) shows, without any other conditioning variables, that large firms and firms that are part of a group have a higher probability of innovating than small firms and firms that are not part of a group of firms (first column in Table 4.1).

However, as we saw above, there is a large diversity of innovative performance across manufacturing sectors. Still, when industry dummies are added to the model (second column in Table 4.1) none shows up as significant. This can be interpreted by saying that the sector effects are not strong determinants of innovation (when the size of the firm and whether the firm is part of the group are included).

However, when we considers only two groups of firms – those that are high or medium high technology, on the one hand, and those that are low or medium low technology, on the other – the results show that firms in the high/medium high technology group do indeed exhibit a much higher probability of innovating that the average firm (note that the coefficient associated with the dummy for the low/medium low technology firms is not significant).

The results indicate, once again, the existence of duality. Note how large and statistically significant the coefficient associated with high/medium high technology is, even after controlling for the size of the firm and the fact that it may belong to a group. Thus, more sophisticated firms in markets with higher demand seem to have a substantially higher probability of innovating than other firms. This is not tied, one should stress, to a mere 'sector effect' (the sector dummies were not significant), it is really a characteristic of a large group of sectors that have in common belonging to the high/medium high technology category. The duality here is clearly substantiated.

Naturally, other factors, beyond size and belonging to a group, influence innovation. We tried out a further, more sophisticated model, to test the robustness of the previous conclusions. The new model has, in addition to the variables of the first model, also the firm level of productivity and the importance of exports. Both of these variables are known to have important effects on innovation. The results of this second model are shown in Table 4.2.

Of course, the models above have merely descriptive value; we do not make any claims in terms of causality, much less explanation. They are understood as showing the correlations among the variables included. It is known, for example, that several of the variables are simultaneously determined (namely innovation and productivity; on this see Conceição and Veloso, 2002). Thus, the point we make is that, even controlling for a number of characteristics that influence innovation, still there is a clear duality in terms of probability of innovating when one considers technology intensity as a criteria for differentiating firms.

Table 4.1   Regression results on the characteristics of innovative firms: first model[2]

Factor	Unconditioned (1)	Industry dummies (2)	Technological intensity (3)
Intercept	-1.576** (0.2448) [0.0000]	-9.104 [-0.0001] [1.0000]	-1.773** [0.2562] [0.0000]
Firm is part of group	0.529** (0.1423) [0.0002]	0.318* [2.0834] [0.0372]	0.474** [0.1435] [0.0009]
Log of number of employees	0.213** (0.0613) [0.0005]	0.262** [4.0365] [0.0001]	0.224** [0.0625] [0.0003]
High/ medium high technology		Conditioning Industry dummies None is significant	0.757** [0.138] [0.0000]
Low/medium low technology			0.163 [0.1163] [0.1614]
Concordant observations	84% 820	87% 820	85% 820

4.6   FOSTERING INDUSTRY–SCIENCE RELATIONSHIPS TOWARDS INNOVATION

The analysis above considered research excellence independently of its structure, so in this section we look at the different actors funding and performing research. The ultimate objective is to build on our conceptual framework concerning the need to promote social capital, together with specific competences, if a true European innovation area is to be considered (and to include countries such as Portugal). The analysis is based on the integration of policies relating to education, science and technology, and social and economic development, but also on the diversification of actions to support the creation and diffusion of knowledge, in order to achieve the objective of stimulating the development of a system of innovation in Portugal integrated at the European level. Rather than relying exclusively on high technology sectors, we favour the broad innovation framework of Smith (2000), in that the knowledge bases of mature and traditional industries are cognitively deep and complex, as well as institutionally distributed. This is particularly applicable to Portugal, with the practical consequence that growth will not be based just on the creation of new sectors, but on the internal transformation of sectors which already exist, namely by exploiting their distributed knowledge bases.

Table 4.2   Regression results on the characteristics of innovative firms: second model[2]

Factor	Unconditioned (1)	Industry dummies (2)	Technological intensity (3)
Intercept	-5.297**	-13.745	-5.201**
	[0.5784]	[157449]	[0.5922]
	[0.0000]	[0.9999]	[0.0000]
Firm is part	0.095	-0.039	0.070
of group	[0.1612]	[0.171]	[0.1626]
	[0.5551]	[0.8188]	[0.6674]
Log of	0.211**	0.241**	0.224**
number of	[0.0645]	[0.0676]	[0.0653]
employees	[0.0011]	[0.0004]	[0.0006]
Log of	0.423**	0.410**	0.390**
productivity	[0.0584]	[0.0661]	[0.0593]
	[0.0000]	[0.0000]	[0.0000]
Share of	0.018	0.112	0.048
exports	[0.1451]	[0.1674]	[0.1488]
	[0.9031]	[0.5019]	[0.7493]
High/		Conditioning	0.621**
medium high		Industry	[0.1409]
technology		dummies	[0.0000]
		None is significant	
Low/Medium			0.152
low			[0.1214]
technology			[0.2106]
Concordant	84%	88%	85%
observations	820	820	820

In this context, much has been written in recent years on the increasing challenge of promoting the relevance of research and of linking it more closely to the needs of society, and various instruments have been developed to encourage research with industrial applications (for example OECD, 2000a, b). With this in mind, structural mechanisms to support and stimulate industry-science relationships and partnerships for innovation should be designed on the basis of international experience, particularly in OECD countries. Leading practices include the Partnerships for Innovation programme (http://www.ehr.nsf.gov/pfi/) of the National Science Foundation, which was also recently set up with the aim of promoting public/private partnerships (P/PPs), to involve firms and university centres, particularly those located outside the major American research universities, and directed towards new products and services, as well as to encourage education and training activities in the areas of innovation and technology transfer. Among other aspects, analysis (for example Meyer-Krammer and Shomoch, 1998; Mowery, 1998; Hall and van Reenen, 1999; Siegel et al., 1999, Rosenberg, 2000, 2002) reveals three critical factors for the structuring of consortium research and of partnerships for innovation in general, namely:

- *inter-institutional mobility* as a critical factor for success in the relationship between firms and the science and technology system;
- the need to promote *licensing* and agreements for the use of the *intellectual property of universities*;
- incentives for the *creation of companies and university spin-offs* as an effective means of transferring knowledge.

While the first factor has been central to all the initiatives in progress in the majority of OECD countries, the other two have been evident almost exclusively in the USA, and recently in the United Kingdom, despite being repeatedly referred to in OECD reports. In general, the intensity and quality of industry-science relationships (ISRs) play an increasing role in determining returns on investment in research, in terms of competitiveness, growth, job creation and quality of life (Mowery, 1998; Hall and van Reenen, 1999). They also determine the ability of countries to attract or retain highly mobile qualified labour (Rommer, 2000). But the point to be made is that while ISRs are undergoing fundamental changes prompted by globalisation and other factors as part of an overall trend towards accelerated development of a market for knowledge, there is accumulating evidence that many OECD countries are lagging behind in the modernisation of ISRs (OECD, 2000a).

Under this framework, Figure 4.12 shows the share of gross domestic expenditure on R&D (GERD) among government, business and higher education sectors for 2000, or the latest year available, which clearly demonstrates a large diversity of national situations. It is also clear that countries' R&D funding and performance structure have other different characteristics that might distinguish them further (Smith, 2001). One of these characteristics is a relatively high share of funding from abroad (particularly for Ireland and Sweden, but also for UK), which also supports our argument for the need to consider policy integration, but together with action diversification across Europe.

The evidence emphasises the need for integrated science and economic policies, in that research activity lies at the interface between the discovery-driven culture of science and the innovation-driven culture of engineering, creating a synergy between science, engineering, and industrial practice.

Based on the analysis of Schuetze (2000) and Polt et al. (2001), among others, technology transfer as it has been conventionally understood is only a part of a larger system of knowledge creation and application, involving many forms of communication and interaction between university and community. Knowledge transfer must involve opportunities for learning of all kinds, requiring technical universities to consider cooperative research and organised learning as twin activities (Mowery and Rosenberg, 1989; Nelson and Romer, 1996).

Against the background of the initiatives described above and the comparative results of Figure 4.12, the process of technology transfer in Portugal has consistently been considered from a short term perspective and has been based on specific contracts, mainly of a consultancy nature. Today, it is clear that science and technology cannot be promoted independently of an innovation policy and that in turn innovation determines and is determined by the market. However, it is also clear that research and innovation are structurally distinct activities, each with its own incentives, which are complementary but not interchangeable. In fact, the evidence of duality discussed before is enhanced through the considerably low level of science-industry relationships derived from the results of Figure 4.12, which reflect systemic failures but, above all, an overall lower capacity for building social capital. Specific policies for building industry-science relationships and partnerships for innovation in general, require incentives that take the following factors into account:

- *time*: a relatively long term perspective, with ongoing efforts to promote research and development;
- *scope*: promoting international relationships and opening up cooperation in science and technology, particularly within Europe but also with a transatlantic dimension;
- *context*: taking into consideration specific regional and sectoral aspects, thus promoting a diversified environment;
- *value*: promoting market strategies and encouraging market-oriented technological cooperation, particularly through developing clusters in key sectors of the economy.

In particular, the diversified actions to be set out should be designed to foster links between the science and technology system and the productive sector so as to promote the development of national skills in science and technology, while at the same time enabling the scientific base to be strengthened through institutional cooperation at various levels, particularly through alliances that develop the capacity of existing resources within a system of innovation. Following Porter and Stern (1999):

Traditional thinking about management of innovation focuses almost exclusively on internal factors – the capabilities and processes within companies for creating and commercialising technology. Although the importance of these factors is undeniable, the external environment for innovation is at least as important. For example, the striking innovative output of Israeli firms is due not simply to more effective technology management, but also to Israel's favourable environment for innovation, including strong university-industry linkages and a large pool of highly trained scientists and engineers.

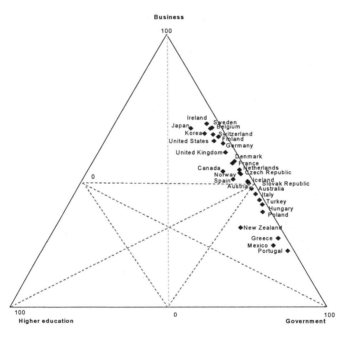

Note: The triangle shows the respective contributions of government, business and higher education to R&D funding. Example: In Ireland 75 per cent of funding is coming from business (to be read along the vertical axis), 24 per cent of funding is coming from government (to be read along the downward-leading diagonal axis). The remaining funding is coming from higher education (to be read along the upward-leading diagonal axis). The central point would represent a perfect co-funding of the three sectors.

Source: OECD, S&T databases, Sept. 2001

Figure 4.12   *Government, business and higher education sectors in R&D funding*

4.7   CONCLUSIONS

In this chapter we reviewed the Portuguese path in terms of its standing and evolution on science and innovation indicators and assessments. The message clearly conveyed is that, on average, Portugal has a weak position in terms of its standing. However, averages are misleading. We have shown clearly the existence of a duality in Portuguese society, with excellence coexisting with low performance. Additionally, in dynamic terms the evolution has been remarkable, with a clear dynamic of catching up and convergence.

Our analysis of the complexity of the Portuguese situation suggests that to identify poles of scientific and technological excellence quantitative indicators are clearly insufficient. In particular, relying on quantitative indicators can severely bias the characterisation of the scale and quality of scientific and technological activities in countries such as Portugal, as well as in the so-called peripheral and less favoured European zones. Rather than argue that there is scientific excellence in Portugal per se, we attempted to provide an illustration of how building on the national efforts aimed at characterising the country's scientific systems can significantly enrich the information on existing excellent research competences and high quality R&D centres.

To this end, the chapter provides an extended description of the concept behind the evaluation of research excellence in Portugal as one stage in an ongoing process that aims to stimulate development of the scientific and technological system in less favoured European zones. This process, based on independent assessments by international experts, has stimulated critical debate on research activities and their strategic importance for national development and progress, as well as the reorganisation and reorientation of research units in a climate of growing international competitiveness.

From a more normative point of view, we argue that building dynamic national science bases, linked through international networks of excellence and partnerships for innovation, is crucial if the diversity of countries is to be respected, and the potential of excellence to be explored. The major challenges presented by the implementation of public/private partnerships (P/PPs) are identified, particularly in terms of the need for ongoing funding to ensure the quality of the supply and to develop the necessary markets, which must take into account crucial factors such as individual mobility, protection of the intellectual property rights of universities and the encouragement of entrepreneurship.

It is clear that patterns of scientific strength and weakness are strongly influenced by the nature of the societal and technological problems to be solved (Freeman and Soete, 1997; Gordon, 2000). In any case, current understanding of the complexities of the knowledge bases that underlie future technological knowledge is very limited, so that building dynamic and diversified national science bases should be an important issue in European science policy. One important implication is that a unified policy goal of building a European innovation area needs to consider decentralised capacities (at national and/or regional levels), together with international criteria, to identify poles of research competences, and to build networks of excellence, as enablers of new competences and excellence in the coming decades. Thus, despite a unified policy, there is a need for action diversification.

NOTES

1. Data in this paragraph come from the E U Benchmarking of Science and Technology Policies Report, European Commission (2001).
2. Dependent variable: 1 if the firm has introduced any type of innovation, 0 otherwise. Standard errors in brackets, p-values in square brackets. ** significant at 1% or less. Logistic regression. Results with a normally distributed link function (Probit) were not dramatically different. Manufacturing only.
3. Dependent variable: 1 if the firm has introduced any type of innovation, 0 otherwise. Standard errors in brackets, p-values in square brackets. ** significant at 1% or less. Logistic regression. Results with a normally distributed link function (Probit) were not dramatically different. Manufacturing only.

REFERENCES:

Bruton, H.J. (1998). 'A Reconsideration of Import Substitution', *The Journal of Economic Literature* 36 (June): 903–36.

Caraça, J., Conceição, P., and Heitor, M.V. (2000). 'Suggesting a Public Policy Towards the Research University in Portugal', *Higher Education Policy* 13: 181–201.

Carneiro, R. and Conceição, P. (2002). 'Beyond Formal Education: Learning-by-Doing, ICT Adoption and the Competitiveness of a Traditional Portuguese Sector', *European Journal of Education*, 37(3): 263–80.

Cohen, W.M. and Levinthal, D.A. (1990). 'Absorptive Capacity: A New Perspective on Learning and Innovation', *Administrative Science Quarterly* 25: 128–52.

Conceição, P. and Ávila, P. (2001). *Community Innovation Survey in Portugal – 1998,* (in Portuguese), Lisbon: CELTA Publishers. Also available through http://www.oct.mct.pt.

Conceição, P., Gibson, D.V., Heitor, M.V. and Sirilli, G. (2001). 'Knowledge for Inclusive Development: The Challenge of Globally Integrated Learning and

Implications for Science and Technology Policy', *Technological Forecasting and Social Change* 66: 1–29.

Conceição, P. and Heitor, M.V. (1999). 'On the role of the University in the Knowledge-Based Economy', *Science and Public Policy* 26(1): 37–51.

Conceição, P. and Veloso, F. (2002). 'Is Investing in Innovation Unproductive? A Time to Sow and a Time to Reap', submitted for publication.

European Commission (2000a). *European Research Area*, COM(2000) Brussels: The Commission.

European Commission (2000b*). Pathways for European Research*, Brussels: The Commission.

European Commission (2001). *Benchmarking R&D policies in Europe*, Brussels: The Commission.

Freeman, C. and Soete, L. (1997), *The Economics of Industrial Innovation*, Cambridge, MA: MIT Press.

Glaeser, E.L. (2000). 'The Formation of Social Capital', Paper presented at the International Symposium on the Contribution of Human and Social Capital to Sustained Economic Growth and Well-Being, Québec City, Canada, 19–21 March.

Gordon, R. (2000). 'Does the "New Economy" Measure Up to the Great Inventions of the Past?', *Journal of Economic Perspectives*, forthcoming.

Hall, B. and van Reenen, J. (1999). 'How Effective are Fiscal Incentives for R&D? A Review of the Evidence', NBER Working Chapter N°. W7098.

Heitor, M.V. (2000). 'Evaluation of Research Units, 1999/2000 – Final Report', Observatory for Science and Technology, Portuguese Ministry of Science and Technology.

Lundvall, B.-Å. (2000). 'Towards the Learning Society: Challenges and Opportunities for Europe', Presentation at the Research Seminar 'Towards a Learning Society: Innovation and Competence Building with Social Cohesion for Europe', Lisbon, 28–30 May Available at http://in3.dem.ist.utl.pt/ learning2000/default.htm.

Lundvall, B.-Å. (2001). *Innovation, Growth and Social Cohesion: The Danish Model*, Cheltenham and Northampton, MA: Edward Elgar.

Meyer-Krammer, F. and Shomoch, U. (1998). 'Science-Based Technologies: University-Industry Interactions in Four Fields', *Research Policy* 27: 835–51.

Mowery, D. (1998). 'The Effects of Bayh-Dole Act on US University Research and Technology Transfer', OECD/TIP Workshop 'Commercialization of Government-Funded Research', Canberra, 25 November.

Mowery, D.C. and Rosenberg, N. (1989). *Technology and the Pursuit of Economic Growth*, Cambridge: Cambridge University Press.

Nelson, R.R. and Romer, P. (1996). 'Science, Economic Growth, and Public Policy', in B.L.R. Smith and C.E. Barfield *Technology, R&D, and the Economy*, Washington, DC: Brookings, 49–74.

North, D. (1990). *Institutions, Institutional Change and Economic Performance*, Cambridge and New York: Cambridge University Press.

OECD (1998). *Education Outlook*. Paris: OECD.

OECD (1999). *Science, Technology and Industry Scoreboard: Benchmarking Knowledge-Based Economies*, Paris: OECD.

OECD (2000a). *Industry-Science Relationships: Interim Report*, DSTI/STP/TIP(2000)6, Paris: OECD.

OECD (2000b). *Knowledge Markets and Innovation Systems: Nurturing the Institutions of Innovation*, DSTI/STP/TIP16, Paris: OECD.

OECD (2001). *S&T Databases, Sept. 2001*, Paris: OECD.

Olson, M. (1982). *The Rise and Decline of Nations: Economic Growth, Stagflation, and Social Rigidities*, New Haven CT: Yale University Press.

Pavitt, K. (1998). 'The Social Shaping of the National Science Base', *Research Policy* 27(8): 793–805.

Pavitt, K. (2000). 'Why European Union Funding of Academic Research Should Be Increased: A Radical Proposal', *Science and Public Policy* 27(6): 455–60.

Polt, W., Rammer, C., Gassler, H., Andreas, S. and Schartinger, D. (2001). 'Benchmark Industry-Science Relations: the Role of Framework Conditions', *Science and Public Policy* 28(4): 247–58.

Porter, M. and Stern, S. (1999). *The New Challenges to America's Prosperity: Findings from the Innovation Index*, Washington, DC: US Council on Competitiveness.

Putman, R.D. (1993). Making Democracy Work: Civic Traditions in Modern Italy, Princeton, NJ: Princeton University Press.

Rommer, P. (2000). 'Should the Government Subsidize Supply or Demand in the Market for Scientists and Engineers?', NBER Working Chapter N°. 7723.

Rosenberg, N. (2000). 'America's University/Industry Interfaces – 1945-2000', University of Stanford, Department of Economics.

Rosenberg, N. (2002). 'Knowledge and Innovation for Economic Development: Should Universities be Economic Institutions?', in *Knowledge for Inclusive Development* P. Conceição, D. Gibson, M. Heitor, G. Sirilli and F. Veloso (eds), Westport, Connecticut: Quorum Books, pp. 35–47.

Santos, F., Heitor, M.V., and Caraça, J. (1998). 'Organizational Challenges for the University'. *Higher Education Management* 10(3): 87–107.

Schuetze, H.G. (2000). 'Industrial Innovation and the Creation and Dissemination of Knowledge: Implications for University-Industry Relationships', in *Knowledge Management in the Learning Society*, Paris: OECD, pp 161–74.

Siegel, D., Waldman, D. and Link, A. (1999). 'Assessing the Impact of Organizational Practices on the Productivity of University Technology Transfer Offices: an Exploratory Study', NBER Working Chapter N°7256.

Smith, K. (2000). 'What Is the Knowledge Economy? Knowledge-Intensive Industries and Distributed Knowledge Bases', Discussion paper, DP 2002-6,

Institute for New Technologies, INTECH, The United Nations University. Available from www.intech.unu.edu/publications/.

Smith, K. (2001). 'Comparing Economic Performance in the Presence of Diversity', *Science and Public Policy* 28(4): 267–76.

Temple, J. (2000). 'Growth Effects of Education and Social Capital in the OECD', Paper presented at the International Symposium on the Contribution of Human and Social Capital to Sustained Economic Growth and Well-being, Québec City, Canada, 19–21 March.

Wright, G. (1999). 'Can a Nation Learn? American Technology as a Network Phenomenon', in N. Lamoreaux, D.M.G. Raff and P. Temin, (eds*). Learning by Doing in Markets, Firms, and Countries,* Chicago and London: University of Chicago Press.

PART TWO

Promoting organisational learning

Introductory note: Innovation and organisational change

Edward Lorenz

The performance effects of organisational change have become increasingly central to the policy debate on the sources of European competitiveness. Indeed, it is doubtful whether one can any longer characterise enterprise organisation as the neglected factor in policy discussions on achieving European competitive advantage (Andreasen et al. 1995). One reason for this is the growing recognition that ICT investments alone generally fail to deliver improved enterprise performance. Rather, what works is combining ICT investments with a set of HRM practices designed to take advantage of ICT's potential for facilitating richer horizontal and vertical communication and the enhanced involvement of employees in organisational problem solving and decision making.[1] The chapters in this section, focusing on the diffusion and impact of 'high involvement' or 'flexible' work practices are thus especially relevant to the issues of competence building and social cohesion in Europe.

The above argument linking HRM and investments in ICT to competitive performance overly simplifies what is a complex set of interrelations. Comparative estimates based on national survey evidence point to significant differences in the penetration rates of participatory work practices across European nations,[2] and Gjerding's study (Chapter Six) shows that even among the Nordic countries there are importance differences in the degree to which such practices as job rotation, quality circles and multidisciplinary team organisation are adopted. While the literature within the 'societal effects' or 'varieties of capitalism' traditions would instruct us to focus on the way national institutional arrangements mediate the diffusion of new work practices, giving rise to national hybrids, it is far from clear that national effects account for all, or even most, of the observed international variation. Sector determinants and differences in industrial structure across nations may be equally or more important. Or, as Gjerding's study suggests, differences in diffusion rates may simply reflect issues of timing. Norway and Sweden, for example, initiated policies to promote flexibility at the workplace as early as the 1960s, while similar schemes only appeared in Denmark and Finland some twenty years later. Further, as Wickham stresses (Chapter Five), if we focus on the types of practices being adopted, rather than on diffusion rates, a significant body of literature points to convergence in organisational methods across Europe, associated with the pressures of globalisation. Yet, here as well, caution is needed in interpreting the evidence. The increasingly universal managerial jargon used to describe on going organisational changes may mask significant differences between nations. Any definitive answer to this question will require additional evidence, based on more satisfactory measures of organisational change, with a Europe-wide coverage comparable to that of the Community Innovation Surveys.

The question of the performance effects of the diffusion of high involvement work practices is also a matter of debate. If, as Wickham observes, most studies find a positive correlation with some measure of productivity, the relation to financial performance is more in doubt. Of particular relevance to the issue of competence building is the relation between organisational change and innovative performance. The Danish DISKO studies find convincing evidence of a positive link between product innovation and the adoption of new work practices. A recent study based on the WERS survey of workplace employment relations has come up with a similar result for the UK (Michie and Sheehan, 1999). This issue is of particular relevance to the EU Sixth Framework Programme's focus on the economic impact of the transition to a knowledge-based society and it can be hoped that further empirical studies focusing on the innovation/organisation link will be forthcoming.

Even more contentious than the issues of diffusion rates and performance effects is that of the impact of new organisational practices on worker outcomes. There are a number of French studies, for example, positively linking workplace stress and an intensified pace of work to such practices as the delegation of responsibility and multi-skilling (Gollac and Volkoff, 2000). Moreover, new organisational practices are more often than not introduced by management without the employment guarantees that many observers, based on the Japanese model, argued were a necessary condition for achieving high levels of employee commitment. One possibility is that the impact of new HRM practices on worker outcomes is mediated by the strength of formal systems of employee representation, with a tendency towards positive outcomes in countries like Denmark or Sweden where the unions' role remains strong. This would imply, from the point of view of worker outcomes, positive complementarities between formal and informal forms of participation. Unfortunately, as Wickham reminds us, there is no necessary link between formal and informal forms of participation. Indeed, in some countries, such as the US and the UK, the increased adoption of informal forms of participation appears to have gone hand-in-hand with a decline in union representation.

Another key issue is the impact of organisational change on employment and the demand for skills. New participatory work practices arguably put a premium on hiring workers with formal qualifications and may bias employment against those without vocational training. Lundvall and Christensen's study (Chapter Seven) based on the DISKO survey of Danish enterprises provides a novel take on the issue of a skill bias in current organisational changes. Basically what the DISKO results show is that for firms facing increased competitive pressure, workers without vocational training generally fare worse than those with such training. Nonetheless, it appears that especially dynamic firms, that have followed the prescription of combining ICT investments with the introduction of participatory work practices, are able to compensate for the negative impact on employment of workers without vocational training. This result, which confirms the hypothesis of positive complementarities between organisational change and ICT investments, is important from the policy angle and it is hoped that similar studies will be carried out for other European nations.

It is often claimed that contemporary organisational innovations improve both performance and worker outcomes. Wickham's paper introduces a note of scepticism, saying in essence that there is no such thing as a free lunch and that increased participation and greater social cohesion at the workplace may be expensive luxuries rather than sources of competitive advantage. But of course history is full of counterexamples to that overused aphorism. Technological progress, if not a free lunch, is certainly a rather cheap one, in the sense that it has produced increases in output more than commensurate with the effort and cost undergone. Any answer to the question of whether today's organisational innovations constitute another counterexample to the science of scarcity will require additional research based on improved empirical measures. The two empirical studies in this section move in that direction by helping to elucidate the complex relation between organisational change, economic performance and worker outcomes.

NOTES

1. One recent study estimated that in successful companies the value of accumulated intangible assets associated with expenditures on worker training and organisational change outstrips the amount invested in ICT by at least a factor of 4. See Brynjolfsson and Hitt (2000).
2. See, for example, Coriat (2001).

REFERENCES

Andreassen, L., Coriat, B., den Hertog, F. and Kaplinsky, R (eds) (1995). *Europe's Next Step: Organisational Innovation, Competition and Employment*, London Frank Cass.

Brynjolfsson, E. and Hitt, L. (2000). 'Beyond Computation: Information Technology, Organisational Transformation and Business Performance', *Journal of Economic Perspectives*, 14(4): 23–48.

Coriat, B. (2001). 'Organisational Innovation in European Firms: A Critical Overview of the Survey Evidence', in D. Archibugi and B-Å. Lundvall (eds), *The Globalizing Learning Economy*, Oxford: Oxford University Press, pp. 195–215.

Gollac, M. and Volkoff, S. (2000). *Les Conditions du Travail*, Paris: La Découverte.

Michie, J. and Sheehan, M. (1999). 'HRM Practices, R&D Expenditure and Innovative Investment: Evidence from the UK's 1990 Workplace Industrial Relations Survey (WIRS)', *Industrial and Corporate Change*, 8(2): 211–34.

5. Understanding technological and organisational change

James Wickham

5.1 INTRODUCTION

The subtitle of this book includes the words 'social cohesion' and 'Europe'. If 'Europe' has any positive meaning to its citizens, it means some vague combination of 'social cohesion', parliamentary democracy and economic growth. Social cohesion is therefore central to 'Europe' as a political entity and to European identity in a way that is not the case for the identity of the individual member states.

Other bases for European identity are remarkably weak. Appeals to European culture are attractive to elites and to professional art historians, but notoriously have little popular purchase. In 1999 Crouch argued that for ordinary Europeans, the most decisive difference between us and the USA and Japan is simply that we play football and they do not (Crouch, 1999) – and after World Cup 2002 not even that is completely true. Appeals to our common history seem rather bleak once we go back before 1950. The Europe of the first half of the 20th century was hardly a model of good governance (Mazower, 1998). And when European cities are defined by their grand public buildings, it is often forgotten how much of this depends on a shared history of colonialism. It is perhaps emblematic that this is clearest in Brussels, whose grandiloquent architectural statements were built by King Leopold with the loot of the Congo to show how that the city was now a truly European capital (Hochschild, 2000).

Social cohesion is therefore important for Europeans, but it is also controversial. On the one hand there is the view, particularly strong in the Anglo-American business media, that European social protection (especially in the labour market) is the cause of Europe's slow economic growth. On the other hand there is the view (often put forward by the European Commission itself) that social cohesion is not only compatible with economic growth, but is actually crucial to it. This chapter explores one aspect of this debate, namely the implications of changes in work organisation, in particular those involving information and communication technologies (ICTs), for social cohesion at work. At its simplest, the chapter asks: Does information and communication technology undermine the European social model in the workplace?

The chapter attempts to answer this question in two stages. I begin by clarifying some conceptual issues: the meaning of this term 'social cohesion', the role of political choice, the relationship between ICTs and entrepreneurialism. I then use the results of some recent work within the European Commission's Targeted Socio-Economic Research (TSER) programme to ask whether current changes in work, technology and organisations are making the combination of economic growth and social cohesion more or less likely. Does the research show any evidence that ICTs are being chosen in order to improve the quality of work? Does work with ICTs require not just new skills and knowledges, but commitment and trust? And what are the implication of ICTs in the workplace for a better balance between work and non-work life?

5.2   CONCEPTUAL ISSUES: COHESION, CHOICE AND ICTs

5.2.1   Defining Social Cohesion

'Social cohesion' is one of those terms the meaning of which has become less clear the more it has been used. The term was added into the European Treaty by the Single European Act, which enjoined the member states to develop 'cohesion' with the poorer states (Gold, 1993; Bainbridge and Teasdale, 1995). During the 1990s it came to mean more than just equality between richer and poorer areas and at times, for example in discussions of poverty issues, seemed to be simply a codeword for reducing social inequality. Alternatively, social cohesion is used to describe something closer to the Durkheimian ideal of 'organic solidarity': the sense that all members of society have different roles but share a common fate and mutual responsibility.

Given this multiplicity of meanings, it is useful to distinguish between the vertical and the horizontal aspects of 'social cohesion'. By vertical I mean inequalities of income, wealth and power. Such inequalities may generate social exclusion and even social conflict, but this is not necessarily the case (many very unequal societies have also been very stable). By horizontal social cohesion I mean a sense of mutual trust and responsibility between members of society. At its simplest a 'cohesive' society in this sense is a society in which you don't worry if you forget to lock the backdoor at night.

It is often assumed that the two aspects of social cohesion vary together. The USA is a fairly clear example of this. Thus on the 'vertical' dimension the USA has levels of income inequality which far exceed any found in Europe, even in the UK (as nearly always, the closest within Europe to the US case). Furthermore, such inequality also has a political legitimacy that is inconceivable in Europe. Equally on the 'horizontal' dimension: the high level of crime (especially random crime) and the US prison population of two million (Christie, 1998) would certainly convince Durkheim that this was an extremely anomic society. Indeed, in the USA much crime is within the most excluded groups, notoriously but hardly uniquely 'black on black' (Wacquant, 1996). This lack of both vertical and horizontal cohesion is the image of the USA that is the silent guest at conferences where Europeans discuss their social cohesion.

Yet of course the story is not that simple. In terms of the horizontal dimension of cohesion there are many counter arguments. In his journeys to the strange new land in the early 19th century de Tocqueville (*Democracy in America*) stressed the high level of voluntary participation in public life in the USA. Such citizen involvement is part of the American way of life. Equally, the apparent resurgence of social involvement by the US corporate sector is precisely a resurgence (think of Carnegie, Rockefeller and even Ford). Conversely, some participants in the debate on the welfare state in Europe have claimed how the institutions of the welfare state (schools, hospitals, social work) which were created to ensure cohesion end up being run for the benefit of their employees rather than their 'clients'. Especially in Scandinavia, it has been argued that such institutions actually destroy social cohesion because they undermine the simple decencies of ordinary charity. The sufferings of our fellow citizens become the concern of the state, and nothing to do with us.

On the vertical dimension there is some evidence that income inequality is now being reduced in the USA. However, it remains indisputable that in terms of income inequality at least the USA remains far less 'cohesive' than Europe. Yet in terms of other sorts of inequality the USA can often claim to be more cohesive than Europe. For example, it really does have to be stressed that for all its racial tensions, the USA has welcomed new citizens in a way that has shamed Europe ever since the Irish famine. Which European state could ever have erected at its frontier the Statue of Liberty with its inscription: 'Give me your tired, your poor, your huddled masses yearning to be free'?

At this macro level of the whole society, the fundamental issue at the moment is whether social cohesion and economic growth are compatible.

Scholars of the regulationist school understood the 'Golden Years' (Hobsbawm, 1994) of the third quarter of the last century in Europe as showing that in fact social cohesion was not just compatible with economic growth but one cause of it. From this perspective, Keynesianism was not just an economic policy but also an institutional system (above all the welfare state itself) delivering the high levels of consumer demand and the suitably 'qualified' labour force that the boom required.   Now of course such institutions of regulation are widely seen as contributing to labour market inflexibility. This is the point at which our American guests start to speak, contrasting American dynamism with European sclerosis. But before we discuss the role of organisations here, we do need to ask our guests a question. If we Europeans worry about how we can maintain social cohesion and gain economic growth, surely Americans should wonder whether their economic growth has been purchased at the cost of the destruction of all aspects of social cohesion?

Such a discussion is posed at the level of the entire society. However, questions of social cohesion also involve organisations, and in two different ways, what I term the internal and the external aspects. We can ask to what extent the organisation is itself socially cohesive (internal aspect). We can also ask what contribution an organisation makes to social cohesion – or the lack of it – in the wider society (external aspect).

The simplest impact the enterprise makes on social cohesion in the wider society is through its reward system. If firms operate a relatively egalitarian wage policy (there is a relatively narrow range of gross wages and salaries) and if furthermore the remuneration package of their senior managers is relatively small, then the enterprise contributes directly to 'vertical' cohesion in the wider society. A related but more complex issue is the type of employment offered. If some employment is not only low paid but also irregular, unpredictable, or short term, then clearly the economic position of the employees is weakened. Vertical cohesion is undermined.

Much more difficult to conceptualise is the contribution of the enterprise to 'horizontal' cohesion in the wider society. One aspect is the sort of personalities and the forms of behaviour enterprises reward. For example, if enterprises reward only short term commitment, provide only short term rewards and reduce all interaction to market calculation, then their members are surely likely to behave in such a way in other areas of their lives. Enterprises, in other words, are not just passive recipients of individuals produced by socialisation processes located elsewhere in society. They are also agents of socialisation in their own right. And the results of this socialisation may strengthen or may undermine the 'horizontal' social cohesion of the wider society.

The key concern of this chapter is however with cohesion within organisations. Just as at the macro level, social cohesion within the organisation can be understood as having a vertical and a horizontal aspect. The vertical aspect is about inequality of power, while the horizontal aspect involves notions of community and trust. Although they are often conflated, they are analytically and sometimes empirically distinct.

On the vertical dimension it is clear that European organisations are more 'cohesive' than those in the USA. European employees have more rights and therefore a greater ability to constrain the actions of management. In terms of representation, union membership has fallen in the USA to an extent that has virtually no parallel in Europe. In many European countries where union membership is low, unions are still involved in national or sectoral level bargaining that shapes the conditions of union and non-union employees alike. As a result union density figures usually under estimate the influence of European trade unions, unlike in the USA. Furthermore, the European tradition of rights of collective representation within the firm has no US equivalent. This originates in the inter-war period, expanded enormously in the immediate aftermath of World War Two and has grown by fits and starts since then. It culminates in the European Works Council Directive. Such workplace citizenship in the form of works councils, board level representation and even workplace assemblies has no counterpart in the USA (or for that matter, East Asia). At an individual level European legislation provides protection in terms of health, safety, parental leave, restrictions on working time and the protection of equal opportunities which, once again, are very different to the US situation.[1]

On the horizontal dimension however the story appears to be very different. US enterprises have been increasingly concerned to create a team spirit of commitment within the workplace. Although such exertions have a long history, they became formalised in the renaming of personnel management as 'human resource management' (HRM) in the 1980s and in the simultaneous growth of the management of culture. In the 'strong culture' company management ensures that employees take responsibility for their work and for their contribution to the company as a whole – a clear example of 'horizontal' social cohesion at the micro level. It appears that as the world outside becomes more unequal, more brutal and more dangerous, American managers are trying to turn their workplaces into cosy communitarian islands in a sea of anomie.

The novelty here is not the attempt to ensure that employees identify with the firm, because 'paternalism' has a long history. The novelty is the attempt to ensure this identification through active involvement in decision making in areas which immediately effect employees, through the delegation of authority downwards, and the removal of intermediate layers of supervision:

practices that can all be summed up in the term 'empowerment'. Using the terminology of the European Foundation's EPOC project, this 'direct participation' can be contrasted with the older 'indirect participation' of participation through representation (Krieger and O'Kelly 1998; Sisson, 2000).

To the extent that it generates normative constraints on the actions of managers, such horizontal cohesion does also generate vertical cohesion. In other words, managers who strive to involve employees in decision making know that they are unlikely to gain such active involvement if they behave in despotic ways: their attempts to create community restrain their actions as well as those of their employees. Conversely, vertical cohesion can also generate horizontal cohesion. Thus co-determination and *betriebliche Mitbestimmung* in West Germany (as well as the narrow wage spread) helped to ensure that German employees identified with their enterprise through the long post-war boom. Furthermore, long before management discovered HRM, German employees were given far more responsibility in the day to day organisation of their work than was normal elsewhere in Europe (Lane, 1989). The relationship between vertical and horizontal cohesion is by no means straightforward however. In some situations, such as for example during the shop stewards movement in Britain in the 1950s and 1960s, relative equality of power can go together with overt conflict within the enterprise.

An enterprise that is, in these terms, internally cohesive has both vertical and horizontal cohesion. Historically the (West) German experience shows that this is possible and that furthermore it can be combined with economic success. For many contemporary managers, the problem with trade unions and other forms of representation is that they actually hamper participation in the workplace: in my terms, vertical cohesion is said to undermine horizontal cohesion. As such, the European version of social cohesion in the workplace is under challenge.

It is certainly claimed that direct participation gives employees more influence on their normal work than indirect participation. This is partly why it is described as 'empowering'. However, unlike some forms of indirect representation, this empowerment involves no rights. The empowerment of direct participation, to the extent that it actually occurs, is entirely within the gift of management. What management gives, it can also take back. Furthermore, the rationale for the introduction of direct participation is also different. Indirect participation and individual protection were argued for as ends in themselves. Workers *should* participate in the running of their firm, workers *should* have adequate safety protection, and so on. For this very reason they have been formulated as *rights* (either granted or still to be won) to be enshrined in legislation. They might also have beneficial effects for the firm, just as Keynesianism benefited employers as well as employees, but that is a secondary issue. Rights cannot depend on management strategy. By contrast, direct participation is a management strategy and a means to an end. The next subsection of this chapter examines this relationship between ends and means in more detail.

5.2.2   Spurious Pragmatism

Discussion of work organisation is an example of how political and empirical arguments are often conflated. Authors justify objectives which they actually support on political grounds not in terms of their own political values, but in terms of the alleged further consequences of these objectives. In other words, ends are treated as means. This is not a naïve plea for a completely value free social science. It is simply to suggest that some things have to be argued for on ethical and moral grounds, and not in terms of what I term a spurious pragmatism.

One argument for cohesive organisations is that they produce learning and innovation and hence economic growth. Thus the European Commission's Green Paper *Partnership for a New Organisation of Work* (European Commission, 1997) argues that firms need to become more participatory if they are to compete effectively. It goes on to argue that this participation can best be achieved by a combination of what this chapter has called 'direct' and 'indirect' participation. A rather similar argument is often put forward by national governments. For example, in Ireland national economic policy is largely the result of a formal 'national agreement' between the government, the trade unions, the employers' organisations and other major economic interest groups. The three year 'Partnership for Prosperity and Fairness' explicitly promotes 'partnership' at enterprise level in order to improve the quality of employment and economic competitiveness (Government of Ireland, 2000).

It would of course be very pleasant if the only way to achieve economic growth was by creating micro level cohesion, but social science has to insist that this relationship is an empirical matter. As Cappelli and Newmark (2001) point out, the idea that good jobs are a way to good profits is almost as old as industrialisation itself. Currently the focus of interest is on ways in which work can be reorganised to harness workers' own ideas as to how they could work more effectively: Total Quality Management (TQM), quality circles, job rotation, self-managed teams, and so forth. The extent to which such 'high performance work practices' do actually contribute to improved performance is by no means clear. While most studies do find some relationship to improved productivity (for example MacDuffie, 1995; Sisson, 2000), the impact on actual financial performance is more tenuous (Cappelli and Neumark, 2001).

Equally, any relationships that do occur may be entirely spurious, in that both participation and economic growth may be the result of some other feature (such as state policy, national level concertation or whatever). Finally the relationship may be the other way round, and participation may be the result of efficiency and not the cause. So efficient firms generate resources which they can then spend on the 'luxury' of participation. This is not as implausible a strategy as it sounds. There is evidence that there is a growing divergence between people's living standards as conventionally measured by income and their sense of personal and social well-being: measures of GDP are decreasingly informative about the quality of life in a society (see discussion in Osberg and Sharpe, 2000). If this is the case, then firms may reward people with participation, so participation becomes more akin to a benefit in kind rather than a direct means to greater efficiency.

The implication is that we need to be much clearer about the actual empirical argument we are making, and furthermore not conflate moral choices with empirical arguments. In the early 1950s many German Christian Democrats were gloomily convinced that communism was more efficient than capitalism and a planned economy in Germany would inevitably be more successful than free enterprise. However, they argued that free enterprise was morally superior because it alone opened the possibility of political freedom. Their choice was based on a political value judgement which they recognised as such. Such clarity of thought and such political courage would be useful today.

5.2.3   ICTs and Entrepreneurialism[2]

'Spurious pragmatism' is hardly restricted to those concerned to defend 'social Europe'. Similar issues arise on the other side of the political spectrum in terms of the relationship between information and communication technologies (ICTs), entrepreneurialism, labour market deregulation and organisational form. As above all Gadrey (2000) has pointed out, it is now taken for granted that ICTs spread fastest in an economic environment with entrepreneurial initiative, flexible organisations and a deregulated labour market. Once again something that is actually held to be desirable for political and moral reasons (entrepreneurial initiative) is justified in terms of its alleged empirical consequences (diffusion of ICT).

Within this discourse a second theme emerges, namely the importance of individuals being able and willing to change not just jobs but also employers and even being able to set up their own enterprises. Once the centre of the discourse is the 'e-economy', then the focus shifts completely from the organisation to the individual. Here the image of the organisation is as an open network rather than a closed building. In the more extreme formulations the individual with a career in an organisation is replaced by the entrepreneurial individual with a network of connections.[3] In this vision the social structure of the 'New Economy' involves a radical de-institutionalisation.

Social scientists are rightly sceptical of such arguments. It only requires a minimal awareness of different social interests to note that if employees accept responsibility for their own employment and unemployment, managers can, in the terms of the previous subsection, conveniently achieve horizontal cohesion without having to accept any constraints upon their own arbitrary power. Equally, it is easy to point out that data on job tenure across Europe do not show any dramatic decline (Crouch 1999; Doogan, 2001) or that graduate students entering the labour market still predominantly seek 'bureaucratic' careers (Brown and Scase 1994). Consultants and management gurus have a vested interest in announcing dramatic changes – to which they alone can provide the appropriate response.[4] One role for social science, as opposed to consultancy prophesy, is precisely to carefully delineate the extent and nature of these changes. The TSER projects discussed below can potentially contribute to this task. However, two other more ambitious points need to be made.

Firstly, social scientists should be more sceptical in principle about any automatic linkage between technology and societal form. Such 'technological determinism' has been criticised extensively in the sociology of science and technology since the 1970s. It is salutary to consider the fate of other and older 'obvious' views, such as what used to be the self-evident linkage between computers, the 'information society' and technocratic planning (Daniel Bell in the 1970s). And has nobody noticed that today the European economies which are moving fastest into ICT usage and development are those well known centres of neoliberalism, Finland and Sweden?[5]

Secondly, ICTs and of course above all the internet are often said to require or even cause a pure market. Thus in a moment of product diversification from software supplier to societal guru, Bill Gates has prophesied that the internet ushers in the 'consumer paradise' of a 'frictionless market' (Gates, 1995). The problem here is that a pure and self-supporting market is a conceptual impossibility. Any market requires institutional structures to support it, to enforce laws of contract, to provide means of exchange, and so on. Above all a market requires the unspoken trust on which all formal exchanges are based. Long ago Durkheim called these the 'non-contractual elements' of contract. If you want to see what a pure market society looks like, you need look no further than Russia. A market society, as even the World Bank is now discovering, requires market institutions and governance. Markets require societies, markets require 'friction'. The relationship is contradictory, but one implicates the other. To the extent that ICTs are used to justify the fantasy of an all-embracing market, they become props of a new ideology.

5.3 LEARNING FROM THE TSER PROJECTS

I now examine these issues through a discussion of the results of a group of research projects funded by the European Commission's TSER programme. The TSER programme as a whole funded a total of 162 projects; the six discussed here all focus on the organisation of work and technology. The TSER itself was the first EU research programme specifically allocated to social science, which is a small and relatively novel component of the EU's overall research funding overall (see Peterson and Sharp, 1998; Brine, 2000). The TSER research projects are important because they are European in several senses: they all draw their data from several European countries, and all of them attempt to pose their research questions in terms of Europe as a whole, rather than as simply comparing different European countries. They are part of an emerging *European* social research tradition. Here formal academic publishing is not always valued as highly as in the Anglo-American world, so the projects' results are only now beginning to filter through in terms of conventional academic publishing. Consequently I cite from the project reports which are available on the web; the websites of the projects are listed at the end of this chapter. I refer to the projects by their acronyms rather than the names of individual researchers.

5.3.1 Looking for the Ghost in the Machine

One of the reasons why the linkage between ICTs and a pure market economy seems so plausible is that now there appears to be no alternative. Globalisation makes the American way appear the only way. Technology and social institutions appear locked together as they travel along a predetermined path.

In this context, the social shaping of technology research tradition (Mackenzie and Wacjman, 1985) is important. Researchers have shown how social institutions shape technology, and how therefore technology varies depending on its social context. If this can also be shown for ICTs today, then it undermines the claim that there is no alternative to the particular configuration of institutions and technology that characterises the Anglo-Saxon 'New Economy'. Several TSER research projects on ICTs and organisations come out of the social shaping of technology research tradition.

Projects FLEXCOT, PRECEPT and SERVEMPLOI in particular assume the variability of technology. Rejecting technological determinism, they have an a priori commitment to tracing and explaining technological variation.

Project PRECEPT applies the social shaping of technology approach to the management practice of BPR (Business Process Re-engineering). BPR was the gangster rap of management guruism. Its proponents specialised in violent slogans such as 'Don't automate, obliterate!' (Hammer, 1990), arguing that ICTs can now be used to completely redesign the business processes of the organisation. PRECEPT traces how this practice has been taken up and utilised in Europe. It argues that the practice will be socially shaped at every stage by intermediaries, so that BPR in Europe will differ substantially from the original American programmatic statements.

PRECEPT shows that it is possible to trace the evolution of BPR and that this evolution is shaped by different social groups. This is hardly surprising. What is far more important is the tentative conclusion that it may be 'less instructive to look for differences between "national arrays" than to examine differences between different carriers (e.g. consultant versus academic; human resource management specialist versus information technology supplier)' (Slack et al, 1999; 25) Traditionally some of the key social differences that it has been possible to locate in the development of technology have been national differences. PRECEPT is suggesting that in a globalised world national differences become less important, but some other divisions become more important. These divisions however are themselves rather informal and rather uninstitutionalised, not least because BPR has been transmitted into Europe almost entirely through private sector channels, rather than through government agencies.

A similar indeterminacy can be found in project FLEXCOT. The research here was designed to locate linkages between ICTs and flexible work practices, with the ultimate policy objective of developing socially 'sustainable' flexible work practices. The project focused on four economic sectors in six countries (Belgium, Denmark, France, Italy, Spain and the UK); it used national sectoral overviews and case studies. The researchers insist that:

> There is no ICT-work-organisation logic. ICTs are both a driver of change and an enabler of change, but they *interact in complex ways with other inter-related drivers of change* (Vendramin et al 2000; 8 emphasis in original).

This is a clear rejection of technological determinism. Yet the FLEXCOT research results show that across sectors and countries, management is using ICTs in very similar ways and with very similar consequences. Management appears increasingly driven by short term goals of competitiveness. These goals not only ignore social issues but may even be economically counterproductive in the long term. There is not just a move towards short termism, but towards achieving these aims in broadly similar ways.

The 'varieties of capitalism' tradition (Crouch and Streeck, 1999) argued that the different institutional structures of the different European countries pushed or pulled management to achieving its objectives in different ways. Management acted differently because its actions were context-specific and these contexts differed. Yet according to Project FLEXCOT, national regulations have at most affected the pace of change, not the direction. Change is towards greater flexibility in the use of labour, whether through flexible working time, work location, contracts, outsourcing or functional flexibility. This flexibility does take different forms in different sectors, and does have different consequences for different groups of workers, but what is dramatic is the lack of any significant national differences.

Project SERVEMPLOI is a study of women's work in retail and in retail financial services and includes some of the same sort of workplaces as FLEXCOT. In both retail financial services and the retail sector itself, so the project argues, it is difficult to find any nationally specific developmental path. National systems of regulation in financial services have traditionally configured the national financial services sectors in very different ways. Now with the advent of the Single European Market and with the accompanying deregulation of financial services similar processes of restructuring, work organisation and technological development are occurring across Europe. For example, everywhere bank workers are being redeveloped from bank clerks into sales agents, routine clerical functions are being automated and then moved to centralised call centres and the 'front line' staff are becoming one channel through which the bank sells its (new) financial products.

While both FLEXCOT and SERVEMPLOI projects insist that these developments cannot be 'explained' by technology, there is no denying the erosion of national differences as managers pursue increasingly similar strategies. While there may well be alternatives to the status quo, it is becoming difficult to locate them. In this sense, research in the SST tradition has become a desperate search for the ghost in the machine: social choice is an axiomatic principle rather than an empirically observable result.

5.3.2   Knowledge, Reflexivity and Organisation

We have already seen that a long tradition within employment research claims that successful organisations require employee participation and involvement. The novelty is that participation is now linked to the stress on flexibility and ICTs. Two TSER research projects appear to develop this argument further by arguing that the effective use of ICTs requires the workforce to have 'reflexivity' (SOWING) and 'work process knowledge' (WHOLE).

As in the projects discussed above, WHOLE and SOWING do not see ICTs as an autonomous force acting on the organisation (they reject 'technological determinism'). At the same time, SOWING goes further than the other projects in insisting on the new organisational reality implicated in ICTs.   Quoting Castells (1996; 31), SOWING sees ICTs 'not as an exogenous source of impact [on work processes], but as the fabric in which such activities are woven.' Just like that of the proponents of BPR but from a very different perspective, this argument insists that ICTs are far more than simply discrete technologies. In a typology of 'Perspectives on ICTs', ICTs are reported to have been described variously as a tool, an automation technology, a means for control and surveillance, an information technology, an organisation technology, a medium and communication technology. To a large extent this can be seen as a developmental hierarchy, so that ICTs were tools to carry out discrete existing tasks, but have now become crucial to strategic objectives, driven by users' market needs rather than technological development per se.   Project SERVEMPLOI similarly insists that ICTs now involve more than 'islands of automation' and that even the cash desk operator in the supermarket now works in an 'informatised' workplace.

But what are the implications for organisational work? Project SOWING argues that in this new context, the 'reflexive organisation' is a new 'Leitbild' (or paradigmatic model) for contemporary organisations faced with the need to restructure. Relating (implicitly) to similar ideas in both the sociology of 'postmodernity' and in the management consultancy literature, organisations, so it is argued here, need to be able to continually reinvent themselves. This requires however reflexivity both at the individual and the organisational level, as people and rules are seen as constituted and hence reconstitutable. This in turn requires new forms of qualification. Rather than any simple shift 'from' technical 'to' social skills, SOWING suggests that we can see shifts occurring within a range of different forms of qualification. Nonetheless, the project does support those other arguments (see for example Brown and Scase, 1994) that stress the growing importance of qualifications other than purely technical skills. SOWING argues that this creates the possibility of new forms of social exclusion since many social groups do not have access to these new qualifications.

Technical skills are relatively easy to identify and evaluate; as such they can be 'taught'. Social skills and aptitudes are more the product of socialisation, they are more difficult to acquire in instrumental fashion and are more easily linked to class, ethnic or gender stereotypes. SOWING alerts us to the importance of these 'skills' in ICT-based work. However, the project may inadvertently exaggerate the role of ICTs here. For example, the pioneering work of Warhurst et al. (2000) has shown how the growth of up-market restaurants and designer retail outlets has created a new demand for 'aesthetic labour' by 'cool' workers. This in turn generates new forms of social exclusion in the labour market. Yet the growth of this form of work has more to do with structural shifts in the economy and the growth of the service sector, and very little to directly to do with ICTs.

New forms of social exclusion are the downside of what is fundamentally a new version of the optimistic tradition. However, this argument remains tentative given the current stage of the research in SOWING. Furthermore, the argument ignores many other more dystopian strands in the research literature which are picked up in other research projects. This lacuna occurs for two reasons. Firstly, the project appears to focus on one type of workplace, but without either any argument as to why such workplaces are important or any comparison with other less ICT-dependent workplaces. Secondly, the workplace is studied in isolation from the wider social structure, from the labour market and even from the overall ownership of the enterprise itself.

A similar problem of context also applies to the very rich case studies reported in the WHOLE project. This thematic network is based on research studies covering a range of sectors, from different areas of manufacturing to a wide variety of service sector activities (from air traffic control to industrial laboratory work). The key argument here is the importance of 'Arbeitsprozesswissen' or 'work process knowledge'. This involves an understanding of work roles in other parts of the organisation, an awareness of the interdependency of work activities, and a workplace culture which promotes providing service to the internal customer. As developed by the WHOLE network, such knowledge is seen as including both tacit and explicit (and even theoretical) knowledge. In particular work process knowledge is collective – knowledge is not a 'thing' to be owned[6] but is 'a process of participation in communities of practice'. Understanding knowledge in this way, so WHOLE argues, has implications for training, since most training practices focus on knowledge that is only individual and explicit. Developing work process knowledge does require the blurring of occupational boundaries and a flexible organisation, but unlike many adherents of the optimistic tradition, the WHOLE group are clear that the development of such knowledge-intensive organisational forms is far from inevitable. Indeed, they stress that more 'traditional' (Fordist/Taylorist) modes of organisation often have competitive advantages.

Project SERVEMPLOI and in particular project FLEXCOT highlight more negative aspects of the new forms of work. The results from FLEXCOT show that all over Europe flexible employment increasingly has aspects which are negative for employees (individualisation of working time, temporary employment contracts, outsourcing, and so on). Project FLEXCOT stresses that ICTs are powerful enablers of these changes, although they cannot be seen as causing them. Like other research, FLEXCOT stresses that at the same time and sometimes in the same places we can find what would normally be seen as improvements in the quality of work: team working, more internal flexibility, more responsibility. However, unambiguous improvements in the quality of work seem to be restricted to professional groups in quite narrow niches (such as design professionals in civil engineering).

In fact the findings of FLEXCOT fit with much other employment research which finds that the new flexible and ICT-intensive workplace is profoundly ambiguous for employees. Within the workplace more responsibility brings more pressure. Both are often related to ICTs – on the one hand access to more information and more decision making, on the other hand tighter time constraints, more demands for immediate action and more intrusive transparency. More fundamentally, the new insecurity (downsizing, outsourcing and temporary employment) ends what has usually been considered to be an essential prerequisite for high trust organisations (Osterman, 1998). Employees, so the FLEXCOT results show, are now being asked to be flexible and adaptive, but are no longer offered secure employment in return.

The restructuring of work organisation is interwoven with (but hardly reducible to) rapid restructuring of ownership. Mergers and acquisitions are now becoming the norm in what used to be termed the 'Rhineland capitalism' of Continental Europe. Despite the attention devoted to this change in the business press, only project SERVEMPLOI gives this any analytical importance (by stressing the rapid growth of takeovers and mergers in the financial services sector in particular). Yet once the workplace becomes an entity that can be bought and sold, then 'shareholder value' replaces the role of 'stakeholders'. This can accentuate employees' insecurity and so, again, undermines trust within the organisation. Furthermore, initial results from SERVEMPLOI also show how mergers and acquisitions undermine employees' tacit knowledge and disrupt path-dependent technological trajectories. We therefore face a paradox. At precisely the point at which one strand of research literature is stressing the importance of trust and collective knowledge, another is documenting how what are usually understood to be the preconditions for trust and collective knowledge are being destroyed.

The research also shows a clear loss of power and initiative by trade unions. According to these reports unions 'at best' fight a rearguard action and/or protect the interests of a declining number of existing members while new employees face less satisfactory conditions. Both SERVEMPLOI and FLEXCOT document that ICTs are an important enabler here, since they facilitate a greater locational flexibility. And finally, only SERVEMPLOI asks what the changes mean for women and questions of gender equality, and comes to a fairly gloomy conclusion. Where women have traditionally been employed in routine work, such as retail shops and retail financial services, the changes in work organisation merely reinforce the non-recognition of women's skills and women's position at the bottom of the employment hierarchy.

5.3.3   Paid Work, Unpaid Work and Social Life

Conventional research on ICTs and organisations focuses on the organisation of work and is largely gender-blind. As one of the contributors to project SERVEMPLOI has documented, there is however a subversive tradition which raises the issue of gender in relation to information technology and in particular to the role of ICTs in the workplace (Webster, 1996). The gender dimension is dealt with better in more recent projects which cover the link between work organisation, working time and the location of work. Thus in different ways projects NESY, FLEXCOT and SERVEMPLOI discuss how ICTs are interwoven with changes in working hours and with the different spatial location of work. For example, the ICTs enable enterprises to manage more complex and variable shift systems and are central to the way in which enterprises have reorganised work into new and distant spatial locations – epitomised of course by the development of the call centre.

There is an extensive literature on the way in which women's domestic labour shapes their ability to participate in the labour market. This literature is particularly well summarised in various papers from the NESY project. Within this tradition, SERVEMPLOI specifically considers women's total relationship with the labour market through its panel studies of repeated interviews with a group of women in the service sector. Another novel contribution to the debate is made by project NESY which inverts the usual relations. Instead of studying only how domestic labour impacts on paid labour, NESY shows how the extensification of work impacts on the non-work sphere of people's lives. NESY in particular locates trends towards on-call working, longer shifts, 24 hours working, teleworking and so forth. In this way changes in work organisation impact on people's ability to carry out unpaid work, in particular the work of caring for children and older dependants. Even more intriguingly, projects SERVEMPLOI and NESY illuminate the way in which many new forms of service work 'commodify' emotions and utilise this aspect of the non-work sphere in the sphere of paid employment. And of course this applies particularly, but not exclusively, to women.

Even more fundamentally, research on ICTs and work organisation may throw new light on the relationship between the 'information society' and citizenship. Here the optimistic position is of course that ICTs enable greater political participation, while the more dystopian perspective focuses on issues such as over-individualisation, alienation, the gap between the information-rich and the information-poor. A perspective that starts from the organisation of work suggests some rather different issues, even if these are to date largely implicit in the research results. Thus the extensification of work presumably impacts on people's ability to engage in social life as citizens, and while this has long been documented for the inhabitants of Silicon Valley (Rogers and Larsen, 1984), there is relatively little research on this aspect of high technology work for more ordinary people. Clearly this relates to the more general issue of over-individualisation and entrepreneurialism discussed above and in more detail by one of the contributors to the NESY project (Gadrey, 2000).

Finally, results of project SOWING suggest that the need for social knowledge in the new workplace may generate new forms of social exclusion. It is worth considering whether citizenship in the 'information society' requires knowledges and competences which are increasingly generated in specific workplaces. Consequently exclusion from such workplaces generates new forms of social incompetence and marginality, from political participation through to access to particular technologies and services supplied outside the workplace.

5.4   CONCLUSION: REFORMULATING THE LEARNING ORGANISATION?

Everybody apparently wants social cohesion. But unpacking the term shows that this is not necessarily true. This chapter has shown that both vertical and horizontal cohesion are in fact incompatible with many features of American society. Within the workplace cohesion is even more problematic. American (or Anglo-American?) management is increasingly opposed to vertical cohesion (employee rights) and as such wants horizontal cohesion (community and commitment) on its own terms. An alternative, European social model in the workplace is perfectly plausible. One historical version existed in West Germany at least until the 1980s, and a more contemporary version has been put forward in various European Commission proposals.

However, the concept of spurious pragmatism shows that it is intellectually dishonest to assume such workplace cohesion can be achieved without overt political choice – just as it is dishonest to assume any inherent linkage between the spread of ICTs and the triumph of free market individualism. Empirical research within the TSER programme has shown that the reality of ICT-based workplaces is more ambiguous and complex than either ideological position would have us believe. The research does show that in the current situation there are clear trends undermining national distinctiveness within Europe. The research also shows that for employees these trends are not entirely positive. ICTs facilitate new forms of responsibility and knowledge, but also flexibility that is imposed by employers in ways that rarely benefit employees. Furthermore, the impact of changes at work upon citizenship (and hence for social cohesion) in the wider society seem to be largely negative.

Of course such results are not what the naïve proponents of the 'information society' would like to hear, but good empirical research often challenges our presuppositions. Who knows, it may even indicate the spaces for political choice?

Table 5.1   Websites for TSER research projects discussed in this chapter

Project acronym and name	Website
FLEXCOT: Flexible Work Practices and Communication Technology	http://www.ftu-namur.org/flexcot/
NESY: New Forms of Employment and Working Time in the Service Economy	http://www.iatge.de/index.html?pro jekt/am/nesy-engl.html
PRECEPT: Process Re-engineering in Europe: Choice, People and Technology	http://www.its.dtu.dk/faggr/tesoc/pr ecept/menu.htm
SERVEMPLOI: Innovations in Information Society Sectors – Implications for Women's Work, Expertise and Opportunities in European Workplaces	http://www.tcd.ie/erc/Servemploi/
SOWING: Information Society, Work and the Generation of New Forms of Social Exclusion	http://www.uta.fi/laitokset/tyoelama /sowing/frontpage.html
WHOLE: Work Process Knowledge in Technological and Organisational Development (thematic network)	http://www.education.man.ac.uk/eu whole/home2.html

NOTES

1. However, some commentators suggest that in the area of individual rights in the workplace US law is in advance of European (see for example Robert Taylor, *Financial Times* 19 May 2000).
2. After presenting the initial version of this paper I received a copy of Jean Gadrey's book (Gadrey, 2000) which discusses similar issues but far more elegantly and systematically.
3. Most famously in Reich (1993); similar arguments in Handy (1993).
4. For a critique of such 'rupturism' see Burrell (1996). Benders and van Bijsterveld (2000) point out that as (we) social scientists increasingly seek interaction with 'users', in order to achieve credibility we are obliged to engage with and give credibility to those forms of knowledge which our new audience considers 'leading edge'.
5. Scandinavia has the highest level of PC usage and the highest level of internet connection amongst the population within Europe. One explanation has been the narrow income distribution! Furthermore, Sweden and Finland are the places of origin of the only two European companies (Nokia, Ericcson) which are global players in mobile telephone technology.

6.   The new management fad (?) of 'knowledge management' understands knowledge in precisely this 'lump of stuff' mode.

REFERENCES

Bainbridge, T. and Teasdale, A. (1995). *The Penguin Companion to European Union*, London: Penguin.

Benders, Jos and van Bijsterveld, Mark (2000). 'Leaning on Lean: the Reception of a Management Fashion in Germany', *New Technology, Work and Employment* 15(1) (March): 50–64.

Brine, J. (2000). 'TSER and the Epistemic Community of European Social Researchers' , *Journal of European Social Policy* 10.3(August): 267–82.

Brown, Philip and Scase, Richard (1994). Higher Education and Corporate Realities: Class, Culture and the Decline of Graduate Careers. London: UCL Press.

Burrell, Gibson (1996). 'Hard Times for the Salariat?' in Harry Scarbrough (ed.), *The Management of Expertise*, London: Macmillan, pp. 48–65.

Cappelli, Peter and Neumark, David (2001). 'Do "High Performance" Work Practices Improve Establishment-Level Outcomes?' *Industrial and Labor Relations Review* 54 (4) (July): 737–75.

Castells, Manuel (1996). *The Rise of the Network Society*, Oxford: Blackwell.

Christie, Nils (1998). 'For a penal geography', *Actes de le Recherche en Science Sociales* 124 (Sept): 68–74.

Crouch, Colin (1999). *Social Change in Western Europe*, Oxford: Oxford University Press.

Crouch, Colin and Streeck, Wolfgang (eds) (1999). *Political Economy of Modern Capitalism*, London: Sage.

Doogan, Kevin (2001). 'Insecurity and Long-term Employment', *Work, Employment and Society* 15 (3) (September): 419–41.

European Commission (1997). *Partnership for a New Organisation of Work – Green Paper*, Bulletin of the European Union Supplement 4/97.

Gadrey, Jean (2000). *Nouvelle Economie, Nouveau Mythe?* Paris: Flammarion.

Gates, Bill (1995). *The Road Ahead*, New York: Viking.

Gold, M. (1993). 'Overview of the Social Dimension', *The Social Dimension*, London: Macmillan, pp 10–40.

Government of Ireland (2000). *Programme for Prosperity and Fairness*, Dublin: Stationery Office.

Hammer, M. (1990). 'Re-engineering Work: Don't Automate, Obliterate', *Harvard Business Review* 90 (July–August): 104–12.

Handy, Charles (1993). *The Empty Raincoat: Making Sense of the Future*, London: Hutchinson.

Hobsbawm, Eric J. (1994). *Age of Extremes: The Short Twentieth Century 1914-1991*, London: Michael Joseph.

Hochschild, Adam (2000). *King Leopold's Ghost*, Basingstoke: Macmillan

Krieger, Herbert, and O'Kelly, Kevin (1998). 'The Extent of Participation in Europe', *Transfer* 98(2): 214–29.

Lane, Christel (1989). *Management and Labour in Europe*, Aldershot: Gower.

MacKenzie, Donald, and Wacjman, Judy (eds) (1985). *The Social Shaping of Technology*, Milton Keynes: Open University Press.

MacDuffie, J.P. (1995). 'Human Resource Bundles and Manufacturing Performance', *Industrial and Labor Relations Review* 48 (2): 197–221.

Mazower, Mark (1998). *Dark Continent: Europe's 20th Century*, London: Allen Lane The Penguin Press.

Osberg, Lars and Sharpe, Andrew (2000). 'Comparisons of Trends in GDP and Economic Well-Being – The Impact of Social Capital', Paper presented at the Symposium on the Contribution of Human and Social Capital to Sustained Economic Growth and Well-Being, Québec City, 20 March 2000.

Osterman, Paul (1998). 'Changing Work Organisation in America: What Has Happened and Who Has Benefited?' *Transfer* 98(2): 246–63.

Peterson, J. and Sharp, M. (1998). 'Technology Policy in the European Union', London: Macmillan.

Reich, Robert (1993). *The Work of Nations: Preparing Ourselves for 21st Century Capitalism*, London: Simon & Schuster (First edition) 1991.

Rogers, Everett M. and Larsen, Judith K. (1984). *Silicon Valley Fever*, New York: Basic Books.

Slack, R., Williams, R., Graham, I. and Lloyd, A. (1999). *Literature Review*, Project PRECEPT, http://www.its.dtu.dk/faggr/tesoc/precept/menu.htm.

Sisson, Keith (2000). *Direct Participation and the Modernisation of Work Organisation*, Luxembourg: Office for Official Publications of the European Communities.

Vendramin, P., Valdenduc, G., Rolland, I. et al (2000). Final Report, Project FLEXCOT http://www.ftu-namur.org/flexcot/.

Wacquant, Loic (1996). 'Red Belt, Black Belt: Racial Division, Class Inequality and the State in the French Urban Periphery and the American Ghetto', E. Mingione (ed.), *Urban Poverty and the Underclass: A Reader*, Oxford: Blackwell, pp. 234–74.

Warhurst, Chris, Nickson, Dennis, Witz, Anne and Cullen, A. M. (2000). 'Aesthetic Labour in Interactive Service Work: Some Case Study Evidence from the "new" Glasgow', *Services Industries Journal* 20(3) (July): 1–18.

Webster, Juliet (1996). *Shaping Women's Work: Gender, Employment and Information Technology*, London: Longman.

6. The flexible firm: new concepts and differences between the Nordic systems of innovation

Allan Næs Gjerding

6.1 INTRODUCTION

The point of departure of the present chapter is the idea that it is difficult to sustain competitiveness in a contemporary setting without striving for flexibility. By 'flexibility' we mean the ability of the firm to exploit changes in the environment and turn them into opportunities that lead to sustained favourable market positions. Consequently, flexibility implies that the firm must explore new opportunities in order to adapt to or prepare for new events, but succeeds commercially only to the extent that it is able to exploit these new opportunities. Thus, flexibility rests on some sort of balance between exploration and exploitation. While exploration often requires that existing lines of activities are put aside or deleted from the organisational repertoire, exploitation rests on the organisational ability to institute behavioural regularity. The intricacy of this balance, which has been referred to as a flexibility-stability dilemma (Gjerding, 1992, 1996a) or a paradox of flexibility (Volberda, 1998), represents a challenge that is not easily met. Exploration and exploitation may require not only distinct competences, but also distinct types of organisational behaviour, especially regarding ways of perceiving the world, activity time horizons, and tolerance towards ambiguity (March, 1991). The managerial task of reconciling these conflicting requirements is far from trivial.

From an organisation design point of view, it has been argued that organisations may assume different forms at different points of time, that is, being in a state of experimentation and flux when needed and, contrarily, instituting production and order when needed. The logic of this suggestion, for example when labelled as differentiation in time and space (Holbek, 1988), is captured by the classic unfreeze-change-freeze sequence (Lewin, 1951) by which flexibility reflects the ability of the firm to master the change process. The change process is envisaged as triggered by disequilibrating forces that upset the behavioural patterns of the firm, and change occurs until an equilibrium between forces of drive and restraint is achieved. This sequential approach presupposes that the firm moves in and out of equilibrium in a way where the organisational repertoire is, alternately, stable and unstable, and although this may be a fairly adequate description of organisational behaviour in some circumstances, it does introduce two conceptual problems. First, the ability of the firm to perform in and out of equilibrium movements is sensitive to the frequency with which the movement is needed. If the movement is performed frequently, the organisational repertoire may never settle down. Second, it is assumed that forces of change can be separated from forces of stability. This is true only to the extent that the management of change is a rational process where events are analytically decomposed into clearly defined cause and effect chains that can be adequately predicted in the absence of ambiguity.

The present chapter reflects the point of view that ambiguity is rarely absent. It is inspired by the notion of creative tensions (Leonard-Barton, 1988) and adopts a position favourable to the postmodern rejection of stability as a permanent phenomenon and to insistence on a continuous clash between stability and change (Hatch, 1997). In consequence, the organisational repertoire never settles down, but is always in a state of disequilibrium. This does not mean that the organisational repertoire is devoid of stable elements. Stable elements do exist, such as operating procedures and planning routines. Even though they are challenged by occurring problems and new ideas, and thus continuously subjected to change, they serve as stable social institutions that guide the directions of change going on. This is part of the organisational sensemaking (Weick, 1995) by which the organisation members try to understand what they are and have been doing. Furthermore, as argued by Jensen (1998) with reference to Ahmed et al. (1996), flexibility depends on result-oriented competences that institutionalise stability, and consequently flexibility requires an ongoing process of learning since the existing organisational repertoire and knowledge base determine the direction and limits of flexibility.

The focus on learning as part of achieving flexibility may be traced back to the seminal contributions by Peters & Waterman (1982) and Kanter (1983) that formed such an important part of the 1980s debate on competitive excellence. Some, like Porter (1980, 1985), believed that competitive excellence could be achieved through careful analysis of the competitive environment based on an assessment of the strengths and weaknesses of the firm. While Porter's approach was rooted in comparative statistics, other researchers, like Pedler, Boydell & Burgoyne (1989) adopted a more dynamic perspective and argued that firms need to develop a capacity to continuously transform themselves. This line of thinking led to the concept of the learning company (Pedler, Burgoyne and Boydell, 1991) that combined different disciplines, such as total quality management (Deming, 1986) and organisational learning (Argyris and Schon, 1978). The concept of the learning company shares with the emphasis on flexibility the temptation of arriving at two conclusions that actually challenge the concept itself. First, as explained by Nymark (1997), although most researchers within the learning organisation field recognise that the learning organisation is a means rather than a goal, the concept has often been interpreted as if we are dealing with controllable organisation design. In consequence, the design, and not the learning process institutionalised by the design, becomes the focus of managerial attention. Second, the need for continuous transformation tends to dominate the discussion of managerial implications. In consequence, the emphasis on change squeezes out the stability issue and, furthermore, overlooks the fact that change may not always be justified – in fact is counterproductive in circumstances where change is not warranted (Gjerding et al., 1997; Lundvall and Kristensen, 1997).

Accepting a critical approach to the concept of the learning organisation, the chapter reflects on some Nordic empirical research (Gjerding et al., op. cit; NUTEK, 1999) in which the author has taken part, and questions the theoretical premises of that research. The need for such reflection is great, since the research in question has played an important part in contemporary industrial policy reasoning, notably in Denmark, Sweden and Finland. 'Flexibility' has become a buzzword for industrial policy makers and consultants who often argue in favour of a single conception of flexibility, and thus there is a need for questioning the existence of such single solutions. Furthermore, there is another reason why questioning is warranted. Often research and policy debate has associated striving for flexibility with the evolution of learning organisations. However, as the analysis proceeds the reader will find that flexibility takes forms that are quite different from what characterises learning organisations. Section 6.2 presents the empirical research retrospectively in terms of a Swedish, a Danish and a joint comparative Nordic study, while Section 6.3 discusses the main theoretical basis for the research in question. Consequently, a typology presenting different types of flexible competitive behaviour is proposed. The concluding Section 6.4 discusses some implications for research and policy.

6.2 SOME NORDIC EMPIRICAL RESEARCH ON FLEXIBILITY

Following upon the G7 meeting on job creation in 1994, the OECD was commissioned to do a study on technological and organisational change and labour demand with an emphasis on the human resource implications of the creation and diffusion of flexible enterprises. Within this framework, the Swedish National Board for Industrial and Technical Development undertook a survey in 1994 of 707 private business workplaces with at least 50 employees (NUTEK, 1996). The survey focused on human resource management, work organisation, and technological and organisational change, including questions on competitive pressure and relations with important external actors, notably customers and suppliers. In order to create a quantifiable focus of the analysis, NUTEK (ibid.) arrived at a flexibility indicator, comprised of two dimensions.

The first dimension related to organised skills improvement and simply covered those firms that indicated that they had elements of organised skills improvement in ordinary work. The reason for including this aspect was the assumption that the existence of organised skills improvement reflects the firm's 'capacity for continuous transformation of the workplace and the ability to meet customers' demands in a rapidly changing market' (ibid. p. 88).

The second dimension related to the level of decentralisation, where an index value described the extent to which employees were able to influence the daily and weekly planning of their own work, quality control, maintenance, customer contacts, budgeting and purchase policy (ibid., pp. 89–91).

Flexible firms were defined as those belonging to the upper half of the decentralisation index that had organised skills improvement. In effect, about one quarter of the sample could be described as flexible organisations, and in comparison with the remaining three quarters of ('traditional') firms, the flexible firms were shown to be more productive, less pestered by employee absence, more skills demanding, and less predisposed to labour turnover.

6.2.1 A Danish Flexibility Score

Inspired by the Swedish study, a group of researchers at Aalborg University undertook a Danish survey of 1900 private business firms during 1996. The Danish survey (Gjerding et al., 1997) was part of a major Danish study on strengths and weaknesses of the Danish national system of innovation (Lundvall, forthcoming). While NUTEK (1996) focused on numerical, functional and wage flexibility, Gjerding et al. (op. cit.) focused primarily on functional flexibility and more or less neglected numerical flexibility. Following Atkinson (1985), numerical flexibility refers to how the firm adjusts the labour input in response to product market demands, that is, by varying the number of employees, the number of working hours, the intensity of work, and the use of part-time or temporary employees. Wage flexibility, often denoted as financial flexibility, refers to the adjustment of wages according to performance and variations in labour supply and demand. Functional flexibility denotes the ability of the firm to reallocate employees among tasks and prepare them for new tasks, for instance by job rotation, team building, and training and retraining. The Danish study defined flexibility as the ability of the firm to respond to a turbulent environment by product and process innovation, based on an integrative organisation and a corporate culture of renewal and learning (Gjerding et al., op. cit., p. 10).

Internal flexibility factors	
Structure	Cross-occupational working groups Quality circles/groups
Process	Rotation between functions Integration of functions Continued vocational training Educational activities tailored to the firm Long term educational planning
Culture	Delegation of responsibility Employees' weekly planning of own work Employees' evaluation of own work
External flexibility factors	
Technology	Introduction of new ITC technology Introduction of other forms of new technology
Product	Introduction of new products and services
Market	Attempt to conquer new foreign customer groups

Sources: Lund and Gjerding (1996, p. 14) and Gjerding et al. (1997, p. 106)

Figure 6.1   Different components of flexibility

Subsequently, the survey data were processed in different ways, displaying different types of organisational integration, product innovation management and human resource management (op. cit., Chapters Three to Six), and eventually a unified analytical approach to flexibility was attempted (ibid., Chapters Seven to Eight), see Figure 6.1.

The unifying approach reflected a separation of flexibility into internal and external factors. While the internal factors described organisational structure, process and culture, the external factors described process, product and market innovation. The internal factors reflect the point of view that an organisational structure enabling mutual adjustment of goals and aspirations is flexible if horizontal and vertical integration are combined with the empowerment of employees and continuous upgrading of human skills. The external factors reflect the idea that flexibility is achieved by innovation in technology and markets. The factors in Figure 6.1 represent fourteen measurement points in the sense that the responding firms could answer affirmatively or not to the questions associated with each factor, and thus each firm could obtain a value ranging from zero to fourteen. Actually, the distribution of firms was quite bell-shaped, as depicted by Figure 6.2, with about two per cent at each of the extreme ends of the flexibility score.

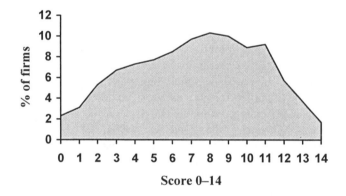

Source: Lund and Gjerding (1996, p. 14)

Figure 6.2 The Danish flexibility score, percentage distribution

The summation in Figure 6.2 reveals the extent to which the different firms in the sample employ none or some of the fourteen factors. However, it does not show the extent to which firms are biased towards internal or external flexibility. Consequently, the firms were regrouped, as shown in Figure 6.3, with a group of static (non-flexible) firms and three different types of flexibility. Although all firm sizes and sectors were represented in each group, some general patterns appeared, apart from the group of mainly internally flexible firms that were quite evenly scattered across sectors and firm sizes. The group of static firms was dominated by small firms in the trade, construction and transportation sectors while the small group of mainly externally flexible firms was dominated by small and medium sized firms and biased towards the manufacturing sector. Finally, the group of dynamic firms was dominated by the manufacturing and business service sectors, biased towards firms with at least 100 employees (Gjerding, 1999).

External flexibility	Internal flexibility	
	High	Low
High	Dynamic (25%)	Externally flexible (8%)
Low	Internally flexible (26%)	Static (41%)

Source: Adapted from Gjerding et al. (1997, p. 119)

Figure 6.3   Three types of flexibility in the Danish private business sector

Based on the analyses of organisational integration, product innovation management and human resource management (Gjerding et al., 1997), the Figure 6.1 inventory of flexibility factors seemed to capture the most important issues. In retrospect, this impression gains strength from the comparison by L'Huillery (1998) between studies in Denmark (Gjerding, 1996b; Lund and Gjerding, 1996), the UK (Ostermann, 1994, Waterson et al., 1997), France (Greenan 1995; Greenan, 1996a, 1996b; Coutrot, 1996), Sweden (NUTEK, 1996) and Germany (Kinkel and Wengel, 1997). Furthermore, the impression was verified by subsequent case studies of organisational change in 24 of the responding firms (Jørgensen et al., 1998). Compared to the indicator originally used in the Swedish survey, the Danish method captured more aspects of the flexible organisation and at the same time revealed different combinations of flexibility.

6.2.2   A Comparative Nordic Study

During 1997, an initiative to undertake a comparative Nordic study (NUTEK, 1999) organised by NUTEK was taken by a group of researchers belonging to NUTEK, the Danish Research Unit for Industrial Dynamics (DRUID), the Norwegian Institute for Social Research (ISF) and the Finnish Ministry of Labour. The fact that similar surveys on the diffusion of flexibility were in progress in Finland (Antila and Ylöstalo, 1999a, 1999b) and Norway (Olsen and Torp, 1998) stimulated the initiative. However, the comparative study encountered several difficulties. While the Finnish study had been designed to allow comparisons with both the Swedish and Danish studies, the Norwegian study had been designed to focus mainly on internal and external labour markets, and wage formation. Furthermore, a number of questions were put differently in the different national studies, thus creating uncertainty as to how the answers could be compared. In consequence, the comparative study *involved two steps.* First, where possible, two or more countries were compared along the dimensions of numerical, wage and functional flexibility. Second, a comparative indicator on flexibility inspired by the original Swedish one (NUTEK, 1996) was developed, but confined to functional and wages flexibility since the Danish survey more or less neglected numerical flexibility, as mentioned previously.

It had to be taken into account that the sample differed across the studies. The Swedish, Finnish and Danish studies focused on the private business sector and covered, respectively, 707, 810 and 1900 firms. The Norwegian study, covering 2130 firms, included public workplaces as well. Furthermore, while the Danish, Norwegian and Finnish studies covered firms with at least ten employees, the minimum firm size in the Swedish study was 50 employees. In consequence, public workplaces were omitted, and analysis was undertaken with respect to 10+ and 50+ employees. The following refers only to private business firms with at least 50 employees.

Regarding the first step, the comparison mostly revealed similar patterns in the four Nordic countries. However, some interesting differences appeared. First, it appears that Sweden is ahead regarding the use of work teams, and that job rotation is more frequent in Sweden and Finland than in Denmark and Norway. To some extent, this may reflect the existence of large national and private policy schemes to that effect. Second, the use of skills development plans is comparatively more widespread among Norwegian firms. Third, the use of temporary workers is extremely common in Finland and also extensively used in Norway and Sweden. Corresponding figures do not exist in the Danish survey, but a comparison between official labour market statistics reveals that the proportion of temporary workers in Denmark is comparatively small (NUTEK, 1999). These differences may reflect that the Danish labour market is regulated to a smaller degree than in the rest of the Nordic countries, and that Swedish, Finnish and Norwegian firms cope with labour market regulations by emphasising temporary contracts to a higher degree.

Regarding the second step, an indicator composed of five factors was developed. Wages flexibility entered the measure in terms of the use of a *compensation system based on results or quality.* Functional flexibility was represented by four factors, thus reflecting the main emphasis of the study. The four factors referred to the delegation of responsibility and the use of skills development plans, working teams and job rotation. The purpose of the indicator was to distinguish between two groups of firms, that is, a group of so-called front runners where all five factors were present, and the remaining group of firms. By applying a strict definition like that, the group of researchers hoped that differences between the Nordic countries would appear more clearly.

The measurement of the delegation of responsibility was intricate. In all four studies, the respondents were asked to indicate whether the responsibility for tasks lies with the employees, middle management, top management, or conjointly, and some studies even asked if the responsibility lies with teams. Furthermore, all studies allowed the category of 'other'. It was decided to construct a responsibility index where employees and/or teams were given the value of +1, the management/top management the value of −1, and the remaining options the value of zero. Subsequently, if the value of the responsibility index was larger than or equal to −0.5 the firm would be included in the front runner group.

Regarding the issue of skills development plans, questions had been put differently in the different studies. The only way to compare was to include affirmative answers that the firm had skills development plans for each employee in direct production in the cases of Norway and Sweden, and skills development plans for each employee in the case of Finland. In the Danish study, the presence of skills development plans was not covered so Danish firms were included in the front runner group if they affirmed that long term educational planning was of *great* importance in order to make sure that employees continuously develop their skills.

It appeared that while approximately 13 per cent of the firms in Sweden, Denmark and Finland could be categorised as front runners, the corresponding Norwegian figure was only five per cent, see Figure 6.4. The reason for the low Norwegian figure was not attended to in the Nordic study, but we may suggest two partial explanations. First, the Danish study showed that organisational renewal and the development of flexibility are closely related to the degree of competition (Lundvall and Kristensen 1997). This issue has been investigated in the Danish, Finnish and Norwegian studies, and it appears that the Norwegian firms have experienced an increase in competitive pressures to a smaller extent (NUTEK, 1999, p. 106).[1] Second, job rotation is more rarely used in Norway (NUTEK, 1999, Appendix 1, pp. 13–14).

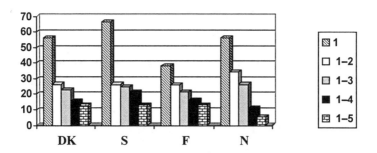

	Denmark	Sweden	Finland	Norway
1. Responsibility index ≥ -0.5	56.1	66.4	38.1	56.2
2. Skills development plans (1+2)	26.4	26.2	26.0	34.5
3. Work teams (1+2+3)	22.8	24.5	21.6	26.4
4. Job rotation (1+2+3+4)	15.7	21.3	16.1	10.9
5. Compensation system (1+2+3+4+5)	12.7	13.2	13.1	5.4

Source: Adapted from NUTEK (1999, p. 78)

Figure 6.4   *Stepwise application of the front runner criteria ,% share of firms*

Beside the special Norwegian position, some important differences actually exist across the Nordic countries, reflecting the fact that flexibility, on average, assumes different forms in the different countries. Tracking how the number of front runners decreases according to the number of measurement factors applied highlights the differences. Figure 6.4 displays a Swedish lead regarding the delegation of responsibility (1), while Finland seems to lag behind. When we add the factor of skills development plans (2) as a criteria for belonging to the group of front runners, positions change dramatically, with Norway now the leading country. This change reflects the fact that the use of skills development plans are more widespread in Norway than in the other Nordic countries. Furthermore, a significant number of Danish and Swedish firms drop out, which implies that the delegation of responsibility is a 'stand-alone' phenomenon in Denmark and Sweden to a larger extent than in Norway and Finland. Norway maintains its leading position when the use of work teams (3) is included, while there is virtually no drop out of Swedish firms. These observations reflect the fact that the use of teams is closely related to the use of skills development plans, and that teams are more frequently used among Swedish firms. When we add the use of job rotation (4), Norway suddenly lags behind, reflecting the previously mentioned smaller emphasis on job rotation. Finally, the use of compensation systems based on quality and/or performance (5) has a stronger exclusion effect in the case of Sweden and Norway, implying that wage flexibility is more closely related to functional flexibility in Denmark and Finland than in Norway and Sweden.

6.3   THE CONCEPT OF FLEXIBILITY

The unifying indicators on flexibility used in the Nordic studies reflect two normative prescriptions that have been pursued in the empirical research. First, that the organisational structure must allow cross-functional and cross-hierarchical integration that combine top-down direction with subordinate autonomy. Second, that the purpose of integration is to ensure requisite variety. The main idea is that the organisation becomes self-organised in the sense that the management provides a sense of direction, but allows ample room for emerging solutions. Translating these prescriptions into recent managerial ideas, we might say that strategy making must rely on umbrella concepts (Mintzberg, 1994) while the organisation structure should be like a holographic design (Morgan, 1986), perhaps even like a hyper-text organisation (Nonaka and Takeuchi, 1995). The variety of flexible solutions presented in Section 6.2 clearly shows that flexibility is a multi-faceted phenomenon that involves different types of problem solving and search, combined in various ways. However, the empirical studies presented are not clear as to what characterises the problem solving and search involved. The present section attempts to provide clarification retrospectively, in two steps. First, the studies are characterised in terms of some dominant approaches that may be identified within the literature on flexibility (Volberda, 1998). Second, these approaches are briefly criticised, and an alternative approach suggested and applied to the empirical studies.

A unifying theme of the literature on flexibility, as reviewed by Volberda (op. cit.) and to some extent by Gjerding (1996a), is that flexibility is important because firms find themselves in circumstances where they are subjected to change, thus leading to unsatisfactory levels of goal attainment unless the firm changes, too. In an early (seldom noticed) contribution, Zaltman et al. (1973) identified this situation with the occurrence of *performance gaps*. Initially, they defined performance gaps as 'discrepancies between what the organisation could do by virtue of a goal-related opportunity in its environment and what it actually does in terms of exploiting that opportunity' (p. 2). Later on they rephrased the definition as discrepancies between 'what the organisation is doing and what its decision makers believe it ought to be doing' (p. 55). Actually, these two definitions are not entirely similar. While the first emphasises an adaptive response to environmental change, the second focus on the perception and enactment of organisational behaviour. The application of the first definition may lead to a discussion of how organisations reactively or simultaneously cope with environmental change, while the application of the second definition would imply proactive behaviour as well. Taking these two definitions as our point of departure, the following discussion aims at describing how flexibility may be defined in different ways, based on a combination of Gjerding (1992, 1996a) and Volberda (1998). The purpose of this discussion is to show that the nature of flexibility is not only proactive and reflective, but that flexibility may occur even in cases where the organisational behaviour is more or less routinised.

6.3.1 Dominant Approaches to Flexibility

The diversified approach of Zaltman et al. (1973) provides a nice starting point, because it reflects the main discussion within the flexibility literature, in two respects. First, it relates to the question of whether flexibility should be conceived as proactive behaviour, or whether we may include reactive behaviour as well. Second, it raises the issue of whether the attainment of flexibility is a matter of conscious goal-oriented activity, or whether flexibility could be attained by allowing organisational action to emerge. As portrayed by Figure 6.5, the combination of these points of view leads to different perceptions of flexibility. In the conscious goal-oriented case, the organisational behaviour is planning-oriented, either reactively by way of dealing with occurring events or proactively by way of predicting and preparing for events that might take place. In the emerging case, reactive behaviour implies an element of surprise where employees are confronted by problems they have to solve or opportunities they have to pursue, while proactive behaviour signifies that the employees are constantly looking for new opportunities. The latter may be described as *opportunistic surveillance*, in other words a behaviour that 'does not wait to be activated by a problem and which does not therefore stop when a problem solution has been found' (Thompson, 1967, p. 151). These four cases are all captured by the Nordic empirical studies presented in Section 6.2, although there is a tendency to focus on prerequisites for proactive behaviour. Reactive behaviour is not excluded, but it is mainly perceived as quasi-proactive behaviour in the sense that flexible firms may behave reactively when faced with environmental changes, but they tend to prepare themselves for these events by instituting organisational changes.

Perception of behaviour	Perception of activity	
	Conscious goal-oriented	Emerging
Reactive	Ex post planning	Action by confrontation
Proactive	Ex ante planning	Opportunistic exploration

Source: Elaborated from Volberda (1998, Chapter One)

Figure 6.5   Different types of flexible organisational behaviour

In his work on flexibility, Volberda (op. cit.) has identified three main approaches in the flexibility literature (see Figure 6.6) that may assist a further understanding of the Nordic studies. The *general approach* attributes the need for flexibility to an accelerated pace of change in the competitive environment and argues that flexibility is needed in order to adapt to these changes or to stimulate innovation. The general approach comprises both reactive and proactive behaviour, and includes static, comparative static and dynamic descriptions as well. In effect, the typology presented in Figure 6.5 belongs to the general approach. The *functional approach* assumes that flexibility can be attributed to different segments of the organisational activity, in other words, that flexibility can be achieved in one line of activity while others remain non-flexible. For instance, the firm may change its production core by aiming for flexible production equipment while the rest of the organisation goes unchanged. The functional approach is partial and deals with such different issues as flexible wage contracts and 'make or buy' decisions. Finally, the *actor approach* deals with the nature of individual stakeholders assumed to be able to influence the direction of organisational behaviour. The approach discusses such topics as the relationship between entrepreneurs and conservative managers, risk profiles, and employee tolerance towards uncertainty. The actor approach is partial in the sense that it explains organisational behaviour by individual traits.

Approach	Main reason for flexibility	The purpose of flexibility
General	Accelerated environmental change	Change leading to innovation
Functional	Activities can be segmented	Local economic efficiency
Actor	Flexible individual stakeholders	Utilising individual enthusiasm

Source: Elaborated from Volberda (1998, Chapter One)

Figure 6.6   Three main approaches to the analysis of flexibility

All of the Nordic studies, both the individual country studies and the comparative study, belong to the *general* approach in the sense that they try to create unifying dynamic descriptions where changes in the competitive environment are argued as stimulating change, either through direct influence or through management perception. The role of competitive pressures as perceived by management plays an important role in the Danish study and is also present in the Finnish study. In the Swedish and Norwegian studies, and the comparative study, the role of competitive pressure is less clear and mainly present in the form of a discussion of the contingencies prompting changes that lead to flexibility. However, to some extent a *functional* approach is applied in partial analyses, as part of an analytical division where aspects of functional, numerical and wage flexibility are singled out for detailed analysis before they are summarised in a general approach. This is especially the case in the Norwegian and Finnish studies where partial analyses detached from the general approach appear, while partial analyses are less detached and more guided by the general approach in the Swedish, Danish and comparative studies. Finally, the *actor* approach is more or less absent. Most prominently, it appears in the Danish study, but primarily in the form of an analysis of obstacles and stimuli to change that complements the analysis within the general approach.

6.3.2 An Alternative Approach

None of the three dominant approaches described above is entirely satisfactory. First, the general approach presupposes that change leads to innovation, and that innovation is needed. However, change does not necessarily lead to innovation, and innovation may not be warranted if the firm operates in stable environments. Second, the functional approach is based on a segmentalistic logic that fails to notice the dynamic relationships between the different parts of the organisation and the organisational activity. Third, the actor approach pays too much attention to personal aspects of flexibility and underrates the impact of managerial and organisational structures and cultures. In consequence, Volberda (op. cit.) proposes a typology that combines technological, structural and cultural aspects of organisational behaviour, see Figure 6.7. The main idea is that flexibility rests on the creation of dynamic capabilities that facilitate both reactive and proactive responses because they are based on broad and deep knowledge bases within an organisational framework that allows experimentation and higher level learning, that is deutero learning (Bateson, 1942) that implies that the firm is able to balance single loop and double loop learning (Argyris and Schon, 1978).

Variety of capabilities	Speed of response	
	High	Low
High	Strategic	Structural
Low	Operational	Steady state

Source: Volberda (1998, p. 117)

Figure 6.7   Three types of flexibility

Flexibility is absent in the *steady state* case, which may be described as a situation where the firm employs static procedures aimed at the optimisation of a relatively stable throughput. *Operational* flexibility is dominated by routinised behaviour that allows a fast reactive response to changes with which the firm is familiar, while *structural* flexibility refers to slow adaptation of the organisation structure and the incumbent decision and communication processes. Finally, *strategic* flexibility refers to non-routine organisational behaviour where the firm faces unfamiliar changes of the nature of organisational activities. Although Volberda (op. cit.) is not explicit as to the extent to which reactive and proactive behaviour are involved in the cases of structural and strategic behaviour, we may argue that both types of behaviour can occur. However, the distinction becomes blurred. In the case of structural flexibility, the response may be either reactive or proactive, and in the long run they may substitute for one another. In the case of strategic flexibility, we would normally find or assume proactive behaviour, but a type of reactive (or quasi-proactive) behaviour may occur in the sense that firms embark on unfamiliar activities in order to prepare for future events, thus being ready to act on environmental changes.

The notion of performance gaps introduced earlier implies that flexibility denotes the ability of the firm to search for and implement solutions to problems that occur or are anticipated. Consequently, being flexible is search-based problem solving. Problem solving may be reproductive, that is, more or less a replication of past experience where the firm utilises previously applied solutions, or productive in the sense that new solutions are created (March and Simon, 1958). The search process may take the form of the opportunistic surveillance introduced in section 6.3.1, or be related to occurring problems, in other words, problemistic search 'that is stimulated by a problem (usually a rather specific one) and is directed towards finding a solution to that problem' (Cyert and March, 1963, p. 121). Combining these dimensions with the classification proposed by Figure 6.7, we arrive at the four types of flexibility depicted in Figure 6.8.

Problem solving	Search	
	Problemistic	Opportunistic
Reproductive	Routine Operational flexibility	Quasi non-routine Structural flexibility
Productive	Non-routine Structural flexibility	Non-routine Strategic flexibility

Source: Adapted from Gjerding (1992, p. 108) and Figure 6.7

Figure 6.8   Four types of flexibility – Figure 6.7 revisited

Figure 6.8 suggests that while operational and strategic flexibility may be uniformly described in terms of search and problem solving processes, the description is less clear in the case of structural flexibility. Routinised activities where known solutions are applied to occurring problems lead to operational flexibility, while the creation of new solutions by opportunistic search enables the firm to be strategically flexible. The situation of strategic flexibility may be defined as a case of solutions looking for problems, as described by the classic garbage can model (March and Olsen, 1976). Slow adaptation of the organisational repertoire may take the form of reproductive problem solving based on opportunistic search, in other words a case where we look for new opportunities to apply known solutions. This is a quasi-non-routine activity in the sense that we impose familiarity on unfamiliar settings. However, it may also take the form of productive problem solving based on problemistic search where solutions to occurring problems are searched for in fields beyond the existing organisational repertoire. This is a case of non-routine activity where we expose ourselves to unfamiliarity in a setting of ambiguity and are unable to determine the ensuing results.

At the outset, it is difficult to describe the Nordic studies in terms of Figure 6.8 since none of them was conducted with specific reference to the combination of problem solving and search activities. However, some interpretation is possible, although it does not yield any clear cut impression. The main purpose of the Swedish and comparative flexibility indicators is to give an impression of the variety of organisational capabilities where flexible (NUTEK, 1996) and front runner (NUTEK, 1999) firms are supposed to be highly positioned. Thus, the main emphasis is on strategic and structural flexibility. The same approach characterises the Finnish study where an indicator similar to the Swedish is used as a unifying element (Antila and Ylöstalo, 1997). To some extent, the strict definition applied by the comparative study (NUTEK, 1999) implies that we are observing the extreme case, in other words the focus is on strategic flexibility. In the case of the

Danish flexibility indicator (Lund and Gjerding, 1996) the focus is on the variety of capabilities and, furthermore, by distinguishing between internal and external flexibility the Danish indicator includes, indirectly, the element of speed of response. We may argue that high levels of both internal and external flexibility lead to rapid response, while the case is less clear regarding a bias towards either internal or external flexibility. Thus, the dynamic firms in Figure 6.3 are characterised by strategic flexibility while the externally flexible and internally flexible firms may cover cases of strategic or structural flexibility. The Norwegian study (Olsen and Torp, 1998) is more difficult to classify since the main focus is on internal and external labour markets. However, the study does include an analysis (Olsen, 1998) of combinations of functional and numerical flexibility. Olsen (ibid.) finds it difficult to verify that functional and numerical flexibility are combined, but at the same time they are not totally separated. Instead, the surveyed firms tend to employ either functional flexibility in combination with some aspects of numerical flexibility, or numerical flexibility in combination with some aspects of functional flexibility. These results indicate that the Norwegian firms mainly focus on operational and structural flexibility, and it may explain the low proportion of Norwegian front runners since front runner firms are characterised by strategic flexibility.

6.4   IMPLICATIONS FOR RESEARCH AND POLICY

If we were to point out a single overall message sent by the present volume, it would be that contemporary social cohesion takes place within the framework of a learning society. The present volume is inspired by the contribution of Lundvall and Johnson (1994) who argue that it is intellectually more fruitful to speak of the learning economy instead of the knowledge economy as often referred to in recent research and policy debates. The idea of a learning economy implies that we are dealing with dynamic processes of construction and destruction of knowledge and social institutions that are the outcome of continuous collective competence building and not merely a process of individual knowledge accumulation. Thus, we must expect to observe *different* industrial practices not only across countries but also within countries. This applies to the phenomenon of flexibility as well. Contrary to what is often argued, the present chapter shows that there does not exist one best way to organise for flexibility. Instead, flexibility must be analysed as a *diverse phenomenon* that assumes different forms in different industrial and national settings. The evidence from the Nordic studies shows that firms arrive at different solutions for flexibility, and points to the importance of taking *differences in industrial practice* into account when comparing solutions for flexibility.

Two observations may underline this argument. First, while changes in the intensity of competition played a major role for the development of flexibility in the Danish case, and to some extent in Finland as well, there is no indication that this is the case in Norway (Schøne, 1999) or Sweden (NUTEK, 1999). In order to explain this observation, which actually contradicts what could be expected on theoretical grounds (see for example Gjerding, 1999; Lundvall, 1999), we may observe the timing of efforts to stimulate the development of flexibility. Industrial policy schemes to that effect were initiated in Norway and Sweden as early as in the 1960–70s, while similar schemes did not occur in Denmark and Finland until some twenty years later (NUTEK, 1999). Thus, the strategic pursuit of flexibility is a more recent phenomenon in Denmark and Finland than in Norway and Sweden where firms have focused for a longer period of time on developing various types of flexibility. Second, the pursuit of flexibility by combining the use of teams with schemes for developing employee skills is important in all of the Nordic countries. However, while associating this effort with the delegation of responsibility is especially important in Norway and Finland, the delegation of responsibility is to a higher extent a stand-alone phenomenon in Denmark and Sweden. Similarly, while job rotation is associated with remuneration schemes especially in Denmark and Finland, job rotation is more likely to be associated with the use of teams in Sweden, and less likely to occur in Norway.

The existence of flexibility as a diverse phenomenon may not come as a surprise to scholars studying systems of innovation where the diversity of the institutional set-up, industrial specialisation and learning patterns play an important role in explaining the dynamics of different types of innovation systems (Lundvall, 1992; Nelson, 1993; Edquist, 1997). Different systems of innovation are characterised by different types of practices and interactions, at the levels of firms, industries, markets and the economy. Thus, differences in the way in which firms develop and sustain flexibility are to be expected, even between small high income economies of close cultural proximity such as the Nordic countries. The ensuing importance of not focusing on one best way to organise for flexibility has important implications for the way in which flexibility is understood, especially when policy making is concerned. Unfortunately, but understandably, policy makers prefer single concepts that lead to uniform policy measures. To some extent this is the reason why the Swedish, Finnish and comparative studies aim at defining a single subset of flexible firms, as these analyses were undertaken in close proximity to policy making bodies. The same phenomenon also occurred in the first application of the Danish survey data where the concept of *the* flexible firm was advocated by the Danish Ministry of Industry and Trade (Erhvervsministeriet, 1996). When flexibility is discussed, both in research and in policy debates, there is often a tendency to focus on the type of strategic flexibility portrayed by Figure 6.8. However, as argued in this chapter, strategic flexibility represents the extreme case. Actually, the pursuit of flexibility may be less ambitious, as in the case of operational flexibility, or represent intermediate cases, as when structural flexibility is achieved by opportunistic search based on reproductive problem solving *or* by problemistic search based on productive problem solving.

Often research and policy debates have associated striving for flexibility with the evolution of learning organisations. However, this chapter has shown that flexibility takes forms that are quite different from what characterises learning organisations, as in the cases of operational and structural flexibility, and this observation underlines the importance of being critical towards the concept of the learning organisation as previously explained in subsection 6.3.1. Furthermore, a critical stance is warranted, not only on theoretical grounds, but on policy grounds as well. In the present volume Wickham (Chapter Five) argues that the evolution of learning organisations – which he describes in terms of the reflexive organisation becoming the dominant paradigm for organisations facing restructuring – imposes flexibility upon the employee that may not be beneficial and may even endanger the employee's role as a citizen in the wider society. Lundvall (forthcoming) has pointed out that the emphasis on learning is beneficial to those with a capacity for learning, while citizens with a low capacity for learning are forced to occupy insecure positions in the labour market. While it is, obviously, important to enhance competitiveness by stimulating processes of learning and competence building within firms, it is equally important to realise that policy schemes to that effect have a social exclusion effect. In consequence, a social cohesion perspective would imply that learning enhancing policy schemes must be based on a broad understanding of the national system of innovation that integrates industrial and labour market policy with educational and social policy, for instance along the lines described by Lundvall and Christensen in the present volume (Chapter Seven) and by Lundvall (forthcoming).

NOTES

1.   Actually, the Norwegian results remind one of the Finnish results. However, before the national survey was undertaken, the Finnish economy went through a period of severe crisis and restructuring (Antila et al., 1999). Prior to the survey, pressures for renewal has already exerted a very important influence on the development of flexibility in the Finnish economy, and in consequence the relationship is less likely to appear among the surveyed firms.

REFERENCES

Ahmed, P.K., Hardaker, G. and Carpenter, M. (1996). 'Integrated flexibility – Key to Competition in a Turbulent Environment', *Long Range Planning* August, 562–71.

Antila, J. and Ylöstalo, P. (1997). *Flexibility, Cooperation and Workplace Success in Finland*, Helsinki: The Working Environment Division Research Unit of the Ministry of Labour. Paper presented at the conference on Networking in Business – Interaction in Working Life, University of Vaasa, November: 24–25.

Antila, J. and Ylöstalo, P. (1999a). *Enterprises as Employers in Finland*, Labour Policy Studies No. 205, Helsinki: Ministry of Labour.

Antila, J. and Ylöstalo, P. (1999b). *Functional Flexibility and Workplace Success in Finland*, Labour Policy Studies No. 206, Helsinki: Ministry of Labour.

Antila, J., Kauppinen, T. and Ylöstalo, P. (1999). 'Flexibility in Finland in the 1990s', in NUTEK (1999).

Argyris, C. and Schon, D.A. (1978). *Organizational Learning: A Theory of Action Perspective*, Reading, MA: Addison-Wesley.

Atkinson, J. (1985). *Flexibility, Uncertainty and Manpower Management*, Brighton: Institute of Manpower Studies, University of Sussex.

Bateson, G. (1942). 'Social Planning and the Concept of Deutero-Learning', in Bateson, G. (1972), *Steps to an Ecology of Mind*, New York: Ballantine Books, 159–76.

Coutrot, B. (1996). 'Gestion de l'Emploi et Organisation du Travail dans les Enterprises Innovantes: Une Approche Statistique des Practiques d'Etablissements', *Les Dossiers de la DARES*. 3–4: 201–7.

Cyert, R.M. and March, J.G. (1963). *A Behavioral Theory of the Firm*, Englewood Cliffs; NJ: Prentice-Hall.

Deming, W.E. (1986). *Out of the Crisis*, Cambridge, MA: MIT Press.

Edquist, C. (ed.) (1997). *Systems of Innovation*, London: Pinter.

Erhvervsministeriet (1996). *Erhvervsredegørelse 1996* (Industrial Account 1996), Copenhagen: Erhvervsministeriet.

Gjerding, A.N. (1992). 'Work Organisation and the Innovation Design Dilemma', in Lundvall, B.-Å. (ed.), *National Systems of Innovation*, London: Pinter.

Gjerding, A.N. (1996a). *Technical Innovation and Organisational Change: The Innovation Design Dilemma Revisited*, Aalborg: Aalborg University Press.

Gjerding, A.N. (1996b). *Organisational Innovation in the Danish Private Business Sector*, DRUID Working Paper No. 96-16, Aalborg: Aalborg University.

Gjerding, A.N. (1998). *Innovation Economic, Part II: The 'New' Innovation Economics*, International Business Economics Working Papers No. 27, Aalborg: Centre for International Studies, Aalborg University.

Gjerding, A.N. (1999). 'Flexibility in Denmark: Pressures for Renewal and Change in the Danish Private Business Sector', in NUTEK (1999), 151–77.

Gjerding, A.N. (ed.), Jørgensen, K., Kristensen, F.S., Lund, R., Lundvall, B.-Å., Madsen, P.T., Nielsen, P. and Nymark, S. (1997). *Den Fleksible Virksomhed* (The Flexible Firm), Copenhagen: Erhvervsudviklingsrådet.

Greenan, N. (1995). 'L'Organisation de la Production dans l'Industrie', *Les 4 pages* 43 (January).

Greenan, N. (1996a). 'Innovation Technologique, Changements Organisationnels et Évolution des Compétences', *Economie et Statistique*, No.298, pp.15–33.

142   *Promoting Organisational Learning*

Greenan, N. (1996b), 'Progrés Technique et Changements Organisationnels: Leur Impact Sur L'Emploi et les Qualifications', *Economie et Statistique*, No.298, pp. 35–44.

Hatch, M.J. (1997). *Organization Theory*, New York: Oxford University Press.

Holbek, J. (1988). 'The Innovation Design Dilemma: Some Notes on Its Relevance and Solutions', in K. Grønlaug and E. Kaufmann (eds), *Innovation: A Cross-Disciplinary Perspective*, Oslo: Norwegian University Press, 253–77.

Jensen, B.H. (1998). *Flexibility in a Market-Oriented Organisation*, MAPP Working Paper No. 56, Aarhus: Centre for Market Surveillance, Research and Strategy for the Food Sector, The Aarhus School of Business.

Jørgensen, K. Kristensen, F.S., Lund, R. and Nymark, S. (1998). *Organisatorisk Fornyelse – Erfaringer fra 24 Danske Virksomheder* (Organisational Change – Experiences from 24 Danish Firms), Copenhagen: Erhvervsudviklingsrådet.

Kanter, R.M. (1983). *The Change Masters*, New York: Simon and Schuster.

Kinkel, S. and Wengel, J. (1997). 'New Production Concepts: One Discussion Does Not Make a Summer', in ISI Fraunhofer, Karlsruhe, *News from the Manufacturing Innovation Survey*, No. 4.

Leonard-Barton, D. (1988). 'Implementation as Mutual Adaptation of Technology and Organization', *Research Policy*, 17: 251–67.

Lewin, K. (1951). *Field Theory in Social Science*, New York: Harper and Row.

L'Huillery, S. (1998). *Les Enquêtes Nationales sur le Changement Organisationnel*, Centre de Recherche en Economie Industrielle, Working Paper No. 98-04, Paris: Université Paris XIII.

Lund, R. and Gjerding, A.N. (1996). *The Flexible Company. Innovation, Work Organisation and Human Resource Management*, DRUID Working Paper No. 96-17, Aalborg: Aalborg University.

Lundvall, B.-Å. (ed.) (1992). *National Systems of Innovation*, London: Pinter.

Lundvall, B.-Å. (1999). *Det Danske Innovationssystem* (The Danish System of Innovation), Copenhagen: Erhvervsudviklingsrådet.

Lundvall, B.-Å. (forthcoming). *Innovation, Growth and Social Cohesion: the Danish Model*, Cheltenham and Northampton, MA: Edward Elgar.

Lundvall, B.-Å. and Johnson, B. (1994). 'The Learning Economy', *Journal of Industry Studies*, 1–2: 23–42.

Lundvall, B.-Å. and Kristensen, F.S. (1997). *Organisational Change, Innovation and Human Resource Development as a Response to Increased Competition*, DRUID Working Paper No. 97-16, Aalborg: Aalborg University.

March, J.G. (1991). 'Exploration and Exploitation in Organizational Learning', *Organization Science*, 2: 71–87.

March, J.G. and Olsen, J.P. (1976). *Ambiguity and Choice in Organizations*, Oslo: Universitetsforlaget.

March, J.G. and Simon, H.A. (1958). *Organizations*, New York: John Wiley and Sons.

Mintzberg, H. (1994). *The Rise and Fall of Strategic Planning*, London: Prentice-Hall.

Morgan, G. (1986). *Images of Organization*, London: Sage.

Nelson, R.R. (ed.) (1993). *National Innovation Systems*, New York: Oxford University Press.

Nonaka, I. and Takeuchi, H. (1995). *The Knowledge-Creating Company*, New York: Oxford University Press.

NUTEK (1996). *Towards Flexible Organizations*, Stockholm: NUTEK, B 1996:6.

NUTEK (1999). *Flexibility Matters: Flexible Enterprises in the Nordic Countries*, Stockholm: NUTEK, B 1999:7.

Nymark, S. (1997). 'Læring, Forandring og Organisation – et Kritisk Perspektiv', (Learning, Change and Organisation – A Critical Perspective), in A. Christensen (ed.), *Den Lærende Organisations Begreber og Praksis* (Concepts and Practice of the Learning Organisation), Aalborg: Aalborg Universitetsforlag, 59–80.

Olsen, K.M. (1998) 'KombineresUlike Typer Fleksibilitet?' (Are Different Types of Flexibility Combined?), in Olsen and Torp (1998), 117–26.

Olsen, K.M. and Torp, H. (1998). *Fleksibilitet i Norsk Arbeidsliv* (Norwegian Labour Market Flexibility), ISF Rapport 98:2, Oslo: Institutt for Samfunnsforskning.

Osterman, P. (1994). 'How Common Is Workplace Transformation and Who Adopts It?', *Industrial and Labour Relations Review*, 47: 173–88.

Pedler, M., Boydell, T. and Burgoyne, J. (1989), 'Towards the Learning Company', *Management Education and Development*, 20 (1): 1–8.

Pedler, M., Burgoyne, J. and Boydell, T. (1991). *The Learning Company: A Strategy for Sustainable Development*, London: Mc-Graw Hill.

Peters, T.J. and Waterman, R.H. (1982). *In Search of Excellence*, New York: Harper and Row.

Porter, M.E. (1980). *Competitive Strategy*, New York: The Free Press.

Porter, M.E. (1985). *Competitive Advantage*, New York: The Free Press.

Schøne, P. (1999). 'Flexibility in Work Organizations. The Norwegian Case', in NUTEK (1999), 201–16.

Thompson, J.D. (1967). *Organizations in Action*, New York: McGraw-Hill.

Volberda, H.W. (1998). *Building the Flexible Firm*, New York: Oxford University Press.

Waterson, P.E., Clegg, C.W., Bolden, R., Pepper, K., Warr, P.B. and Wall, T.D. (1997). *The Use and Effectiveness of Modern Manufacturing Practices in the United Kingdom*, ESRC Centre for Organisation and Innovation, Sheffield: University of Sheffield.

Weick, K.E. (1995) *Sensemaking in Organizations*, Thousand Oaks: Sage Publications.

Zaltman, G., Duncan, R. and Holbek, J. (1973). *Innovations and Organizations*, New York: John Wiley and Sons.

7. Broadening the analysis of innovation systems – competition, organisational change and employment dynamics in the Danish system

Bengt-Åke Lundvall and Jesper Lindgaard Christensen

Traditionally, innovation systems have been analysed as rooted either in the R&D system or in the production system. This chapter suggests a broader approach, seeing them as rooted in the national production and human resource development systems. The argument is linked to the literature on innovation systems and illustrated by empirical data from a study of the Danish innovation system (the DISKO project). A simple 'macro-micro-macro model' is used to structure the analysis. It is shown how the transformation pressure affects the behaviour of firms in terms of hiring and firing. The effects on aggregate employment of firm behaviour are then considered.

It is shown that the intensity of competition has a major impact on employment at the level of the single firm. But it is also shown that firms that engage in product innovation and in the introduction of new forms of organisation can compensate for the job losses imposed by increased competition. It is shown that increased competition does not seem to affect the relative position of workers without vocational training at the level of the firm. But it is also shown that massive job losses for workers without vocational training tend to take place in those firms that do not respond to increased competition by introducing new products or new forms of organisation.

7.1 INTRODUCTION

The concept of national systems of innovation goes back to Friedrich List, who criticised what he called the 'cosmopolitan' approach of Adam Smith as too focused on competition and resource allocation to the neglect of the development of productive forces (List, 1841). The analysis of national systems developed by List took into account a wide set of national institutions including those engaged in education and training as well as infrastructures such as networks for transportation of people and commodities (Freeman, 1995).

The modern revival of the concept some 12–15 years ago gave rise to different, more or less broad (often implicit) definitions of innovation systems. The US approach (Nelson, 1988) linked the concept mainly to high tech industries and put the interaction between firms, the university system and national technology policy at the centre of the analysis. Freeman (1987) introduced a broader perspective that took into account national specificities in the organisation of firms – he emphasised for instance how Japanese firms increasingly used 'the factory as a laboratory'. The Aalborg approach (Lundvall, 1985: Andersen and Lundvall, 1988) was inspired by the analysis of national production systems pursued by the French structuralist school in Grenoble. It looked at national systems of innovation as rooted in the production system and it also emphasised the institutional dimension, where 'institutions' were defined theoretically either as norms and rules or as materialised in the form of organisations (Johnson, 1992). Porter (1990) brought in regimes of competition as important dimensions of national systems.

Looking at some of the major recent contributions on innovation systems (Freeman 1987, 1997; Porter 1990; Lundvall, 1992; Nelson, 1993; and Edquist, 1997) the focus remains on the production and innovation system while much less attention is given to the part of the economy engaged in the development of human resources. Going back to List and, not least, to Marshall, who emphasised that regional competence was rooted in the workforce, this remains a rather narrow perspective. Especially in a period when it is recognised that more and more of economic dynamics depends on the creation, dissemination and use of knowledge, it is natural to put more focus on the human resource dimension.

The obvious alternative to new definitions of innovation systems is to give stronger emphasis to the fact that education systems and labour markets are nationally constituted and play a key role in competence building and in shaping the foundation for innovation processes; and, further, to recognise that there are national specificities in the formation of skills and in the national labour dynamics as well as economic and cultural barriers to the free movement of labour across national borders. There are important changes taking place that increase the international mobility of highly skilled labour but there is little doubt that 'human capital' and labour remain the least mobile of the resources used in the production process.

Starting from a different tradition that, historically, has put less emphasis on technical innovation and more on macro economic dynamics, regulation school economists have been among the first to introduce the human resource dimension when pursuing comparative analyses of national systems (Boyer, Amable and Barré, 1997). In their factor analysis of international differences, four out of the nine indicators used are related to the human dimension. Also, in the parallel work on 'national business systems' pursued by Whitley and others there is a strong emphasis on national specificities in human resource development systems and labour markets (referred to as the 'labour system' in Whitley, 1996).

We can thus identify at least three different ways of delimiting the innovation system. The first is the innovation system as *rooted in the R&D system;* the second is the innovation system as *rooted in the production system;* and the third is the innovation system as *rooted in the production and human resource development system.*

One reason to prefer this broader perspective is that it makes it possible to analyse the interaction between technical change, organisational change and competence building. At the level of the firm, the links between technical innovation, organisational change and human resource development are crucial for understanding both the dynamics and the performance. Some old and new debates on the role of information and communication technologies illustrate this fact. The so-called Solow paradox – the observation that there is limited evidence of a positive productivity impact from the new information technologies – has returned onto the agenda after the disappointing performance of high technology firms following the 'new economy' euphoria (OECD, 2000a). As demonstrated by Paul David, the Solow paradox tends to dissolve when it is taken into account that the new technologies will give rise to enhanced performance only after a prolonged period of adaptation of skills and organisations (David, 1991). It has been argued that the most important 'next step' for Europe is to develop an industrial policy aiming at promoting organisational change (Andreasen, et al., 1995). This contrasts with current EU policies too one-siddedly focused on promoting the diffusion of ICT solutions.

To show the usefulness of this broad definition of the innovation system it is especially illustrative to apply it to the Danish system. Denmark is quite weak in science-based activities. Few radical innovations take place in Denmark. Most of the R&D content in Danish products comes from abroad – much of it as embodied in imported products. At the same time Denmark, in spite of its low tech specialisation, is characterised by successful competence building and remains among the five countries in the world with the highest GNP per capita. We therefore believe that the Danish case may be well suited to illustrate the general importance of institutional and organisational change as opposed to technical change. More specifically the Danish case demonstrates that there are alternative ways of creating wealth in the so-called new economy. Denmark is the country in the world with the most equal income distribution and is in strong contrast to the US and UK models of growth based on growing inequalities.

A related reason for taking the broader view has to do with the basic assumption about the 'learning economy' developed in connection with the collective Aalborg book on innovation systems (Lundvall, 1992). In Dalum, Johnson and Lundvall (1992) and in Lundvall and Johnson (1994) we argued that the last decade had witnessed a change in the mode of competition, which implied that interactive learning (and forgetting) had become the most important process for determining the position of individuals, firms, regions and countries in competition. This hypothesis also pointed to the need to give stronger emphasis to the analysis of the development of human and organisational capabilities.

In what follows we briefly summarise a selection of results from an analysis of the Danish innovation system, the DISKO project.[1] First we present structural characteristics of the Danish economy. Here we draw upon a combination of empirical analysis as pursued in the DISKO project and on OECD material. In the second section of the chapter we analyse the dynamics of the system using data from the DISKO project. Here, the focus is on how the transformation pressure at the macro level affects the behaviour of firms and, vice versa, on how changes at the level of the firm result in changes in aggregate employment and in a weakening in demand for workers without vocational training in the economy as a whole. We finally derive policy conclusions from these analyses and from the broad perspective on innovation systems.

7.2   STRUCTURAL CHARACTERISTICS OF THE DANISH INNOVATION SYSTEM

Income distribution statistics from Eurostat show that Denmark has a smaller proportion of poor people (11 per cent have an income below 60 per cent of median income) than any other European country and Gini coefficients also show that the most equal income distribution is to be found in Denmark. The OECD study on 'economic growth in the new economy' (OECD, 2000a) groups Denmark – together with Australia, Ireland, the Netherlands, Norway and the US – among the countries demonstrating good growth performance in the new economy of the 1990s. It is obvious that the Danish type of new economy differs from the US type and when looking for a European benchmark for policy making it is therefore useful to give some attention to the Danish case.

Denmark is a rich country with a population working long hours but with low and stagnating productivity. According to OECD statistics Denmark ranked number five in terms of GNP per capita 1998 (OECD, 2000a). The Danish economy has a high GNP per capita but this reflects primarily the fact that active participation in the formal economy is much higher than in most other European countries. The participation rate of women specially is very high. The average Danish citizen delivers about 30 per cent more working hours per year than the average European citizen.

As compared to other European countries labour productivity is not high in Denmark and, especially in manufacturing and in construction, productivity growth has been stagnating for a longer period. One major factor behind the high income per capita is thus the capability to mobilise people in the labour market.

Danish export and production is strongly specialised in low technology products. We find a low technology specialisation in several other small high income countries but Denmark stands out as an extreme also among these (until recently together with Finland). There are some high technology islands in the Danish economy and especially the sector producing pharmaceuticals (dominated by NOVO) is extreme in its strong connection to science.

Denmark is especially successful in the production and export of 'low' and 'low medium' technology goods. This includes food products, furniture and clothing. It has successful niche products in telecommunication (mobile communication), windmills and process regulation. Within all these fields firms are successful in absorbing and using technology from abroad including information technology. Incremental product development characterises both the high technology and the low technology firms.

Within firms there is a growing emphasis on the interaction across departments, between colleagues and between management and workers. Danish manufacturing firms interact with customers and suppliers more frequently than firms in other countries. On the other hand, the interaction with universities is less developed in Denmark than abroad (Christensen et al., 2001). To a certain degree this reflects a rather well functioning system of technological institutes that communicate new technological insights to firms. But it is also true that the university system has historically been strongly geared toward the needs of the public sector both regarding education and research.

Historically, most of the academically trained workforce has been employed in the public sector. This has gradually been changing through the last decade where business services especially have absorbed a growing proportion of the candidates. But still a big proportion of private firms have no or few academics in their workforce.

7.3   CHARACTERISING THE SYSTEM IN TERMS OF HUMAN RESOURCE DEVELOPMENT

It is difficult to change the pattern of specialisation in the direction of science-based and high technology products within a short time horizon (Dalum et al., 1998). One reason is that the pattern of human resource development is connected to it in a systemic way. The Danish human resource development system (the school system, vocational training and the efforts made by firms to develop the skills of their employees) is quite unique. And, in certain respects, it matches quite well the Danish incremental approach to innovation in the low and medium technology sectors. Therefore an upgrading and a stronger emphasis on formal knowledge (as contrasted to practical experience-based knowledge) in the production system must involve changes in education and training.

The Danish education system fosters independent and responsible workers with weak formal competences. Young people are expected to be independent and responsible in Denmark. International studies show that they spend little time on homework but a lot of time on small jobs to get their own income. When finished with high school they take a year off and work or go abroad before starting higher education. Previously they have rated quite weakly (the extent and causes are still under debate among educationalists) in international tests on skills in reading and mathematics. But they seem to be extremely well prepared for working in a turbulent economy where there is a need to delegate responsibility to the lower levels in the organisation. They are also used to communicating directly and freely with authorities (with teachers as well as employers).

The Danish labour market gives weak incentives to firms to invest in training their own personnel. The Danish labour market is characterised by high inter-firm mobility (as high as or higher than in the US) but a more limited geographical mobility. Danish firms invest less in training their own personnel than firms in other countries. On the other hand, the public sector has built a unique and quite resource-intensive system for training adults. This means that Danish workers on average get more time for training within a year than workers in most other countries. Firms contribute through a wage tax to the financing of public training and an important part of it is organised at the regional level by tripartite bodies representing labour, industry and the public sector. This specific division of labour reflects among other things the fact that there are many small firms in the Danish economy that could not take on the responsibility for training their personnel on their own. But it has also resulted in bigger firms using less resources on internal training than their foreign counterparts.

The Danish labour market is flexible and efficient but it is also characterised by polarisation, to the disadvantage of unskilled and foreign workers in terms of job opportunities. There are a number of unique features of the labour market that need to be taken into account when considering the working of the overall innovation system. The substitution rate of unemployment support has been higher and support less restricted in time than in most other OECD countries and this fact explains some of the pecularities. It may explain the high participation rates and the fact that workers in Denmark, in spite of high mobility, feel more secure in their jobs than their colleagues in other European countries with much less mobility.

High mobility reflects to a certain degree the fact that employers meet almost no legal restrictions when it comes to firing personnel. But it also reflects the fact that workers at all skill levels are less afraid of getting lost between jobs when looking for new job opportunities. OECD and labour market economists have emphasised the negative impact on job incentives of 'generous substitution rates' but in Denmark an 'irrational' willingness to work seems to overcome this negative incentive (see Duncan Gallie's contribution in Chapter 12 of this book). Among women, for instance, 20–30 per cent work for a wage in spite of the fact that economically they would be almost as well off staying at home. The Danish labour market is performing well also in terms of low and falling rates of respectively structural, long term and youth unemployment.

There is one area where it does not fare as well, however. Workers without vocational training and foreign workers are much worse off than the rest of the labour force in terms of job opportunities and employment. Here Denmark is, if anything, worse off than most other OECD countries. DISKO data also show that the training initatives inside firms tend to reinforce the polarisation. The chance for workers without vocational training to get training in-house in firms is much less than for other categories of employees. This is the major down side of the homogeneous Danish welfare society and its major challenge for the future.

7.4 FROM STRUCTURE TO DYNAMICS – TRANSFORMATION PRESSURE, EMPLOYMENT AND INNOVATION

What is the connection between intensified competition in product markets and changes in the labour market in terms of aggregate employment and skill requirements? To what degree can the weakening of the relative position of low skilled workers be explained by intensified competition? Is the introduction of new products and new forms of organisation undermining the relative position of these groups? In what follows we will demonstrate that in the Danish context responses to these questions lead us to less pessimistic conclusions than normally expected. In the following subsection we outline the basic characteristics of the analytical approach to be used.

7.4.1 The Basic Model of Transformation, Innovation and Structure

So far the focus has been on some basic characteristics of the structure and functioning of the Danish innovation system. One way of testing the quality of a technical system is to see how it reacts when it is put under external pressure. The same kind of test can be pursued when it comes to analysing the dynamic capabilities of a national system of innovation.

In what follows we will illustrate the importance of mechanisms of transformation by data referring to the Danish economy. Our starting point is a simple model where we link to each other the transformation pressure and the economic structure at the level of the whole economy, on the one hand, and on the other hand, the adjustment and innovation processes at the level of the firm.[3] The empirical analysis is incomplete since it refers exclusively to the transformation taking place in existing and surviving firms for a five year period and does not include the process of destruction and creation of firms. The basic model is shown in Figure 7.1.

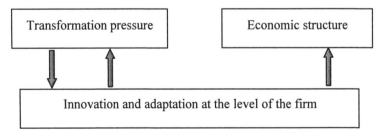

Figure 7.1   *The basic model – from macro to micro and back to macro*

One of the most fundamental factors affecting the transformation pressure is *technical change*. New technology in the form of new products and new processes offers new opportunities as well as new threats to the single firm. A second major factor is the *competition regime*. New entrants into markets and extensions of markets bringing in new competitors are factors that increase the transformation pressure. *Governance regimes* – the role of ownership and finance in managing the firms – affect the intensity but also the direction of the transformation pressure. Finally the *macroeconomic stance* affects transformation pressure. For instance a situation characterised by deflationary policies and an overvalued currency rate implies strong transformation pressure, as do aggressive trade union wage policies. Some of these factors affect all parts of the economy (the macroeconomic stance) while most of the others (technical change and the competition regime) are, at least to some degree, sector-specific.

7.4.2   Different Types of Firm Reactions to an Increased Transformation Pressure

Firms may react to an increasing transformation pressure in a number of ways. They may go on as before without implementing any kind of change. They might combine sticking to the old routines with attempts to reduce the 'fat' of the organisation. That will typically include strategies of 'quantitative flexibility': firing some of the personnel. Sometimes such strategies will succeed and sometimes they will lead to a closedown of the firm and its activities.

A second set of strategies have to do with functional flexibility. Firms may adapt to the increasing pressure by moving resources from less promising to more promising activities. The capability to do so will reflect the degree of 'functional flexibility' of the firm. A more ambitious second order strategy is for the firm to engage in organisational change aiming at increasing its functional flexibility.

A third set of strategies focus on the efficiency of process technology. The firm may introduce more efficient process technology and it may introduce organisational change aiming at increasing its efficiency in the use of the new technologies.

A fourth set of strategies have to do with change in the output and marketing of output. The firm may introduce product and service innovations that make it possible to sidestep and thereby reduce the intensity of competition in its product markets.

A fifth alternative is to look for a new positioning within industrial networks. Establishing closer relationships to customers and suppliers and to knowledge organisations may both enhance the functional flexibility of the firm and make it possible to speed up innovation.

National systems differ in terms of the degree to which they support these different, more or less reactive and proactive strategies at the level of the firm. Different sectors differ in terms of the opportunities they offer when it comes to pursuing the different strategies. Technological opportunities differ between sectors and the same is actually true for 'organisational opportunities' (see below).

7.4.3   Skills and Transformation

Perhaps with the exception of the first set of strategies, all the changes provoked will influence the skills required within the firm. A stronger emphasis on functional flexibility and innovative capacity will increase the demand for general personal skills of cooperation and communication and it will also imply a stronger need for delegating responsibility.

Technical change and product development will increase the demand for specific skills and call for new skills. A speed-up of the innovation process will increase the rate of creative destruction of skills and competences. This will increase the need for lifelong learning in the whole economy and at the level of the firm it will make it more necessary to move toward a 'learning organisation'.

7.4.4   From Firm Strategies Back to the Whole Labour Market

When firms adapt to the increased transformation pressure and adjust their demand for labour and skills accordingly, the aggregate demand for labour and for different types of labour will change. Firms with different strategies for coping with the increased transformation pressure will differ also in terms of their hiring and firing strategies. This implies that changes in the overall labour market dynamics may be seen as aggregate outcomes of technical and organisational change in specific firms and in how the alternative strategies are distributed in the population of firms. What happens in this respect in big firms will, of course, have a greater impact than what goes on in small ones.

7.5   EMPIRICAL ILLUSTRATION OF THE DYNAMICS OF TRANSFORMATION

In what follows, we will introduce results from combining data from one of the surveys in the DISKO project with labour market statistics. We will start by analysing the relative weight firms ascribe to different factors affecting the transformation pressure. Second, we will demonstrate that the increased transformation pressure affects technical and organisational change. Third, we will investigate the direction of these changes. Fourth, we will analyse how the transformation pressure affects the change in the demand for labour at the level of the firm and how the aggregate demand for labour is shaped by the changes at the firm level. We will conclude by a discussion of the implications for Danish and European policy making.

7.5.1   The DISKO-data

What follows is based on a unique combination of two data sets. The first is a Danish survey originally addressed to somewhat less than 4000 Danish firms. We had close to 1900 useable responses from firms in manufacturing, transport, construction and service industries. In most cases management representatives filled out the questionnaire. The response rate was 48 per cent. Of the firms included 1200 had less than 50 employees. The sample was stratified to include all the large firms and only approximately one fifth of small firms. The data in what follows are not weighted to adjust for this skewing and should therefore be interpreted as being valid for the specific group of firms in the sample rather than for all Danish firms.

The firms were asked about their use of different forms of organisational structures, their investments in human resources and their activities in terms of technical innovations.[4] Most of the questions included in the analysis below refer to what changes had been experienced or initiated in the period 1993–95.[5]

The second set links data from the Danish IDA labour market database on such factors as employment, training, creation and destruction of jobs, to the firms in the sample.[6] When firms include more than one production unit we get a matching problem between the two data sets. This match has been established by coupling employment data from the single biggest production unit to the questionnaire of its mother firm. In order to be included firms had to have existed both in November 1990 and in 1997. After this, and after excluding firms which ceased to exist, there are 1610 production units with a total employment of more than 140 000 in this data set.

The subset of firms included in the DISKO survey covers the private business sector, excluding agriculture. These sectors employed 947430 persons in 1993 (total employment in Denmark was close to 2 500 000). In terms of number of employees our realised sample is thus big in comparison to the total population. It can also be shown that employment in the sub-aggregate develops in parallel with total employment in the business sector. When analysing the aggregate effect on employment this may be more important than the fact that the sample, with its over-representation of big firms, is not representative.

7.5.2   Transformation Pressure as Viewed from the Firms

One of the questions in the survey gives an idea of how firms assess the relative importance of different factors affecting the transformation pressure. Firms were asked what conditions had played a major role in changing the work content of employees.

Table 7.1   Proportion of firms responding 'high extent' to the following question: 'To what degree have the following conditions contributed to changes in work content of the employees during the period 1993–95?'

Condition	Percentage of all firms
1. Sharper competition	30.2
2. Introduction of new technology	28.1
3. Need for better contacts with customers.	23.6
4. Better possibilities for development of new products or services	13.0
5. Need for better contacts with sub-contractors	9.7
6. Demands and wishes of employees	9.7
N= 1869	

Table 7.1 shows that among the factors evoked in the questionnaire the one referred to most frequently is 'sharper competition'. The other factors given strong weight relate to the introduction of new technology and the need for better contact with customers. In what follows, we will use the response to a question about a change in the intensity of competition to illustrate how a change in the transformation pressure affects the behaviour of firms.

One way to make the transformation pressure variable operational is thus to take the experiences of firms as a starting point. Here we will use the firms' response to the question about whether they had or had not experienced an increase in the intensity of competition for the period 1993–95 (see box 7.1).

Of all firms responding to this question (1869 firms) 40 per cent reported that the competition pressure had been strongly increased, 33 per cent that it had increased somewhat, while 24 per cent reported no change or a milder competition pressure (three per cent responded that they did not know).

Table 7.2 shows that the increase in competition is not experienced evenly in the private sector. It is signalled most strongly by bigger firms, and firms in some sectors are less prone to refer to it than firms in other sectors. Firms in manufacturing and business services refer to much stronger competition more frequently, while firms in the construction sector do so less than the average.

BOX 7.1   INCREASED COMPETITION PRESSURE IN THE 90S?

Can management representatives be expected to judge correctly 'the real changes' in the competition pressure they have been exposed to? Is it reasonable to assume that the period 1993–95 was characterised by such a massive intensification of competition in Denmark? It may be argued that management will tend to overestimate the rate of increase in competition in the same way as farmers might tend to regard this year's weather as being worse than last year's.

There might be such a bias in the average response. But as we shall see there is a difference between firms responding that there is much stronger competition and the rest, not only in what they say they do – they actually perform differently in terms of, for instance, job creation. Also, if management representatives believe that competition has been intensified they will adjust their behaviour and strategies accordingly.

Therefore we believe that the 'subjective' measure of competition used here is a very useful complement to 'objective' indicators referring to concentration ratios, market shares and barriers to entry. We propose an interpretation of the response 'much stronger competition' as signalling that some old routines need to be changed in order to survive. The reason may be deregulation, entrance of new producers as well as innovative initiatives among competitors in terms of increased efficiency or more attractive new products.

Table 7.2 illustrates the fact that changes in the transformation pressure may be distributed unevenly in the economy. It is especially interesting that both smaller and bigger firms in the construction sector experience much less of an intensification in the transformation pressure than manufacturing firms more exposed to international competition.

Table 7.2   Share (%) of the firms responding 'much stronger competition in the period 1993–95', by size categories and sectors

Firm Size	Manu-facturing	Cons-truction	Trade	Trans-port	Business services	The whole economy
Less than 50 employ-ees	39.9 100	23.3 58	35.2 88	41.5 104	39.5 99	40.0
More than 50 employ-ees	49.4 124	32.4 81	48.2 121	43.2 108	45.3 113	100

Source: Questions 20, 1, 26a and 26b in the DISKO survey on organisation and qualifications at the firm level. See Lund and Gjerding (1996) for an account of the questions posed.

7.5.3   Competition, Innovation, Organisational Change and Network Positioning

How does an increase in the transformation pressure affect product innovation, organisational change and positioning in industrial networks? In the survey, firms were asked if they had introduced new products or services, if they had gone through major organisational change and if they had established closer cooperation with customers and suppliers in the period 1993–95. In Figure 7.2 we present the share that responded yes according to how they characterised the change in competition for the same period.

Figure 7.2 illustrates the fact that the firms experiencing much stronger competition were more frequently involved in product innovation and organisational change. The differences are even more significant when it comes to establishing a closer collaboration with customers and suppliers. Apparently there is a connection between increased competition and closer vertical cooperation among firms.

These results may be interpreted in two different ways. Although there has been no explicit analysis of causality, the most obvious interpretation is that intensified competition 'is the cause of' or triggers change in the different dimensions (new products, new forms of organisation and a change in network positioning). An alternative (or complementary) interpretation is that, in the period studied, competition had intensified especially in those sectors where there (normally) is a lot of change going on in terms of technology and organisation. This second interpretation would, actually, indicate a tendency toward a polarisation of the economy. At the one pole we would find sectors characterised by accelerating change and intensified competition and at the other we would find sectors with little change and little increase in the competition pressure.

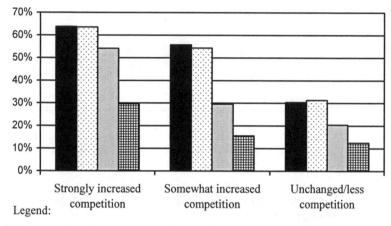

Legend:

■ Introduction of new products 1993–95 (share of firms that answered yes)

☐ Introduction of new organisational forms 1993–95 (share of firms that answered yes)

☐ Closer cooperation with customers 1993–95 (share of firms that answered 'to a great extent')

⊞ Closer cooperation with suppliers 1993–95 (share of firms that answered 'to a great extent')

Source: Gjerding (1996), Appendix 1, Question 20, Question 1 and Questions 26a and 26b.

Figure 7.2   Technical and organisational change in firms that reported increased or unchanged competitive pressure during the years 1993–95

One way to get a first idea about whether the second mechanism may be at play is to compare the change in the competition pressure with the rate of organisational change across sectors and across firms of different sizes. In Table 7.3 we present the share of firms in different size categories and sectors that reported that they had introduced organisational change in the period.

Table 7.3   Share (%) of firms which introduced organisational change at least once in the period 1993–95, by size and sectors

Firm size	Manu-facturing	Cons-truction	Trade	Trans-port	Business services	The whole economy
Less than 50 employ-ees	52.0 99 (100)	28.5 54 (58)	43.1 82 (88)	28.3 54 (104)	52.3 100 (99)	52.3
More than 50 employ-ees	75.2 144 (124)	52.9 101 (81)	64.9 124 (121)	64.4 23 (108)	66.7 128 (113)	100 (100)

Source: Questions 20, 1, 26a and 26b in the DISKO survey on organisation and qualifications at the firm level.

The frequency of organisational change is clearly highest in big firms in manufacturing and business services. Within parentheses we give the index number from Table 7.2 so that we can see how far, in these broadly defined sectors, there is a match between the relative transformation pressure and the frequency of organisational change. We find a rather good match and that means that we cannot disregard the complementary hypothesis. Sectors characterised by frequent organisational change are normally also characterised by intensified competition.

But it is also important to note that the match is not perfect. The small transport firms experience an increased competition pressure to more than an average degree (index = 104) but they introduce organisational change much less frequently than the whole population of firms (index = 54). This may be taken as an illustration of the fact that 'organisational opportunities' may differ between sectors. 'Transport' includes not only transport in a narrow sense but also for instance restaurants, and there might be limited possibilities for small firms in 'transport' – typically a small trucking firm or a grill bar – to reorganise activities. It is important to note that at this stage we only aim at illustrating some fundamental mechanisms of transformation and routes for exploring this issue further – it is not our errand to demonstrate statistically specific relationships.

Our conclusion is that the evidence tends to support the general idea that increased competition triggers changes in products as well as changes in internal organisation and network positioning. This is compatible with a theory of the firm where firms are satisfiers rather than optimisers – they stick to old routines in good times but engage in change when their survival is threatened.

7.5.4   The Direction of Organisational Change

We are interested in the direction of organisational change in firms exposed to a stronger transformation pressures. Firms were asked if they had expanded the use of certain specific practices and organisational techniques. In Table 7.4 we compare firms reporting a much stronger competition with the firms reporting respectively somewhat stronger (SSComp) and unchanged/ weakened comp (UWComp).

Table 7.4   *Proportion of firms responding 'yes' to the following question: 'Has the firm extended its use of the following organisational traits during the period 1993–95?'*

Organisational trait	MSComp-firms	SSComp-firms	UWComp-firms	All firms
Delegation of responsibility	63.25% 111	58.36% 102	46.48% 81	57.23 (N=1653)
Interdisciplinary work groups	55.38% 106	55.75% 107	43.39% 83	52.19% (N=1029)
Quality circles/groups	51.78% 108	48.56% 101	42.51% 89	47.93% (N=845)
Integration of functions (such as sales production/service, finance)	51.98% 113	48.40% 105	31.97% 70	45.91% (N=1222)
Performance-based pay	43.62% 102	45.99% 108	36.88% 86	42.69% (N=855)
Planned job rotation	46.84% 112	45.14% 107	27.40% 65	42.00% (N=781)
Systems for the collection of proposals from employees	48.38% 118	36.89% 90	34.07% 83	41.10% (N=978)

Source: Questions 8 a–g first part in the DISKO survey on organisation and qualifications at the firm level. N refers to the total number of responses to the question. N varies because the questions were addressed only to the firms that had introduced the practice in question before or after the period referred to.

Table 7.4 shows (see the 'All firms' column) that increased delegation of responsibility is the form of change most frequently referred to. But several of the other, more advanced, forms of organisational change – such as bringing in integration of functions – are also widely introduced and extended. The firms experiencing a much stronger or somewhat stronger intensity of competition had been more active in terms of organisational change in all the categories compared to firms that reported unchanged competition.

It is interesting to note that the difference between the three categories is most clear when it comes to 'integration of functions' and 'planned job rotation'. These are some of the core characteristics of the functionally flexible and innovative organisation. The analysis thus gives some support to the hypothesis that increased competition triggers not only adjustment in terms of re-allocating resources. They also tend to drive firms toward forms of organisation that are functionally flexible. The alternative hypothesis is more awkward here. It would be that 'exogenous' waves of organisational change in certain sectors would give rise to an intensification in competition in those same sectors.

7.5.5 The Transformation Pressure and Employment – from Micro to Macro

We have demonstrated that an increase in the transformation pressure, experienced as an increase in the intensity of competition at the firm level, seems to be related to changes in products and organisational forms. There is apparently a link between the increase in the transformation pressure at the macro level and the behaviour of the firms in these respects. Now we will turn to the opposite mechanism and see what happens at the level of the firm may affect the whole labour market.

In Table 7.5 we compare the employment development in three sub-aggregates of firms differentiated on the basis of how they have experienced[7] the change in competition pressure.

It is an interesting issue whether the firms that have introduced elements of functional flexibility are in a position where they can cope with increased competition with less negative effects on employment. In Table 7.6, in order to keep the presentation simple we have separated firms into two groups. One includes firms exposed to much stronger competition and the other group covers the rest of the firms. Each of these sub-aggregates has been divided into two – one including firms that reported a minimum number of organisational traits that are regarded as important for establishing functional flexibility, and one including the rest of the firms.

Table 7.5   The development in employment 1992–97 for three groups of firms arranged according to change in competitive pressure (index of the number of employees, 1992 = 100)

Change	Nov. 92	Nov. 94	Nov. 96	Nov. 97
Strongly increased competition	68.440=100	102.5	100.1	102.1
Somewhat increased competition	46.141=100	103.3	102.1	103.1
Unchanged/less competition	19.071=100	103.8	104.3	103.5
Total	133.662=100	103.1	101.6	102.7

Source: IDA data combined with DISKO survey

Table 7.5 shows that firms belonging to the three groups only differ marginally regarding their employment development for the period 1992–97. Firms that referred to much stronger competition had less employment growth between 1992 and 1997 while those referring to unchanged or weakened competition had expanded their employment more than the average. For the period 1996–97 there is a catch-up in employment in the firms referring to much stronger competition, while the number of employees is stagnating in the two other groups combined. This pattern is compatible with a combination of firms that downsize when confronted with increased competition and firms that succeed in compensating for the increased transformation pressure by engaging in technical and organisational change.

Table 7.6 shows an interesting pattern. It is in the group exposed to much stronger competition where functional flexibility makes a major difference in terms of job creation. While the functionally flexible firms in this category tend to create more new jobs than the average especially in the long run, those that are not functionally flexible lose jobs both in the short and the long run. This pattern indicates that, at least in Denmark, organisational characteristics associated with functional flexibility may reduce the need to resort to numerical flexibility in terms of downsizing when the firm is exposed to more intense competition.

Among the strategies to cope with an increased transformation pressure we pointed to the introduction of new technologies and the development of new products and services as a possible response. We also saw above that firms that get exposed to stronger competition tend to engage in product development more frequently than those not so exposed. In Table 7.7 we have once again separated firms into two main groups, one including firms exposed to much stronger competition and another covering the rest of the firms. Each of these sub-aggregates has been divided into two – one including firms that have reported a certain minimum effort in terms of technological change, product development or market creation and one including the rest of the firms.

Table 7.6   Comparing employment development 1992–97 in firms that are more or less functionally flexible and more or less exposed to stronger competition

Competition/ flexibility	Nov. 92	Nov. 94	Nov. 96	Nov. 97	Diff.
Much stronger competition (MSComp-firms)					
• Functionally flexible firms	55 668=100	103.3	102.0	105.0	+2764
• Non-functionally flexible firms	12 804=100	98.6	91.6	89.0	-1413
Somewhat stronger competition or unchanged or weakened competition (SSComp-firms and UWComp-firms)					
• Functionally flexible firms	48 480=100	103.6	102.8	103.7	+1772
• Non functionally flexible firms	16 705=100	103.1	104.3	102.1	+355
Total	136 428=100	103.1	101.5	102.7	+3638

Source: IDA data combined with DISKO survey

Among the strategies to cope with an increased transformation pressure we pointed to the introduction of new technologies and the development of new products and services as a possible response. We also saw above that firms that get exposed to stronger competition tend to engage in product development more frequently than those not so exposed. In Table 7.7 we have once again separated firms into two main groups: one including firms exposed to much stronger competition and another covering the rest of the firms. Each of these sub-aggregates has been divided into two – one including firms that have reported a certain minimum effort in terms of technological change, product development or market creation and one including the rest of the firms.

Table 7.7 demonstrates that firms that engage in innovation and market creation create more jobs than firms that do not engage in such initiatives. It also shows that the difference is much more clear for firms exposed to much stronger competition than it is for firms living a more protected life. In the period studied job losses took place in those firms that were exposed to much stronger competition that did not engage in innovation. It might be argued that in these firms we have 'technological unemployment in reverse'. The lack of technical change and of efforts to create new markets results in job losses.

Table 7.7   Comparing employment development 1992–97 in firms that are more or less active in terms of technological innovation and in creating new markets (and more or less exposed to stronger competition)

Competition/ innovation	Nov. 92	Nov. 94	Nov. 96	Nov. 97	Diff.
Much stronger competition (MSComp-firms)					
• Innovative firms	44 846=100	103.1	103.4	107.0	+3134
• Non-innovative firms	23 626=100	101.1	93.8	92.5	-1783
Somewhat stronger competition or unchanged or weakened competition (SSComp-firms and UWComp-firms)					
• Innovative firms	32 177=100	103.3	102.7	104.8	+1772
• Non-innovative firms	33 408=100	102.4	101.6	100.6	+190
Total	136 428=100	103.1	101.5	102.7	+3638

Source: IDA data combined with DISKO survey

These results seem to reinforce a standard assumption in mainstream economics. Intensifying competition seems to trigger changes that increase the competitiveness of firms. That would, in the context of an open economy, result in positive effects on international competitiveness and domestic employment.

There are a number of caveats that need to be taken into account before concluding that intensified competition results in such positive dynamic effects. First, it should be considered that we are studying a single case.

There are signs that Denmark has been characterised by a weak competition pressure in several sectors including the construction and service sectors. Second, the period 1992–97 was one with stable growth and it is not certain that the patterns characterising such a long upswing would stay the same in a downswing. Third, we have only captured the surviving firms. In order to estimate the overall employment effect it would have been more satisfactory to include the deaths and births of firms in the analysis. Finally, as already pointed out, the capacity to cope with an increased transformation pressure will reflect technological and organisational opportunities as well as the functional flexibility of the firms. The good policy mix seems therefore to be one that on the one hand promotes the diffusion of new organisational practices and enhances technological opportunities and on the other hand ensures a suitable competition pressure for the private sector.

In the analysis we have separated the impact of organisational characteristics on employment from the impact of technical innovation and market creation. In other calculations using the same data set the hypothesis of complementarities among these elements in tested (Laursen and Foss, 2003). It was hypothesised that new work practices would spur product innovation. It was also tested whether new practices stimulate innovation to a larger extent when adopted as a system rather than in isolation. The hypothesis was tested by means of factor analyses and probit regressions. It was found that, indeed, the human resource management practices seem to complement each other and work more efficiently if implemented in combinations rather than in isolation. And it was also found that innovation was most frequent among the firms using several of the HRM practices.

Based on the same data, ordered probit regressions (Vinding, 2001) show that human resource practices significantly influence the innovative performance of firms in the sample. Thus, Vinding differentiates the innovative performance of firms as the dependent variable and includes in his model human resource management practices and, for the present purpose equally interesting, the development in competition pressure. Both these variables are shown to be significantly and positively related to innovative performance. Therefore, Vindings results confirm at a general level those of Laursen and Foss (op. cit.). The important finding by Vinding is that there is also a significant positive relationship from competition to innovation. The strength of the relationships varies between sectors, however.

We have now established the relations shown in Figure 7.3. Moreover, the dominant causalities between the elements have been argued for, namely the arrows from functional flexibility to innovation and from competition to innovation and functional flexibility.

We can thus conclude that increased competition will on average tend to have a negative effect on the growth of employment in the short run. Firms with organisational and management practices that promote functional flexibility and human resource development will be more successful in coping with increased competition. They will also be more innovative.

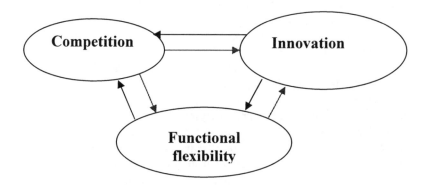

Figure 7.3   Relationships   between   competition   innovation   and   functional flexibility

And the increased competition will in itself promote product innovations and the creation of new markets. In our data set firms introducing new products and services tend to be much more successful in terms of job creation than those that do not do so.

Table 7.8 indicates that the major effect on job creation from product innovation comes not immediately but with a substantial time lag. Some of the job creation in firms introducing a new product in the period 1993–95 did not take place until 1996–97 and the same is true for the job losses in the firms that did not innovate. This implies that efforts to promote innovation in firms as well as in public policy need to have a certain time horizon.

Table 7.8   *Employment 1992–97 in firms with and without product and service innovations 1993–95 (index 1992 = 100)*

Product/service innovation	Nov. 92	Nov. 94	Nov. 96	Nov. 97
P/S innovative	92 764= 100	103.6	103.1	105.5
Non-P/S Innovative	42 368= 100	102.5	98.6	97.1

Source: IDA data combined with DISKO survey

7.5.7   Changes in the Content of Work

We have now linked competition, functional flexibility and product innovation to trends in aggregate employment. In this part of the chapter the focus will be on the skill dimension of the labour market. The weakening of the position of low skilled workers is a general problem that was growing in almost all OECD countries in the period 1985–95. The explanations given refer either to international trade with low wage countries or to technology as skill-biased (OECD, 1994). In what follows we will see how far the phenomenon can be explained by a more intense competition.

As pointed out, one weakness with the Danish labour market is that workers without vocational training in terms of employment opportunities and unemployment are worse off than workers with more training. With its very even income distribution the Danish economy may be seen as a prototype of the European dilemma where equality in terms of incomes may result in exclusion of workers with low skill levels.

A series of questions in the survey refers to changes in the content of work and in the demand for skills. In what follows we will compare firms reporting a much stronger competition pressure in 1993–95 with the whole population in this respect. Table 7.9 shows how firms with different experiences in terms of a change in the intensity of competition report changes in work content.

Table 7.9 shows that almost 50 per cent of all firms report that there has been an increase in work tasks which are demanding in terms of work-related ('occupational') qualifications. But even more important for the whole population of firms (see the 'All firms' column) is the increase in the demand for general qualifications such as work autonomy and cooperation with management.

None of these are the factors that distinguish the MSComp-firms from the rest most clearly, however. MSComp-firms stand out as characterised by a strong *reduction* in routine work and specialised labour (figures not reported in the table). They also stand out in reporting that more and more of their tasks relate to communication inside and outside the firm (see the categories 2, 4, 5, 7 and 8 in the table).

Together this gives a picture of change in the work process where a more rapidly changing environment recorded as an intensification of competition puts a premium on skills to cope with and to interact with others in coping with change. In this context, experts not prepared to adapt to new conditions and to communicate with peers who command different kinds of expertise

Table 7.9   *Proportion of firms responding 'more' to the following*
              question: 'Has the content of work changed for the
              employees during the period 1993–95 with more emphasis on
              factor?'

Work content	MSComp-firms	SSComp-firms	UVComp-firms	All firms
1. Work autonomy	63.93 115	57.70 104	41.40 75	55.38 100
2. Cooperation with management	56.93 120	49.02 104	31.97 68	47.30 100
3. Occupational qualifications	52.76 113	49.51 106	34.92 75	46.71 100
4. Cooperation with colleagues	53.03 121	46.23 106	27.89 64	43.71 100
5. Contact customers	49.39 121	41.97 102	29.02 71	40.98 100
6. Specialisation	32.71 108	29.84 99	27.89 92	30.18 100
7. Contact subcontractors	34.72 128	26.23 97	17.46 65	27.02 100
8. Contact other firms	24.09 124	19.02 98	13.15 68	19.37 100
9. Routine content of work	6.33 92	6.07 89	9.30 136	6.85 100

Source: Question 20 in the DISKO survey on organisation and qualifications at the firm level.

will not be very useful. It might be argued that the focus on learning is especially strong in the MSComp-firms.[8]

These data on work content can be complemented with data on skill requirements. As can be seen from Figure 7.4, for the whole population, there is a strong increase in the demand especially for general competences such as responsibility, flexibility and capability in communicating. It also shows that the more strongly firms have experienced increased competition the more prone are they to point to a need for more qualifications in all these respects. In our survey we found that firms themselves see this factor as the most important when it comes to explaining changes in skill requirements. The increase in skill requirements for the MSComp-firms is especially strong in relation to flexibility and communicative abilities. This pattern of response gives further support to the hypothesis that intensified competition is a major force behind the shift in the demand for labour toward a workforce which can adapt to a rapidly changing environment by being responsible, able to communicate and cooperate.[9]

So far we have demonstrated how the intensified transformation pressure goes hand in hand with organisational and technical change. Firms respond to the increased pressure by introducing product innovations and by introducing new forms of organisation within the firm and with external parties that increase their functional flexibility.

We have also shown that firms experiencing a stronger transformation pressure are the ones that change their requirements for skills most strongly. They distinguish themselves from the others, especially, when it comes to reducing routine labour and the degree of specialisation and when it comes to requiring more general personal skills related to cooperation, communication and taking responsibility. Now we will turn to an explorative analysis of labour market statistics – the same limitations of the data as pointed out in earlier sections should be taken into account for what follows.

7.5.8   Competition and the Relative Employment Opportunities for Workers without Vocational Training

In this section we explore the question: how does an employment pattern for the workers without vocational training develop as compared to that for all workers? Specifically, we will analyse how this pattern develops in the three sub-aggregates related to the change in the intensity of competition. We assume that workers without vocational training have a more limited capability to learn because they have not 'learnt to learn' in the formal education system. We should thus expect them to experience a relative weakening of their position especially in firms experiencing a much stronger competition. Our results indicate, however, that this tendency is quite weak and that such a hypothesis may be too simplistic in relating the capability to learn to the formal training of the worker.

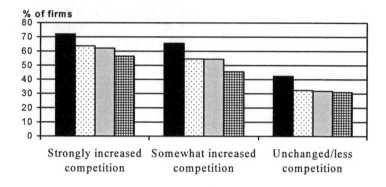

Source: Gjerding (1996), p. 67.

Figure 7.4   *Share of firms that answered 'greater' to the question 'Has the firm altered its demands for qualifications in connection with hiring 1993–95?' by change in competitive pressure*

By combining survey responses regarding competition with the IDA labour market data, we can see what has actually happened to workers without vocational training in the three groups of firms.

Table 7.10 shows a substantial decrease in the share of workers without vocational training during the five year period 1992–97 (from about 41 per cent to less than 39 per cent). Most of the reduction (two thirds of a net loss of 1588 jobs) took place in firms that had experienced a strong increase in competition, while the rest took place in the intermediate group. But the relative worsening of the position of workers without vocational training was actually quite similar in the three categories.

The fact that the relationship between competition and a weakening of the relative position of the workers without vocational training, in the register data, is much less strong than the link between competition pressure and shift in demand for skills, as registered in the survey, is interesting. It may be taken as an indication of the fact that, at least in Denmark, these workers are far from 'unskilled' in an absolute sense and that formal training is not all that matters in the learning economy.[10] This may be sustained by our case studies where we found a number of instances where workers without vocational

Table 7.10   Employment of workers without vocational training and all
              workers 1992–97 in groups of firms experiencing varying
              degrees of increased competition during the period 1993-95

Competition		Nov. 92	Nov. 94	Nov. 96	Nov. 97
Strongly increased competition	All	68 440=100	102.5	100.1	102.1
	Unskilled	28 070=100	100.2	95.1	96.2
Somewhat increased competition	All	46 141=100	103.2	102.1	103.1
	Unskilled	18 426=100	99.9	97.2	97.5
Unchanged/decreased competition	All	19 071=100	103.8	104.3	103.5
	Unskilled	8254=100	103.2	100.1	98.1
Total	All	133 662=100	103.1	101.6	102.7
	Unskilled	54 750=100	100.8	97.0	97.1

Source: Lundvall and Nielsen (1999)

training have been more easy to integrate in connection with the introduction of new forms of organisation than skilled workers (Gjerding et al., 1997). But the same case studies also demonstrate that a lack of general skills, in terms of ability to read, write and calculate, may be barriers to change toward forms characterised by functional flexibility and delegation of responsibility to operators (Voksted, 1998, 1999). Strengthening such general skills among 'unskilled' workers through a system for adult training may be an important element in reducing the tendency toward polarisation in the economy.

But the pattern observed leaves us with an open question regarding what is driving the polarisation in the labour market where workers without vocational training tend to become much less in demand. One possible explanation could be that the introduction of functional flexibility and innovative activities are going hand in hand with an upgrading of the labour force in terms of formal skills. In order to illuminate this hypothesis we have divided the firms into two extreme groups. The 'dynamic firms' combine elements of functional flexibility with elements of innovation and market creation. The 'static firms' have gone less far in both these respects (see box 7.2).

BOX 7.2 DEFINING   STATIC   AND   DYNAMIC FIRMS

The distinction between dynamic and static firms stems from a ranking of firms according to whether they have in the period undergone a number of different organisational changes (like interdisciplinary work groups, integration of functions and so on) and a number of different technological changes (like new ICTs, new products or services and so on). If the firm had introduced more than five out of ten organisational new traits and more than two out of four technological changes, they were classified as dynamic. Vice versa, static firms are those that score low on both of these two kinds of changes.

In Table 7.11 we have divided workers without vocational training into two groups also according to the change in the pressure of competition. We will now compare how employment of workers without vocational training has developed in 1992–97 in the two types of firms.

Table 7.11 shows that the dynamic firms in the longer run (between 1992 and 1997) were able to compensate for the negative impact of much stronger competition on employment of workers without vocational training. But it also shows massive job losses (25 per cent over five years) for workers without vocational training in firms exposed to much stronger competition that neither used new forms of organisation nor introduced new products. The more than 1000 jobs lost in this rather small part of the economy correspond to more than half of the total net job loss for workers without vocational training.

This gives rise to a more complex hypothesis regarding the causes of job losses for workers without vocational training. The hypothesis would be that it is the combination of an increased transformation pressure and a limited organisational capability to engage in change at the level of the firm that results in massive destruction of jobs for workers without vocational training.

This gives rise to a more complex hypothesis regarding the causes of job losses for workers without vocational training. The hypothesis would be that it is the combination of an increased transformation pressure and a limited organisational capability to engage in change at the level of the firm that results in massive destruction of jobs for workers without vocational training.

Table 7.11   *Employment of workers without vocational training in dynamic and static firms 1992–97*

Competition	Nov. 92	Nov. 94	Nov. 96	Nov. 97
Strongly increased competition				
Dynamic firms	16 500=100	100.3	96.9	102.1
Static firms	4218=100	92.3	81.9	75.0
Somewhat increased or milder competition				
Dynamic firms	11262=100	101.5	98.5	102.0
Static firms	5862=100	99.3	97.0	93.5

Source: IDA data combined with DISKO survey.

The transition to more highly developed organisational forms does not in itself make workers without vocational training more vulnerable, rather the opposite. Policies aiming at promoting competition need to be combined with policies enhancing the ability to innovate and introduce organisational change. When such enhancement cannot be realised there is a need to leave competition pressure at a more moderate level.

We have made an attempt to explain one of the most important macro trends in the labour market – the relative weakening of the position of unskilled labour – by aggregating the reactions of firms to an intensification of competition. There are important methodological problems in generalising to the macro level the dynamics observed at the firm level. The functionally flexible and innovative firms do affect the environment of the more static firms. Therefore, adverse effects on employment of speeding up change may be experienced by those who cannot keep up with the high rate of change, not by the firms that take the lead. Still, in the open economy, there are economy-wide competitiveness effects to be reaped from making firms 'more dynamic'. Also, at least in the context of the Danish economy, there seem to be quite strong incentives for all categories of employees to take a positive part in changing 'their own' firm in this direction.

7.6   CONCLUDING REMARKS AND POLICY IMPLICATIONS

The general purpose of this chapter has been to demonstrate the fruitfulness of a broader approach to national innovation systems that takes its starting point in the national production and human resource development systems. In the first part of the chapter we indicated, by illustrations from the Danish economy, that it might be difficult to change important characteristics of the innovation and production system without radical reform of the human resource development system. The two dimensions are closely connected and it is difficult to understand the dynamics in one of the dimensions without taking into account what goes on in the other.

In the second part of the chapter we made an attempt to illustrate new analytical perspectives that might be evoked by this broader approach. It was shown that the general economic climate in terms of the transformation pressure and the intensity of competition has a major impact on what firms do by way of technical innovation and organisational change. Looking at things the other way around, we demonstrated that it is possible to gain new insights regarding the macrodynamics by starting from what is taking place within the firm. We illustrated this with an analysis of how the behaviour of firms affects aggregate employment, but a similar exercise could have been pursued regarding economic growth and productivity. But besides these general results we believe that some policy lessons can be learnt from the analysis both at the national and the European levels.

For a Danish-type innovation and production system with high income equality there is a special need to invest in the learning capability of those without vocational training. Different general programmes giving employees access to leave for getting training should be made more selective and aim at enhancing the skills of the least skilled workers.[11] This kind of 'new new deal' is not only a question of social justice. If nothing is done to upgrade the skills of workers without vocational training and of those with rigid skills, a growing proportion of the labour force will disappear from the labour market with bottleneck problems as the result.

Another even more difficult challenge is to integrate workers with a different cultural background into the labour market. The Danish mode of innovation and production is intense in its use of 'national social capital' and in terms of often somewhat implicit communication. Therefore it becomes increasingly important to give special emphasis to the problems of integrating workers without vocational training and foreign workers into working life. There is a need to give foreign workers a more efficient introduction to Danish culture and to the Danish language. Time-limited special schemes making it possible to hire workers have been excluded from the labour market for a longer period at a cost lower than the minimum salary may be necessary to make integration a success. To avoid the 'working poor' problem government could subsidise such workers for the entrance period.

Some lessons can be drawn also for the European community. Our results strongly support the intentions of the authors of the book *Europe's Next Step* (Andreasen et al., 1995). They point to the need to focus European policy on stimulating organisational change in European firms. The Danish case indicates that there is a great potential in such a project and that it can be realised without sacrificing the job security of workers without vocational training. It could actually have trade unions and employer organisations as important partners.

The other key implication is the need to strengthen policy coordination both nationally and at the European level. Historically there has been a sharp sectoral division of responsibility between macroeconomic and competition policy on the one hand and education, labour market and innovation policy on the other hand. If anything the division has become even more accentuated in Brussels with Commissioners and directorates referring back to a specific national sectoral interest. According to the analyses above, this is highly problematic. Promoting competition may be quite constructive if, but only if, the capacity to cope with change has been developed. Functionally flexible firms that engage in product and service innovations are the ones most successful in coping with an increase in the transformation pressure. To promote organisational flexibility and innovative capability is therefore a necessary complement to competition policy.

Finally, we believe that the Danish case is useful in demonstrating that using the US as a benchmark for Europe's entrance into 'the new economy' and all kinds of e-activities (e-learning, e-commerce and so on) is a political choice and not at all a necessary analytical outcome. There is no simple relationship between economic equality and economic efficiency. Some might prefer the luxury of social cohesion to a society where the most rapid increase in employment is that of jail and security guards. But before the Danish type of innovation system can be seen as a benchmark the challenge to integrate those who are cultural outsiders has to be tackled.

NOTES

1.   The DISKO-project has been divided into four distinct modules each focusing on a specific level of the innovation system: 1. Technical change, organisational change and human resource development within firms. 2. Product innovation and inter-firm collaboration. 3. Firms' interaction with the knowledge infrastructure and with factor markets. 4. Mapping knowledge intensity and knowledge flows in the whole economy. Additional information on the project may be obtained from www.business.auc.dk/disko.

2.   It would be even more interesting to compare how different national systems react and perform when exposed to a similar transformation pressure. For instance it would be interesting to analyse the different development paths of Denmark and Sweden over the last decade or so. Both systems have experienced a strong transformation pressure reflecting the combined impact of rapid technical change and globalisation but they have responded quite differently in terms of economic performance. There has, for instance, been a remarkable change in the relative position of the two economies. In the middle of the 80s, GNP per capita was 20 per cent higher in Sweden while, in the mid 90s, there had been a change in the ordering and now GNP per capita is 20 per cent higher in Denmark. Does the relative success of Denmark primarily reflect different strategies in terms of regulating the transformation pressure coming from globalisation (intelligent Danish macroeconomic policies or restrictions on devaluations imposed by the EMS) or is it rather structural and institutional characteristics (the innovation system) that explain these major differences?

3.   A similar idea has been used to demonstrate the need for policy coordination in 'the learning economy' (Lundvall, 2002).

4.   The definition of technical innovation follows the Oslo manual standard. However, firms were also asked about their introduction of new information and communication technologies and their possible organisational innovations.

5.   For a detailed presentation of the data set see Gjerding (1996) and Lund and Gjerding (1996).

6.   In fact, a third data source adds information on the accounts and investments of the firms. This has been done by Statistics Denmark using their registers of official statistics, but in this case at the firm level. Here we only use the DISKO survey data and the employment data.

7.   It should be emphasised that the perception of the firms does not necessarily correspond to the actual development. In fact, objective indicators of the competition pressure in the 1990s show that there are hardly any changes (Konkurrencestyrelsen, 2001, Chapter Two). However, what matters for the behaviour of firms is precisely the perception of the development rather than the actual development.

8.   This may be one reason why the weakening of the relative position of workers without vocational training is only marginally affected by the change in the pressure of competition (see the comments to Figure 7.4).

9.   The fact that the shift in the demand for labour is not mainly for more skilled people but rather for workers with a high learning capability is emphasised in the recent OECD analysis of technology, productivity and job creation, where it

is stated that '... technical change is less biased against certain types of skills than against the inability to learn'(OECD, 1996, p. 9).
10. See, for instance, footnote 7 to this chapter
11. We argue that older workers without vocational training should retain the opportunity to leave the labour market at an age lower than the standard retirement age.

REFERENCES

Andersen, E.S. and Lundvall, B.-Å. (1988). 'Small National Innovation Systems Facing Technological Revolutions: An Analytical Framework', in C. Freeman, and B.-Å. Lundvall (eds) *Small Countries Facing the Technological Revolution*, London: Pinter, pp. 9–36.

Andersen, T. Dalum, B., Linderoth, H. Smith, V. and Westergård-Nielsen, N. (2001). *The Danish Economy*, Copenhagen: Djøf Publishing.

Andreasen, L., Coriat, B., den Hertog, F. and Kaplinsky, R. (eds) (1995). *Europe's Next Step. Organisational Innovation, Competition and Employment*, London: Frank Cass.

Boyer, R., Amable, B. and Barré, R. (1997*). Les Systèmes d'Innovation à l'Ere de la Globalisation*, Paris: Economica.

Christensen, J., Schibany, A. and Vinding, A. (2001). *Collaboration Between Manufacturing Firms and Knowledge Institutions, in Innovative Networks*, Paris: OECD.

Dalum, B., Johnson, B. and Lundvall, B.-Å. (1992). 'Public Policy in the Learning Society', in B.-Å. Lundvall (ed.), *National Innovation Systems: Towards a Theory of Innovation and Interactive Learning*, London: Pinter, pp. 296–317.

Dalum, B., Laursen, K. and Villumsen, G. (1998): 'Structural Change in OECD Export Specialisation Patterns: Despecialisation and "Stickiness"', *International Review of Applied Economics* 13: 3 447–67.

David, P. (1991). 'Computer and Dynamo: The Modern Productivity-Paradox in a Not-Too-Distant Mirror', *American Economic Review*, 90(2).

Edquist, C. (ed.) (1997). *Systems of Innovation: Technologies, Institutions and Organizations*, London: Pinter.

Freeman, C. (1987). *Technology Policy and Economic Performance: Lessons from Japan*, London: Pinter.

Freeman, C. (1995). 'The National Innovation Systems in Historical Perspective', *Cambridge Journal of Economics*, 19: 1 5–24.

Freeman, C. (1997). 'Innovation Systems: City-State, National, Continental and Sub-National', mimeo, Paper for presented to Montevideo Conference, December 1997, SPRU, University of Sussex, Falmer, Brighton.

Gjerding, A.N. (1996). 'Organisational Innovation in the Danish Private Business', DRUID Working Paper, No. 96-16, Aalborg: Department of Business Studies, Aalborg University.

Gjerding, A.N., Jørgensen, K., Kristensen, F.S., Lund, R., Lundvall, B.Å., Madsen, P. Nielsen, P.T. and Nymark, S. (1997). *Den Fleksible Virksomhed: Omstillingspres og Fornyelse i Dansk Erhvervsliv*, DISKO report no. 1, Copenhagen: Industry and Trade Development Council.

Johnson, B. (1992). 'Institutional Learning', in B.-Å. Lundvall (ed.), *National Innovation Systems: Towards a Theory of Innovation and Interactive Learning*, London: Pinter, pp. 23–44.

Konkurrencestyrelsen (2001). *Konkurrenceredegørelse 2001*, Copenhagen: The Ministry of Industry.

Laursen, K. and Foss, N. (2003). 'New HRM Practices, Complementarities, and the Impact on Innovation Performance', *Cambridge Journal of Economics*, 27(2): 243–63.

List, F. (1841). *Das Nationale System der Politischen Ökonomie*, Basel: Kyklos (translated and published under the title *The National System of Political Economy*, by Longmans, Green and Co., London, 1841).

Lund, R. and Gjerding, A.N. (1996). 'The Flexible Company, Innovation, Work Organisation and Human Resource Management', DRUID Working Paper No. 96-17, Aalborg: Department of Business Studies, Aalborg University.

Lundvall, B.-Å. (1985). *Product Innovation and User-Producer Interaction*, Aalborg: Aalborg University Press.

Lundvall, B.-Å. (ed.), (1992). *National Systems of Innovation: Towards a Theory of Innovation and Interactive Learning*, London: Pinter.

Lundvall, B.-Å. (2002). *Innovation, Growth and Social Cohesion: The Danish Model of a Learning Economy*, Cheltenham and Northampton, MA: Edward Elgar.

Lundvall, B.-Å. and Barras, S. (1998). *The Globalising Learning Economy: Implications for Innovation Policy*, Brussels: DG XII, European Commission.

Lundvall, B.-Å and Johnson, B. (1994). 'The Learning Economy', *Journal of Industry Studies*, 1(2): 23–42.

Lundvall, B.-Å and Nielsen, P. (1999). 'Competition and Transformation in the Learning Economy – the Danish Case', *Revue d'Economie Industrielle* 88: 67–90.

Nelson, R. R. (1988). 'Institutions supporting technical change in the United States', in G. Dosi, C. Freeman, R.R. Nelson, G. Silverberg and L. Soete (eds), *Technology and Economic Theory*, London: Pinter, pp. 312–329.

Nelson, R.R. (ed.) (1993). *National Innovation Systems: A Comparative Analysis*, Oxford: Oxford University Press.

OECD (1994). *The OECD Jobs Study*, Paris: OECD.

OECD (1996). *The OECD Jobs Strategy: Technology, Productivity and Job Creation*, Paris: OECD.

OECD (2000a). *A New Economy? The Changing Role of Innovation and Information Technology in Growth*, Paris: OECD.

OECD (2000b). *Beyond the Hype*, Paris: OECD.

Porter, M. (1990). *The Competitive Advantage of Nations*, London: Macmillan.

Vinding, A, (2001). 'Absorptive Capacity and Innovative Performance: A Human Capital Approach', Paper presented to DRUID seminar, Aalborg, Nov. 29th.

Voksted, S. (1998). *Efteruddannelsessystemets rolle og muligheder i det danske innovationssystem*, Copenhagen: Erhvervsfremmestyrelsen.

Voksted, S. (1999). *Kan kurser ændre holdninger?*, Copenhagen: Erhvervsfremmes tyrelsen.

Whitley, R. (1996). 'The Social Construction of Economic Actors: Institutions and Types of Firm in Europe and Other Market Economies', in R. Whitley (ed.), *The Changing European Firm*, London: Routledge, pp 39–66.

PART THREE

Building competences

Introductory note: Innovation and competence building

Manuel V. Heitor

The chapters included in this part of the volume clearly highlight the link between competence (skills, education), and innovation (technological change) towards inclusive learning. The connection between education, skills and competence, on the one hand, and the learning society, on the other, must consider the manifold interconnections between competence and the learning society and link them with the broader context of the anxieties and concerns, hopes and expectations that we live with today.

An important issue is to know what it takes to be part of the learning society. We may not know exactly what the learning society is, but we do know that there are requirements to be part of it. We need, in particular, to build competence, of which skills are a part. However, for some cases, the need for new skills is not associated with technological change, but with an organisational change, and the new skills provided are not particularly intensive in specialised knowledge. It is important to stress this point because the discussion can easily be drawn into the skill-biased technological change discussion. Naturally, technological change does indeed play a role in increasing the demand for 'a higher order of skills', but there are other elements of change driving this demand. What is hardly questionable is that those that do not possess either the skills or the ability or possibility to acquire them become excluded.

Carneiro (Chapter Eight) is particularly effective in presenting a clear definition of competence. It is worthwhile citing a passage of his chapter in which this definition – and a contrast with more canonical definitions of education and skills – is provided in a striking way: 'Instead of requiring a skill, which they see as still too narrowly linked to the idea of practical know-how, employers are seeking competence, a mix, specific to each individual, of skill in the strict sense of the term, acquired through technical and vocational training, of social behaviour, of an aptitude for teamwork, and of initiative and a readiness to take risks'.

Many instances can be given converging the importance of building competence. Carneiro chooses a few, from the resurgence of the 'human capital' literature – which has percolated into the language of everyday life – to the very idea of the knowledge-based economy – the commonplace concept that we referred to earlier in this introductory chapter.

Carneiro also explores the implications of the importance of competence building to the individual and to the dynamics of innovation and presents the idea that it is important to nurture vocational identities. Vocational identities include, but are more than just, the individual knowledge base and the portfolio of competences. These include attitudes revealing a preference for learning, in which 'competence building' considers also aspects such as the strengthening of identity and of a foundation of emotional stability and of self-esteem. Thus, the idea of competence building is, in this context, viewed in a much more comprehensive and deeper way, encompassing the individual in several dimensions. The link with innovation is made through the distinction between adaptive and generative learning, which are connected with the Schumpeterian cycle of creative destruction.

Carneiro traces the evolution towards the learning society as a third stage of a process that was preceded by the 'clockwork orange' age and by the 'knowledge age'. Here again, we see that the idea of a learning society is, indeed, different from that of the knowledge economy. While Carneiro is able to describe the other two remaining 'ages' in some detail, the learning society remains a mystery. It remains a mystery, basically, because it needs to be constructed.

Steedman (Chapter Nine) addresses the requirements for skills in the context of changing organisations and the emergence of new technology. The first important thing that needs to be stressed to understand Steedman's argument is that skills here take on a rather broad connotation. We are not thinking exclusively about very highly qualified skills, but rather of new skills. For example, Steedman gives the example of a privatised railway firm that started to provide training in social and communications skills to employees without formal qualifications (to better prepare the employees to interact with customers). In this instance, the need for new skills is not associated with technological change, but with an organisational change, and the new skills provided are not particularly intensive in specialised knowledge as I remarked at the outset.

Steedman identifies the groups that are most at risk of being excluded as being those that are predominantly composed of adults and in which at least half of the group has been in employment at any one moment in time. The at-risk group is typically composed of individuals who have acquired no further education or training qualifications following the end of compulsory schooling.

Thus, Steedman argues, policies to promote the learning necessary for skill and competence upgrading cannot ignore the potential of the workplace and the strong incentives for upgrading that employers can provide. Also, the shorter or longer periods that the at-risk group spends out of the workplace must be utilised to the full to promote upgrading. Concluding, Steedman defends the need to define and promote a 'minimum learning platform', in which all are involved, from schools to employers, from the government to other institutions such as financial organisations.

Niemi (Chapter Ten) takes a more pragmatic view, in contrast with the analytical and policy-oriented perspective of Steedman, and analyses the idea of lifelong learning. Niemi's twist is to suggest that what is required is lifewide learning, which means that beyond the time perspective (learning over time, for ever) there is a need to add the idea of learning all the time. This, again, links well with Steedman's perspective, who also argues that learning must be assumed during work and beyond. Niemi takes an approach that draws from the education literature.

A specific instance of an organisation (or, rather, institution) that has not been created with the explicit intention of promoting education is taken by Booth (Chapter 11). Booth sees competence building as a bridge between the often contradictory requirements of flexibility and social guarantees. Competence building does contribute to efficiency and may decrease the demands for less flexibility and, at the same time, does contribute to increased social cohesion, since it reduces the likelihood of being part of an at-risk group, to go back to Steedman's terminology.

Finally, Booth's analysis is made within the context of change that unions are facing. She seeks to understand what roles unions can play in this new context of increasing demands for both flexibility and social cohesion. Her main argument is that trade unions must cease being, and having an image of being, reactionary, but rather have a forward-looking perspective, working towards social inclusion and the integration in a skills-based economy of an ever larger portion of the workforce.

8. On knowledge and learning for the new millennium

Roberto Carneiro

There is no question that there are deep analogies between mindlike artefacts and human minds. There are also deep disanalogies. The deepest of these, we think, is the functional one: how thought is shaped to serve our intentions and the settings in which we are compelled to operate as culture-reliant human beings.

Bruner et al. (1990), pp. xv.

8.1 INTRODUCTION

Seldom has humanity shared such a deep sense of urgency.

Against a legacy of notable progress we shoulder a growing burden made up of issues that vex humanity daily – ethnic conflict, warfare, endemic poverty, environmental depletion, plague-stricken continents, organised crime, anomic conduct at the heart of modern cities.

Indeed, there is a well documented catalogue of human achievements. We take a common pride in it: the advancement of science and technology; progress in human rights, freedom and democracy; new wealth creation paradigms; extended lifespan. Hence, the windows of opportunity appear to be wide open.

Paradoxically, though, people feel increasingly wedged into a maze of global anxiety. The plight of suffering fellow citizens of the world occupies ever increasing proportions of our daily news. Perils facing global governance reinforce the overall disbelief in politics. Volatility in the economy and in capital markets generates widespread uncertainty. The wholesale risk society is marked by powerful jolts. It exercises intractable pressures on our daily lives.

While profoundly split on the appropriate policy remedies or the best societal directions, one potent idea appears to bridge disparate views. To a large extent, learning is recognised as the key attribute of developed communities and individuals; likewise, education is the unique provider for sustainable human prosperity.

Everything operates as if the perfectibility principle has regained confidence: however uncertain and perilous the context, the quality of human life and the limits of human comprehension can undergo indefinite improvement.

In a knowledge-driven world, where the economy itself has turned into an *ecognomy*, human intelligence inequities and differential opportunities to learn establish the fundamental divide between peoples and countries. Our beleaguered world is a showcase of fierce knowledge competitions. Proprietary knowledge soars in value, whether speaking about frontier research or state of the art defence technology.

Is it possible to single out one domain of human endeavour that escapes this paradigm? Is economic growth separable from human development and from the accumulation of intangible assets? Will technology not subside into incremental upgrades – from generation X to generation X+1 – unless it becomes more learner-friendly? Is it not that the fate of cultures remains ultimately associated with their learning and evolving capabilities? Can social institutions – as corporate organisations – succeed in assimilating advanced adaptive and generative learning functions?

8.2 OUR NEW AGENDA IS FRAUGHT WITH LEARNING CONDITIONALITIES

The generation and sustainability of learning communities, learning cities, learning governments, learning organisations, lifelong learning individuals and ever learning schools, constitutes the overriding challenge to be undertaken in the wake of a new millennium. Knowledge and learning have only just begun to operate together. It is expected that they will partner even further to determine our common predicament.

The sheer fact that the human capital discourse – which has been dominant over the last five decades – has acquired a second momentum is in itself significant. The rise of a knowledge-driven economy, and the concomitant premium allotted to intangible assets, have stretched the debate on education and training; these institutions remain the single major source of human capital formation and of knowledge production and dissemination in our global age.

Never before have our developed societies been grounded in such high levels of educational attendance. Ironically, it is also fair to notice that seldom in history have we witnessed such paramount signs of dissatisfaction with the outcomes of our educational systems. What's going wrong?

Parents, students, teachers, employers, unions, politicians, media, often complain of declining standards or express concerns about the uneven quality of our schools. Our so-called developed societies express in various ways a mounting concern with the inertia of educational systems in arriving at higher standards of achievement, relevance and outcomes. Comparative assessment exercises have thrown light on the existence of wide disparities across systems and countries. We shall not enter into a discussion on how fair or unfair these critiques may be. In any case, disagreements are compounded when attempting to discuss remedies or when designing a rationale for structural reform.

One inescapable fact is that economic priorities have tended to subsume both the education and learning enterprises and their internal fabric during most of our terminal century.

Human capital – or its postmodern surrogate concept: knowledge management – is the mighty expression of that utilitarian approach. The economics of education has supplied most of the key rationale for ambitious reforms that swept our educational systems throughout most of the 20th century. Some prominent international organisations have acted as champions in leading the new debate on human capital.

Hence, the upsurge of knowledge as a key production factor in the new economic lexicon has contributed to 'hardening' what was always regarded as a most relevant asset both to society and to the corporate world. As a consequence, knowledge theory underpins a feverish period of creative search. Where and how is it produced? How best can it be disseminated? How can we characterise the most favourable nurturing environments? Which are the key factors warranting timely application and market exploitation of new knowledge? What are the enablers to convert knowledge into problem solving competences and skills?

The latter question is not just an abstract exercise for the delectation of intellectuals. On the contrary, the value of knowledge is, not surprisingly, closely tied up with that of competences. Knowing is a necessary condition but only knowing-how provides for the sufficient complement required by an industrious and promethean society.

The UNESCO Commission on Education for the 21st Century[1] associates this trend with the vibrant demand for higher skills at all levels:

> Instead of requiring a skill, which they see as still too narrowly linked to the idea of practical know-how, employers are seeking competence, a mix, specific to each individual, of skill in the strict sense of the term, acquired through technical and

vocational training, of social behaviour, of an aptitude for teamwork, and of initiative and a readiness to take risks. (pp. 89)

In the utilitarian legacy of the 20th century problem solving and innovation-driven society, the overriding criterion for knowledge assessment is value creation. From this perspective, knowledge production and management address a host of complex concerns, otherwise alien to the time-honoured traditions of the education mill. It is worth mentioning, inter alia, the following domains currently under exploration:

- accessing existing knowledge and appropriating critical flows of new knowledge (stock and flow management);
- developing objective indicators to measure the impacts of knowledge on wealth creation;
- discerning how ICTs influence the formation and spread of new knowledge;
- managing the working triangle of knowledge processing and circulation: education, R&D, innovation;
- measuring and accrediting non-formally acquired competences (work-related skills);
- fine-tuning learning and unlearning strategies – customised to the purpose of balancing active vs inert knowledge;
- relating personal and vocational identities to alternative knowledge paths;
- balancing adaptive and generative learning.

This list adds far more to the research agenda on knowledge, and its social and individual functions, than just paying tribute to a *new economy* hype. Let us take the last two points, for instance.

8.3   NURTURING VOCATIONAL IDENTITIES

Who am I? What are my core competences? Do I 'own' proprietary knowledge? Regardless of where and how I work is there continuity in my professional career? Where do I seek new learning experiments? Am I able to formulate a knowledge ambition? Do I understand the social networks that add value to my knowledge pool? Have I a strategy to bolster my working self? What traits do I value as a lifelong learner?

Vaulting volatility marks our working context. The market puts a premium on multicompetences and mobility. The spread of tele and e-work calls on novel self-management competences. Likewise, the central tenet of autonomy and self-determination resorts to the critical issue of personal and vocational identity.

These questions do help us understand the extent to which charting a fully fledged vocational identity is a formidable enterprise. Unless organisations are identity enhancers they will struggle to find the effective path toward collective knowledge and community learning.

Giving credence to this pursuit, it is now possible to devise a theory on the emergence of vocational identities, a sort of hybrid - *homo sapiens et faber*. Each human repertory at stake would necessarily include some, or all, of the following features, with allowance for different combination patterns. Each particular combination reveals a specific stage in a developing vocational self:

- a knowledge base (the cognitive genome);
- a portfolio of competences;
- a preference for learning strategies;
- a discernible path towards the strengthening of identity (construction of *self*);
- a foundation of emotional stability and of self-esteem;
- a set of strategies to enhance personal assets;.
- a commitment to both the vision and priorities of the relevant organisations, regarded as learning opportunities;
- a conscious evolution – including the social dimensions of identity formation.

Consciousness – brain research findings conclude – revolves around intricate mechanisms of knowledge processing and selection upon value carried out in the two components of our forebrain: the limbic system and the cerebral cortex. Purposeful conduct recalls the assistance of semantic memory, motivation and awareness.

Conscious evolution sets the stage for autonomy and meaning making in the process of vocational identity formation. Placed at the summit of a long personal evolutionary chain it stems from a robust landscape of consciousness[2] grappling with the deepest, most intractable dilemmas of vocation and identity, and grows increasingly wary of shallow activism.

In the absence of consciousness and vocational identity learning lacks purpose, work is remotely associated with personal development and the drive to learn is erratic.

Intent is the direct consequence of vocational identity. Professional fulfilment is its main outcome.

8.4   ADAPTIVE AND GENERATIVE LEARNING

'New economy' and 'constant adaptability' are increasingly synonyms.

Ever shorter *creative destruction* cycles are compressing the time length of competitive advantages resulting from innovation. The Schumpeterian description of business cycles applied to the internet age sets the background for a high pace of productivity gains, thriving in extreme and inhospitable competition. Instancy is at the cutting edge of new knowledge application and of unprecedented demands on the human ingenuity to adapt. The buzzword in the tech-savvy communities is 'time to market': that is to say the speed at which ideas are transferred into business models, the readiness to apply research outcomes and new knowledge in corporate innovation.

In this unstable landscape, new learning theories often surrender to conjunctural flexibility. This discourse is emphatically praised by the prevailing views on learning organisations.

However, in our increasingly unpredictable, dynamic and blurred world it is no longer possible to rely on someone who can 'figure it all out at the top'. Empowering the individual learner and agent of change becomes the challenge. Flexibility and generativity both at the institutional and individual levels become evermore critical. Senge[3] spells it out in a neat formulation:

> The prevailing view of learning organisations emphasises increased adaptability. But increasing adaptiveness is only the first stage in moving toward learning organisations. The impulse to learn in children goes deeper than desires to respond and adapt more effectively to environmental change. The impulse to learn, at its heart, is an impulse to be generative, to expand our capability. This is why leading corporations are focusing on generative learning, which is about creating, as well as adaptive learning, which is about coping. Generative learning, unlike adaptive learning, requires new ways of looking at the world. (pp. 413).

This is not ornately composed prose for the internal consumption of a chosen few.

Human beings have been designed for learning. Children come fully equipped with an unassailable drive to explore and experiment rather than conservatively to avoid mistakes. Conversely, our primary institutions of education have been designed to teach and to control. The same reasoning applies to our prevailing systems of management, which are quite frequently eager to reward mediocre obedience and rote conformity to norms.

Survival instincts are often commensurate with adaptive learning capabilities: the reaction to external stimuli, dealing with threats and behaving in accordance with standards of flexibility.

The visionary person, but also one who remains committed to effective change, looks beyond adaptability. Creative tension – measured by the gap between vision and current reality – acts on expanding capabilities, devises ways to encapsulate strong inference, and addresses multiple competing hypotheses.

Table 8.1   Characteristics of adaptive and generative learning

Adaptive Learning	Generative Learning
❑ Responding to environmental change ❑ Coping with threats ❑ Reacting to symptoms ❑ Capturing trends and incorporating early signs of change ❑ Eliciting flexibility as prime value	❑ Expanding capabilities ❑ Enhancing creativity ❑ New ways of looking at the environment ❑ Addressing underlying causes ❑ Thinking differently ❑ Anticipating futures

The best blend of adaptive and generative learning remains a matter of scholarly dispute. Adaptive skills are useful in a context of constant but continuous or incremental change; generative capacities define the leaders in the response to radical innovation and systems depart swiftly from their notorious disequilibrium in search of a new state of equilibrium.

In any case, one outcome is evident. If our schools are to evolve into genuine learning organisations rote adaptability should not outstrip generative learning concerns. The comprehensibility of a multidimensional universe and the skills to unravel complex systems are contingent on a fresh mindset, one which remains open to discontinuous reasoning and prepared to welcome quantum leaps toward discovery.

Creative instead of merely adaptive learning demands a greater investment in *seminality*. Valuing ideas that establish new paradigms is the lever to bypass the *binary instinct of the human machine*. Seminal patterns of thought will tend to bypass linear reasoning; they will always prefer alternative thinking or non-standard approaches when addressing complexity or the unexpected.

Seminality creates *meme,*[4] – units of meaning nurturing the 'universals of culture' minutely listed by George Murdoch in his monumental categorisation. These, in turn, are critical to the formation of semantic memory – the lasting patterns serving as anchors to interpretation and enhancers of meaning making.

For centuries, education thrived on an industrial paradigm. Learning, in turn, appeals to a service-minded strategy designed to maximise knowledge acquisition.

Switching from the industrial mode of teaching to learning-friendly schools and institutions will require a lot more than the customary resolve to produce simple or incremental change.

8.5   NEW KNOWLEDGE PARADIGMS

While recognising the omnipresence of economic considerations surrounding knowledge management theories one could not ignore some potent signs of disquietude. It is now commonplace to remark a deep current in the quest for a paradigm change: drifting away from dispensed teaching in large educational machineries; giving way to distributed and demand-driven 'action learning'; and resorting to decentralised networks of institutions.

Three archetypes of new knowledge will shape the next stages in knowledge theories. They form a web of 3 Cs: Chaos, Complexity, Consilience. Let us briefly allude to them as prime sources of new thinking. 'Newton's mathematic organisation of the middle world – from molecules to stars – reveals serious deficiencies in a number of respects'. This is how Van Doren[5] introduces chaos analysis as a high sensitivity approach to slight variations in initial states. Chaos theory is fraught with a new lexicon: fractals, strange attractors, Mandelbrot sets, multibody systems. This new science is equipped to deal with a world of a subtle God – even a careless God – not a malicious One, in Einstein's own words. Disorder is not necessarily contrary to the attainment of a new order state. Quite often the former acts as a prerequisite to the latter.

Complex thinking reclaims a new canon in thinking and knowledge management. It springs from attempts to explain how complexity can follow non-linear and discontinuous paths to arrive at higher orders. This would be the case with Krugman's punctuated equilibrium theories of self-organising systems[6] and with Kaufman's NK models in molecular and evolutionary biology. Complexity places itself at the 'edge of chaos', the thin borderline between perfect internal order and total disorder to trace breakthrough developments.

Consilience is advocated by Edward Wilson,[7] a renowned scientist who retrieves William Whewell's[8] 'jumping together' of knowledge by the linking of facts and fact-based theory across disciplines to create a common ground of explanation. In line with the Ionian enchantment of Ancient Greece, consilience seeks the key to the unity of knowledge; taking on board the fundamental premise that the ongoing fragmentation of knowledge and resulting chaos in philosophy are not reflections of the real world but artefacts of scholarship. Consilience resumes a positivistic faith in scientific knowledge to add meaning and explanatory power to human intervention in the surrounding world.

A search into the realm of this evolving universe allows us to discern five paradigmatic mutations. Among other key features this structural change aims at crossing the Rubicon of exclusion, a dividing line that was never breached during the industrial age, notwithstanding the most vigorous denouncements fired at the educational perpetuation of an underclass of non-achievers and the low skilled in successive generations.

Constructivism sheds new light on the role of intersubjectivity vis-à-vis social learning: knowledge is elevated to the category of personal and social construct, indivisible from cultural conditionalities and their forceful interplay. The road to knowledge and cognition is thus contingent on memory, history, language, ethnicity and affection.

Culture, in itself, acts as a powerful marker of knowledge appropriation and transmission. Symbolic language pervades the entire universe of knowledge; speech – naming things – is intertwined with thought. Knowledge results from the internalisation of social interaction. Language is the material foundation of thought.[9]

'Knowledge is love and light and vision' – those are the expressive words of Helen Keller, an admirable personality of our last century. Each and every piece of new knowledge is a treasure disclosed.

Mastering the tools of comprehensive learning is a true cultural – perhaps multicultural – adventure, epitomised in democratic achievements such as freedom of thought and of opinion.

We have reached, at this junction, nothing other than a largely expected consequence. The sources of knowledge are rapidly changing; the ways in which we understand knowledge appropriation are equally undergoing dramatic evolution.

Theoretically speaking, knowledge availability increases exponentially in the world of the internet and global networks. Notwithstanding this recognition, the world of learning is still a landscape of major differences, a source of unfair competition and unequal distribution.

Once education is regarded as the fundamental lever of societal progress or regress, inclusiveness becomes the major policy issue to be tackled in the near future. Both equity and efficiency approaches demand from learning systems an enhanced capacity to deal with the socially deprived and with the low ability groups whom the industrial mode of education systematically excludes from the organised benefits of human advancement.

In a cognitively fashioned society, knowledge carries the potential of becoming a more powerful discriminator of human fate than in the former industrial society. To put it in other words, the premium awarded on knowledge and competences nowadays demands better attention to those groups of low achievers that are falling through the loopholes of our basic education systems.

Table 8.2   The way to inclusive knowledge

Classical approach		New approach
What to teach How to teach	⟶	Where to learn When to learn
Initial education For a lifetime	⟶	Flexible learning throughout life
Fragmented knowledge	⟶	Holistic knowledge
Status-ridden knowledge	⟶	Inclusive knowledge
'Have - nots'	⟶	Haves

In a cognitively fashioned society, knowledge carries the potential of becoming a more powerful discriminator of human fate than in the former industrial society. To put it in other words, the premium awarded on knowledge and competences nowadays demands better attention to those groups of low achievers that are falling through the loopholes of our basic education systems.

The quest for a new knowledge paradigm is not separable from the goal of a more equitable distribution of knowledge in societies.

8.6   THE FUTURE OF LEARNING – A BIG PICTURE

These contrasting views lay down the ground for a broad vision of the future of learning.

Departing from education and flowing through the knowledge-driven age we arrive at scenarios of a learning society as an enthralling proposition designed to overcome the shortcomings both of a bureaucratic vision and of the economic domination over the education sphere.

A fully comprehensive model will consider the intersections of three key variables: paradigm shifts; delivery modes; driving forces (Figure 8.1). In turn, each of these key variables is allowed to declinate longitudinally throughout time. Thus, they are permitted to unfold into three dimensions: past; present; future. A summation of the 3x3 resulting combinations could be briefly described in the following matrix.

Paradigm shifts: from industry (past), to globalisation (present thrust), and moving toward a New Renaissance period (utopian vision).

Delivery modes: from uniform, rote systems (past), to segmented distribution (present market-driven trend), and gradually accommodating increasing levels of personalisation/customisation (utopian vision).

Driving forces: from bureaucracy-led (past preference for *national or state-controlled* systems), to market-led arrangements (present move), which, in turn, should give way to empowered communities (utopian vision of radical devolution to civil society).

My submission is that we are swiftly moving from a Clockwork Orange education to a Knowledge Age, championed by a combination of a global order with market segmentation in distribution channels. The latter doctrine stems from the belief in a promethean knowledge: a knowledge generation capable of releasing humankind from bondage and of realising a supreme order of wealth.

The Big Picture that we favour does not end here. Economic theory, on its own, is grossly unsatisfactory for addressing a grounded humanistic and societal dream. The end of history would be too clumsy without a further horizon to aspire to.

Hence, our concept of a Learning Society as the realisation of the unity of learning. It is a vision made up of robust learning communities fully empowered to conduct the business of education and training in accordance with their communal identities.[10] A civil society of this calibre exercises its prerogatives to the farthest limits of subsidiarity. That is to say, any state intervention is contained within the primordial rights of aware and self-determining communities.

Exorcising the demons of utilitarian colonialism that have curtailed proper *educere* – in the purest Latin understanding – is a central tenet of this dream. This is a decisive move only comparable, perhaps, to the chasm that separates prescientific from scientific knowledge.

The proposition of a Learning Society remains a '*mysterium tremendum*'. It is a powerful appeal to the realm of human will and consciousness to reach beyond simple knowledge as a panacea and a new consumption commodity to be managed in our daily portfolio of conveniences.

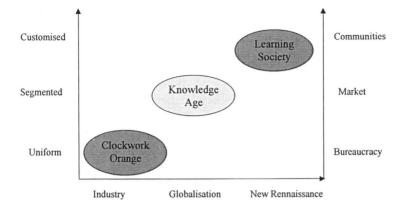

Figure 8.1   Towards the learning society – a comprehensive model considering the intersection of three key variables: paradigm shift, delivery modes, driving forces

Our Western-biased human story witnessed two major knowledge explosions. The first began in Greece *circa* 600 BC. It encompassed all fields of enquiry from mathematics to philosophy, covering the physical and the human sciences. The second also originated in Europe some five centuries ago – leading into a remarkable age of discovery and scientific achievement.

Both ancient Greek and modern knowledge systems have made serious errors and perpetrated awesome mistakes. The present state of our planet bears testimony to that.

In both cases the errors originated in human arrogance, overbearing pride or 'a kind of overweening presumption implying an impious disregard for the limits that an orderly universe imposes on the actions of men and women'. Greeks had a name for this human deviance: *hubris (*or *hybris)*. Hubris was a sin and the Greeks worshipped a goddess, Nemesis, who punished those who committed it. This was the case with Icarus. Indeed, this is the weakness to which many of the great and gifted are most susceptible. The signs of Nemesis are all around us today. Just read the daily press for documented evidence.

Insofar as globalisation imposes new dependencies, nowadays knowledge hubris is not confined to those who practise it – it entails profound implications for the entire planet, affecting some of the primordial equilibria at work in our fragile planet. Bridging the gulf between knowledge and learning equates with the way to overcome a tragic flaw of our modern age. The more knowledge seems generalised, insofar as information appears to become accessible to all at the reach of our bare fingertips, the gulf separating a developed world and an underdeveloped sub-world widens every day when measured by effective learning opportunities. The consolidation of a Global Learning Village unequivocally places the issues of differential learning opportunities and knowledge disparities in the front line of international action. Major knowledge gaps and learning inequalities are fundamental breaches in the social brokerage systems of information.

The lessons delivered by our recent past show that welfare gaps stand a strong chance of widening in the new economy. We need to move beyond the technological fallacy of a connected world. The real challenge is to realise a bonded world. Connectivity – or the death of distance – ought to translate into greater personal proximity: the realisation of a global world where the affluent minorities are unequivocally committed to the fate of their fellow citizens in the deprived areas, those who are the bearers of intergenerational poverty and inherited exclusion.

Debt swaps for education, better flows of scientists and researchers, re-orienting development aid to learning and human development, democratising access to a digital culture and to the use of ICT, investing in brain-gain favouring the poorest regions and countries – these constitute some of the priorities to be followed by international and national organisations charged with the responsibilities of conducting cooperation and development policies. In particular, e-learning software, content and services should enhance learning opportunities in the educationally underserved communities and regions rather than targeting the already affluent markets.

The UNESCO Commission for Education in the 21st Century[11] proposed four pillars to inspire the new learning ventures in the coming century: Learning to Be, Learning to Know, Learning to Do, and Learning to Live Together.

Living together in harmony and nurturing social capital are equivalent to weaving interdependency – a natural construct on a planet made smaller and closer. Sharing a common sense of belonging to society is innate to the human condition – we continuously display 'great intensity of mutual concern and tremendous dependency on each other', as Michael Carrithers well notes.[12] The author further remarks: "The fact that we are social animals is not just an adventitious, accidental feature of our nature, but lies at the very core of what it is to be human. We simply could not live, could not continue our existence as humans, without our sociality. As Maurice Godelier wrote, "humans in society, they produce society in order to live".... We cannot know ourselves except by knowing ourselves in relation to others.'

Otherwise, what is furthermore peculiar about human sociality is its surprising variability. The diversity of humans and of human social life is infinite; it surpasses any codifiable capacity known to humanity. Diversity unfolds before our eyes and appeals to our systematic observation endeavours in every possible manner. Thus, watching and reflecting upon diversity is our prime source of discovery – our raw material for learning throughout life.

Cultures that celebrate diversity are generators of natural learning environments. From this key angle, learning cultures act on permanence to nurture plural citizenships: learning to live together addresses and recognises the inevitability of valuing a multicultural global village. Moreover, learning cultures understand the need to engage in permanent knowledge ventures.

By living together we acknowledge difference. Most importantly, by appreciating diversity we learn to learn and to grow together. A global learning village contains the potential for a safer and a better place to live.

8.7   LEARNING THROUGHOUT LIFE AND NEW CITIZENSHIP: FOUNDATIONS OF A NEW SOCIAL CONTRACT

It directly follows that *learning throughout life* – a proposition widely endorsed by governments and international organisations – is highly contingent on the formation of vibrant cultures, both at individual and societal levels.

Continuous learning poses a formidable challenge to all knowledge-driven societies. Seldom are individuals equipped with the skills necessary to self-organise and self-manage long term knowledge paths. Therefore, underpinning metacognitive competences and skills from the very early stages of formal education is becoming all the more important.

Learning to organise multiple sources of information; learning to learn from experience (experiential knowledge); dealing with the social dimensions of knowledge formation; learning to self-regulate the effort to learn; learning to forget and to unlearn whenever necessary and making room for new knowledge; combining – in adequate dosage – codified and tacit knowledge; permanently converting inert into active knowledge – these are but a few of the pressing challenges that form part of a learning culture.

A comprehensive vision of personal learning as vitally important to all stages of one's life span will address three different development goals:

Personal and cultural development – related to sense, meaning making and spiritual wealth.

Social and community development – related to citizenship, participation and sociality.

Professional development and sustainable employability – related to production, job satisfaction, material welfare and economic pursuits.

Learning in the new millennium is expected to make a major contribution to the realisation of the third aim – *grosso modo*, the traditional goal set by the economics of education. The evolution of our world towards complexity and interdependency, however, brings out the necessity to provide a broader frame for lifelong learning: putting upfront personal and cultural advancement, as well as citizenship development – two further human development needs that are far from being concealed within a narrow economic approach.

Moving from rhetoric to actual implementation is still far from being achieved. Permanent and lifelong education has pertained to the educational lexicon for decades. Hence, it is necessary to open new avenues exploring life as a fundamental learning asset – not strictly in an expanded time horizon sense, but profiting from life's unique experience as an invaluable subject of reflection. Learning is inevitably a consolidation of dense inner journeys, it appeals to *'The Treasure Within'*.

There is no quick fix inventory of magical solutions.

The UNESCO Commission on Education for the 21st century (Delors et al.) alludes to a number of overriding priorities. A renewed new policy thrust would contemplate, inter alia, four cardinal areas:

- offering study time entitlements for all after compulsory education;
- carefully examining the strong features of the dual system and extending its strengths to overcome the current 'trust gap' between companies and schools;
- developing networked learning and strong partnerships to enhance lifelong learning opportunities;
- putting teachers and educators at the centre of the learning society and providing them with incentives to embark on lifelong learning strategies.

Schools, universities and teachers have throughout time been the 'knowledge pillars' of human and social progress. Dreaming of a learning society without catering for their contribution sounds inadmissible. Schools still provide the best embryo of multipurpose learning centres; universities are central knowledge hubs, irreplaceable factories of new knowledge and homes of advanced learning. Teachers meet the core requirements to occupy the forefront of lifelong learning enterprises. The all-learning society relies on teachers as leaders, not laggards.

The traditional *associationist* theory – brilliantly designed under Thorndike's genius – influenced the entire pedagogical preferences of the 20th century. Under these assumptions, drill and practice coupled with bonds and rewards would suffice to address a core theory of aptitude distribution; the Bell curve provided with the undisputed statistical dogma. Teachers would qualify as semi-skilled workers with the prime duty of carrying out instructions designed by curriculum experts.

New learning theories emphasise a 'new core' constituted by knowledge constructivism and learners who actively engage in self-management of cognitive processes.

Intelligence ceases being treated as a natural and inelastic endowment. Research shows that long term immersion in demanding environments can favour the acquisition of robust 'habits of mind'. Incremental expansion of intelligence is attainable through generative learning: a balanced combination of effort and ability, appealing to expert instruction and competent mentoring. Teachers' abilities become critical and themselves expansible through effort and ongoing professional development.

The hallmark of a learning school, then, is its *ethos* to continually seek new knowledge and to provide the leadership enabling a new teacher professionalism. Teachers are fundamentally learners, eager to engage in the institutional negotiation of improvement goals and in the strengthening of solid vocational identities.

From this fresh perspective teachers are no longer required to display a standard set of abilities. Externally prescribed performance benchmarks can be met in a variety of ways. As lifelong learners teachers are expected to target moving learning goals and to commit themselves to constantly expanding a package of core skills. Figure 8.2 summarises some of the knowledge challenges for teachers in a learning society, which may translate into enhanced teaching competences and in improved classroom delivery.

L. Resnick[13] phrases the challenges of a new teacher professionalism in a particularly eloquent way:

> Although professionals in many fields are required to participate in a certain amount of continuing education in order to keep their licenses or certificates current, educators often perceive that, to admit that one is still learning, is to announce a professional weakness. This understanding of professionalism suggests a performance goal orientation and the associated view of ability as immutable. In the effort-based environment of nested learning communities, where ability is seen as an expandable repertoire of skills and habits, professionals are defined as individuals who are continually learning, instead of people who must already know. Their roles include both teacher and learner, master and apprentice, and these roles are continually shifting according to the context.

In a global learning environment, Education as a Right finds a natural partnership in Learning as a Duty. In other words, the new millennium is a kind of void canvas that the theorists of the natural state so eloquently described. From Plato to Rousseau, Hobbes to Rawls, social philosophy has sought supreme harmony through the formation of stable and lasting social contracts; contracts that are freely negotiated and that establish codes of conduct based on a balanced interplay between rights and duties in society.

It is worth mentioning, at this juncture, another remarkable human trait: that, unlike common animal sociality, human social existence stems from the genetic propensity to nurture long term contracts that evolve by culture into moral precepts and laws.

We engage naturally in lasting covenants; moreover, we accept the necessity of securing them for survival: long-term friendship, family bonding, belonging to a community, cultural links. Learning is also an enterprise of the communal mind; one of its fundamental principle is ethics and catering for our foundational institutions of sociality.

Thus, a learning society posits a sovereign opportunity: to establish a new equilibrium between social rights and individual duties; also, a time to reconcile individual and collective – or cultural – rights.

During an address to high-ranking representatives of the European social partners, assembled in Thessaloniki, we proposed the following concept:[14]

> The social contract is mostly an implicit agreement, accepted by all parties concerned. The post-war social contract, which lasted successfully for some 50 years, is at present grossly outdated. This terminal stage is becoming apparent in a number of assumptions that no longer hold today: stable and full employment; the benefits of the welfare state; a limitless economic growth machinery; absolute faith in democratic governance; a strict separation between constitutional powers.
>
> There remains little doubt that unless a new concerted effort is put into practice to produce a different social contract, tailored to serve the complex information society and to make the most of the learning challenges, our societies will run into growing difficulties. In this new contractual approach, the economy will go on playing an important role; however, it is neither the sole nor the primordial factor. Full citizenship standards, striking a right balance between duties and rights, will increasingly call upon values such as justice, fairness, equity and solidarity in both our national and international orders.

Conscious citizenship lies at the root of participatory democracy. Participation demands a threshold level of social capital and trust capable of upholding higher order common purposes. This sphere of public interest surpasses the simple rights of individuals to difference.

This is why democratic rule is at the heart of citizenship education. Making allowance for a learning society is closely tied in with deepening democratic beliefs and committing future generations to perfecting democracy.

Schools and universities are – and have always been – bastions of sociality. They are social institutions to the marrow and the seedbeds of societal governance. Education establishments and educators are at the forefront of a new society. They are the engines of a brave new world. They carry the prime responsibility of making possible a better society: building the foundations of a new social contract that elicits education, knowledge and learning, as the key ingredients of a new deal. It is time to retrench around dreams of greatness – survival is no longer sufficient.

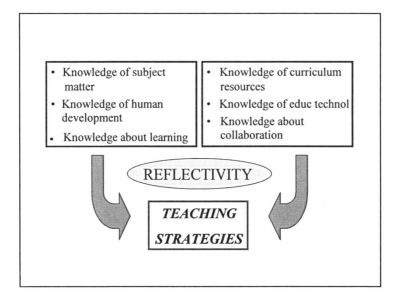

Figure 8.2   Knowledge challenges for teachers in a learning society

Addressing the theme 'priorities for the new millennium' is a call to rebellion. Likewise it is a cogent call to duty in each and every educational establishment, in the conscience of each and every educator. Likewise, educational, social and political leaders face once again a formidable challenge: delivering a new millennium of advanced knowledge, lifelong learning and supreme wisdom.

A widely acclaimed artist and film-magician of our times – George Lucas – sees in education the cornerstone of our society, the foundation of our freedom and a vital building block of our democracy. In the preface to *Learn and Live*, a publication of The George Lucas Educational Foundation, pp. v, he writes:

Our leaders have to make difficult choices every day, dealing with issues as complex as health care, transportation, and the infrastructure. We cannot afford to

let education be left out of the national debate. If we share a common love of
learning throughout our lives, then the nation's enormous resources can be
brought to bear in this important endeavour.

Human dream is the prime lever of change and progress. Utopia always
preceded the feasibility design of alternative futures.
Or, to put it in Shelley's words:

Poets are the unacknowledged legislators of the world.

NOTES

1. Delors et al. (1996).
2. We make use of Jerome Bruner's illuminating distinction between two critical
    landscapes in his analysis of the human condition: consciousness and action
    (Bruner, 1986).
3. From Senge (1996).
4. 'Meme' refers to the notion of a culture unit, the most elementary component of
    semantic memory, dubbed by different authors as mnemotype, idea, idene,
    sociogene, concept, culturgen and type.
5. Van Doren, C. (1991).
6. For an abridged presentation of punctuated equilibrium theories see: Krugman
    (1996).
7. Wilson, E. (1998).
8. Whewell. (1840).
9. Vygotsky (1986).
10. Here we refer to Castells' concepts of communal identities and cultures of
    resistance that are shaping a new international order. See Castells (1997).
11. Delors et al.(1996).
12. Carrithers (1992): 1.
13. Resnick has produced a consistent body of thinking in extending the concept of
    learning organisations to schools and education establishments.
14. Carneiro, (1999): 56.

REFERENCES

Bruner J., Goodnow, J. J. and Austin, G. A. (1990). *A Study of Thinking*, New
    Brunswick and London: Transaction Publishers.
Bruner, J. (1986). *Actual Minds, Possible Worlds*. Cambridge, MA: Harvard
    University Press.
Burness, P. and Snider, W. (1997). 'Nicasio: The George Lucas Educational
    Foundation', *Learn & Live,* pp. v.
Carneiro, R. (1999). 'Achieving a Minimum Learning Platform for All', in *Agora IV,
    The Low-Skilled on the European Labour Market: Prospects and Policy Options*,
    Thessaloniki: CEDEFOP:47–57.

Carrithers, M. (1992). *Why Humans Have Cultures*, Oxford: Oxford University Press.

Castells, M. (1997). *The Information Age: Economy, Society and Culture; Vol. I: The Rise of the Network Society; Vol.II: The Power of Identity; Vol. III: End of Millennium;* Maldom, MA and Oxford: Blackwell Publishers.

Delors, J. et al. (1996). *Learning: The Treasure Within.* Report to UNESCO of the International Commission on Education for the Twenty-First Century. Paris: UNESCO.

Krugman, P. (1996). *The Self-Organizing Economy*, Malden, MA and Oxford: Blackwell Publishers.

Resnick, L.B. and Hall, M.W. (1998). 'Learning Organizations for Sustainable Education Reform'. Daedulus, Vol. 127, No. 4, 89–118, pp. 110.

Senge, P. M. (1996). 'The Leader's New Work: Building Learning Organisations', in H. Mintzberg and J.B. Quinn, (eds), *The Strategy Process – Concepts, Contexts, Cases,* Englewood Cliffs N J: Prentice - Hall.

Van Doren, C. (1991). *A History of Knowledge*, New York: Ballantine Books.

Vygotsky, L.S. (1986). *Thought and Language*, Cambridge, MA: MIT Press.

Whewell, W. (1967). 'The Philosophy of the Inductive Sciences: Founded upon Their History', *The Sources of Science (41)*, Johnson Reprint Corp.

Wilson, E. (1998). *Consilience – The Unity of Knowledge*, New York: Vintage Books.

9. Low skills – a social problem for Europe

Hilary Steedman

9.1 INTRODUCTION

The aim of this chapter is to explore some of the many issues which arise for our societies from change in the technological and organisational features of working life.[1] In particular, the chapter will focus upon the implications of these changes for social cohesion. The chapter will draw upon results of a number of research projects on European labour markets carried out within the Targeted Socio-Economic Research (TSER) programme of the European Commission (DGXII) and on other research where relevant. Within such a short chapter the research mentioned cannot cover the whole range of relevant work. Nevertheless it is hoped that the results and findings used here to illustrate these issues will be appropriate and to the point.

This chapter is structured as follows. Section 9.2 briefly identifies those aspects of technological and organisational change in working life that have particular implications for social cohesion by increasing the risk of social exclusion. Section 9.3 focuses upon the implications for skill and competence acquisition, in particular for learning-promoting institutions. Section 9.4 outlines some key features of a 'minimum learning platform' and concludes.

9.2 THE SKILL AND COMPETENCE IMPLICATIONS OF TECHNOLOGICAL AND ORGANISATIONAL CHANGE IN WORKING LIFE

The emerging knowledge-based economy offers an increasing supply of well paid abstract job tasks, often under flexible labour market contracts, requiring significant education and training (Eliasson, 2000). The potential of technological advance and change intensifies and complements competitive pressures which affect both the traded goods sector of the economy (globalisation) and the non-traded goods sector (privatisation leading to competitive pressures and heightened consumer expectations). Soete (1996) warns that important policy challenges arise from this shift in the focus of the economy towards knowledge-based products. In particular, he warns that it is likely that *large parts* of the labour force will be excluded from the process of wealth generation by virtue of their inadequate levels of skill and competence. Understanding of the practical implications of these changes can be helped by concrete examples.

As part of the work carried out for the TSER NEWSKILLS programme, Houtkoop (1999a) analysed a series of case study visits made to firms in Sweden, the UK and the Netherlands employing a predominantly low skilled workforce. In the newly privatised UK railway company visited for the project – whose staff were predominantly without formal qualifications – intensive training in social and communication skills was being provided for staff with direct contact with customers (formerly passengers!).

In a privatised UK water company, new EU water quality standards required the introduction of IT equipment on a very large scale in an industry where the workforce was also predominantly without formal qualifications. This precipitated redundancies and early retirement and significant investment in the training and upgrading of the remaining employees.

In the Netherlands one of the case studies concerned a major brewery. Over the past seven years the brewing process has become more complex because of automation and centralised process management. In earlier times, employees merely carried out routine tasks, connecting tubes, closing valves, or, in packaging, loading cardboard into the machine. Now, the brewing process is monitored and directed from a central process terminal. In packaging, the employee not only loads cardboard but operates the machine as well. Parallel to these technological developments, the company initiated organisational change in a push for more cost-effective production. As a consequence the organisation moved away from a line organisation, and individual workers had to assume more responsibility themselves. Employees had to learn how to work as a self-directing team whereas before there had been one responsible supervisor for each team who told them what to do. The number of supervisors was halved. Thanks to the profitability of the company and the possible negative repercussions of mass layoffs, the company decided to massively upgrade the skills of the existing workforce.

A final example, also taken from the NEWSKILLS project concerns employees in the footwear sector in Portugal (Carneiro and Conceição, 1999). In this study it was found that, on the one hand, a *traditional* sector (shoe and leather industry) has been able to prosper by generating competitive firms, by incorporating critical advanced technologies and by securing and expanding jobs while employing skilled craftsmen but with very low levels of formal education. On the other hand, a *modern* industrial sector, the electric and electronics industry, has only been able to remain competitive by developing and incorporating technology, in conjunction with the absorption of comparatively much higher levels of human capital, and with the adoption of information technologies. We try to interpret the asymmetric behaviour of these two representative Portuguese industrial sectors by hypothesising that they have suffered different learning dynamics. While the traditional sector has relied on informal methods of knowledge accumulation (basically, learning-by-doing dynamics), the modern sector has based its competitiveness on formal education and institutionalised innovation activities.

Case study material of this type strongly suggests the hypothesis that workers' skill levels are crucially important for the innovation and technological capacities of firms. Evidence supporting this hypothesis is found in two papers from recent TSER research programmes. In the TSER Schooling Training and Transitions programme (STT) Salvanes and Forre (1999) working with Norwegian data conclude that there is strong evidence of skill-biased technical change as an explanation for the observed change in the skill composition of the workforce. They also find that trade has played a significant role, in that plants exposed to greater import competition experience higher rates of job displacement. In the TSER NEWSKILLS programme, Mellander (1999a), in a study of manufacturing in Sweden, found technological change to be an important factor explaining the fall in demand for the low skilled group. In a subsequent paper (Mellander, 1999b) a decomposition analysis was performed to show how much of the demand shift against the low skilled in Swedish manufacturing could be accounted for by technical change. Technical change was found to be the single most important factor while (unfavourably developing) relative wages was the second most important factor.

The TSER NEWSKILLS programme concluded that, with the exception of Portugal, labour market demand for individuals with no education or training beyond compulsory schooling (henceforth ISCED 0-2) has continued to fall – relative to the average of demand for all skill levels – in the European countries included in the study (McIntosh and Steedman, 2000).[2] In all countries where this fall in demand has occurred it has been accompanied throughout this period by reduction in the supply of skills at the ISCED 0–2 level. This fall in supply can be interpreted as a response from the supply side to falling demand. However, the fall in supply has been outstripped by the fall in demand.

Evidence from the NEWSKILLS project which analysed changing employment shares of the ISCED 0–2 group over time shows that the group is under-represented in high tech manufacturing. Most of the manufacturing sectors in which the ISCED 0–2 individuals are over-represented are 'low-tech' and have been contracting over the last ten years. In the service sector, prospects for the ISCED 0–2 group are less bleak than in manufacturing. Certain service sectors where the ISCED 0–2 group is over-represented are growing in most or all of our five EU countries (notably hotels and catering and retailing) (Kirsch, 1999). However, difficulties encountered by mature workers in moving from manufacturing to service sector employment were also highlighted by TSER research. At a seminar which brought together researchers and representatives of the social partners (CEDEFOP, 2000) it was emphasised that those working in manufacturing have not had the opportunity to develop the 'softer' social skills required to respond appropriately in face to face contact with customers.

Except in Portugal, the work of Kirsch (op. cit.) showed that the ISCED 0–2 group was rarely *maintaining* its share of employment in the expanding sectors of the economy. This section opened with a reference to the warning from Soete that the 'new economy' poses a substantial threat to social cohesion by excluding those with insufficient skills and competences from sharing in the wealth generation process. The evidence from these research projects underlines the danger of labour market and associated social exclusion for the substantial proportion of the EU population – currently 40 per cent of the 25–59 age group – with qualifications at or below the ISCED 2 level. In the following section recent research is again used to outline the challenge that this poses to our societies and governments and the institutional and other change that this suggests.

9.3   IMPLICATIONS FOR SKILL AND COMPETENCE ACQUISITION

While the *average* for those at ISCED 2 and below for all 15 EU member states is 40 per cent, this hides a significant dispersion of values across the member states and between age groups. In Germany less than 20 per cent are at this level while for the 25–29 year olds in both Germany and Sweden the figure is below 15 per cent. This provides a credible benchmark to justify asserting that the first challenge to policy makers and government is to reduce overall by at least one half the proportion of the EU population with no education and training qualification beyond compulsory education. It might be argued, using a credentialist thesis, that the upgrading of skills and qualifications merely shifts demand to higher levels of the qualifications hierarchy, but this is not borne out by the evidence available from recent studies. In a working paper produced for the STT programme of research (Gurgand, 1999) the empirical tests run in the paper found no evidence of shifting of demand to higher levels of the qualification hierarchy for identical jobs. A comparison of employment/population ratios by skill level across countries having very different proportions at the ISCED 0–2 level carried out by the OECD also supports this view (Table 9.1).

Two fundamental points emerge which should serve to focus policy discussion. First, the at-risk group is predominantly composed of adults: second, in all countries at least half is in employment at any one moment in time. It follows, therefore, that policies to promote the learning necessary for skill and competence upgrading cannot ignore the potential of the workplace and the strong incentives for upgrading that employers can provide. It also follows that the shorter or longer periods that the at-risk group spends out of the workplace must also be utilised to the full to promote upgrading.

Preventing the perpetuation of an at-risk group must also be a high priority. In all EU countries the younger age groups have a greater chance than the older age groups of continuing in education and training to at least the level of upper secondary education. Nevertheless, on average across the EU 15 nearly a third have not done so.

The current high levels of adults without further education and training and the continuing flow of young people without the minimum educational level required for labour market participation are the product of European education systems as they operated over the past 50 or 60 years and as they currently operate. A research project funded by the European Commission within the LEONARDO programme concluded that 'our school systems are proving powerless to achieve the declared aim of compulsory education: success for all. This means that there is an obligation of presence rather than results' (Planas, 2000, 59–61). Casal, Garcia and Planas (1998) conclude that 'Second chance experiments [for young people] are having disappointing results because of all the negative factors accumulated by their "clients" during the long period of compulsory schooling.' A first priority must be to fundamentally refocus the efforts of those providing initial education so as to produce willing and eager lifelong learners rather than discouraged learners.

Entitlement (currently expressed in terms of numbers of years of schooling) should be redefined to refer to the acquisition of a basic minimum or platform without reference to a set period of time or a given input of resources (CEDEFOP, op. cit.). The difficulties of such a fundamental reorientation of educational priorities constitute a first challenge to policy makers.

A second challenge is to ensure that when young people and adults are not in employment the skills and education already acquired are maintained, and contact with the most recent technological and organisational innovations is not lost. For economically active young people and adults long periods out of the labour market constitute a special case of social exclusion – exclusion from work which maintains skills and offers opportunities to acquire familiarity with technological innovation. Publicly financed programmes of training and upgrading are essential to help bridge the skills gap created by periods of involuntary inactivity. Recent European research helps us to understand what does and does not work when such programmes are put into practice.

Table 9.1   Employment/population ratios by educational attainment for persons aged 25–64, 1994 (percentages)

Country	Ratio	Less than upper secondary education	Upper secondary education	Tertiary level education
France	Employment/population	51.8	73.9	81.2
	Unemployment rate	14.7	10.5	6.8
Germany	Employment/population	49.0	70.2	83.4
	Unemployment rate	13.9	8.8	5.4
Netherlands	Employment/population	51.3	73.4	81.9
	Unemployment rate	8.2	4.8	4.3
Portugal	Employment/population	67.3	79.1	90.1
	Unemployment rate	6.0	6.2	2.5
Sweden	Employment/population	78.6	83.3	89.2
	Unemployment rate	8.8	7.6	3.6
United Kingdom	Employment/population	55.5	75.2	85.8
	Unemployment rate	13	8.3	3.9

Source: OECD Employment Outlook July 1997, Statistical Annex Table D

The TSER STT programme shows that results of government intervention to provide opportunities for unemployed young people have had variable results (Dolton, 1999) and points out in terms similar to those of Planas that a person's educational and personal history is important in conditioning the probability of their successful transition. Nevertheless, some firm conclusions have emerged. Based on an analysis of UK programmes for the young unemployed, Dolton concludes that the long run effects of this training can be beneficial – specifically in relation to employment enhancement for women. Furthermore he found that government training policies which had a higher structured training content with a higher degree of compulsion are more effective. The STT programme also found that apprenticeship was helpful in easing the labour market transition of young people.

The TSER programme 'Effectiveness of Labour Market Oriented Training for the Long Term Unemployed' (Brandsma, 1999) provides some interesting pointers as to 'what does and does not work' in programmes to upgrade the skills of the long term unemployed. Case study material from the project suggested that the chances of dropping out of such training increases with the flexibility of the curriculum. This finding fits with other work, including that of Dolton mentioned above, which suggests that for young people and adults motivation is lost in highly individualised learning environments. This can be interpreted as meaning that those with little experience of adult learning require clear structures and frameworks and need to function within a community of learners at a similar stage. The same TSER programme also suggests that care needs to be taken in providing guidance and counselling – too much or too little increases the risk of dropout.

But the challenge of social exclusion cannot be tackled from within the initial education and training system or by publicly funded schemes alone. The at risk group is mainly composed of adults, the majority of whom are in work for most of the time. It is in the workplace that action is required and that change must be brought about. Both the STT and the NEWSKILLS project have produced new research which has confirmed that (leaving aside apprenticeship training for young people) the supply of training provided to employees is biased towards the skilled and highly skilled in all European countries studied (McIntosh, 1999; Vicinay, et al., 2000). Leuven and Oosterbeek (1999a and 1999b) analyse International Adult Literacy Study (IALS) data as part of the NEWSKILLS programme and, rather more surprisingly, show that low skilled workers offered training are more reluctant to take up the offer than higher skilled workers. In other words the low skilled workers perceive the incentives to train as insufficient to overcome the negative aspects of undergoing training (including the psychological barriers produced by unsuccessful or unsuitable first schooling experiences).

This research places the question of finding effective incentives to persuade the at risk group to make the transition to being learners at the centre of the issues discussed here today. Many still work in jobs which are repetitive, provide little or no contact with information technology and require little initiative or contact with the wider public. The nature of these jobs may well explain reluctance to invest in training or accept it if offered since little immediate benefit can be perceived. Encouraging every workplace to develop into a workplace where learning is built in to the work process and provides incentives for individuals to invest in their own development constitutes the major challenge to policymakers to combat social exclusion. Incentives to invest in learning provided by employers can be complemented by government intervention to encourage and part-fund 'learning/competence accounts'. This policy, currently under active consideration in the UK and Sweden, encourages individuals to save in order to finance full- or part-time study leave. Accounts may be topped up by employers and/or from public funds as appropriate.

9.4 THE MINIMUM LEARNING PLATFORM AND CONCLUSIONS

The danger of increased social exclusion as a direct result of the effects of the 'new economy' on skill needs and, through skills, on earnings, is very real. As pressure to manage domestic economies more efficiently increases (through privatisation/contracting out of public services) there will be few 'sheltered' sectors of the economy where the at risk group can continue to hope for an acceptable level of earnings. This at-risk group can be clearly identified as being situated principally within the 40 per cent of the EU adult population which has acquired no further education or training qualifications following the end of compulsory schooling. Most of those in this group who are economically active are in employment for most of their adult lives and the challenge of eliminating the 'non-learning workplace' lies at the heart of the policies needed to combat exclusion from participation in the 'new economy'. The main challenge is to the social partners to ensure that not only are formal and informal learning opportunities offered to all employees but that incentives to participate in such learning are developed and put in place. One important way in which this can be carried out is the recognition and accreditation of the process of 'tacit learning' that takes place when skills are acquired informally in the workplace. Formal accreditation of such learning could provide a powerful incentive to individuals to acquire skills in the workplace.

However, incentives need to extend beyond workplace learning to motivate all members of our societies to invest their own time and other resources in developing their skills and potential. Carneiro (2000) has suggested that what is needed is a new social contract which emphasises the responsibility of the citizen to participate actively in the learning society. 'There remains little doubt that unless a new concerted effort is put into practice to produce a different social contract, tailored to serve the complex information society and to make the most of the learning challenges, our societies will run into growing difficulties', pp. 47–56. The concept of a 'minimum learning platform' – defined as the set of skills and knowledge required for full participation in society and in work and further learning – could help to focus the efforts of individuals and of the social partners on the new and ongoing investment in learning that is needed (CEDEFOP, op. cit.).

The NEWSKILLS TSER project investigated some of the current national initiatives in this field (Houtkoop, 1999b) and concluded that common aims and elements underpinned these initiatives. In a number of countries there is already strong evidence of interest in a 'minimum level'. Naturally, this is not always the term used, but there are striking similarities between countries. In the Netherlands there has been a policy discussion over the last five years on the topic of the so-called 'minimum starter qualification'. In Sweden there is a tradition that the curriculum of the compulsory school should aim to provide skills necessary for daily life.

The identification of the importance of personal and social skills or the 'softer skills' for effectiveness in the workplace has been an important feature of the debate about a minimum learning platform over the past ten years. Adequate levels of literacy and numeracy are now seen as necessary for employability but only really effective if accompanied by a range of 'softer skills'.

In the UK, employer organisations have taken the lead in emphasising the importance of these skills. From September 2000, all post-16 students, those studying an 'academic' as well as those studying a vocational course, will be encouraged to obtain a qualification in specified key skills. In 1999 a report entitled *A Fresh Start – Improving Literacy and Numeracy* was published by a government-appointed commission chaired by Sir Claus Moser (The Moser Report). This led to a number of recommendations; most notable in this context is the proposal that, for the first time, a National Basic Skills Curriculum for Adults should be set out with a range of levels clearly defined. This curriculum would concentrate on the three main key skills: literacy, numeracy and IT skills.

In Portugal, researchers working with the Ministry of Education have defined the desired profile of a young person at the end of 12 years of education. This profile stresses citizenship, and social skills as well as academic attainments, and has acted as a guide to the development of the curriculum. In France targets have been set which have as their aim that all young people should obtain a recognised national qualification before leaving the period of initial education.

To summarise, in the countries considered here, some points of convergence are already apparent:

- Communication in all its forms including quantitative literacy and skills of self-presentation are now considered to be necessary for employability. This requires a solid foundation of language competence and knowledge of basic mathematics.
- In non-English speaking countries some ability to work in a foreign language, normally English is increasingly required – and achieved – for most employees.
- In all countries emphasis is placed on familiarity and basic understanding of information and communication technology (ICT).

Personal and social skills are increasingly valued and a number of countries seek to develop these skills during courses of education and or training – these include:

- the ability to learn independently;
- the capacity to react to and deal effectively with uncertainty and unpredictability in the work environment;
- the capacity to manage interpersonal relations successfully;
- the ability to manage time and own work in an autonomous manner.

The approaches adopted in trying to define a 'minimum platform' differ widely across countries.

Differences are also emerging in the role that the education system is expected to play. Finally, we can also detect differences of emphasis on the respective roles of government and business and industry in delivering a minimum platform. However, there can be no doubt that achieving this range of skills for all learners should and will undoubtedly become a high priority for firms, governments and individuals in the coming decade.

But institutions will need to change also. Schools must redefine their aims and values so as to make raising the threshold level of achievement of their students their prime objective. In other words, schools too must embrace the concept of the 'minimum learning platform' as an entitlement and as an aim. Other institutions, for example those providing financial support for those willing to work but unable to do so, will also need to be rethought. A new social contract as outlined here would lead to expectations that periods out of work should become a natural 'window' where learning and skills upgrading can take place.

If all this can be achieved, we can hope to create not only a healthy growing economy but societies in which human capital endowments are much more equal than in the past and where human lives are enriched as a consequence.

NOTES

1. Helpful comments on this chapter were received from Erik Mellander, IUI, Stockholm, Catherine Sofer, Université de Paris 1 and participants in the Seminar 'Towards a Learning Society – Innovation and Competence Building with Social Cohesion for Europe', held in Quinta da Marinha, Guincho, 28–30 May 2000. Errors are, of course, my own. The Centre for Economic Performance receives financial support from the Economic and Social Research Council.
2. France, the Netherlands, Portugal, Sweden and the UK.

REFERENCES

Brandsma, J. (1999). 'TSER Programme of Research "Effectiveness of Labour Market Oriented Training for the Long-Term Unemployed"', Final Report to DGXII of the European Commission, Brussels: The Commission.

Carneiro, R. (2000). 'Achieving a Minimum Learning Platform for All – Critical Queries Influencing Strategies and Policy Options', in CEDEFOP AGORA IV, *The Low-Skilled on the European Labour Market: Prospects and Policy Options – Towards a Minimum Learning Platform*, Thessaloniki, 29-30 October 1998, 25–31.

Carneiro, R. and Conceição, P. (1999). 'Learning-by-Doing and Formalized Learning: A Case Study of Contrasting Development Patterns in Portuguese Industry' Working Paper No. 1009, Centre for Economic Performance, London School of Economics; STET.

Casal J., Garcia M. and Planas, J. (1998). 'Les Réformes dans les Dispositifs de Formation pour Combattre l'Échec Scolaire et Social en Europe: Paradoxes d'un Succès'. *Formation-Emploi: 62.*

CEDEFOP (2000). AGORA IV, *The Low-Skilled on the European Labour Market: Prospects and Policy Options – Towards a Minimum Learning Platform*, Thessaloniki, 29-30 October, 1998.

Dolton, P. (1999). 'Youth Unemployment, Reservation Wages and the YTS Scheme', TSER-STT Working Paper 33–99.

Eliasson, G. (2000). 'Developments in Industrial Technology and Production – Competence Requirements and the Platform Theory of On-the-Job Learning' in CEDEFOP AGORA IV, *The Low-Skilled on the European Labour Market: Prospects and Policy Options – Towards a Minimum Learning Platform*, Thessaloniki, 29-30 October 1998, 25–31.

Gurgand, M. (1999). 'Is There Job Competition in the French Labour Market?', STT Working Paper 40–99.

Houtkoop, W. (1999a). 'The Position of the Low-Skilled in Firms'. Max Goote Centre, University of Amsterdam, mimeo, TSER-NEWSKILLS Working Paper No. 3.

Houtkoop, W. (1999b). 'Progress Towards a Minimum Learning Platform in Europe' Max Goote Centre, University of Amsterdam, mimeo, TSER-NEWSKILLS Working Paper No. 26.

Kirsch, J.L. (1999). 'Devenir des Bas Niveaux de Qualification: Comparaison des Situations Nationales', mimeo, CEREQ, Marseille TSER-NEWSKILLS Working Paper No. 8.

Leuven, E. and Oosterbeek, H. (1999a). 'The Demand and Supply of Work-Related Training: Evidence from Four Countries', *Research in Labour Economics* 18; TSER-NEWSKILLS Working Paper No. 10.

Leuven, E. and Oosterbeek, H. (1999b). 'Demand and Supply of Work-Related Training: Evidence from Five Countries (Results for the United Kingdom)', Faculty of Economics, University of Amsterdam, mimeo; TSER-NEWSKILLS Working Paper No. 14.

McIntosh, S. (1999). 'Vocational Training in Europe: Individual and Institutional Determinants', *The European Journal of Vocational Training* 18, TSER-NEWSKILLS Working Paper No. 19.

McIntosh, S. and Steedman, H. (2000). *Low Skills: A Problem for Europe.* Final Report to DGXII of the European Commission on the NEWSKILLS Programme of Research, Centre for Economic Performance, London School of Economics and Political Science, http://cep.lse.ac.uk/homepage/tser/publications. html.

Mellander, E. (1999a). 'The Multi-Dimensional Demand for Labour and Skill-Biased Technical Change', mimeo, Industriens Utredningsinstitut, Stockholm, TSER-NEWSKILLS Working Paper No. 20.

Mellander, E. (1999b). 'Varfr har efterfrgan fallit plgutbildad arbetskraft svensk tillverkningsindustrie?', Research Report 1999:8, Institutet för arbetsmarknadspolitisk utvärdering (IFAU), Stockholm.

OECD (1997). Employment Outlook, July.

Planas, J. (2000). 'Arriving at a Minimum Platform for All: The Political Options and Strategies', in CEDEFOP AGORA IV, *The Low-Skilled on the European Labour Market: Prospects and Policy Options – Towards a Minimum Learning Platform,* Thessaloniki, 29-30 October 1998, 59–61.

Salvanes, K. and Forre, S.-E. (1999). 'Job Destruction, Heterogeneous Workers, Trade and Technical Change: Matched Worker/Plant Data Evidence from Norway', TSER-STT Working Paper 22–99.

Soete, L. (1996). 'Globalisation, Employment and the Knowledge-based Economy', in OECD, *Employment and Growth in the Knowledge-Based Economy,Paris:* OECD.

Vicinay, J.-C., Clark, A., Dolton, P., Elias, P., Groot, W., Levy- Garboua, L., Lommerud, K.-E., McKnight, A. and Sofer, C. (2000). *Final Report to DGXII of the European Commission on the TSER Schooling Training and Transitions programme* (STT), LEO-CRESEP Faculté de Droit, d'Economie et de Gestion de l'Université d'Orléans.

10. Competence building in life-wide learning

Hannele Niemi

10.1 INTRODUCTION

> The report of the OECD (1998) Human Capital Investment stresses that
> Expectations for human capital investment to deliver key economic and social
> goals are now high, but also wide-ranging in nature. They concern countries,
> companies and individuals striving to maintain an edge in intensely competitive
> situations in which knowledge and skills are critical. At the same time, they
> concern strategies to overcome unemployment and foster social cohesion. (OECD
> 1998, 8). Learning has been acknowledged lately in Europe as the very core of
> economic development (see for example Lundvall, 2000; Oliver, 1999; White
> Paper, 1995; Cochinaux and de Woot, 1995, p. 52).

Learning and the acquisition of competence and skills are the most important
tools for achieving individual or organisational goals. People should learn to
seize the opportunities for improvement in society and for their personal
empowerment. There is a strong optimistic trust in the power of knowledge
and learning.

But there is a growing concern: who is becoming empowered and who is
not? It seems to be a dilemma between the ideals of competence building and
reality in people's lives. At the same time, when emphasising capacity
building, we hear the voices that warn us that there are a lot of people who
are in danger of exclusion (White Paper, 1995; Young, 1998). There is a
growing polarisation between people who have rich learning environments
and the abilities to learn new competences, and people who are not in these
circumstances and do not have these skills. In this chapter, the concepts of
learning and research on learning, from a life-wide perspective, will be
explored. Thereafter, the question of how to create meaningful learning

spaces for knowledge creation and for enhancing different people's competence building will be elaborated on.

10.2 LIFE-WIDE LEARNING: VERTICAL AND HORIZONTAL DIMENSION OF LEARNING

In many European documents and discourses a concept of life-long learning has been a common metaphor during the past years (Oliver, 1999; Alheit and Kammler, 1998; White Paper, 1995; Cochinaux and de Woot, 1995, p. 52). It implies that human beings require the capacity to learn throughout their lives. Life-long learning means that learning new knowledge and skills starts early in childhood and continues in adulthood: and even among older people learning skills are needed. The lifespan of knowledge is shorter and shorter. People need to learn new skills and competences in their work and also in their everyday life because of rapid technological innovations and new knowledge production in different areas of society and culture. Learning to learn has become one of the core competences that people should adopt and internalise as early as possible in their school years. Learning to learn is a continuous process, and it should also be an important target in many companies. Tasks in work life are changing rapidly. The learning skills of the personnel are key factors in the success of organisations. Knowledge creation and innovations are the basic demands for companies and organisations to survive and make progress in a global world, where risks and problems as well as opportunities are growing at an accelerated speed.

The concept 'life-long learning' has been used to describe the vertical learning dimension, namely throughout all ages. It is an essential part of the learning concept, but it does not cover the whole phenomenon. We need a complementary dimension, which is the horizontal one. Life-wide learning consists of the vertical and horizontal dimensions of learning. The horizontal dimension means that we are learning in different situations and life areas which are cross-boundary. Learning and knowledge are no longer only a monopoly of the school, not even of the university. In our late modern societies, there are many other forums of learning which may be called learning spaces. Working life and work organisations are important learning spaces. People also learn in their leisure time, for their own sake, or because of capacity building for their future. Information technology, with the internet and virtual communication and learning spaces, creates a powerful arena for learning, both in the formal and informal settings of education. Also media, such as traditional mass communications and new forms of electronic media, especially with interactive digital TV, provide many learning opportunities.

Life-wide learning	
The vertical dimension of learning	• Learning throughout life • Learning challenges at different ages • Learning skills at different ages, supporting a continuous learning capacity
The horizontal dimension of learning	• Learning in different cross-boundary areas of life (such as school, working life, leisure, home, IT environments) • Transfer between different areas • Learning skills in different areas, supporting a continuous learning capacity

Figure 10.1   Life-wide learning consists of the vertical and horizontal dimensions of learning

10.3   WORKING LIFE AS A LEARNING SPACE

Working life is becoming a more and more important learning environment. People are learning for work and at work. For working life learning means that the personnel will increase their capacity for new tasks either in their work or in formal educational settings. Many companies see that an investment in the development of employees will bring advantages later on although according to Lundvall (2000) only a small minority of all firms (10–15 per cent) have introduced the major traits of the learning organisation. He also warns that it is tempting for firms to focus skill upgrading only on those who are rapid learners. Recent research on learning has also revealed that the whole working community should be committed to the development process. It does not make a real change in the working culture if only some individuals are learning. Real changes in organisations necessitate new constructions in beliefs, values and practices (see for example Hooper and Potter, 2000).

Learning at work means that new skills are learnt through work processes. Most tasks of working life produce new questions and unanswered problems which need to be solved. Learning from work experiences is most likely when individuals are presented with challenging situations. Opportunities for learning are provided by new or uncertain situations and the facing of conflicting demands (Ruohotie, 1996, pp. 54–5). People who have internalised learning skills will confront new challenges as learning spaces. The work in advanced companies and other organisations often consists of cooperative processes. If people have learnt to work collaboratively and share ideas though participation they can together make new findings and target purposefully towards innovations. Life-wide learning means that people learn more and more in teams and in other collaborative groups. Learning is partly an individual process, but increasingly also a process which is based on sharing and participation with different partners in a learning society.

Life-wide learning means that there are continuous processes of learning, vertically throughout various ages, and horizontally in cross-boundary spaces of life. It provides open doors for new competence building and growth processes of individuals and communities. But who are life-wide-learners and what is needed to become a life-wide learner? For this we need a new research on learning which takes into consideration the breadth of learning spaces and the differences of learners and learning communities. We also have to tackle the question of why some people are excluded from learning paths. Recent research on learning has produced valuable knowledge of life-long learning at an individual level or in different groups. It provides a basis to seek what different learning paradigms have revealed for supporting life-wide learning, and what new concepts and approaches are needed in future learning research.

10.4   WHAT HAS THE RESEARCH ON LEARNING ACHIEVED UP UNTIL NOW?

During the last decades there have been several different explanations for what learning is and how knowledge is created through learning (Reynolds et al., 1996). Case (1996) has analysed paradigms of research on learning and knowledge. He introduces three different philosophical views of knowledge and their impact on educational research and practice. The traditions are empiricist, rationalist and sociohistoric. A differentiating factor is that of what is seen as the main agent in knowledge creation. The empiricist tradition sees that knowledge is created by the experience that we have with the environment with which we are interacting. The rationalist tradition assumes that knowledge is created in our minds, while the sociohistoric tradition sees that knowledge is socially constructed.

The empiricist tradition has had a clear manifestation in the behaviouristic approach. The external factors are determinants in explaining what learning is. The mind is a device for detecting patterns in the world, and operating on them. Our knowledge of the world is a repertoire of patterns that we have learned to detect, and operations that we can execute on these patterns. Learning is a process that generates knowledge; it begins when we are exposed to a new pattern, continues as we learn to recognise and respond to that pattern in an efficient manner, and generalise our response in an appropriate manner.

The rationalist tradition sees the mind as an organ whose function is the acquisition of knowledge. Knowledge is seen as something that is constructed by the mind and evaluated according to rational criteria, such as coherence, consistency and parsimony. The constructivist tradition, as a representative of the rationalist tradition (Case, 1996, p. 79), emphasises the importance of the structures of knowledge that are domain-specific. Knowledge is viewed as having its own internal structure. The optimum educational process is seen as being one in which guided discovery, not direct instruction and practice, plays the major role. Learning is seen as the process that takes place when the mind applies an existing structure to new experience in order to understand it. Development is seen as the longterm change that takes place in the structures with which new experience is assimilated.

A third perspective is offered by the sociohistoric tradition. The human mind is seen as being distinctive from the minds of all other species in its capability for developing language, tools and a system of education. Knowledge is seen as the creation of a social group, as it engages in its daily interaction and praxis, and both adapts to and transforms the environment around it. Learning is seen as the process of being initiated into the life of a group, so that one can assume a role in its daily praxis. Development is seen as involving the emergence and training of capacities that make this sort of initiation possible.

Patricia Alexander (1996) also speaks about different generations in the learning research of the last decades. In the 1960s, during the dominance of behaviourism, learning research focused on external, traceable manifestations that mattered, rather than the thoughts and emotions that fostered or propelled them.

In the second generation of learning research such terms as situation, motivation and environments emerged. Not only was knowledge more often treated unidimensionally in the first generation studies, but the possible interactions that arose between knowledge and related variables were also more apt to be treated as experimental nuisances rather than critical insights. To many contemporary knowledge researchers, it is this very form of interaction that captures the imagination and sparks inquiry. In the late 1980s, for example, researchers were likely to pursue studies that explored the interactions between knowledge and strategies, knowledge and interest, or knowledge and beliefs. Knowledge was no longer treated simply as a cognitive variable, separated from any motivational or affective dimension. In the second generation, new research designs entered. Earlier linear designs and predictions were supplanted by nonlinear and multidimensional models. Another shift in the current notions of knowledge is a greater acceptance of the incompleteness of knowledge, its relativity and its potentiality to mislead. Sometimes one's informal knowledge is in opposition to the formal or scientific concepts that are the foundation of the instructional enterprise. Knowledge is domain-specific, situational and contextual. (Alexander, op. cit.)

Alexander (ibid.) reviews the way in which each earlier tradition has been necessary for our understanding of what learning is. She also leaves the future open and gives an impression that new approaches are needed for many unanswered questions. Case concludes (1996, p. 84) '… it is possible to observe the influence of the three evolving epistemologies with a gradual but incomplete shift taking place from an empiricist, to a rationalist, and most recently to a sociohistoric point of view'. Case (ibid. p. 82) raises an interesting question with regard to the future of the empiricist and rationalist positions: namely to what extent the sociohistoric approach to development and education is likely to replace its predecessors. His own view is that it will not replace them. It is like its predecessors, only a partial approach, which must ultimately be supplemented with insights from the other two traditions. In order to appreciate the complementarity of the three positions, rather than just the polarised stances that they have taken toward each other's work, Case (ibid., p. 93) welcomes a dialogue between the three existing perspectives. If a process of dialogue is initiated, it also seems likely that each tradition will have something special to contribute to the ultimate outcome.

We may see a transition from external to more internal determinants in learning paradigms, from unidimensional to multidimensional research designs and explanations, from decontextual to more specific, situational and contextual knowledge, and from static to more individually and socioculturally constructed knowledge. The research on learning is in a transitional stage. There are many good foundations, but the picture is still too fragmented and narrow if learning is explained or researched only from one perspective or tradition. All these approaches have been necessary for the recent understanding of learning, but we must build a more comprehensive and multifaceted picture of learning. What we need is a more holistic and comprehensive research paradigm of learning which really takes into account different learners in different social and cultural contexts, and which also covers different learning spaces: what is available in our everyday life or in the educational and working life settings. The needs and challenges of our European societies are so huge that we require a learning concept and research on learning which confronts the new learning environments and human beings' differences in knowledge and competence creation.

In the next exploration, the question of learning skills in life-wide learning will be examined. The author regards learning skills as the basis of acquiring new competences. Learning skills are metaskills for learning and they reflect the important aspects of the learning concept. We need the broad concept of learning skills which covers the cognitive, emotional and social nature of learning. The other important issue is the concept of learning space and how to connect it with learning skills in life-wide learning.

10.4.1   Learning Skills in Life-Wide Learning

In learning psychology, we have a long tradition which provides clear evidence that there are big differences between learners. Even in the 1960s and 1970s, many research studies explored how individuals have different aptitudes and how they use different learning styles or strategies. In the 1980s the concept of self-regulated learning emerged as a promising tool for human learning behaviour. It means that individuals must have the skills to steer their own learning processes.

Wolters (1998: 224) concludes based on a large earlier body of research (Pintrich and Garcia, 1991; Schunk and Zimmerman, 1994; Winne, 1996) that self-regulated learners are generally characterised as active learners who efficiently manage their own learning experiences in many different ways. In theory, self-regulated learners have a large arsenal of cognitive and metacognitive strategies that they readily deploy, when necessary, to accomplish academic tasks. Also, self-regulated learners have adaptive learning goals and are persistent in their efforts to reach those goals (Schunk and Zimmerman, 1994). Finally, self-regulated learners are proficient at monitoring and, if necessary, modifying their strategy use in response to shifting task demands. Self-regulated learners are motivated, independent and metacognitively active participants in their own learning (Pintrich and Ruohotie, 2000).

The concept of self-regulated learning includes the ideal that people take responsibility for their own learning. The educational system or training in companies in itself cannot guarantee empowerment. Learners are also expected to take responsibility for their own progress (Dohmen, 1999). In competence building they must have the capacity to steer their own learning and to build learning environments which are suitable for their own learning, using traditional information sources and learning materials as well as modern information and communication technology.

The learning process should be an active process in which the learner has ownership and initiates. However, there is a mutual interaction between how learning environments, for example organisations and working places, support learners to learn and how learners become effective learners. Adults' learning skills are often seen as self-evident capacities. Very often we overestimate their self-regulatory skills (Mandl, 1997). However, there is much evidence that many adults have problems in steering their learning. And even in higher education, we find that students need support in developing learning skills (Boud, 1995; Niemi, 2000; Richardson, 2000; Simpson, 2000).

A necessary condition of competence building is that people have learnt to learn and they can self-regulate their learning (see for example Dohmen, 1999). But what are learning skills if we view them in the framework of recent learning paradigms, trying to create a more comprehensive picture of learners? The following summary of learning to learn is elaborated from cognitive, emotional and social aspects.

10.4.2 Metacognitive Skills

There has been a long body of research on metacognition since the 1980s. (for example Flavell, 1979; Biggs, 1988; Pintrich, 1995; Borkowski, 1996; Winne, 1996; El-Hindi, 1997; Stewart and Landine 1998). Usually it is assumed that it consists of two broad components: (1) knowledge about people's cognitive states and processes and (2) the ability to control or modify these states (Corkill 1996). At a general level we may define the concept of metacognition as does Pekka Ruohotie (1994, p. 33):

> The term metacognition is often used to mean the conscious selection and assessment of strategies in learning. Metacognition can be subdivided into knowledge and skills. The knowledge component is an individual's understanding of his/her own schemes, strategies and processes as well as his/her own understanding of him/herself as a learner ... Metacognitive knowledge (executive control) directs choice of the strategy to be applied in any given situation. Selection of a strategy presupposes that it will be accurately interpreted and skillfully applied.

Researchers of metacognition emphasise that metacognitive knowledge and skills are interactive.

John Borkowski (op. cit.) introduces a three dimensional concept of metacognition referring to Pintrich, Wolters, and Baxter. Three interrelated aspects of metacognition are: (1) metacognitive knowledge; this knowledge is usually about person, task, and strategy variables and their interactions, (2) metacognitive judgements and monitoring; they reflect ongoing activities and processes that learners engage in while performing a task. This category consists of learning judgements, feelings of knowing, comprehension monitoring, and confidence judgements; and (3) self-regulation, representing the highest level of metacognitive activity. It means changing cognitive skills and strategies in response to new or changing task demands.

We have research that offers evidence that there are differences in individuals' metacognitive monitoring and control (Corkill, 1996; Winne,

1996). What causes this are such things as people's earlier knowledge of domain, their knowledge of tactics and strategies and their dispositions and styles for approaching tasks in stable and enduring ways. But many research designs are fairly narrow and the picture is still fragmented. The results reflect how different actions may reflect a single metalevel model applied in metacognitive monitoring. We need new research on more complicated learning spaces and on problems that people confront in their lives. We also need more knowledge about bootstrapped and maladapted forms of self-regulative learning. It seems that some learners adopt destructive forms of self-regulative learning (Winne, 1996). For instance, some learners use a self-handicapping strategy, such as choosing not to study. So there is already an excuse for academic failure. The knowledge of how to overcome this problem would be of absolutely importance when targeting competence building in Europe. Also, we would need more knowledge of how metacognitive strategies and skills can be taught and mediated to different age groups in working organisations and educational institutions. There are research results which show that the learners were able to gain a sense of personal autonomy over learning through training strategies for monitoring and regulating their own understanding of skills and concepts (McInerney et al., 1997). But we also have information that learners may not receive instruction which is explicit enough about metacognitive knowledge and skills in schools and in working life settings (Winne, 1996; Boekaerts, 1997; Niemi, 2000). How metacognitive knowledge can be thought of and learnt at different ages and in complex learning and working situations, are key questions in competence building.

10.4.3   Metamood Skills – the Emotional Viewpoint on Learning Skills

Shortly after metacognitive research began, it emerged that learning to learn and self-regulation are not only a cognitive process. Individuals are in a very different position regarding the willingness and volition to learn. We must acknowledge that the capacity to learn is not only a cognitive phenomenon. It is also an emotional and social process.

Linda Elder (1997) has emphasised that the human mind is comprised of three basic functions: thoughts, feelings and desires. The cognitive component includes mental actions traditionally linked with thinking, such as analysing, comparing, assuming, inferring, questioning, contrasting and evaluating. The feeling (or emotional) function is that part of the mind which is our internal monitor, which informs us of how we are doing in any given situation or set of circumstances.

Our motivation could be viewed as our mind's engine, which moves us forward toward some action or slams on the brakes so we can avoid some behaviour. As our driving force, motivation plays a substantial role in determining the behaviour in which we engage or fail to engage (Elder op. cit.). These three basic mental functions, although theoretically distinct, operate in a dynamic relationship, continually influencing one another in mutual and reciprocal ways. When searching for the ingredients necessary for a rational life, it is crucial not to underestimate the role of the affective dimension of the mind. To engage in high quality reasoning, one must have not only the cognitive ability to do so, but the drive to do so as well. What is more, it is evident that to learn to solve problems effectively, one must have the desire to do so. One must be committed to doing it. Thus, the affective dimension, comprised of feelings and volition, is a necessary condition and component of high quality reasoning and problem solving.

The concept of metamood also helps us to understand the emotional nature of learning. It implies the learners' awareness of their emotions in learning processes and the readiness to steer the learner for effective learning. The concept 'metamood' comes from Salovey (Salovey et al., 1995), but it has something in common with Goleman's emotional intelligence concept. Goleman (1995) and Salovey and Mayer (1997) have introduced it in order to break down the modern concepts of reason and rationality. They consider that Western psychology has neglected the meaning of emotion and emotional experiences in our thought and behaviour. They criticize the fact that emotions and rational processes have been viewed almost as being antagonistic towards one another.

Salovey points out that emotions can serve as a source of information to individuals and that individuals may be more or less skilled at processing this kind of information (Salovey et al., op. cit. p. 126). Salovey and his research group have focused on emotional skills that are likely to be related to the use of feelings to motivate, plan and achieve in life. Goleman (op. cit., pp. 36–37) defines the concept of emotional intelligence as having abilities such as being able to motivate oneself and persist in the face of frustrations; to control impulses and delay gratification; to regulate one's moods and keep distress from overwhelming the ability to think, and to empathise and to have hope. Goleman criticises the idea that, unlike the notion of IQ, with its nearly one hundred year history of research with hundreds of thousands of people, emotional intelligence is a new concept.

Goleman (op. cit., pp. 46–7) has presented the following description of emotional intelligence:

Knowing one's emotions: Self-awareness – recognizing a feeling as it happens – is the keystone of emotional intelligence.
Managing emotions: Handling feelings so they are appropriate is an ability that builds on self-awareness.

Motivating oneself: Marshalling emotions in the service of a goal is essential for paying attention, for self-motivation and mastery, and for creativity. People who have this skill tend to be more highly productive and effective in whatever they undertake.

Recognizing emotions in others: Empathy, another ability that builds on emotional self-awareness, is the fundamental 'people' s skill'.

Handling relationships: is, to a large part [sic], skill in managing emotions in others. Social competence, and the specific skills involved in human relationships, are preconditions for popularity, leadership, and interpersonal effectiveness.

Some years earlier, Howard Gardner presented his theory of the multiplicity of intelligence and introduced the concepts of interpersonal and intrapersonal intelligence (Gardner and Hatch, 1989; Gardner, 1993). The former means the ability to understand other people: what motivates them, how they work, how to work cooperatively with them. It also includes the capacities to discern and respond appropriately to the moods, temperaments, motivations and desires of other people. The latter is a capacity to form an accurate, veridical model of oneself and to be able to use that model effectively in life. It is a key to self-knowledge, access to one's own feelings and the ability to discriminate among them and draw on them to guide behaviour.

Meta-mood skills have a close interaction with motivation, and through it with metacognition. Many researchers stress that motivational strategies have a very important role in self-regulated learning processes (Ruohotie 1994; Boekaerts 1997; Pintrich 1999; Pintrich and Ruohotie 2000). Pintrich defines self-regulated learning as the strategies that students use to regulate their cognition as well as the resource management strategies that students use to control their learning. Positive self-efficacy and task value beliefs can promote self-regulated behaviour. Ruohotie (1994, pp. 35, 39) emphasises volitional processes of individuals in work organisations. The term 'volition' means strength of will and it is understood to be a continuum with the lack of willpower at one end and strong will at the other. Volitional processes are part of a larger self-regulating system which includes motivation and related cognition and emotion. Boekaerts (1997) has introduced a six component model to describe self-regulated learning. In her model, motivational strategies mean that students create a learning intention; they have coping processes to alter stressors; they have the ability to reduce negative emotions; they have prospective and retrospective attributions; they use avoidance strategies meaningfully; and they have the ability to use social resources.

Monica Boekaerts emphasises that it is important that a distinction be made between short-term increments in domain-specific competence and long-term increments in multiple forms of self-regulation skills, in relation to that domain. These include: (a) metacognitive skills that guide and direct the learning process in that content domain; (b) metamotivational skills that create favourable internal conditions for initiating, sustaining, and disengaging from a learning activity swiftly and flexibly (motivation and action control); and self-management skills that help learners to interpret increased levels of arousal when working in a domain and handle emotions and stress swiftly (emotion control). She recommends that, in the initial stages of a learning process, learners should be supported by instructional techniques that keep the demand-capacity ratio in balance (in other words teachers should provide adequate cognitive and emotional scaffolding), whereas this scaffolding should fade in the later stages of the behavioural change process. (Boekaerts, 1995).

The emotional component of learning broadens our views of the problem of why some people are learning and others are not. It depends very much on their emotions, values and motivation. If the learning situation is too demanding in relation to one's own competence, the reaction may be avoidance to sustain self-respect. Very often low achievers want to escape from the learning tasks which they experience as a threat to their ego.

10.4.4   Social Nature of Learning and Participatory Skills

Cobb (1994) wants to make the distinction between social constructivism and cognitive constructivism. The former places the emphasis on the influence of the social context on the construction of knowledge. The latter examines how individuals construct their own understanding of the world though problem-solving with objects and with others. He writes:

> Both highlight the crucial role that activity plays in learning and development. However sociocultural theorists typically link activity to participation in culturally-organised practices, whereas contructivists give priority to individual students' sensory-motor and conceptual activities. Further, sociocultural theorists tend to assume from the outset that cognitive processes are subsumed by social and cultural processes. (pp.14)

Social perspective theorists' views of knowledge are as varied as the disciplines that have inspired them. However, there are some common traits in that these theorists reject the traditional information processing view that knowledge is acquired by transmission from one knower to another, and then represented solely within the mind of the knower. Rather than use the terms 'acquisition' and 'representation', social perspective theorists view knowledge as construed by, and distributed among, individuals and groups as they interact with one another and with cultural artefacts, such as pictures, texts, discourse and gestures. (Cole, 1991; Reynolds et al., 1996: 98).

Social perspective theories emphasize the role of social and cultural contexts in cognition. They highlight the effects of the social framework on our beliefs, concepts and construction of knowledge. Learning has increasingly been seen as embedded within a social context and framework (Slavin, 1997). Social perspective theories have been variously called social constructivism, sociocultural perspective, sociohistorical theory, and socio-cultural-historical psychology. Although social perspective theorists' views are diverse, each theorist posits that learning occurs through the mediation of social interaction. Knowledge is not an individual possession, but socially shared and emerges from participation in sociocultural activities (Reynolds et al., op. cit. 1996, p. 98). Learning requires also social skills. This means that learners will need skills which make them capable of social interaction.

Educational psychologists have predominantly taken the individual perspective, often neglecting the social and cultural environments within which learning takes place. However, there are approaches which open the social perspectives on learning. One of the promising frameworks for understanding a collaborative knowledge construction within a systemic approach is an activity theory in cultural-historical psychology. The activity theory sees the dynamics of human activities as the integration of various interdependent relations in a dialectical process, where mental and external processes continuously force each other forwards. In this framework, Yrjö Engeström's theory of 'learning by expanding' provides a model for members of developing organisations to help them organise the description, analysis and reflection of their practices and guide the transformations of the system (Engeström, 1995; Hansen et al., 1999, p. 184). Other social component approaches emerge from models of professional development in learning organisations. These frameworks aim at finding conditions in which professional growth is the best possible. Social support and an open, innovative organisational atmosphere are very important factors in advancing people's working and learning capacities (Ruohotie, 1996).

We also have interesting research projects around help seeking in learning difficulties (for example Butler, 1998; Newman, 1998; Ryan et al., 1998), which show the importance of social and cultural aspects. They have revealed that many learners do not actively seek help with their academic task when needed. Learners with low self-efficacy are more likely to believe that others will think that their need for help indicates that they lack ability, and, therefore they are less likely to seek help. In contrast, when students who have high self-efficacy encounter failure or difficulty, they do not worry that others will attribute it to their lack of ability. The learners who do not feel capable of doing their work are the ones most likely to avoid asking for help. It is a question of culture in learning settings. Learning and working environments characterised as caring, supportive and friendly are likely to make learners feel more comfortable interacting with tutors and trainers and other learners. Positive relationships that encompass both academic and social concerns are likely to support learners' effort to seek help when it is needed.

Social and participatory learning skills are also needed in evaluation processes. The changes taking place in the concept of learning and in our societies call for new approaches to evaluation. The important question is how to support high quality learning through evaluation. The learning environments where evaluation is primarily for control and measuring performances create a culture of avoidance of seeking help, and of defending ourselves. Learning environments which are oriented to problem solving, cooperation and continuous learning require evaluation that is a tool for development, a continuous communication process. Evaluation should help people to understand cultural, social and interpersonal dynamics in educational settings and in their lives. Evaluation should reveal the areas which need improvement. Evaluation should also have a function of anticipation – helping people to orient themselves towards the future, in increasingly unsettled times, and empowering them to make their impact on the culture and society. Thirdly, evaluation should build communication and partnerships – helping people to work together for transformation to achieve high quality learning.

This new approach to evaluation is served by communicative evaluation (Niemi, 1996; Niemi and Kemmis, 1999). Communicative evaluation attempts to make students and teachers aware of how they may together influence the teaching and learning culture. Evaluation can be a continuous debate, seeking new methods and new practices in teaching and learning. It does not aim to rank people, it aims to seek reasons why they are confronted with barriers to learning and competence building. Evaluation may be a joint effort to create collaborative, encouraging and meaningful learning spaces. This means that learners will need skills which make them capable of interacting in evaluation processes.

We may see that people's participatory skills are essential learning skills. Learners need communication and dialogue skills, empathy and other interpersonal skills as well as skills of sharing, for example, knowledge and emotions. European scenarios stress the social nature of learning, indicated by concepts such as cooperative learning, and collaborative problem solving, sharing and promoting interaction. Social perspective theories give an important impulse to develop organisational cultures towards more cooperative knowledge creation. The new demands of learning emphasise teamwork and networking as necessary tools for high quality learning and knowledge creation. Learning is a social practice, along with its cognitive and emotional nature. We need more research into how to promote learners' capacities for participation and sensitivity to cultural differences. These abilities do not develop as self-evident qualities and we need more knowledge as to how they can be learnt and mediated.

10.4.5 Cross-Boundary Learning Spaces

Learning and knowledge creation are individually and socioculturally constructed processes. In our European societies, learning and knowledge construction must be purposefully mediated and supported. This means that educational infrastructures, companies and workplaces should provide optimal conditions for learning. They need the knowledge of how people learn and how to combine people's capacity to learn with a comprehensive view of life-wide learning skills. But learning is not only supported by providing high quality learning skills. The other aspect of supporting learning is organising the cultural structures of systems.

Japanese researcher, Ikujiro Nonaka, asks what the fundamental conditions for knowledge creation are. Where is knowledge creation located? To address these questions, he (Nonaka and Konno, 1998) introduces the Japanese concept of *ba,* which roughly translates into the English word 'place'. *Ba* can be thought of as a shared space for emerging relationships. This space can be physical (such as an office, dispersed business space), virtual (such as e-mail, teleconference), mental (such as shared experiences, ideas, ideals) or any combination of these. What differentiates *ba* from ordinary human interaction is the concept of knowledge creation. *Ba* provides a platform for advancing individual and/or collective knowledge. *Ba* is a shared space that serves as a foundation for knowledge creation. *Ba* exists at many levels and these levels may be connected to form a greater *ba.* Just as the *ba* for an individual is the team, the organisation, in turn, is the *ba* for the teams. To participate in a *ba* means to get involved and transcend one's own limited perspective or boundary. This exploration is necessary in order to profit from the 'magic synthesis' of rationality and intuition that produces creativity. *Ba* is the world where individuals share feelings, emotions, experiences and mental models.

The concept of *ba* gives a good basis for understanding how learning is individually, socially and culturally constructed and how we may create spaces which support knowledge creation. According to Nonaka, leaders have to embrace and foster the dynamism of knowledge. The role of top management is to provide *ba* for knowledge creation. Their task is to manage knowledge emergence. The success of knowledge creation depends on management's assumption of responsibility, justification, financial backing and caring (Nonaka and Konno, op. cit.).

Ruohotie (1996) summarises several learning organisation studies. He emphasises that learning has become increasingly important to the success of organisations. By achieving high quality learning, 'core learning', and core competence building, the organisation may gain a permanent competitive advantage. He uses the concept 'core learning' to refer to collective learning and mastery. Core learning requires high learning skills and commitment to common goals, beyond regular norms. Team organisation supports business activity based on core learning, but it is difficult, if not impossible, to accomplish core learning in a hierarchical organisation. The concept of core competence includes the following ideas: collective skills; diverse social abilities; the skill to communicate and transfer skills both vertically and horizontally within the organisation and to associated interest groups; the ability to unify innovatively the existing skills, and to create new knowledge of the organisation's processes or products.

Ruohotie (1996, p. 49) gives this definition:

> The learning organization is a community which is able and willing to question its performances and customs, thus providing creative conflict. Questioning is the positive catalyst for change. This requires a culture within the organization which sees questioners as a positive force; that is, a prerequisite for and not a brake on development. A learning organization can adopt its structure and behaviour to meet the requirements of the situation, it develops its skills continuously to influence its own future, and it is always involved in improvements of its performance and in learning from its experience.

An environment which encourages creativity and innovation is characterised by, among other things, freedom, good project leadership, sufficient resources, support and encouragement, a flexible schedule, challenge and a certain healthy amount of pressure as well.

We need a strong cultural change in learning environments. It means moving towards encouragement and sharing – a culture which allows risk taking and open collaborative problem solving. We have to be aware that competence building necessitates a metacognitive and metamood knowledge of learning and participatory skills. To build new competences we also need changes in system-level conditions. We have to make them support life-wide learning.

We are an integral part of our contextual cultures and traditions, and we reproduce them through our own acts. Schools and working life live with their cultures which originated in their earlier history. These cultures contain a lot of common wisdom, but also many irrelevant practices or concepts which do not support students' or workers' growth into active learners. We also carry our learning culture from the earlier times of our own school life, and it forms our concepts and ideals which we regard as aims of learning (Niemi, 2000). We also must be critical, and seek new values and practices for learning, if the earlier structures seem to prevent more than support the learning of different individuals and groups.

10.5   LEARNING AND COMPETENCE BUILDING IN HUMAN BEINGS' LIVES

Competence building in life-wide learning means both an individual and a social perspective to learning. People should learn to learn using different strategies to steer their own learning processes. They need metacognitive skills, metamood skills and participatory skills. Learning to learn is a long lasting, continuous process which starts at an early age in school and continues throughout life, at different ages. Educational institutions and working life should pay more attention to people's learning skills and support them in advancing their capacity to learn. This vertical learning dimension, throughout life, should also help people to become more self-regulated in their learning. If people are self-regulated and have many sided learning skills, they can also transfer their learning strategies and capacity from learning contexts or areas to new situations in their lives. Learning has also the horizontal component. Learning is more and more cross-boundary: school, working life, home, leisure time, hobbies, and virtual learning environments are all learning spaces which may support learners' capacities. But we must see that learning is also an essential value question (Niemi, 1999). It is not only a rational and intellectual process. It is a holistic process, which touches learners' emotions and values and also has a social component. If we accept this approach, we may ask questions related to the meaningfulness of learning: why do people want to learn and why do they not want to learn? There may be many individual reasons based on earlier learning experiences – encouraging and depressing. But meaningfulness also comes from the social atmosphere in companies or educational institutions. A supportive and flexible infrastructure is needed. We need system-level structures which respect humanity and the real needs of people. Learners need a lot of human support and encouragement. But they also need a sense that they can give something to others, share something. They need a feeling that they are needed for what they are, that they are of value to the community. Their competence is an important part of the wholeness. We have to ask critically what we should renew in our systems to get them, more interactively, to support learners to become empowered by learning. We should see people as holistic, moral, emotional and intellectual agents, who need each other, and meaningfulness and purpose in their lives, also in competence building.

REFERENCES

Alexander, P.A. (1996). 'The Past, Present and Future of Knowledge Research: A Re-Examination of the Role of Knowledge in Learning and Instruction. Editor's Notes to a Special Issue on the Role of Knowledge in Learning and Instruction.' *Educational Psychologist* 31(2): 89–92.

Alheit, P. and Kammler, E. (eds) (1998). *Lifelong Learning and Its Impact on Social and Regional Development*. Contributions to the first European Conference on Lifelong Learning Bremen, 3–5 October 1996, Bremen: Donat.

Biggs, J. (1988). 'The Role of Metacognition in Enhancing Learning', *Australian Journal of Education* 32: 127–38.

Boekaerts, M. (1995). 'Self-Regulated Learning: Bridging the Gap Between Metacognitive and Metamotivational Theories', *Educational Psychologist* 30(4): 195–200.

Boekaerts, M. (1997). 'Self-Regulated Learning: A New Concept Embraced by Researchers, Policy Makers, Educators, Teachers, and Students', *Learning and Instruction* 7(2): 161–86.

Borkowski, J.G. (1996). 'Metacognition: Theory or Chapter Heading', *Learning and Individual Differences* 8(4): 391–402.

Boud, D. (1995). *Enhancing Learning Through Self Assessment*. London: Kogan Page.

Butler, R. (1998). 'Determinants of Help-Seeking: Relations Between Perceived Reasons for Classroom Help-Avoidance and Help-Seeking Behaviors in an Experimental Context', *Journal of Educational Psychology* 90(3): 630–43.

Case, R. (1996). 'Changing Views of Knowledge and Their Impact on Educational Research and Practice', in D.R. Olson, N. Torrance (eds), *The Handbook of Education and Human Development. New Models of Learning, Teaching and Schooling*, London: Blackwell, pp. 75–99.

Cobb, P. (1994). 'Where is the Mind? Constructivist and Sociocultural Perspectives on Mathematical Development', *Educational Researcher* 23(7): 13–20.

Cochinaux, P. and de Woot, P. (1995). *Moving Towards a Learning Society. A CREERT Forum Report on European Education,* Geneva: CRE and Brussels: ERT.

Cole, M. (1991). 'Conclusion' in L.B. Resnick, J.M. Levine, S.D. Teasley (eds), *Perspectives On Socially Shared Cognition*. Washington, DC: American Psychological Association, pp. 398–417.

Corkill, A. (1996). 'Individual Differences in Metacognition', *Learning and Individual Differences* 8(4): 276–80.

Dohmen, G. (1999). 'Lifelong Learning for All – Innovative Perspectives of Continuing Education', *Lifelong Learning in Europe* 4(2): 154–158.

Elder, L. (1997). 'Critical Thinking: The Key to Emotional Intelligence', *Journal of Developmental Education* 21(1): 40–41.

El-Hindi, A.E. (1997). 'Connecting Reading and Writing: College Learners' Metacognitive Awareness', *Journal of Developmental Education* 21(2): 10–6.

Engeström, Y. (1995). 'Innovative Organizational Learning in Medical and Legal Settings', in L. Martin, K. Nielsen and E. Tobach (eds), *Sociocultural Psychology: Theory and Practice of Doing and Knowing*. Cambridge: Cambridge University Press, 64–103.

Flavell, J. (1979). 'Metacognition and Cognitive Monitoring: A New Area of Cognitive-Developmental Inquiry', *American Psychologist* 34: 906–11.

Gardner, H. (1993). *Multiple Intelligences! The Theory in Practice*. New York: Basic Books.

Gardner, H., and Hatch, T. (1989). 'Multiple Intelligences Go to School', *Educational Researcher* 18(8): 4–9.

Goleman, D. (1995). *Emotional Intelligence: Why It Can Matter More Than IQ*, New York: Bantam Books.

Hansen, T., Dirckinck-Holmfeld, L., Lewis, R. and Rugelj, J. (1999). 'Using Telematics for Collaborative Knowledge Construction', in P. Dillenbourg (ed.), *Collaborative Learning. Cognitive and Computational Approaches*, Oxford: Pergamon, pp. 168–96.

Hooper, A. and Potter, J. (2000). *Intelligent Leadership: Creating a Passion for Change*, London: Random House.

Lundvall, B-Å. (2000). 'Towards a Learning Society. Innovation and Competence Building with Social Cohesion for Europe: Europe and the Learning Economy – on the Need for Reintegrating Strategies of Firms, Social Partners and Policy Makers'. Background notes for presentation at the Lisbon seminar, 28–30 May. Aalborg: Department of Business Studies, Aalborg University.

Mandl, H. (1997). 'How Should We Learn to Really Learn? Interview', *Lifelong Learning in Europe* 2(4): 195–9.

McInerney, V., McInerney, D.M. and Marsh, H. (1997). 'Effects of Metacognitive Strategy Training Within Cooperative Group Learning Context on Computer Achivements and Anxiety: An Aptitude-Treatment Interaction Study', *Journal of Educational Psychology* 89(4): 686–95.

Newman, R.S. (1998). 'Students' Help Seeking During Problem Solving: Influences of Personal and Contextual Achievement Goals', *Journal of Educational Psychology* 90(3): 644–58.

Niemi, H. (1996). 'Effectiveness of Teacher Education: A Theoretical Framework of Communicative Evaluation and the Design of a Finnish Research Project', in H. Niemi and K. Tirri (eds), *Effectiveness of Teacher Education. New challenges and Approaches to Evaluation*, Reports from the Department of Teacher Education, Tampere University, A 6, pp. 11–32.

Niemi, H. (1999). 'Recreating Values', in H. Niemi. (ed.), *Moving Horizons in Education: International Transformations and Challenges of Democracy*, Helsinki: Helsinki University Press, pp. 211–28.

Niemi, H. (2000). 'Why is Active Learning So Difficult?', in Beairsto, B. and Ruohotie, P. (eds) *Empowering Teachers as Lifelong Learners: Reconceptualizing, Restructuring and Reculturing Teacher Education for the Information Age*. Hämeenlinna: Research Centre for Vocational Education, 97–126.

Niemi, H. and Kemmis, S. (1999). 'Communicative Evaluation: Evaluation at the Crossroads', *Life Long Learning In Europe* 1: 55–64.

Nonaka, I. and Konno, N. (1998). 'The Concept of "*Ba*": Building a Foundation for Knowledge Creation', *California Management Review* 40(3): 40–54.

OECD (1998a). *Knowledge, Skills and Competence*. Paris: OECD.

OECD (1998b). *Human Capital Investment: An International Comparison,* Paris: OECD.

Oliver. P. (ed.) (1999). *Monitoring Change in Education: Lifelong and Continuing Education What Is A Learning Society,* Aldershot: Ashgate.

Pintrich, P. R. (1999). 'The Role of Motivation in Promoting and Sustaining Self-Regulated Learning', *International Journal of Educational Research* 31(6): 459–70.

Pintrich, P.R. (1995). 'Current Issues in Research on Self-Regulated Learning: A Discussion with Commentaries', *Educational Psychologist,* Special issue 30(4).

Pintrich, P.R. and Garcia, T. (1991). 'Students Goal Orientation and Self-Regulation in the College Classroom', in M.L. Maer, P.R. Pintrich (eds), *Advances in Motivation and Achievement: Goals and Self-Regulatory Processes,* Greenwich, CT: JAI Press, pp. 371–402.

Pintrich, P.R. and Ruohotie, P. (2000). *Cognative Constructs and Self-Regulated Learning,* Hämeenlinna: Research Centre for Vocational Education.

Reynolds, R.E., Sinatra, G.M. and Jetton, T.L. (1996). 'Views of Knowledge Acquisition and Representation: A Continuum from Experience Centered to Mind Centered. *Educational Psychologist* 31(2): 93–104.

Richardson, J.T.E. (2000). *Researching Student Learning. Approaches to Studying In Campus-Based and Distance Education.* Buckingham: The Society for Research into Higher Education and the Open University Press.

Ruohotie, P. (1994). 'Motivation and Self-Regulated Learning', in P. Ruohotie and P. Grimmett (eds), *New Themes for Education in a Changing World,* Tampere: Career Development Finland, pp. 15–59.

Ruohotie, P. (1996). 'Professional Growth and Development in Organizations', in P. Ruohotie and P. Grimmett, (eds) *Professional Growth and Development. Direction, Delivery and Dilemmas.* Saarijärvi Career Development, Finland, pp. 9–70.

Ryan, A.M., Gheen, M.H. and Midgley, C. (1998). 'Why Do Some Students Avoid Asking for Help? An Examination of the Interplay Among Students' Academic Efficacy, Teachers' Social-Emotional Role, and the Classroom Goal Structure', *Journal of Educational Psychology* 90(3): 528–35.

Salovey, P.and Mayer, J.D. (1997). What is Emotional Intelligence?' in P. Salovey, and D.J. Sluyter (eds) *Emotional Development and Emotional Intelligence. Educational Implications, New York: Basic Books* pp. 3–32.

Salovey, P., Mayer, J.D., Goldman, S.L., Turvey, C. and Palfai, T.P. (1995). 'Emotional Attention, Clarity, and Repair: Exploring Emotional Intelligence Using the Trait Meta-Mood Scale', in J.W. Pennebaker (ed.), *Emotion, Disclosure, and Health,* Washington, DC: APA, pp. 125–54.

Schunk, D. and Zimmerman, B. (1994). *Self-Regulation of Learning and Performance: Issues and Educational Applications,* Hillsdale, NJ: Erlbaum.

Simpson, O. (2000). *Supporting Students in Open and Distance Learning,* London: Kogan Page.

Slavin, R.E. (1997). 'Co-operative Learning Among Students', in D. Stern, G. L. Huber (eds), *Active Learning for Students and Teachers: Reports from Eight OECD Countries,* Frankfurt-am-Main: Peter Lang, pp. 159–73.

Stewart, J. and Landine, J. (1998). Relationship Between Metcognition, Motivation, Locus of Control, Self-Efficacy, and Academic Achievement. Canadian Journal of Counselling 32 (3): 200–212.

White Paper on Education and Training (1995). Brussels: Commission of the European Communities.

Winne, P.H. (1996). 'A Metacognitive View of Individual Differences in Self-Regulated Learning', *Learning and Individual Differences* 8(4), 327–354.

Wolters, C.A. (1998). 'Self-Regulated Learning and College Students' Regulation of Motivation', *Journal of Educational Psychology* 90 (2): 224–35.

Young, M. (1998). 'Can Lifelong Learning Prevent the Breakdown of Society', in P. Alheit E. Kammler (eds) *Lifelong Learning and Its Impact on Social and Regional Development,* Contributions to the first European Conference on Lifelong Learning, Bremen, 3–5 October 1996, pp. 21–9.

11. Trade unions in Western Europe: an overview and prospects for social inclusion and competence building

Alison Booth

11.1   INTRODUCTION

Most policy makers are in agreement about the need to find the right balance between social guarantees – or *social inclusion* – on the one hand, and labour market flexibility on the other. Education and training, or *competence building,* are seen as a means of encouraging growth and reducing unemployment, and thereby increasing the welfare of all members of society.[1] Trade unions in Western European countries have the potential to play a powerful role in affecting output and growth, not to mention social exclusion and competence building. It is therefore interesting to consider how the role of trade unions may be changing, and to summarise the potential of unions to have a positive effect.

At the end of the 20th century, union membership in Western Europe had declined continuously for two decades, and just under one third of Europe's workforce belonged to a trade union. This continuous decline has led to much speculation about the future of trade unions in Europe, and to the coining of a new phrase – 'de-unionisation'. Against this background, the goals of this chapter are the following. The first is to chart the position of trade unions in Western Europe at the start of the 21st century. The second is to consider whether Europeanisation of industrial relations might follow (i) the Europeanisation of monetary policy, (ii) product market integration, and (iii) social policy through the European Commission directives. The final goal is to consider the prospects for unions in Western Europe of playing a role in facilitating innovation and competence building.

The chapter is set out as follows. Section 11.2 examines union membership at the end of the 20th century, while Section 11.3 looks at three other components of union power – coverage, coordination and centralisation.

Section 11.4 investigates the prospects for union density in the future, given the decline observed in the past two decades. Section 11.5 then goes on to speculate on the prospects for pan-European collective bargaining given three important recent developments, while the final section of this chapter considers the prospects for unions of facilitating innovation and competence building with social inclusion.

11.2 UNION MEMBERSHIP AT THE END OF THE TWENTIETH CENTURY

Figure 11.1 plots U.S. and European union density over the last four decades of the 20th century. Union density rates are defined here as union membership expressed as a proportion of employees in work – or 'net' union density.[2] The peak for Western Europe density was 44 per cent in 1979. It now stands at 32 per cent, lower than at any time since 1960. The US density figures make a striking contrast, and the average EU-wide density is still more than twice that of the US.

Concomitant with the decrease in European union density since 1979 has been a decline in militancy, a fall in the share of output going to labour, and a rise in aggregate unemployment. In the European Union, the number of working days lost as a result of labour conflicts fell from 85 million in 1979 to less than seven million in 1996 (CEC, 2000; Ebbinghaus and Visser, 2000). In the past two decades, the rate of increase in real wages has decreased in all EU Member States. Consequently, unit labour costs have fallen, by about six per cent between 1991 and 1998, against a small rise in the US (CEC, op. cit.; Ebbinghaus and Visser, op. cit.).

How does union density vary across the countries comprising the European Union? Table 11.1 gives the cross-country breakdown. Inspection of Table 11.1 reveals a number of interesting facts. First, there is considerable cross-country heterogeneity, reflecting the diversity of institutional arrangements with regard to collective bargaining. In France, density was only ten per cent in 1997, while in Sweden it was 86 per cent. The second lowest density in 1997 was 17 per cent in Spain, one third of whose workforce is in temporary work. The Nordic countries have the highest levels of density, followed by Belgium. This probably reflects the institutional arrangements in these countries for unemployment benefits (the 'Ghent system' whereby unions administer unemployment schemes). Secondly, Table 11.1 reveals that some countries (Austria, the Netherlands, Switzerland and France) peaked in density considerably earlier than others. In Denmark and Sweden the small recent decline in density may well reflect just short term fluctuations rather than some long term trend decline. The Netherlands and

Britain (countries whose workforces comprise a large proportion of part time women) had in 1997 levels of union density of 24 per cent and 30 per cent respectively.[3]

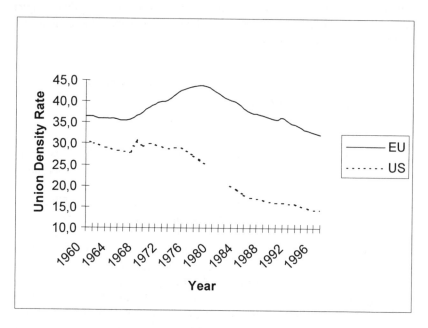

Note: The EU rate is a weighted average of 13 countries, that is, all fifteen current Member States except Greece, Portugal, Spain and Luxembourg, but with Norway and Switzerland. With the four excluded countries (for which no continuous data are available) the current EU density rate would be a few percentage points lower.

Source: Ebbinghaus and Visser (2000).

Figure 11.1   Unionisation EU–US

One important reason for the decline in union density in Western Europe is macroeconomic factors. These include the shift in macroeconomic policy that emerged in the 1980s, when governments and central banks (with a few exceptions such as Sweden), adopted a non-accommodating monetarist stance. This brought about wage restraint through growing levels of aggregate unemployment (Ebbinghaus and Visser, 2000).

Traditional explanations suggest that aggregate unemployment may well have a negative effect on union density. During booms, market forces induce firms to grant wage increases, whereas during recessions employers' bargaining power is strengthened, and they are more likely to reject unions' demands. However, unemployment might be positively correlated with union density, when for example, unions administer unemployment benefit schemes – the so-called 'Ghent system', or may negotiate seniority deals and redundancy packages.

Table 11.1   Union density rates, 1950–1997

Country	1950	1960	1970	1975	1980	1985	1990	1995	1997
Sweden	67	71	67	73	78	82	82	88	86
Finland	30	32	51	65	69	69	73	89	78
Denmark	56	62	63	69	79	78	75	77	76
Norway	45	52	50	52	55	56	56	55	55
Belgium	43	42	42	52	53	51	50	53	..
Ireland	42	50	59	62	64	63	59	52	..
Austria	62	60	57	53	52	52	47	41	39
Italy	45	28	37	48	50	42	39	39	37
United Kingdom	45	45	50	54	56	50	43	36	..
Great Britain	44	44	47	50	52	43	38	32	30
Germany	..	..	..	..	..	..	36	29	27
Germany (West	38	35	32	35	35	34	32	..	..
Germany (East)	..	..	..	..	..	..	47	..	
Portugal	..	..	..	..	52	..	40	30	..
Netherlands	43	42	37	38	35	28	24	24	24
Switzerland	40	39	30	32	31	28	27	24	23
Greece	..	..	..	36..	36	37	34	24	..
Spain	..	..	..	30	8	10	12	18	17
France	30	24	20	22	22	19	14	10	10

Source: Ebbinghaus and Visser (2000).

The decline in union density is related not only to the rise in European unemployment but also to structural changes in labour market participation and employment (such as the growth in 'non-standard' jobs such as temporary work, work done at unusual times or places, and non-standard hours). The proportion of workers in fixed term contracts in France, Italy and Spain increased respectively from 4.7, 4.8 and 15.6 per cent in 1985 to 13.1, 8.2 and 33.6 per cent in 1997. In 1997, of the 150 million workers in the European Union, about 12 percent were employed on fixed term contracts (European Commission, 1999). The Netherlands has the highest proportion of female workers in part time jobs (at approximately 68 per cent), followed by the UK (45 per cent), then Denmark and Germany (OECD, 1999). Greece has the lowest proportion, with Portugal a close second. It seems highly likely that increases in non-standard work have contributed to the decline in union density in Western Europe. Employment in small firms and the service sector has also been expanding.

Fewer young workers have in recent years joined trade unions, and thus the average age of union members has increased. The retirement age across Western Europe has also been declining, and as a result not only is the average duration of lifetime union membership becoming shorter, but a significant proportion of members will leave the unions in coming years.[4] For these reasons, unions will have to run very hard to remain in the one spot.

What about union density and gender? The feminisation of the European labour force is continuing, and it is well known that unions have not always looked after the interests of female workers. And in many countries there is still a considerable gap between male and female unionisation rates (Ebbinghaus and Visser, 1999). However, these gender differences are narrowing, in part because of the fact that women are increasingly likely to join unions, especially when they work in the public sector. We might expect in the future that the inclusion of a formerly excluded section of society might have implications for the bargaining agenda of trade unions.

Of course union density is only one facet of union power – albeit an appealing one because it is easily measured, and it fluctuates considerably over time. There are other important aspects of union strength.

11.3   THE THREE C'S: COVERAGE, COORDINATION AND CENTRALISATION

Other important aspects of union power include the extent of union coverage, the degree of coordination of unions or employers' groups or both, and the degree of centralisation of union bargaining (which might take place at the firm level, the industry level or the national level). The order in which different collective bargains are reached can also provide variation in bargaining structure and may affect union power over wage setting. For example, higher level or first mover bargains can set benchmark agreements, and these can affect the outcomes of subsequent or more decentralised bargains. In many cases, union coverage, centralisation and coordination may have a more profound effect on macroeconomic performance and union wage gains than union density.

Table 11.2 gives union coverage and coordination for Western European countries in 1994. The first column gives union coverage. The coverage variable takes three values, where 3 represents more than 70 per cent of the workforce covered, 2 denotes from 25–70 per cent, while 1 is less than 25 per cent. (Table 11.3 gives a more disaggregated coverage measure.) The second column in Table 11.2 comprises coordination measures (union and employer separately). In each country, the degree of union, then employer, co-ordination is ranked from a low of 1 to a maximum of 3. The most coordinated countries are Austria, Denmark, Norway and Sweden; these countries also have the highest level of coverage (column 2).

Table 11.3 presents union density (column 1) and union coverage (column 2) for 1994, while column 3 gives the difference between the two. Column 3 might be loosely thought of as the proportion of the working population taking a 'free ride' on union membership, since it shows the fraction of workers who receive the benefits of union coverage in terms of higher wages, without incurring the psychic or monetary costs of membership. France has the highest proportion of 'free riders', although this reflects not only very low membership but also very high coverage.

The bargaining structure seems to matter for a country's macroeconomic performance, either because it affects outcomes directly, or indirectly through its interaction with other institutions or with external shocks. The mechanisms through which this may occur are as follows (Calmfors and Driffill, 1988; Boeri et al, 2001). With *decentralised* bargaining, if the decentralised union sets a high money wage, the firm will want to pass this on in the form of higher prices for its product. If the firm is one of many in the industry, the firm's product will be a close substitute for that of other firms. If the firm passes on higher nominal wage costs in the form of higher prices, demand for its product will fall and so too will employment, Thus any real wage gain will be at the cost of higher unemployment. Since a rational union will be aware of this, the decentralised union will not push for too high money wage increases.

In the case of *centralised* bargaining, if the union confederation increases nominal wages, firms will pass this on in the form of higher product prices, and consequently workers' wages will not rise. If the monetary authorities adopt a non-accommodating stance, the real money supply will contract, reducing aggregate demand and thereby increasing aggregate unemployment. Since the union will be aware of the fact that an increase in nominal wages will lead to aggregate unemployment, it will not push for wages that are too high.

Table 11.2   Features of OECD labour markets, 1989–1994

Country	Union coverage index (1994)	Coordination (1994)	
		Union	Employer
Austria	3	3	3
Belgium	3	2	2
Denmark	3	3	3
Finland	3	2	3
France	3	2	2
Germany (W)	3	2	3
Ireland	3	1	1
Italy	3	2	2
Netherlands	3	2	2
Norway	3	3	3
Portugal	3	2	2
Spain	3	2	1
Sweden	3	3	3
Switzerland	2	1	3
United Kingdom	2	1	1

Source: Nickell (1997: Table 5); OECD *Employment Outlook* (1994)

Table 11.3   Union density and coverage in Europe (%)

Country	Union density (1994)	Union coverage (1994)	Extent of 'free riders'
Austria	42	98	56
Belgium	54	90	36
Denmark	76	69	-7
Finland	81	95	14
France	9	95	86
Germany	29	92	63
Italy	39	82	43
Netherlands	26	81	55
Norway	58	74	16
Portugal	32	71	39
Spain	19	78	69
Sweden	91	89	-3
Switzerland	27	50	23
United Kingdom	34	47	13

Source: OECD *Employment Outlook* (1997)

Although centrally agreed wage settlements are supposedly applicable to all sectors of the economy, they are often associated with wage drift (the tendency for certain sectors of the economy to negotiate for themselves wage increases above the central wage agreement). So the success of centralised bargaining in constraining wage increases and maintaining high employment levels depends on the degree to which union confederations can be *coordinated* to avoid wage drift.[5] Coordinated bargaining may also provide a mechanism for the pooling of information about wage-setting, and thereby coordinate expectations. Coordination amongst employers will also restrain wage increases, since firms will find it easier to resist demands for high nominal wage increases if they are acting together (and can also exert pressure on one another).

Intermediate levels of coordination and centralisation seem to have the most harmful effects on wage setting and aggregate unemployment (see Calmfors and Driffill, op. cit.; OECD, 1999). And it seems to be the combination of centralisation *and* coordination that produces the least harmful effects on macroeconomic outcomes. For example, Nickell (1997) regresses aggregate unemployment on various features of labour markets (including union membership, a coverage index, and the union-firm coordination indices reported in Table 11.3), using OECD data. He concludes that only some 'labour market rigidities' cause unemployment. One of these is high union density with collective bargaining and no co-ordination between unions and employers in wage bargaining. However, high union density with collective bargaining *and* high coordination between unions and employers has no adverse effect on aggregate unemployment.

Of considerable interest is the notion that labour market institutions may affect the impact of exogenous macroeconomic shocks on the evolution of macroeconomic outcomes in Western Europe. The idea is that bargaining structure might affect the flexibility of both nominal and real wages, and thus affect aggregate unemployment (Calmfors, op. cit.). Blanchard and Wolfers (2000) find that the responses to negative unemployment shocks have been larger in countries with less coordination of wage setting and higher union density and coverage. Their suggested interpretation is that it may be easier to slow down real wage growth in response to say a reduction in productivity growth if this can be done in a coordinated fashion across trade unions.

11.4.   PROSPECTS FOR TRADE UNION MEMBERSHIP IN THE FUTURE

What is likely to happen to union density in Western Europe in the future? Based on current trends, it seems highly likely that density will continue to fall, owing to the growth in non-standard work and the expansion of the service sector. Moreover, some of the EU Directives may undercut unions' attempts to expand into non-standard work, since the directives provide protection that unions might otherwise have supplied. In the UK, however, it may be that the unions will be able to play a role in monitoring compliance with the EU Directive on, for example, fixed term contracts. Furthermore, the EU Directive on Works Councils may strengthen membership at the local level, and collection of dues and other aspects of organisation may be easier with the new information technology. The integration of product markets might also have quite complex effects, as will be discussed below.

What impact will declining union density have on union influence? Secular declines in union density raise problems for the credibility of the trade union movement, since unions will lose influence with government, especially where there is decentralisation of bargaining. We now turn to speculating on the prospects for pan-European collective bargaining.

11.4.1   Prospects for Pan-European Collective Bargaining

Concomitant with the decline in union density in Western Europe has been a remarkable strengthening of union activity within the institutional framework of the EU, especially within the final decade of the 20th century. The Maastricht and Amsterdam Treaties (1993, 1997) have institutionalised unions and employers as 'social partners', who are not only to be consulted about new Community legislation, but can also start negotiations and conclude an agreement, which preempts – or becomes the basis for – Community legislation (Ebbinghaus and Visser, op. cit.). The Europeanisation of monetary policy has also encouraged a range of union initiatives to coordinate transnational collective bargaining, in conjunction with the so-called Macroeconomic Dialogue, within the framework of the Employment Pact established by the EU in 1999. (This involves the European Central Bank (ECB), the EU Ministers of Finance, the Commission, and European-level union and employers organisations.) At the same time, Western Europe has experienced product market integration, involving the removal of barriers to trade, and the removal of barriers to intra-EU migration. The three developments – product market integration, the Europeanisation of monetary policy, and the strengthening of union activity within the institutional framework of the European Union – are likely to have a profound impact on European trade unions in the 21st century. I now offer some conjectures about how these developments might affect Western European collective bargaining in the future.[6]

11.4.2   Europeanisation of Monetary Policy

Will European integration and monetary unification promote coordination of wage bargaining at the European level? European monetary unification is likely to change the incentives for union wage setting under present institutional conditions, as well as to alter the bargaining structure itself. Calmfors (op. cit.) identifies two mechanisms that work in this direction. First, increased product market competition among countries has weakened the power of unions relative to employers. A natural response of unions would be to cooperate across borders at the sectoral level, in order to prevent national attempts to achieve wage competitiveness leading to a reduction of labour's share of national income.[7] However, attempts to coordinate bargaining transnationally only within individual sectors would be harmful from the point of view of employment, as the competitive forces restraining wages would be weakened (Calmfors, op. cit.; see also Section 11.2 above).

It is possible that a second type of transnational bargaining coordination might be set up, with the objective of establishing at the European level the earlier relationship between German unions and the Bundesbank. Unions from different EU countries might consider coordination in order to become a more equal 'partner' to the ECB (especially within the Macroeconomic Dialogue). More coordination of wage bargaining at the European level could have favourable macroeconomic effects, to the extent that the anticipated monetary policy responses of the ECB to wage settlements could be taken into account. Of course an obvious drawback of such coordination is that it might reduce the responsiveness of wage setting in individual countries to country-specific shocks.

While there are incentives for more transnational cooperation, moves towards this will inevitably be very slow. Bargaining institutions in various countries have developed over a long time and in a variety of ways. As with all institutions, they are characterised by considerable inertia. This suggests that the costs of transnational coordination are likely to be very large.

While formal transnational coordination is probably not very likely in the foreseeable future, what about the establishment of coordination through *pattern bargaining*? This would after all involve much lower coordination costs than formal cooperation. But pattern bargaining will be much more difficult to achieve at the European than at the national level, because each union is very much smaller compared to the total labour market. Potential problems are first, that there is the free rider problem to be overcome. Second, a wage leader has to be agreed upon, and there could be some resistance to German wage leadership. While unions in Austria, Belgium and the Netherlands have used comparisons with German wage setting, it is probable that unions in France, the UK, Spain and Italy would oppose being dominated by German unions (Boeri et al, 2001). Third, even if a leader union in one country could be agreed upon, this union might also have trouble convincing rank and file members that they should take into account European rather than national conditions when formulating their wage demands (Calmfors, op. cit.). Fourthly, the declining importance of the traditional manufacturing sector with its strong unions also makes it much more difficult for a union such as IG Metall to take on the role of wage leader.

11.4.3   The Impact of Product Market Integration

Will European product market integration promote coordination of wage bargaining at the European level? If there is increased product market competition as a result of removal of barriers to trade, then the available surplus to be shared between labour and capital will be lower than before integration. Therefore the expected returns to trade unions from concerted bargaining will be outweighed by the very large costs of coordination, already mentioned.

But on the other hand, if product market integration results in a few large international firms – who may behave oligopolistically – then rents may actually increase (Boeri et al, 2001). Consequently the expected gains to unions from pan-European coordination may outweigh the costs. Moreover, any loss of union power associated with dwindling union membership might induce trade unions to act in concert or even to merge in order to reduce costs.[8] But even if the rents were to increase with product market integration, how can unions induce firms to share this surplus? Booth (1995) emphasised two necessary conditions for unions' ability to negotiate wage increases – there should be some surplus to be bargained over, and the union should have the power to induce the firm to share these rents (perhaps by the ultimate threat of labour withdrawal). If companies are pan-European, the threat of European-wide labour withdrawal will be much greater than the threat of simply national labour withdrawal. However, if companies are actually global rather than pan-European, the effect will be very small.

Of course product market integration may result not only in more trade, but also in increased foreign direct investment (FDI). FDI may occur not only in order to increase profits but also in order to achieve strategic labour market objectives (Naylor, 1999). Having production units in a variety of countries can increase the bargaining power of firms, which can then credibly threaten to shift production during industrial disputes. Product market integration may facilitate the possibility of firms strategically placing various production units in different European – or, as is increasingly likely, Asian and South American – countries, in order to pick off organised labour. This could have the effect of weakening union power at whatever level of coordination at the European level.

However, services are a different matter. In the case of services, firms need to locate close to the product market. Traditionally, unions have tended to be less well organised in service industries than in manufacturing, though there is evidence that this is changing.[9] The geographically tied nature of service industries may enable unions to develop membership and organisation in these industries more effectively than in increasingly foot loose manufacturing industries.

The incentives for unions to move to pan-European collective bargaining – in terms of labour's expected share of any rents – will vary considerably across industries. At the present time, European countries are characterised by very different levels of union bargaining and coordination, ranging from firm level, to industry level to national level. It is not difficult to imagine a scenario in which particular unions who will gain from pan-European coordination move to this, but that in effect this may actually be bargaining at the organisational level. Other unions – for example those in particular services – might gain more from moving to a completely decentralised level of bargaining. So we might actually see a break up of the consensual style of some European countries of the last few years and a shift to a more decentralised system, as is already happening to some extent (see Booth et al., op. cit., Chapter 6).

Of course unions and firms are not the only actors who might be involved in such a move towards or away from pan-European coordination – the European Commission also has an agenda. To this we now turn.

11.4.4   The European Commission and the Social Charter

Will the strengthening of union activity within the institutional framework of the European Union promote coordination of wage bargaining at the European level, or even lead to a new pan-European industrial relations system? The 'social policy' strategies of the European Commission are likely to have a profound effect on European trade unions, not least because many of the EU Directives may arguably be seen as substitutes for union collective bargaining arrangements. In the UK, for example, some unions are currently trying to organise non-standard workers. Since the terms and conditions of these workers are soon to be affected by the provisions of the EU Directives of 2000 (part time work) and 2001 (fixed term workers), it is not clear quite what these workers would gain from union membership. (We use the term 'social policy' in the continental European sense of encompassing both the welfare state and the industrial relations system, and not in the narrower sense used in Britain, referring simply to the welfare state.)

In some countries in which works councils have the most influence, there are strong strictures against direct union participation in them (Booth et al., op.cit., Chapter 5). However, participation is allowed indirectly (German works councils are prohibited from negotiating over wages and benefits normally covered by collective bargaining). More recently, works councils have assumed considerable importance in policy debate, with the European Directive on Works Councils. It remains to be seen if works councils are a substitute for or complement to union activity.

An important question arises as to the relevance of the European Social Dialogue for all groups of society. It has been criticised for its apparent exclusion of other pertinent groups and the absence of citizen involvement, and it is not clear that it represents union members' interests. It certainly cannot be regarded as being a socially inclusive arrangement.

It seems highly unlikely that an EU-wide model of industrial relations will emerge from the cooperation of the social partners and supranational institutions, at least in the medium term. One reason is that national actors are unwilling to lose autonomy to the supranational level, which is viewed as suffering from a weak institutional structure (Keller and Sorries, 1999). However, there are some incentives that might shift the relevant actors towards co-ordination. For example, the introduction of qualified majority voting has meant that one or more governments can be overruled by the majority, which is likely to provide an impetus to trade unions and employers' groups to coordinate their lobbying at the European level. Such coordination will be necessary, in order to persuade a sufficient number of governments of their arguments, and thereby form a majority. While this is very costly, the expected benefits might outweigh the costs.[10]

Another reason why it is improbable that we shall see a central unified system of industrial relations is that it is extremely unlikely to be a feasible option politically (since it would involve centralisation of power). Moreover, this will become even less feasible in the medium term as membership of the European Union is expanded to include more countries, which will increase coordination costs and the diversity of membership.[11]

A further obstacle is that trade unions play a significant role in many European countries in managing heterogeneous national social insurance systems. Thus a double hurdle would have to be crossed to achieve a central European system of industrial relations – convergence of social insurance systems, and centralisation of trade union activities – unless the link between unions and social insurance were to be broken. Such an outcome is highly improbable.

In conclusion, it will probably be a very long time before we observe European coordination in EU-wide collective bargaining over wages. Indeed, if union density continues to decline at its current rate, EU-wide cooperation might never occur. However, in the short term we shall probably observe the paradox of more trans-national coordination of trade union activity through the European Commission at the same time as a continuing decline in union density.

11.5   PROSPECTS FOR UNIONS TO FOSTER INNOVATION, COMPETENCE BUILDING AND SOCIAL COHESION

Now I consider the prospects for unions to play a role in the areas of innovation and competence building with social cohesion, a focus of this volume.

It is clear that union governance can play an important role in affecting social inclusion. Clegg's (1979) taxonomy of unions is still relevant today. At one extreme, unions can be viewed as oligarchic, unresponsive to members' wishes, and with an executive securing a monopoly of power to stay in office with low membership participation and apathy. Alternatively unions may be quasi-democratic, due to the presence of informal parties or factions, growth of workplace organisation, and the existence of workplace or postal balloting. Clearly the more democratic the union, the more *inclusive* it is likely to be, at least with regard to representing its *members'* interests. But as we emphasised earlier in this chapter, in many countries in Western Europe there is a substantial divergence between union membership and union coverage. It is therefore likely that unions are not representing the interests of non-members – not just with regard to wage setting but also with regard to family-friendly policies, and competence building or skills acquisition. It is therefore vital – in the interests of social inclusion – that unions are democratic institutions. It will also be important, if unions amalgamate at the European level in the future as a response to the Europeanisation of monetary policy and product market integration, that issues of union governance and democracy are not forgotten.

Trade unions have the potential to make an important contribution to innovation and to competence building. What impact do unions have on innovation? Economic theory predicts that unions will have ambiguous effects on investment in physical capital and innovation (Booth, 1995). The *negative* effects arise through unions acting as rent seeking organisations that increase wages for union-covered workers at the expense of higher levels of unemployment. They can also arise through the fact that unions may reduce individual motivation and morale, obstruct the efficient organisation of capital and labour by constraining the choice set of management, and sometimes enforce restrictive practices (such as 'overmanning') that are likely to reduce productivity and hinder innovation and investment. The *positive* effects of unions on productivity and innovation may arise through the fact that improvements in procedural arrangements associated with unions may increase worker morale and motivation, and facilitate the transmission of workers' preferences and suggestions to management.

It is therefore important to let the data reveal whether there are positive or negative union effects on innovation and investment across the different countries of Western Europe. However, there is scant empirical evidence as to the impact of unions on innovation and investment. Empirical evidence for the US suggests that unions are associated with significantly less investment in physical capital, innovation and R&D. But for the UK, some studies show a positive impact and some a negative impact. It is clear that more systematic European-wide cross-country work needs to be done in this area.[12]

It is well known that unions reduce worker turnover or quitting. This has a number of benefits, including an increase in on-the-job training. As long as unions reduce labour turnover, long lasting work relationships favour investment in firm-specific human capital (Lynch 1994; Esping-Andersen and Regini, 2000). There can also be an additional effect of unions on training if unions bargain over the level of training as well as wages (Streeck, 1989; Mahnkopf, 1992). Using Britain panel data, Arulampalam and Booth (1998) and Booth et al. (2003) find that union-covered workers receive significantly more training and are less likely to quit than their non-union counterparts. Booth et al. (ibid.) also find that union-covered workers who receive work-related training earn lower wages pre-training and higher wages post-training than do otherwise comparable non-union covered workers. While these findings may be peculiar to Britain, they provide support for the hypothesis that unions can create incentives for human capital investment.

However, to my knowledge, there are no published *cross-country* statistical studies investigating this issue across European Union countries. Moreover, the fact that the European Community Household Panel (ECHP) does not so far ask questions about either individual union status or coverage makes it hard for EU-wide comparisons to be made, in any systematic way, about the impact of unions on competence building.

A crucial point – made earlier in this chapter – is that the level of centralisation *and* coordination of wage bargaining can have a profound effect on macroeconomic outcomes, including of course unemployment. The unemployed are an important component of the socially excluded in our society, in which work is the norm. Thus unions can have a powerful – and not always positive – impact on social exclusion. It is clear that in some European countries unions have been remarkably successful in contributing to macroeconomic stability (see for example the recent experience of Denmark and the Netherlands). But it is also evident that there are fundamental changes occurring in the European Union that may threaten the present equilibrium, as I emphasised above when discussing the Europeanisation of monetary policy and product market integration.

What about the impact of trade unions on another group that might be viewed as socially excluded – non-standard workers? The EU Directives have gone some way to cover non-standard workers, but there are many areas where unions could also play a more interactive role. Of course additional benefits for workers have to be paid for in some way if firms' survival is not to be threatened, and hence the discussion in Section 11.3 is relevant here. If unions are representing the interests of all workers – rather than of a narrower group – they are more likely to adopt more moderate wage setting demands.

One way of ensuring that Western Europe has a cooperative industrial relations system might be through social partnerships, which have worked so well for some European Union countries recently. But this would not work for all European Union countries, which are characterised by very different institutional arrangements.[13]

In summary, it is clear that unions in the European Union can have a powerful effect on the macroeconomy, as well as on innovation, competence building and social cohesion. Trade unions have the potential for being potent forces working towards social inclusion and a skills-based economy. But they can also be reactionary, looking after the interests of only a minority of the more standard sections of the workforce, and fighting technological change and innovation at every step. It remains to be seen how unions will develop in these areas as they respond to the challenges facing them in the next decade.

NOTES

1. Many of the views expressed herein developed while working jointly with Michael Burda, Lars Calmfors, Daniel Checchi, Robin Naylor and Jelle Visser on the report *The Role of Unions in the New Millennium* (Booth et al., 2000). I should like to thank them for our lively discussions without implicating them in the opinions expressed in this chapter.
2. Thus retired, unemployed and self-employed union members are excluded from the density measure. The membership data are from the DUES ('Development of Unions in European Societies') project (Ebbinghaus and Visser, 2000; and CD-ROM) and the labour force data (wage and salary earners in employment) are from the OECD's Labour Force Statistics (see Ebbinghaus and Visser, 2000

in Boeri et al.). The membership figures exclude union members among unemployed, self-employed and retired workers, who make up a total of 14 million members, roughly a quarter of the total union membership in Western Europe (Ebbinghaus and Visser, op. cit.).

3.	Chapter 2 in Booth et al. (2000) emphasises three major institutional conditions conducive to union organisation: union access to the workplace, union involvement in the provision and administration of unemployment insurance, and centralisation of collective bargaining. Where all three of these institutions are (or were) present (as in the Nordic countries and, to a large degree, in Belgium), unions appear able to fight off the negative influence on membership growth caused by unemployment and structural change. See also Ebbinghaus and Visser (1999).

4.	See Chapter 2 in (Boeri et al, 2001) for an extensive discussion of the decline in union density and its causes.

5.	Of course centralised bargaining is also associated with fixed relativities across sectors. It thus prevents firms from adjusting relative wages to attract labour to areas experiencing shortages, and this may prevent allocative efficiency. This argument seems especially compelling among German trade unions. In Britain – a country characterised by many trade unions – there has recently emerged the new 'super-union' Trade Unions for Europe (TUFE).

6.	See also Chapter 6 in Booth et al. (2000), which develops four possible scenarios for future collective bargaining in Western Europe, and argues that the most likely outcome is more decentralised bargaining, possibly at the level of the multinational firm.

7.	This argument seems especially compelling among German trade unions.

8.	In Britain – a country characterised by many trade unions – there has recently emerged the new 'super-union', Trade Unions for Europe (TUFE).

9.	At the present time five German service sector unions are discussing combining to form a new 'super union' – ver.di, which would be larger than Europe's present largest union – IG Metall.

10.	It is also important to consider the distinction between the conclusion of collective agreements and their implementation. It is interesting that the Social Protocol allowed the EU framework agreements to be implemented either by Community legislation or by collective bargaining covering the entire workforce via the social partners. A problem with the latter is that there are not high levels of coverage in all member states. Thus a collective agreement would have to be extended to unorganised workers and firms, by erga omnes provisions (they do not exist in all states). See also Booth et al (op. cit.), Chapter 5.

11.	In 1998 the European Union began negotiations with six Central and Eastern European countries seeking EU membership (the Czech Republic, Estonia, Hungary, Poland, Slovenia and Cyprus).

12.	See Booth (1995, pp. 209–11) for a summary of studies estimating union effects on investment and the introduction of new technology.

13.	See (Boeri et al, 2001) for extensive discussion of these issues.

REFERENCES

Arulampalam, W. and Booth, A.L., (1998). 'Training and Labour Market Flexibility: Is There a Trade-off?', *British Journal of Industrial Relations* 36(4): pp 521–36.

Blanchard, O. and Wolfers, J., (2000). 'The Role of Shocks and Institutions in the Rise of European Unemployment: The Aggregate Evidence', *Economic Journal* 110: C1–C33.

Boeri, T., Brugavini, A. and Calmfors, L. (eds) (2001). *The Role of Unions in the Twenty-First Century*, Oxford: Oxford University Press.

Booth, A.L. (1995). *The Economics of the Trade Union*, Cambridge: Cambridge University Press.

Booth, A.L. and Zoega, G. (2003, forthcoming). 'Industrial and Labour Relations Review'.

Booth, A.L., Francesconi, Marco and Zoega, Gylfi (1999). 'General Training, Rent-Sharing and Unions: Theory And Evidence', CEPR Discussion Paper 2200.

Booth, A.L., Burda, M., Calmfors, L., Checchi, D., Naylor, R. and Visser, J. (2000). *The Role of Unions in the New Millennium*, Report for the Fondazione DeBenedetti, presented in Naples 16 June 2000, forthcoming in Boeri, Brugiavini and Calmfors (eds) (2000), Oxford University Press.

Calmfors, L. and Driffill, J. (1988). 'Bargaining Structure, Corporatism and Macroeconomic Performance', *Economic Policy* 6: 13–62.

CEC (2000). *Industrial Relations in Europe*, Brussels: Commission of the European Communities, DGV.

Clegg, H.A. (1979). *The Changing System of Industrial Relations in Great Britain*, Oxford: Blackwell.

Ebbinghaus, B. and Visser, J. (2000). *Trade Unions in Western Europe Since 1945*, Basingstoke: Macmillan.

Esping-Andersen, G. and Regini, M. (eds) (2000). *Why Deregulate Labour Markets?*, Oxford: Oxford University Press.

European Commission (1999). *Employment in Europe 1998*, Luxembourg: Office of Official Publications of the European Communities.

Keller, Berndt and Sorries, Bernd (1999). 'Sectoral Social Dialogues: New Opportunities or More Impasses?', *Industrial Relations Journal* 30(4): 330–344.

Lynch, L.M. (ed.) (1994) *Training and the Private Sector; International Comparisons*, Chicago: University of Chicago Press for NBER.

Mahnkopf, B. (1992). 'The Skill-Oriented Strategies of German Trade Unions: Their Impact on Efficiency and Equality Objectives', *British Journal of Industrial Relations*, 30: 61–81.

Naylor, R. (1999). 'Union Wage Strategies and International Trade', *Economic Journal* 109: 102–25.

Nickell, S.J. (1997). 'Unemployment and Labour Market Rigidities: Europe versus North America', *Journal of Economic Perspectives* 11(3): 55–74.

OECD (1994) *Employment Outlook*, 'Collective Bargaining: Levels and Coverage',
    Paris: OECD.

OECD (1997). *Employment Outlook*, Paris: OECD.

OECD (1999). *Employment Outlook*, 'Part-Time Work' , pp 13–44 Paris: OECD.

Streeck, W. (1989). 'Skills and the Limits of Neo-Liberalism: The Enterprise of the
    Future as a Place of Learning', *Work, Employment and Society* 3: 89–104.

PART FOUR

Striving for social cohesion

Introductory note: Innovation and social cohesion

Pedro Conceição

The concern with promoting social cohesion (which can also be expressed through the 'double negative' of reducing inequality) has been a hallmark of public policy making in Europe for generations. Welfare and social insurance systems are a European invention now diffused and adopted, although with varying degrees of enthusiasm, around the world. Social cohesion, therefore, reflects a moral or political choice of Europeans, often contrasted with the more decentralised North American economic and political system. Along with a weaker welfare system, an important characteristic of the North American economic system is a stronger reliance on litigation rather than on regulation, corresponding to a weaker role for direct and aprioristic government intervention. Social cohesion, to some extent, can be considered a differentiating feature of European policy design and policy making. As a transversal, identity-connected, policy objective of Europe, social cohesion needs to be thought about within the context of the core themes of this volume, centering on the dynamics of the learning economy. While it will not be possible to explore all the manifold ways in which the learning economy influences and determines the extent of social cohesion the contributions in this part of the volume take a different approach.

However, the characterisation of the previous paragraph simplifies too much. As with all simplifications, the contrast between the European and the North American systems based on the strength and depth of welfare systems and strength of regulation is not only abusive, but can actually mischaracterise reality. For example, during the US progressive era (early 20th century) the hand of the government let its presence be very much felt, in large part through a process in which regulation replaced litigation as the 'principal mechanism of social control of business' (Glaeser and Shleifer, 2001). Later, during the post-Great Depression Roosevelt administrations, the US established some of the institutions of a welfare state, admittedly substantially later than what most European countries had at the time. After

261

World War Two the US government launched itself on the major enterprise of publicly supporting science and technology on a scale unmatched by any European country. It was due to strong US government support that 'the computer' emerged (Flamm 1987, 1988) and it was also due to sustained and intensive government efforts that the academic discipline of computer science was established (Langlois and Mowery, 1996). Not to speak, of course, of the well popularised role of the US government in the creation of the internet.

But if the US government's role as a regulatory and technology inducing leader is widely acknowledged, it is less frequently recognised that US society has equally great concerns about social cohesion. The reason for that goes beyond ethical judgements and assessments of fairness: it can be of importance to efficiency as well, as discussed by Galbraith (2000) and Galbraith, Conceição and Ferreira (1999).

Following the brief note in the Introduction to this volume, the major threat to social cohesion in Europe is, according to Galbraith, the relatively high level of unemployment. In fact, unemployment can be considered the most extreme instance of social exclusion: it is not only that wages are low, people are excluded from participating in the labour market at all. This brings us to the contributions in this part of the book. Gallie (Chapter 12) tackles the problem of unemployment from the perspective of the policies and institutions generating or mediating unemployment, finding, among other important things, that poverty is, indeed, often associated with unemployment. Gallie takes, like Galbraith, a genuine European perspective, in the sense that different European countries are analysed comparatively.

The conclusions reached by Gallie challenge some common understandings about the relationship between welfare institutions and unemployment. Gallie paints a picture in which many assumptions are challenged. For example, one commonly stated view indicates that generous welfare provides disincentives to work. Since people work to get paid, and only to get paid, if they can be remunerated in some other way, they will avoid work. However, the results suggest otherwise, namely that unemployed people would like to work, even if they did not need the money. Additionally, commitment to employment is strong in countries with very generous welfare systems.

Gallie's questioning of the generally held assumptions of the disincentives to work associated with generous welfare is, in a way, turned around. In fact, generous unemployment benefits – in the sense that the standards of living of the unemployed are not greatly affected – can encourage risk taking and personal investments in skills. These two aspects combined can lead to a general improvement in competence, enhance innovation or, at least, lead to better matching between skills and occupations.

Saraceno, in Chapter 13, takes the analysis of social cohesion to yet a different level, focusing on 'local' communities or societies. The spatial patterns of social cohesion are clear and, according to several studies and Saraceno's own perspective, largely self-reinforcing. Saraceno highlights the diversity of experiences that can be shared among people in the same country, even in the same city, according to the place where they live. Thus, within an overall society emerge 'local societies', where the conditions, networks and perceptions are quite diverse from those of a mainstream, more homogenously wealthy, society. Within these local societies also emerge 'local welfare states', meaning that welfare actions are strongly mediated by local contexts, that is, by the demands that emerge and the specific way in which these demands are implemented from the resources allocated to the measures.

Saraceno departs from this general framework to ask questions about the relevance and possibility of developing locally based actions to counteract social exclusion. The conclusions are clear: local targeting of welfare policies can make an important contribution to reducing social exclusion and to promoting social cohesion. Additionally, locally based actions can contribute also to developing new kinds of urban citizenship. The relevance of Saraceno's contribution is manifold, but we would stress the importance of detailing how national policies may be misguided or ineffective when the focus is on the local context. In other words, more than national policies – or at least in addition to national policies – locally based action is important to improve social cohesion. Clearly this is a good complement both to Galbraith's approach, which takes an ultra-macro view of the issue, and to Gallie's, which considers national policies across countries.

Saraceno's balanced treatment does not avoid the problems associated with locally based actions, which are plentiful. Lack of coordination with national and supranational policies, for example, may be harmful and reinforce perceptions of unequal treatment. It can also create the illusion that no national effort is needed. Local action can also provide perverse incentives, encouraging parochialism and increasing national fragmentation.

Finally, Saraceno warns us about the dangers associated with the consequences of benchmarking or attempts to replicate best practices. Clearly, there are risks associated with copying parts or the entirety of policies that work well in a certain context into a different one. The intention is certainly good, and, as Saraceno points out, can even be seen as contributing towards having more homogenous policies and practices, which could, hopefully, be translated into better social cohesion. However, the point is that homogeneity leads also to a 'loss of a capacity to learn', since comparing diversity is one important way to learn.

Blossfeld, in Chapter 14, the last chapter in this part and in the volume, takes us again to an analysis at the country level, looking at the consequences associated with a global tendency – globalisation itself – in different countries. The main argument is that country-specific institutions mould the way in which the impact of globalisation is felt across countries and, since institutions evolve and change, there are also dynamic implications. Different birth cohorts feel the impact of globalisation in different ways.

The conceptual lever sustaining Blossfeld's analysis is the evolutionary approach that sees the interconnection between the exogenous force of globalisation and country-specific institutions as resulting from a process of path-dependence. Thus, the relationship is neither deterministic nor mechanical, but contingent on history and geography. Additionally, Blossfeld maintains that countries engaged in the globalisation process are already 'learning societies', in the sense that they are facing demands to change dynamically at a faster pace.

This context, according to Blossfeld, creates problems for those interested in making rational decisions. If the dynamics of change are continually accelerating and moving in unpredictable directions, the assumptions of stability and the scope of knowledge needed for rational optimisation cannot be met. In this context of change, national and local norms and rules become the anchors of stability that permit rational decisions to be made. This process, thus, contributes to the sustenance of local and national differences, even though many of the forces associated with globalisation are homogenising.

Another consequence of globalisation that results from Blossfeld's analysis is that there may be an intensification of inequalities. The argument is, again, associated with the uncertainty involved with globalisation, which leads people to make less self-binding decisions. The issue of job mobility becomes increasingly relevant in this context. Blossfeld analyses with special care the issue of job mobility, and the way in which differences across institutions in different countries conduce to different outcomes. Specifically, Blossfeld considers the 'institutions' of educational systems, industrial relations between employers and workers, and the structure of the welfare state.

Blossfeld concludes that the interaction between institutions and globalisation, in terms of outcomes associated with inequality, can lead to two outcomes (which are stated as hypotheses suggested by the analyses). In countries with liberal welfare states and open employment relationships, globalisation produces a growing 'service proletariat' because labour market and welfare state institutions do not shield individuals from the forces of rapid global change. In countries with 'closed' employment relationships, globalisation will lead to a division of society into a well protected and a well paid service provider class and a growing, marginalised class of outsiders.

REFERENCES

Flamm, Kenneth (1987). *Targeting the Computer: Government, Industry, and High Technology,* Washington, DC: Brookings Institution.

Flamm, Kenneth (1988). *Creating the Computer: Government, Industry, and High Technology.* Washington, DC: Brookings Institution.

Galbraith, James K. (2000). 'Technology, Inequality and Unemployment in Europe and America', Paper presented at conference on 'Towards a Learning Society – Innovation and Competence Building with Social Cohesion for Europe', Guincho, Lisbon, 28–30 May; http://in3.dem.ist.utl.pt/learning2000/pro.html

Galbraith, James K., Conceição, P. and Ferreira, P. (1999). 'Inequality and Unemployment in Europe: The American Cure', *New Left Review,* 237(September/October): 28–51.

Glaeser, Edward L., Shleifer, Andrei (2001). *The Rise of the Regulatory State.* NBER Working Paper No. 8650. Cambridge, MA: NBER.

Langlois, Richard N., Mowery, David C. (1996). 'The Federal Government Role in the Development of the U.S. Software Industry', in David C. Mowery (ed.), *The International Computer Software Industry: A Comparative Study of Industry Evolution and Structure,* Oxford and New York: Oxford University Press: 53–85.

12. Unemployment, work and welfare

Duncan Gallie

12.1 INTRODUCTION

Until recently, research on unemployment has consisted predominantly of studies within particular countries. This has made it difficult to assess the impact of differences in societal institutions or cultural patterns in either generating unemployment or mediating its impact. The advent of the EU's Framework Programmes has given an important new impetus to systematic comparative research on unemployment. In particular, this has focused on different aspects of the relationship between welfare systems, the experience of unemployment and the chances of returning to stable employment. The results to date raise important questions about some of the conventional understandings of the nature and implications of unemployment. This chapter draws upon the results of a number of the projects that have been funded to consider some of the key issues that have been examined. It looks at arguments about the possible role of the welfare state in heightening the risk of unemployment, at how far welfare provision can mediate the severity of the experience of unemployment and finally at some of the more recent developments designed to facilitate the 'reintegration' of the unemployed.

The projects involved are all comparative, but they have focused on different combinations of countries and have used different research methodologies. With respect to the risks and experience of unemployment, the chapter draws particularly on three projects. The 'employment precarity, unemployment and social exclusion (EPUSE)' research programme compared the situation of the unemployed in eight countries – Denmark, France, Germany, the Netherlands, Ireland, Italy and Sweden. It used large scale samples drawn both from national data sets, which were reanalysed to provide more rigorous comparability, and from the European Community Household Panel. The 'Youth unemployment and processes of marginalisation on the northern European periphery' study focused particularly on unemployed youth in Finland, Iceland, Norway, Sweden, Denmark and Scotland. The overall sample involved 8654 unemployed youth (18 to 24 year olds). Finally, the 'Youth unemployment and social exclusion (YUSEDER)' study was based on matched in-depth qualitative interviews of 50 people per country in six countries – Belgium, Germany, Sweden, Greece, Italy and Spain.

With respect to new policies for labour market integration, the chapter draws principally on the analysis of the trends in policies and their implications provided by the 'Social integration through obligations to work?', the 'Inclusion through participation' and the 'Misleading trajectories' programmes. Between them these provide information on developments in Belgium, Denmark, France, Germany, the Netherlands, Norway, Portugal, Spain and the UK.

It should be emphasised that these projects are still being completed and their findings at this stage must be regarded as tentative. The chapter makes no attempt to summarise the studies as such; the results selected here are taken to address specific issues and are necessarily only part of a much richer body of evidence the studies provide. Finally, the interpretations of these results for the purposes of this chapter must be regarded as a personal viewpoint and not as in any way committing the research teams themselves.

12.2 WELFARE, WORK INCENTIVES AND UNEMPLOYMENT RISKS

A common assumption is that vulnerability to unemployment and, even more, vulnerability to long term unemployment are linked to deficiencies in employment commitment among unemployed people. There are different views about the causes of this. But perhaps the most influential is the argument that it is the result of a calculative response to the incentives or disincentives for work provided by welfare systems. In several countries, this has inspired an attempt by governments to cut back on welfare payments to the unemployed.

The theoretical drive behind most of the research in this area has come very much from the work of economists. The assumption is that work is inherently a disutility, so that the willingness to work will crucially depend on the structure of financial incentives (Lane, 1991). Where the welfare system provides high replacement rates, it is suggested, this will lead both to lower commitment to having a job and to greater inflexibility over job choice. In some countries, studies have been carried out using longitudinal microdata. Although attitudes to work are central to the explanation offered, they are rarely studied directly. The most relevant evidence is thought to lie in the strength of the relationship between the replacement ratio and the duration of unemployment.

It should be noted that, even with respect to this rather indirect test, the results have been far from clear cut (Atkinson and Mogensen, 1993). Arguably, however, the most interesting test of the impact of different levels of welfare provision should come from cross-cultural analysis. While there is much variation in precise estimates, there are very striking differences in the extent to which national welfare systems protect the standard of living of people who are unable to find work. At one extreme, the welfare systems of the 'Northern' European countries have provided relatively good levels of support for a high proportion of unemployed people. At the other end of the spectrum, there are countries such as Italy and Greece, where public financial assistance for the unemployed is minimal. Clearly, if the level of financial assistance is a major determinant of work attitudes, we would expect to see very substantial variations between countries.

The EPUSE (Employment precarity, unemployment and social exclusion) research programme provides comparative data on the commitment to employment of unemployed people in the different countries of the EU as well as on their flexibility about the types of jobs they are prepared to take (Gallie and Paugam, 2000). Is it the case that the unemployed were less committed to employment than those in work and therefore may be to some degree self-selected into unemployment? The survey includes a well tested indicator of non-financial employment commitment that asks people whether or not they would wish to work if there were no financial necessity to do so.

A first point to note is the high level of commitment of unemployed people in the EU as a whole. Nearly two thirds of the unemployed (64 per cent) said that they would want to work somewhere even if there were no financial necessity. Further, it is interesting that not only were the unemployed highly committed in absolute terms but they were more committed than people who were currently in work (Table 12.1). Only 48 per cent of those who were in a job would have wished to continue to work irrespective of financial necessity, compared to 64 per cent of the unemployed. What is particularly striking is the systematic nature of this pattern at country level. In all of the individual country samples the unemployed are more committed than the employed.

This degree of consistency of pattern is relatively rare in comparative research. It is difficult to escape the conclusion that unemployment in some way heightens people's awareness of the advantages of employment. Given the sheer diversity of different types of welfare system across these societies, it seems rather unlikely that it simply reflects the institutional pressures associated with unemployment benefit regulations. The effect is strong even in societies where public welfare provision for the unemployed is fairly negligible (for instance, Italy). More plausibly it may be that unemployment highlights some of the less visible benefits of employment that those in work tend to take for granted. Marie Jahoda (1982) for instance has suggested that employment provides an important source of psychological stability through providing a time structure, participation in a collective purpose and identity and a regular required source of activity. It may be that it is only when there is a rupture in the continuity of employment that people are in a position to fully assess effects of this type.

Even if there are no general grounds for considering the unemployed deficient in employment commitment, do the variations between countries suggest that the relative generosity of the welfare system may have an important impact on work motivation? There is no indication that relatively generous welfare systems give rise to low motivation among the unemployed. Employment commitment was highest among the unemployed in Denmark (85 per cent) and Sweden (82 per cent), while the Netherlands shared joint third position with Britain (81 per cent). The same broad conclusion emerges if the analysis is refined to take account of the fact that there may be compositional differences between the unemployed in the different countries in terms of age, sex and class. This shows particularly high levels of commitment among the unemployed in the Netherlands and Sweden, while Denmark is fifth in order. This somewhat lower ranking of Denmark among the Northern countries is also noted in the North European youth unemployment project – a comparative study of Denmark, Finland, Norway, Sweden, Iceland and Scotland. But, interestingly, the Danes did not have a lower probability of getting a job compared with the young unemployed in other North European countries, possibly reflecting the success of the welfare system in mitigating the factors that usually reduce employability. Overall, it is clear that welfare states that were designed to provide a relatively high level of protection of living standards were associated with relatively high rather than low levels of employment commitment.

How did the relative generosity of welfare systems affect people's willingness to 'trade down' in order to get a job? The EPUSE research showed that most significant variations between countries are with respect to pay flexibility. But again there is no evidence that more generous welfare reduced flexibility. In contrast, all of the three 'high welfare' countries – Denmark, the Netherlands and Sweden – show significantly higher levels of pay flexibility. In contrast, among the 'low welfare' countries, only Italy and Spain had relatively high levels of pay flexibility. The Netherlands and Sweden were again very high in terms of willingness to change skills in order to get a job, but there were signs of greater skills rigidity in Denmark. Finally, countries were remarkably similar in terms of the general unwillingness of the unemployed to change area of residence to get a job.

Table 12.1   *Comparison of employment commitment of the employed and unemployed*

Country	% committed		
	Unemployed	In work	% Unemp/ in work
Austria	66.7	54.0	12.7
Belgium	60.4	44.4	16.0
Denmark	82.8	76.3	6.5
Finland	57.5	55.2	2.3
France	59.4	36.9	22.5
Germany E	69.0	61.2	7.8
Germany W	48.7	43.2	5.5
Great Britain	78.3	53.0	25.3
Greece	74.8	49.4	25.4
Ireland	71.4	62.1	9.3
Italy	75.6	42.7	32.9
Netherlands	80.4	67.3	13.1
Portugal	70.7	58.8	11.9
Spain	51.7	35.8	15.9
Sweden	78.7	75.9	2.8
EU 15	**63.7**	**48.0**	**16.7**
N	**5144**	**7783**	

Source   Gallie and Paugam (2000), p. 113.

It is sometimes suggested that unemployed women are less likely to feel strongly committed to having a job than unemployed men. Neither the evidence of EPUSE nor that of the North European youth unemployment project support this. The latter, using a well established work involvement scale (Warr, Cook and Wall, 1979) found that unemployed women in Finland and Sweden generally had higher work involvement than men in these countries, while there were no gender differences to be found in Denmark,

Scotland or Iceland. The EPUSE data showed that at the level of the EU as a whole, unemployed women were more likely than unemployed men to say that they would want a job even if they did not need the money (68 per cent compared with 60 per cent). Moreover, this was the case for all countries other than Belgium, 'West' Germany, Ireland and Portugal. The overall differences by sex, however, did not reach statistical significance once country, age and class were controlled for. So the safest conclusion is that there was no effective difference in the employment commitment of men and women.

Similarly, there was no overall difference in the impact of benefits on the work commitment of men and women (in both cases it was not significant). However, if the EU societies were divided into those with traditional and non-traditional gender cultures, there was some evidence of contrasting effects of benefits for women, depending on the gender culture. Women in partnerships who received benefit in the traditional societies were less likely to be committed to employment. However, in the non-traditional societies, the reverse is the case and such women are significantly more likely to be committed. The benefit effect is indeed very different between the two types of society.

The comparative evidence then provides little support for the view that the unemployed are less motivated to be in employment than others and, with the exception of married women in gender traditional countries, there is no evidence that such motivation is adversely affected by relatively high levels of unemployment benefit. Overall the emphasis placed on the dangers for work motivation of welfare systems seems to be sharply contradicted by the evidence.

12.3 WELFARE AND SOCIAL EXCLUSION

Does the nature of the welfare system make a fundamental difference to the risk that unemployment leads to social exclusion? Any assessment of this depends upon the specific concept of social exclusion adopted and definitions have varied very widely in the literature. The different EU research projects that examined this issue also provide a range of conceptualisations. The EPUSE project adopted a minimalist definition of social exclusion: 'Social exclusion refers to a situation where people suffer from the cumulative disadvantages of labour market marginalisation, poverty and social isolation.' The 'Youth unemployment and social exclusion (Yuseder)' project followed Kronauer (1998) in adopting a six dimensional view of social exclusion: exclusion from the labour market; economic exclusion; institutional exclusion; cultural exclusion; social isolation; and spatial exclusion.

272 *Striving for Social Cohesion*

However, it also came to the conclusion that three of these dimensions were particularly crucial for people's subjective experiences, namely labour market exclusion, economic exclusion and social isolation (with spatial exclusion also being of major importance in Greece). The North European youth unemployment project focused primarily on four dimensions: long term unemployment, financial insecurity, low social support and three aspects of cultural exclusion (low employment commitment, pessimism and a passive lifestyle). While there is variation then in the breadth of definitions, they share a common focus on the relationship between unemployment, poverty and social isolation.

The general relationship between unemployment and poverty emerges in all of the studies for all of the countries considered. However, it is clear that there were major variations between countries in the extent to which this was the case and this was strongly related to the specific structure of the welfare system. The EPUSE study, using representative national surveys, found that the proportion of the unemployed in poverty (taking the 50 per cent mean equivalised household income line) varied from eight per cent in Denmark to as much as 49 per cent in the UK (Table 12.2). These variations largely reflected the effectiveness of the system of social transfers in particular countries. For instance, the proportions in poverty in Denmark and the UK were very similar when pre-transfer income was considered. However, whereas the Danish transfer system took nearly 90 per cent of the 'pre-transfer poor' out of poverty, this was the case for only 19 per cent in the UK.

The North European youth unemployment study confirmed the exceptional level of protection provided by the Danish system, even among the other relatively generous Nordic welfare systems. Taking as a measure of financial hardship the number of everyday activities that people had to give up due to lack of money, the Danes were consistently less likely than those from any other country to have had to give anything up due to financial hardship. In contrast, unemployed youth in Scotland were more sharply affected by economic hardship than those in any of the Nordic countries.

While the Nordic welfare systems clearly provided exceptionally high levels of financial protection for the unemployed, there was no simple association between welfare generosity and the risk of poverty. Most notably, the risk of poverty was lower in the Southern countries such as Italy, Spain, Greece and Portugal – where the welfare systems left substantial proportions of the unemployed entirely uncovered – than in the UK which provided extensive coverage (albeit at a low level). This was in part because of the role played by the family. The unemployed in the Southern countries were heavily concentrated among young people and young people in the Southern European countries were much more likely to live with their parents than was the case for those in the North. Over two thirds of young unemployed adults aged 20–29 continued to live with their parents in Italy, Spain, Portugal and Greece. The corresponding figures were only 42 per cent in the UK, 29 per cent in Germany and 14 per cent in Denmark.

It is clear that these differences not only reflected the statistical probability of being poor, but also the likelihood of the subjective experience of financial hardship. On the basis of intensive qualitative interviews, the 'Youth unemployment and social exclusion' project concluded that: 'Whereas in the studies from Belgium, Germany and Sweden, the amount of state support seems to be a central determining factor for feelings of poverty among the affected young persons, in Italy, Greece and Spain this might depend to a large extent on the socio-economic situation of the family of origin.' The caveat here is important. The level of financial protection that the family can provide depends upon its own level of resources and the unemployed come disproportionately from poorer families. Indeed, the burden of having to support an unemployed family member, without access to any significant state benefits, may well lead to financial hardship for the rest of the family. Nonetheless, even if family poverty meant that the unemployed in the Southern countries rarely had access to significant everyday income, they were shielded to some degree by the availability of free lodging and food.

Another factor that may have cushioned the financial impact of unemployment is work in the informal economy. This is inherently difficult to explore in formal surveys. However, the 'Youth unemployment and social exclusion' project, which was based on in-depth interviewing, provides some information about the role of the submerged economy in the lives of the unemployed. Its significance would appear to differ sharply between the Northern and Southern countries. Very few were involved in Belgium and Sweden, rising to about 30 per cent of the German sample. In contrast, in Greece, Italy and Spain approximately 80 per cent of the young unemployed interviewed were engaged in some form of informal work. Most of these were temporary or seasonal jobs; they did not make proper use of people's qualifications, the conditions of work tended to be very poor, they gave only a low level of income and, with the exception of Southern Italy, they were not regarded as providing a desirable alternative to a regular job. While helping people to survive financially in countries where benefits were virtually non-existent, such work at the same time posed the risk of locking those involved into marginal employment.

Table 12.2   *Poverty ratios of unemployed persons in the EPUSE countries in the mid-80s and the mid-90s*

Country	50% mean	
Mid-80s	**Mean new**	**Mean old**
Mean*	**26.5**	**26.9**
Denmark	7.6	7.2
Germany[a]	35.5	35.5
France	23.0	24.6
Ireland	37.3	39.4
Italy	37.1	37.8
Netherlands	11.3	13.0
Sweden	27.3	25.0
UK	32.9	32.0
Mid-90s	**Mean new**	**Mean old**
Mean*	**32.0**	**31.2**
Denmark	7.6	7.1
Germany[a]	41.7	36.2
France	23.3	23.9
Ireland	33.4	29.5
Italy	45.7	46.0
Netherlands	25.2	23.8
Sweden	30.4	29.6
UK	49.4	50.6

Notes: *Mean* = unweighted mean of the EPUSE countries in %.*
            a = Figures refer only to West-Germany.

Sources: EPUSE calculations from analyses of national data sets; Gallie and Paugam (2000), p. 39.

The notion of social exclusion implies that the unemployed experience not only deprivation in terms of poverty but also in terms of social isolation. Research in the inter-war period had strongly suggested that unemployment led to the collapse of people's social networks (Jahoda et al., 1972). How far was this picture confirmed by the results of this research? In considering social isolation, it is useful to distinguish three dimensions of sociability: primary sociability (which refers to whether or not there are others in the household); secondary sociability (which relates to the nature of local friendship networks) and tertiary sociability (which concerns whether or not people participate in local associative life).

In its examination of the household situation of the unemployed, the EPUSE project found major differences between the EU countries in the proportions living on their own. The major divide was between Northern and Southern Europe. Whereas in Denmark 40 per cent and in Sweden 38 per cent of unemployed people were living in single person households, the proportions were less than three per cent in Italy, Spain and Portugal and less than five per cent in Greece. This was largely the counterpart of the major differences in the tendency noted above of people (especially young adults) to continue living with their parents. While these differences primarily reflected the wider cultural differences between societies in patterns of household organisation, it is notable that unemployment accentuated the risk of people living on their own in Denmark, France, Britain and the Netherlands, whereas it made no difference in the Southern countries.

While families in the Southern countries clearly provided much higher levels of social support, this was not necessarily entirely unproblematic. The qualitative data of the 'Youth unemployment and social exclusion' project suggested that in Italy 'there are tensions within the family, with conflict and arguments being a commonplace feature of daily life, without this ever getting to the point, however, that a member of the family is "expelled" from within its midst.' With respect to the risk of social exclusion, however, it is clear that the link between unemployment and increased social isolation in household terms was heavily contingent on the societal culture and the unemployed were much better protected in the Southern societies.

The expectation that unemployment would necessarily undercut the frequency of social contacts in the community was also seriously put in question by the EU research. The EPUSE study found that, except in the case of France, there was no evidence that unemployment reduced social networks. The Nordic youth unemployment study also found little difference in the peer and family support networks between young people who had remained unemployed and those who had been able to find work. But the more striking feature was just how variable the level of sociability was for the unemployed *between* different countries. For instance, while only 35 per cent of Danes and 24 per cent of the Dutch spoke to their neighbours on most days, the proportion rose to 52 per cent in Italy and was even higher in the other Southern countries. Similar differences emerged with respect to the frequency of meeting up with friends and relatives outside the household. Interestingly both the survey based and qualitative interview studies indicate that Germany was a country in which the unemployed experienced a particularly high level of social isolation in terms of their friendship networks. Overall, it is clear that the risk of social isolation was heavily conditioned by the broader societal patterns of sociability.

While unemployment had no clear negative effects on the frequency of informal social contacts in the community, it did have implications for the likelihood that people would participate in associative life. The general level of participation in clubs or organisations was very much higher in Northern Europe than in Southern. But the EPUSE project found that in all the countries studied unemployment was negatively associated with participation, and this was statistically significant for all countries other than Portugal and Greece. The North European youth unemployment project also found that young people who had remained unemployed were in general less likely to participate in a range of activities than those who had found work. While associative participation may be less important than other forms of sociability for the emotional support that people may draw on, it has often been seen as of considerable importance for preserving people's integration into citizenship norms (Almond and Verba, 1963; Kornhauser, 1958).

If social exclusion is defined in a minimal way as a situation in which poverty is reinforced by social isolation, then the results of the research suggest that the link between unemployment and the risk of social exclusion varies substantially between the EU countries. The differences in the character of the welfare state are certainly one of the factors that help to account for this. In countries with generous welfare systems, the unemployed were protected from the risk of social exclusion as a result of the relatively low levels of poverty that prevailed. However, the nature of the family and of patterns of sociability in particular societies were also of central importance for the risk of social exclusion. In the Southern countries, although poverty was much more widespread than in Northern Europe, the unemployed were protected from social exclusion because of the social support they received from their parents and friends. The risk of social exclusion was greatest in countries – such as the UK, France and Germany – in which the welfare regime provided low or very uneven financial assistance and where at the same time there was relatively weak social support.

12.4   POLICIES FOR THE 'RE-INTEGRATION' OF THE UNEMPLOYED

The 1990s saw a significant shift in the orientation of welfare policy towards the unemployed in many European societies. At a very general level, this can be seen as an increased emphasis upon 'active' measures designed to provide the unemployed with jobs rather than 'passive' measures concerned with protecting people from hardship while they are without work. However, the specific forms that this change has taken are quite diverse. In particular, there are differences between countries in the extent to which the measures involve compulsion and there are differences in the narrowness or breadth of the definition of activities that are viewed as relevant to reintegration. A number of the EU projects have been concerned with delineating the specific forms that these developments have taken in particular countries and in assessing the opportunities and risks they provide for reintegration.

In the past, the European countries have differed substantially in terms of the relative emphasis they gave to active and passive labour market policies. Sweden was much earlier involved in active intervention than other countries and indeed even in the mid-1990s still spent considerably more on such measures as a proportion of GDP than most other countries. The variations were and still are very substantial. In the mid-1980s, Sweden spent 2.2 per cent of GDP on active measures, whereas Greece spent a mere 0.2 per cent and Spain 0.3 per cent. In the mid-1990s, the Swedish figure had risen to 3.2 per cent, whereas that for Greece had scarcely changed (0.3 per cent). However, taking the overall picture, there was a rise from the 1980s to the 1990s in expenditure on active measures in the majority of the European countries.

However, while the general commitment to increased intervention in the labour market was rising, the period saw growing doubts about the effectiveness of past forms of intervention. This reflected partly the belief that welfare systems had created a motivational problem for the unemployed that could not be resolved simply by improving the information flow about jobs or providing voluntary opportunities for training. But it was also related to the increased preoccupation with the issue of social exclusion and the view that there were categories of the unemployed that were so severely cut off from the labour market that traditional approaches were unlikely to be successful in reaching them or providing effective help.

Among the new initiatives to increase the effectiveness of active labour market measures, the most controversial has been the trend in some countries towards 'workfare' policies in which financial assistance to the unemployed is made conditional upon accepting work. But as the results of the 'Social integration through obligations to work?' project make clear, the notion of 'workfare' can cover a very wide range of institutional realities. The researchers define an idealised workfare model as 'programmes or schemes which require people to work in return for social assistance benefits'. It is characterised by compulsion, the primacy attributed work and a focus on those attached to the lowest tier of public income maintenance. Whereas sanctions for non-cooperation had been introduced in some earlier active labour policies, the fact that these are extended to those on social assistance is particularly draconian in that it potentially removes the last safety net.

In practice, the project's analysis of the nature of the policies introduced in six European countries showed that not only were there substantial differences in the nature of such policies between countries but that in most cases they diverged substantially from the idealised model.

Although such policies were introduced by governments across the ideological spectrum, the differences in the form they took had to be understood in part as flowing from the diverse ideological contexts in which they were formed. The relative importance of the worry about dependency and social exclusion differed considerably between countries. The 'Social integration through obligations to work?' project suggests that France represents the clearest case of an emphasis on the need to combat social exclusion. Policies were conceived in the context of a belief that unemployment was essentially due to structural causes and the state had a duty to assist with the reinsertion of the individual. In contrast Norway represented a particularly extreme case of an emphasis upon the need to combat dependency. In general, where policies derived from a concern with social exclusion there was a stronger emphasis on skill formation, whereas where the concern was primarily about dependency there was a purer 'work enforcement' orientation.

In the majority of countries studied (Denmark, France, Germany, the Netherlands, Norway and the UK), however, the schemes differed from the pure workfare model in a number of important ways. To begin with 'work for benefits' was only one of the alternatives that people were offered (and even then with a top-up payment rather than simply on the basis of normal benefit payment). The schemes usually also provided opportunities for employment in subsidised jobs (where the person received a normal wage), for temporary contracts in publicly created jobs, for some type of training or education or for other non-work activities such as voluntary work. (These were, however, usually conceived as a hierarchy in which paid work was regarded as the preferable path and training and other non-work activities were viewed as paths for those not yet ready or capable of taking up 'normal' work.) The schemes also tended to differ from a pure workfare model in that it was rarely the case that people would lose all of their financial support for non-compliance. For instance, in Denmark, the sanction was the loss of approximately one fifth of benefits and in Germany one quarter.

Nonetheless, while most of the European countries had adopted policies that fell well short of pure workfare, these developments did represent a major shift in the focus of policy, a new bridging of the previously separate spheres of social policy and active labour market policy. Given the resources involved and the very substantial new pressures that they placed on people, what do we know about their outcomes?

It has to be recognised that 'effectiveness' evaluations of the success of such schemes in returning people to regular and stable work are inherently very tricky to conduct in a rigorous way. It is necessary to handle the counterfactual of what would have happened to the participants if they had not entered the scheme. Where schemes affect only part of a target population, the most satisfactory methodological solution is random allocation, thus providing an experimental design. But this poses considerable practical and, arguably, ethical problems. In lieu most serious analyses fall back on the construction of a control group of non-participants through matching techniques, with a careful use of statistical controls to take account of factors that have been shown to affect the likelihood of participation. Developments in the use of 'propensity scores' have also helped to provide a more convincing comparison between the experiences of participants and non-participants. But the very comprehensive nature of the new 'workfare' policies, which in principle are supposed to be applied to all people in a given category, make evaluation even more difficult, since there is no longer a comparison group of non-participants available. While efforts are being made to find ways of getting round this problem (for instance through 'difference of difference' techniques that compare over time the relative outcomes of age groups that are within the scope of the new scheme and those that are not), it is difficult not to believe that there is a considerable loss of precision in the estimates reached.

Reliable evidence on the effects of the new policies may then be very difficult to obtain. But we know from careful analyses of 'partial' schemes that they do appear to have some effect, although its extent is disappointingly small. For instance, the evaluation of effects of the British government's major 'Training for Work' programme for the unemployed over the period 1995–7 showed that, compared to equivalent non-participants, those who had taken part in the scheme spent one extra month in seven in work and this advantage was maintained for at least a year and a half after training (Payne et al., 1999). This was not simply a matter of a higher proportion of people being hived into part time or temporary work. But, taking the hourly wage people received, it was certainly not evident that people secured a more skilled job than those who had not participated. The rather limited effects in terms of longer term employment stability and the quality of jobs that people obtained in this study confirm those from the evaluation of earlier programmes (White, 1998).

The 'Inclusion through participation' and 'Misleading trajectories' projects raise broader questions about the criteria that should be used in assessing the success of such programmes. It is clearly not the case that helping someone find a job can be equated with social integration. Just as the notion of social exclusion was designed to emphasise multidimensional disadvantage, so too an adequate concept of social integration must refer to people's ability to participate more widely in their society.

This is likely to be heavily conditioned by the quality of the jobs they get. The classic evaluation studies tell us relatively little about the nature of the jobs that people obtain. But if these involve routine work, low pay, poor work conditions, limited opportunities for skill development and job insecurity, people are likely to find themselves trapped in a sector of employment that also heavily constrains their ability to participate in the activities of the community. Such programmes can only be judged to have made a substantial contribution to reintegration if they provide people with the skills that make it possible to escape from the secondary employment sector. The provision of real choices that offer people the prospect of more stable and long lasting careers is also likely to be important for the motivation of the unemployed to be involved in such programmes. There may be a resistance to the idea of participation in a programme that is perceived as a form of 'cooling out', attempting to make them reduce their aspirations for a job providing interesting work and good employment conditions.

There is also the danger that some programmes may enhance marginalisation. For instance, they may restrict the range of job opportunities by labelling people as deficient and thus giving greater scope for processes of stigmatisation. Moreover, any compulsory system that affects those on 'safety net' assistance schemes runs the risk of precipitating a further decline into social exclusion for those who, for one reason or another, fail to participate adequately and therefore become liable to loss of benefit. In short, for any serious assessment of the shifts in social policy over the last few years, we would need to know considerably more than some inevitably imprecise estimates of the impact of programmes on rates of job acquisition. We would need to know more about the nature of such jobs and about the fate of those who fell foul of the schemes.

12.5 CONCLUSION

In the course of this chapter, we have seen that there are serious grounds for doubt regarding conventional arguments about the impact of relatively generous benefits on work motivation; that there is much firmer evidence that welfare benefits are one of the significant factors in the risk of social exclusion; and that existing evidence on active labour market policies provides only limited grounds for optimism that problems of social exclusion can be resolved by resort to 'workfare' policies. This raises the question of what other policy directions should be looked to in order to bring about the re-integration of people affected by unemployment.

If the research evidence continues to confirm the lack of any relationship between relatively generous benefits and employment motivation, then there may be good grounds for establishing a policy objective of providing the unemployed with a level of financial assistance that protects them against any drastic decline in their standard of living. This could make sense both in terms of the objective of job acquisition and of wider concerns for social integration. Greater financial security provides people with the resources for more careful job search and for job search over a wider labour market. They can take more time to find an appropriate job and they have the means to travel more easily to explore the opportunities available. The process of good job matching may lead to a longer period before a job is taken, but if that job is better suited to a person's skills and interests they are likely to perform better in it and stay longer. Financial pressures may succeed in pushing people more rapidly into any job that is available but at the cost of low employment stability and recurrent unemployment. Further, the preservation of living standards enables people to continue to participate in the life of their community and in particular in forms of associative life which may involve financial costs. Quite apart from its intrinsic 'citizenship' value, this may have the advantage of ensuring better informational links with the labour market, and it has the more general benefit of reducing the risk of social isolation and its problems for people's self-confidence and social identity.

A second issue that needs to be addressed with respect to social integration is that of the quality of jobs in the lower skilled sector of the labour market. The major factor underlying the risk of unemployment is that of the adequacy of people's skills in a rapidly changing economy. It is asking a great deal of relatively short term active labour market policies to meet what are often very long term deficits in skill formation. The nature of jobs in the low skilled sector usually provides limited opportunities for any natural extension of skills through the everyday work process. Further, studies of the distribution of training invariably show a very uneven pattern, in which training provision is heavily concentrated among those in relatively high skilled work. As a result, those in lower skilled jobs are not only relatively cut off from the wider process of skill development but they are also likely to lose the basic learning skills that are required for skill adaptation. A longer term policy for reducing the risk of social exclusion would need then to find ways both of encouraging employers to improve the quality of work tasks such that they allow people more scope for personal development and also to ensure opportunities for ongoing training in the course of their work careers. In the event of unemployment, this would leave people with the personal resources for a much more rapid acquisition of new skills and thereby reduce the risks of long term marginalisation.

PROJECT REFERENCES

The chapter draws particularly on the following accounts of results of projects funded under the EU Framework Programmes:

- The 'Employment precarity, unemployment and social exclusion (EPUSE)' research programme:
  - Gallie, D. and Paugam, S. (eds) (2000) *Welfare Regimes and the Experience of Unemployment in Europe*. Oxford: Oxford University Press, 2000.

- The 'Youth unemployment and processes of marginalization on the Northern European periphery' research programme:
  - Furlong, A. and Hammer, T. *Youth Unemployment and Marginalisation in Northern Europe*, book manuscript.

- The 'Youth unemployment and social exclusion (YUSEDER)' research programme:
  - Kieselbach T. (ed.) (2000). *Youth Unemployment and Social Exclusion. A Comparison of Six European Countries*. Opladen: Leske and Budrich

- The 'Social integration through obligations to work?' research programme:
  - Loedemel, I. and Trickey, H. (eds) (2000) *An Offer You Can't Refuse: Workfare in International Perspective*. Cambridge: Polity Press.

- The 'Inclusion through participation (INPART)' research programme:
  - Van Berkel R. and Horneman Moller I. (eds) (2002). *Inclusion Through Participation. Active Social Policies in the EU*. Bristol: The Policy Press

- The 'Misleading trajectories: evaluation of employment policies for young adults in Europe regarding non-intended effects of social exclusion' thematic network:

  o Stauber, B. and Walther, A. (1999). *'Misleading Trajectories': Year 1 Progress Report.*

  o Stauber, B. and Walther, A. (1999). *'Misleading Trajectories': Preliminary Results.*

  o Stauber, B. and Walther, A. (1999). *'Misleading Trajectories': Transition Dilemmas of Young Adults in Europe.*

OTHER REFERENCES

Almond, G. and Verba, S. (1963). *The Civic Culture: Political Attitudes and Democracy in Five Nations.* Princeton, NJ: Princeton University Press.

Atkinson, A.B. and Mogensen, G.V. (1993). *Welfare and Work Incentives,* Oxford: Clarendon Press.

Gallie, D. and Paugam, S. (eds) (2000). *Welfare Regimes and the Experience of Unemployment in Europe.* Oxford: Oxford University Press.

Jahoda, M. (1982). *Employment and Unemployment: A Social-Psychological Analysis,* Cambridge: Cambridge University Press.

Jahoda, M., Lazarsfeld, P., and Zeizel, H. (1972). *Marienthal: The Sociography of an Unemployed Community,* London: Tavistock, London (original edition in German, 1933).

Lane, R. (1991). *The Market Experience,* Cambridge: Cambridge University Press.

Kornhauser, W. (1958). *The Politics of Mass Society,* London: Routledge & Kegan Paul.

Kronauer, M. (1998). '"Social Exclusion" and "Underclass" – New Concepts for the Analysis of Poverty', in H.-J. Andress (ed.) *Empirical Poverty Research in a Comparative Perspective,* Aldershot: Ashgate, pp. 51–75.

Payne, J., Lissenburgh, S., Payne, S. and Range, M. (1999). 'The Impact of Work-Based Training on Job Prospects for the Unemployed', *Labour Market Trends,* 107 (7): 355–61.

Warr, P.B, Cook, J. and Wall, T.D. (1979). 'Scales for the Measurement of Some Work Attitudes and Aspects of Psychological Well-Being', *Journal of Occupational Psychology* 52: 129–48.

White, M. (1998). 'Are Active Labour Market Policies Enough?', in J. Morley, A. Storm and M. White (eds), *Unemployment in Europe: The Policy Challenge,* London: The Royal Institute of International Affairs, pp. 39–54.

13. Locally-based actions to counteract social exclusion: what we may learn from TSER research[1]

Chiara Saraceno

13.1   PREMISE

The fact that poverty and social exclusion are not only located in space, but create, so to say, their own physical and social space which then contributes to trapping individuals and groups in a kind of vicious circle is no new insight. Actually, the pioneers of poverty research, Booth and Rowntree, started with area-based, urban studies, which constituted the basis of innumerable studies afterwards in many different countries. Only in relatively recent decades has the availability of national aggregate data somewhat underplayed the relevance of local, ecological, studies for understanding poverty and its dynamics. The focus on local contexts, however, surfaces in the contemporary highly debated studies on the so called underclass (such as Wilson, 1996).

Analogously, as Glennerster et al. (1999) write, the debate about whether area-based strategies are appropriate or not (as against broader, national strategies) runs through the discussion of anti-poverty strategies from the 19th century on, dividing different schools of thought as well as social policy writers, together with that concerning the dividing line between the deserving and undeserving poor.

We might even reinforce this sense of continuity by pointing out that the characteristics of the poor and socially excluded themselves also show a remarkable resemblance over not only the decades, but the centuries: children, women unattached to a man, 'broken families', the ill and the disabled, the frail elderly – all these have persistently made up the bulk of the poor. Today new groups are added to these – the long term unemployed, immigrants, those having risky life styles; but they by no means displace the 'traditional' ones.

Thus, it is the changing processes and actors which shape this apparent continuity which raise, as well as reframe, the 'traditional' research questions. What is the link between people and space in the experience of poverty and social exclusion? What are the mechanisms which produce a 'spatialisation' of poverty and reinforce exclusion processes? What is the responsibility of business, governments and other relevant social actors in producing these mechanisms? What is the local impact of not only local, but national and transnational economic processes and events? What are the role and impact of locally targeted measures as against national ones?

In this perspective the EU plays at least a twofold role which is becoming in itself part of the research questions. On the one hand, through its policy discourse and its research policy it strongly contributes to identifying research priorities and even to developing conceptual frameworks in the scientific community at the international level. The fortune of the very concept of social exclusion in research (not only policy) discourse is widely, if ambivalently, acknowledged as strongly indebted to the EU's initiative. On the other hand, the Commission's initiatives in this policy area constitute an item of the resources, constraints, contradictions, and set of actors which frame both the experience of poverty and social exclusion at the local level and the policies which address them. Thus, the local perspective on social exclusion and on policies to address it also calls attention to the impact of the EU on national and local patterns of governance.

In my reflection on the main issues in this area of research and policy my focus will be on the following themes: (a) the concept of local societies and its usefulness in addressing issues of social exclusion; (b) the virtues and risks of local targeting; (c) the changing patterns of local governance in the development of policies and the impact of/on EU discourses and policies; (d) the virtues and limitations of 'best practice' demonstrative exercises.

One final word of caution: all the studies analysed here,[2] like most recent studies on poverty and social exclusion in EU and OECD countries, address issues of urban poverty and urban policies. Thus there is an increasing convergence between urban studies and studies on poverty and on social policies. There is a kind of virtuous (or rather vicious?) circle between political concern, research funding and policy funding in this. Certainly the high, and visible, concentration of poverty in the urban areas, with the issues of physical degradation and of social unrest and insecurity they raise, is a legitimate ground for this triple focus. In Allen's and associates' (1998, p.7) words:

Whether experiencing economic growth or decline, all major European cities are witnessing the symptoms of growing social exclusion: increasing long term unemployment, male joblessness and the feminisation of an increasingly casualised workforce, widening gaps in income levels, increasing disparities in educational and skill levels, deteriorating health and life expectancies for the poorest members of society. In many cities, these changes are especially visible in the spatial concentration of immigrant and ethnic minority communities and in large areas with deteriorating environmental conditions.

Yet, one might wonder at the virtual disappearance of rural areas from public concern for poverty and social exclusion – a disappearance which might represent in itself a radical form of social exclusion of those very areas.

13.2   CONCEPTUAL AND METHODOLOGICAL ISSUES

More or less explicitly, all the projects I have analysed share the view that the focus on local societies is crucial in understanding both the processes in which and by which social exclusion develops and is subjectively experienced and the patterns of implementation of policies as well as their impact. It is important to observe that this approach is far from supporting the 'culture of poverty' hypothesis, which also is often based on a local community approach. Even when the focus is on poor neighbourhoods, these are understood as deeply embedded in and constructed by the interaction with the wider community: through economic, urban, and social policies which are developed at the municipal, regional, national and even international level. The relevance of 'place' and of spatial concentration of people experiencing phenomena of poverty and social exclusion is stressed as an exclusion inducing factor in itself; yet this is not taken to mean that this produces a self-reproducing 'culture of poverty' which then becomes an autonomous cause. Rather, the focus is on how these links between people and places are constructed 'from without', as well as experienced from within.

Social exclusion, as an experience and a condition which involves not only lack of income, but lack, or strong reduction, of access to fundamental rights combined with some kind of isolation from relevant social networks, is the product of the interplay of locally situated economic, cultural and policy processes. This means not only that different kinds of cities and neighbourhoods may present different 'objective' risks of social exclusion and different ways of spatialising it (for instance not all cities spatially concentrate the poor to the same degree); it means also that not everywhere is the 'same' objective experience culturally and institutionally defined and subjectively experienced in the same way. If it is true that social exclusion is a social construction (Paugam, 1996), this construction has at least two sides: the resources and constraints available to individuals, families and groups, including those deriving from local social assistance patterns; the cultural and political definitions of the situation available in the context in which socially deprived individuals, families and groups live. Both these dimensions may be shaped at the national and international level – through economic policies, through patterns of welfare regime with the concept of citizenship they embody, through immigration policies, and even through international relations (as is pointed out both in Madanipour (1998) and in the interim report of the 'border cities' project). Yet it is at the local level that they are embodied in concrete practices and cultural patterns: in the way the urban space is shaped and segmented in the interplay between business decisions, demographic processes, and urban policies (Madanipour, 1998; URSPIC); in the way crystallised local cultural and political traditions – as they are reproduced within situated interaction processes and spatial contiguity (see for example Peyton Young, 1996) – interpret unemployment; in the way local patterns of social assistance implementation define the poor (or different groups of the poor) and construct life course patterns for them (Becker, 1997; ESOPO, 1998: Leisering and Leibfried, 1999; Payne, 2000).

Thus, all the projects analysed here share more or less explicitly the hypothesis that such a phenomenon as a clearly individuated 'local society' exists. As is well known, the concept of local society owes a great deal to that of 'social formation'. One can speak of a local society when one can identify specific – and lasting over time – constellations of economic conditions, actors and processes, social and political cultures, including patterns of family and kinship arrangements, of organising and participating in civil society and so forth. This core concept of sociological analysis has proven particularly fruitful for analysing specific regional areas within Europe (such as the concept of Third Italy or of 'industrial district' – see Bagnasco, 1997; from a more general perspective see also Giddens, 1983) and has been revitalised as a tool in political analysis by the highly debated work by Putnam (1993) on social capital and civic cultures. From a different perspective, we can retrace it in the most recent conceptualisations of different kinds of cities (see for example Sassen, 1994).

From the concept of local society also that of 'local welfare state' may be developed: as distinguished from, even if not opposed to, that of a merely – or abstractly – national one. It suggests that welfare states, in so far as they deal with personal biographies and interpersonal relationships, are strongly mediated by local contexts: in the kinds of needs which arise, in the patterns of implementation of national policies and rules, in the specific package of resources which is available. The relevance of local contexts in social policy implementation was first pointed out by Lipsky (1980), through the metaphor of street level bureaucracy, although only in respect of the mediating role of social workers and of the specific 'policy cultures' developed within localised services over time. More recently, it has emerged from the awareness of the relevance both of social services and of the so-called third sector in defining welfare state regimes.[3] Social services, in fact, differently from the standard social security provisions (pensions, unemployment indemnity) which are usually administered nationally, are by definition organised locally, even when nationally legislated and regulated. And third sector agencies may vary widely not only intra-country but also cross-country. Also, the kind of partnership and/or competition they develop with public agencies may vary widely-cross, but also intra-country.

At least two projects I analysed use explicitly the concept of 'local welfare states' to indicate the role of locally situated policies and range of actors in shaping distinct social exclusion experiences, 'careers' and perceptions: the ESOPO one and that on 'New social policies against social exclusion in European cities'. The ESOPO project in particular combines a local society approach with a longitudinal one in order to reconstruct and compare social assistance 'careers' in different cities of six European countries. It demonstrates how only a full understanding of the way local welfare states, through their rules, institutional features, patterns of defining problems and subjects, sets of relevant actors and so forth, may make sense of so-called objective data. Cross-country but also cross-city differences in 'careers' are as much, and in certain cases more, the outcome of local welfare systems than of differences between local economic contexts or of differences between individual capacities. Thus, in the German and Swedish cities of Bremen, Halle, Goteborg and Helsingborg over 50 per cent of social assistance recipients are young people under 29. The same is true for only about one quarter of social assistance recipients in the French cities of Rennes and Saint Etiennes, in the Italian cities of Milan, Turin and Cosenza, in the Spanish Vitoria and Barcelona, in the Portuguese Lisbon and Oporto. In Barcelona and Lisbon, in particular, about 48 per cent of social assistance recipients are over 48. At the same time, in the Swedish cities, but also in the German and French ones and in Barcelona the absolute or relative majority of recipients live in one person households, while in Lisbon, Vitoria, Milan, and to a lesser degree Turin, the majority of recipients live in households comprised of three or more members. Childless households are over two thirds of all households receiving social assistance in Bremen, Goteborg, Helsingborg and Rennes, and over half in Barcelona, Halle, Vitoria and Saint Etienne, less than half in Lisbon, Milan and Turin. Job loss is the main reason for entering social assistance in the German cities and to a lower degree also in Barcelona, but 'other causes' (from marital disruption to sickness and handicap or some kind of addiction, as well as insufficient other welfare provisions) are the main route into social assistance in Milan, Turin, Vitoria and Lisbon. As for the duration of social assistance recipiency, Helsingborg and Milan – the two cities with the fastest exiting rate – show a striking similarity, although the two programmes have almost opposite features in terms of coverage, generosity and recipients' obligations.

These cross-, but also intra-country differences, as well as unexpected similarities are both the empirical finding of the ESOPO study and constitute its research question. Where do they come from and how can they be explained on the basis of what we know concerning the incidence of poverty, the unemployment rates by age, the generosity and variety of social assistance systems in the various countries and cities? We cannot argue that the young and childless are more vulnerable to unemployment and poverty in Germany and Sweden than in Portugal, Italy and Spain, and more so in Bremen than in Halle; nor that the economic and labour market context is so widely different between Milan and Turin as to account for the large differences in duration of social assistance between these two cities; nor that joblessness is more serious in Germany than in Portugal; nor that the meagre Milan programme, limited to a small benefit, is as efficient in promoting self-sufficiency among beneficiaries as the generous Swedish income support scheme coupled with a wide range of social and employment services.

The answers to these questions cannot be found by looking only at how national and local systems construct and select social assistance recipients. This certainly involves looking at the incidence of poverty and at the demographic and social characteristics of the poor in the various countries and in the different cities within them; but it involves also looking at the way national welfare systems acknowledge the poor as potential beneficiaries of social assistance and how this acknowledgement is transferred in the actual implementation of policies at the local level, depending on local welfare cultures, but also on local economic, social, and human capital resources.

Comparative studies which rely heavily on aggregate national data often overlook the substantial differences in the way not only national, but also local welfare systems acknowledge and select their beneficiaries at point of entry and also over time, as well as the fact that each individual measure is part of a more or less complex package, within which it takes its specific meaning. On the contrary, both similarities and differences in data must be carefully unravelled to detect the processes and contexts of which they are the outcomes. In the conclusion of the final report of the ESOPO project the authors wrote:

> The cross country and sometime even cross city differentiation in the definition of eligible social assistance recipients which results from the variety of goals, of policies, of patterns of implementation, produces a crucial differentiation in the population of beneficiaries which in turn has consequences for the performance itself of the social assistance measures studied and compared. Our research shows clearly that – legal and *de facto* – eligibility filters have a much more important

impact than any other dimension, not only on the demographic and social characteristics of beneficiaries, but on average duration of dependence on social assistance, risk of recurrent returning, chances of successfully exiting and so forth.

They have an impact both on reasons for entry into social assistance and on reasons for exiting it. Thus, while exiting social assistance in Bremen or Helsingborg means that the beneficiary has terminated his/her need having gained access to other resources, either through work or through social security, in Milan it more often means that he/she has exhausted his/her allotted time in social assistance. At the same time, since in the Italian cities, but also in the Spanish and Portuguese ones, only the most vulnerable and deprived categories are acknowledged as deserving beneficiaries, the chances of 'successfully' exiting social assistance are reduced accordingly.

Similar considerations with regard the methodological and conceptual problems of cross-country but also cross-city comparisons and evaluation arise from within projects aiming at comparing social assistance practices and local action projects. Thus, from within the project on 'New social policies', Payne (2000, p. 82) writes:

> Where social exclusion is concerned macro-level studies are limited to analysis of the impact of social welfare choices upon different social categories ... or perceived structures of disadvantage or oppression – e.g. in relation to race, class and gender ... This leaves questions of agency and structure unanswered, shedding little light upon whether or how social work practices at local level genuinely engage with underlying structural foundations of social exclusion.

Within the same TSER project Turunen (1999) identifies at least three different ways of understanding social work practice in the local strategies proposed, which incorporate different perceptions of citizens' agency, therefore of their role in local development and change. And the ELSES project has found that although there is a growing policy consensus that 'local approaches need to be developed in the intermediary sphere between the private sector, local authorities, local community and/or voluntary groups', 'analysis of the single area-based agencies and their overall objectives makes clear that there are different values behind the local development process'. Thus in order to assess and compare their outcomes one should first detect their explicit and implicit values, goals, assumptions, definition of the problems and of relevant subjects, and so forth.

The concept of local society (and local welfare state), however, may be fuzzy, or too taken for granted. I point to two problems: that of the degree of autonomy of local societies as such and more generally of the linkages and patterns of interdependence between the supra-national, national, regional, urban and neighbourhood levels; and that of the borders which identify a 'local society'. In both cases there is no easy and univocal answer. Autonomy may be great in one sphere, but scarce in another. Different kinds of nation states may acknowledge and institutionalise different degrees of autonomy either at the regional or municipal level or both (see also Payne, 2000). The very finding of relative local autonomy in social policy implementation may have a different meaning if it is found in a country with a strong centralist organisation or a federal one; or if it is found in a country where there are nationally defined and regulated policies or in a country where there is no such thing. Thus, for example in the ESOPO project the distinct features of local welfare packages between Milan and Turin were expected, given the lack of a national framework. Much less expected were differences in the implementation of RMI between Rennes and Saint Etienne, given the highly centrally regulated character of the measure in France. Even there, however, the interplay between the locally specific social and demographic characteristics of recipients and local political cultures, administrative traditions, patterns of collaboration between different social actors shapes differently structured paths. As a consequence, 'social assistance careers' in the two cities appear quite distinct, not only because of the different social-economic contexts, but also because of the different structure of opportunities shaped by social assistance implementation itself (Saraceno, forthcoming). Further, autonomy in social assistance policy making may hide devolution of responsibilities rather than – or without – devolution of resources and decision making processes (see also Roth, 2000; ELSES). Finally, borders identifying communities and relevant actors may shift depending on the dimension one focuses on: even at the administrative level they might differ, depending whether one considers school districts, electoral districts, or health care districts. And policies may even, purposely or not, redesign them (URSPIC).

Thus, both research and policy projects must carefully identify their communities and their more or less shifting borders on the basis not of an ideal and univocal criterion, but of their specific objective. As the ELSES project points out with regard to the ideal setting of local action:

> There is no reason from empirical evidence for giving statistical, administrative or political consideration priority. Rather, the nature of the specific problems and potentials to be addressed and the principal objectives of policies pursued should have a bigger influence on area designation. The size and internal composition of priority areas has an important effect on the kinds of policies pursued in each area.

An analogous reasoning might be developed for selecting research areas, particularly for comparative purposes: what is to be compared should guide the selection of the scale at which the comparative effort should be set. For example, if it is the options and paths offered to those in economic need and at risk of social exclusion, the municipal level as defined by administrative boundaries seems better fitted than the regional or national, but also than the merely neighbourhood one, although one must take into account the interplay with both in the research design. On the other hand, if research is on the impact of local policy the focus should be on the area identified by the specific project itself, and on the way it interacts with existing formal and informal borders.

13.3   LOCAL ACTION AND LOCAL TARGETING: SOME POLICY FINDINGS

All the studies point out that the value of local initiatives can make a useful contribution to improving the quality of life in disadvantaged places, if not to developing a new kind of urban citizenship. More than national policies they are responsive to locally identified problems and are in a position to link 'people-based and place-based strategies' (Cars et al., 1998), instead of abstractly separating them. Also, they may be more open to flexibility, innovativeness, cooperation between different institutional actors; they are able to bring in resources in terms of human capital as well as of funding, and are by definition the better equipped to devise holistic responses, at least at the local level.

To a greater or lesser degree all projects studying local actions, that is social economic and/or urban regeneration policies specifically targeted on identified communities or neighbourhoods, point to a common set of problems from the point of view of policy making and policy designing. In synthesising them I will largely rely on ELSES's executive summary and 'Good Practice Guide', on URSPIC reports and on the conclusions by Cars and associates in the first book of their project.

The first problem concerns the relationship between specific area-based actions and broader social and economic policies and programmes. Research indicates the risk that government may use local action as a substitute for general, mainstream social policy (see also Kleinman, 1999). Thus, for instance ELSES (but see also URSPIC's final report) points out that 'while the UK has taken a lead in area based regeneration schemes, it is also true that the extent and provision of the welfare state in other countries has influenced the nature of problems and the local need for action'. Cars and associates (1998, pp. 286–87) too stress that 'the interrelations between local, national and supranational initiatives are poorly understood, but it is clear that their disjunction is part of the problem. Thus initiatives which do not connect with these wider processes to find local solutions are likely to be ineffective and short lived.' It should be added that sometimes the working of the EU initiatives itself is an element in this process of fragmentation, either because national and local actors poorly coordinate between themselves and with other programmes, or because the EU itself deals directly with local organisations and sets of partners, 'behind the back', so to speak, of national and local governments. Even while reviewing a small number of research projects in this field I couldn't avoid noticing that some cities are systematically present, without there being any explicit linkages with previous or concurrent action projects in the same area. The impression is strong that in many cases each action has its own organising actors and that communication across projects is at best casual. This points to the overall issue of governance which I will address in the next paragraph.

On the other hand, exclusive focus on local action and local actors without a parallel focus on overall coherence, may increase parochialism and fragmentation and even (re)produce social spatial imbalances. This is a central argument in the criticism by URSPIC, on the basis of some of their case studies, of the specific kind of local action which goes under the heading of urban redevelopment. Moreover, the organisational and knowledge competencies required to successfully bid for local, national and EU funding, may exclude precisely the most needy communities and groups, which lack the necessary skills or cannot show competitive rates success. According to the URSPIC researchers, this process occurs throughout many of the European funding schemes. Also ELSES researchers observe that 'competitive local action may trigger displacement effects or zero-sum games within the urban structure'.

A second problem is also connected to issues of governance. The need for local actions to involve some kind of plural institutional arrangements and partnership arises from the nature of actions themselves as well as from the requirements of the funding agencies – be they the state, the region, or the EU. Although the nature of partnerships varies widely according to national administrative and political cultures and to local societies' features, there are common constraints on partnership working. They include differences in objectives and rules of functioning between different levels of authorities as well as between public, third sector and business actors; lack of trust between the various actors; rigid division of competencies (departmentalisation) within local and national authorities, and so forth. As a consequence, often there are strong imbalances between partners and interaction and collaboration may be merely perfunctory or superficial.

A third problem involves a kind of paradox: since local initiatives are essentially targeted on particular populations identified both by their social and demographic characteristics and by their living within an identifiable space, there is an objective risk of stigmatising that same space-neighbourhood and its population, with negative feedback effects at the subjective as well as wider social-cultural level. As the ELSES study reminds us, the reputation of an area is primarily a social construct, which may be reinforced by the very attempts – at the local or national policy level – to legitimise its being a candidate for a special intervention. Thus, arguing for targeted local actions on the basis of number of social assistance recipients, school dropouts, number of lone parent families and so forth may produce both a negative reaction towards those very areas by public opinion and a self-stigmatisation by its inhabitants. But the paradox may be further deepened by the unforeseen consequences of measures taken to unravel it, such as housing schemes for middle class incomes, in order to attract middle class households into a previously degraded and poor neighbourhood, start-up business centres and so forth. Although these measures can help to improve the image of an area and may be essential for enabling social and economic development in the long run, the ELSES study warns that they are no simple solution to stigmatisation; while the URSPIC study indicates that in some cases these improvements may become 'unsustainable' for the poor, in so far as housing becomes too expensive for them and they become disconnected from previous resources (one of their strong examples to this effect is the South Bank in London).

A fourth problem concerns the fact that many projects not only are poorly coordinated with national/regional policies and sometime even with other relevant policies at the urban level; they also are not clear in their long term and middle term objectives, as well as in their overall organisational planning. They also often lack an in-built system of monitoring and evaluating, which on the contrary the studies indicate as an essential part of local actions themselves: as a tool to make organisations accountable to citizens, as a means for developing forms of collective problem analysis, and primarily as a means of policy learning and policy reorientation. Actually both in its synthesis report and in its 'Good Practice Guide' the ELSES project stresses that not only must projects be based on careful research and understanding of contexts, but that they should help develop a culture promoting learning from failure, not only from best practice, and support innovation and effectiveness in local initiatives:

> An established learning culture within local initiative promotes the reformulation
> of work methods, goals and priorities according to changing social realities, local
> needs and problems. Regional and national authorities have a role to play in the
> establishment of structures that promote interaction and collaboration between

local development initiatives, and enhance the transfer of practical experience and learning.

The relevance of developing self-monitoring and self-evaluative procedures within social work is at the core of the project on 'new local policies', although, as noticed above, it incorporates at least three different methods whose differences and possible interplay do not seem fully articulated. Learning by policy is also one of the focuses of the project on 'policies of social integration in Europe'.

A fifth problem is that of time (ELSES, URSPIC) and of the lack of coordination between the timing imposed by the rules imposed by funding arrangements and the time necessary to build the social capital and the local strategic capacity which is needed to develop successful projects. The ELSES project estimates that the process of accumulating local strategic capacity (networking abilities, entrepreneurial attitudes, trust, leadership and so forth) usually takes more than five years, which is much longer than normal funding arrangements allow for. The same could be argued for developing the human capital of those affected by local actions. Actions which finish too early risk wasting not only money, but trust, social and human capital.

With regard to policy recommendations, the following points emerge from these studies: the need to involve local people themselves in the definition of needs and in the development of actions – therefore the need for a flexible, not merely top down approach (see also the project on 'new local policies'); and the need to distinguish multiple paths into inclusion, not only through employment, however much labour market inclusion remains the main route to inclusion (the Dutch social activation model is cited as an example of an approach which offers several footholds for individuals to get involved in societal activity and recognising variable starting points and needs). From this point of view I would also suggest that what is meant by 'learning society' and 'lifelong learning' might usefully be rethought in order to avoid it becoming a socially excluding perspective and concept with regard to those who, because of their individual circumstances, biographies, age, and so forth may make little of the most up-to-date technologies and skills (see also Chapter 7 in this volume). It should be broad enough to include incentives to, and appreciation of, the development of different kinds of skills, as well as of the capability to adapt and deal with changing social and personal circumstances, to develop and maintain meaningful social relations and so forth.

Other suggestions involve the need to 'socially invest' in human resources throughout the lifecycle in order to allow individuals to be able to deal with and take advantage of the increasing flexibility required by the labour market and by changing life circumstances; the increasing role and potential of the social economy and of the third sector in general, both in creating new (often 'tailor-made') jobs and in local revitalising strategies. From the ELSES project, however, also a word of caution comes with regard to this last issue, concerning possible risks of interference with regular jobs or of distortion of competition. Thus they write that 'initiatives must define the specific role of the third sector between a secondary labour market and the regular labour market, between state subsidies and self subsistence'.

13.4   EMERGING NEW PATTERNS OF GOVERNANCE

Both from the analysis of local societies and from that of specific projects there emerge two distinct, if intertwining phenomena.

First, a local society is constructed through the interaction of multiple actors, some of which are locally-based, some of which are regionally – or nationally – based and some of which may be also internationally-based. These distinctions cut across the most acknowledged one: that between private (or business), public and third sector. They imply divisions of interests (such as that an only locally-based enterprise has different interests in the community than one which has a wider basis), of powers, of cultures and so forth, which also interplay with the public-private-third sector one. While analysing the role of third sector agencies in the cities of the ESOPO project, we were impressed by the different scale they might have (Saraceno, forthcoming). This also yields a different negotiating power with local and national public authorities. The 'Misericordia in Lisboa' cannot be compared to a highly dedicated small volunteer agency which works with the homeless in the same city. Moreover, in some cities there may be a full range of these different levels, as well as actors, while in others only a few levels as well as actors are present or play a crucial role. Again in the ESOPO project we found that Caritas plays a crucial role in Milan, but not in Turin. Analogously, the role of the municipality in administering the nationally regulated RMI is widely different in Rennes, where the municipality traditionally plays an active role, and in Saint Etienne, where this role is left to the local branch of the central state.

Thus, local governance patterns are the outcome of a complex and highly differentiated tapestry of actors, with varying degrees of power, of autonomy from other bodies, of national and local relevance, as well as of reciprocal interdependence. The balances – or unbalances – thus created in turn may be redrawn and the actors rearranged due to changes occurring both at the local level and at the regional, national and even international ones.

Second, this multiplicity of formal and informal actors is increasingly focused on by formal funding requirements as well as by the common vocabulary of social partnership, at the EU and national level. Inter-actors and inter-institutional cooperation – that is a kind of formalised governance – are increasingly not only a requirement arising from the complexity of needs addressed, from an eco-social approach to problems, but a formal, top-down normative and even bureaucratic requirement. This requirement, as well as its vocabulary, however, impact on national and local cultures and a set of actors which are quite differentiated. This might produce greater homogeneity, but vice versa also greater differentiation, which should be taken account of both while devising comparative research on the impact of local action projects and in 'best practice' discourses. The ongoing project on 'policies of social integration in Europe' is specifically focused on the diversity of networks working on various projects at the local level: in terms of range of actors involved, of degree of formalisation, division of labour and so forth. Further, this new requirement, and the resources attached to it, certainly encourage the creation of such partnerships between existing actors and even the development of new actors. Yet, particularly in contexts where on the one hand competitive funding is involved and on the other hand the general system of services and guarantees is weak, they may have unforeseen less positive consequences. In the first place, they may shift the power and negotiating balances between the various actors not only on the basis of their higher capacity to develop and manage efficacious projects, but on more casual grounds. Thus a new funding attracted by the presence of an 'interesting' social partner may deprive or displace for no other reason existing projects and consolidated practices and policy networks. As the URSPIC project observes, for instance, the regulatory conditions set by Structural Fund initiatives often require setting up new institutions, partnerships and organisations at the local level. These are often 'established alongside existing institutions of local governance and can lead to mounting tensions with local government, uncertain powers and obscure decision-making procedures', which are further heightened by an absence of transparency in the allocation of funds from the EU to the national, to the regional and to be project level. This may become an element not only of social exclusion, but of lack of trust and therefore of weakening that very social capital which is the basis of cooperation. In the second place, the very requirement of 'innovation' may encourage the fragmentation of projects and the multiplication – often ad hoc – of actors, rather than the accumulating of expertise which is a necessary requirement for innovation to be founded and socially efficacious. In turn, this risks provoking only ad hoc, if not fake, cooperation, rather than a stable pattern of interaction and mutual learning. Thirdly, competitive funding may create greater intra-national imbalances both in power and in resources: depending on the ability of local actors to cooperate, attract and match different funding, therefore producing social exclusion and impoverishment of social capital. The introduction of competitive rules in the access to and provision of basic rights and developmental resorted may certainly encourage local initiative and entrepreneurship, but must be looked at, and recourse to, with great caution. From this point of view, at a more general level Roth (2000) observes that many dimensions of the new active citizenship evoked by concepts of 'urban citizenship' and of bottom-up participation de facto risks being very middle class concepts: 'active citizenship only for the active ones. Self help, volunteering, third sector politics, "Burgerarbeit", "Burgerschaftliches engagement" are booming concepts dedicated to citizens with the necessary resources' (p. 34).

Other authors are less pessimistic (such as Cars et al., 1998) and Roth himself, as well as URSPIC researchers, point to experiences to the contrary: where not only formalised social partnership, but active involvement of people from deprived populations and environment has resulted in an improvement both of individual capacities and social environment, and of collective agency. It is interesting however that the 'good practice' examples imply not only users' involvement, but also the capacity of local and national governments to integrate and support a given local initiative and to coordinate it with their own policies, thus suggesting that local governance must be intentionally and consciously governed, although not necessarily top down. This in turn requires a better harmonisation of requirements and bureaucratic rules, a greater flexibilisation in relationships, as well as a more adequate timing in decision making.

The Communication by the Commission, 'Towards a More Inclusive Europe' (1 March, 2000), followed by the agreement reached at the Lisbon summit, and by the decision to launch an action plan against social exclusion based both on national action plans and on European cooperation, points to a fresh move in the direction of developing some kind of European social benchmarking (an expression used in the Communication). Also the decision by the Commission not to develop another 'top-down' anti-poverty programme to be added to the existing national programmes, but instead to fund inter-country cooperation in developing common standards, may be read within this perspective; although it is also the consequence of the national governments' resistance – in the name of the principle of subsidiarity – to having a European programme in the field of social policy.

13.5   BEYOND GOOD PRACTICE TRANSFERABILITY

The term 'good practice in policy' seems to have become a sort of mediating instrument between the stress on subsidiarity with regard to social policies between the different levels of governance and the formal goal of policy coordination, benchmarking, and so forth. It suggests the hope of a convergence through good deeds and good examples, the grounds of which, however, are at best shaky.

The grounds are certainly strong for arguing that social policies are very delicate and context-specific 'packages', which involve multiple actors and take their meaning in relationship to other parts of the package; therefore they cannot be easily changed in a top-down uniform way; although one might wonder how this acknowledgement can stand side by side with common and rigidly regulated financial and budgetary rules. In any case, precisely the good reasons for supporting a subsidiarity approach to social policies should make us more cautious and self-critical in putting our hopes in the self-evident educational role of best practice – or better analyse exactly what we mean – and may expect – from it.

> There is no straightforward definition of 'good practice'. Generally speaking, good practices or best practices are exemplary 'success stories' as regards defined criteria such as effectiveness and efficiency. The focus is on explaining why particular projects or policies are successful. These do not provide easy answers or readily transferable remedies to problems encountered elsewhere. Policies cannot be literally transferred to other contexts without adaptation. (from the ELSES 'Good Practice Guide', p.4)

This observation from a very sophisticated and complex comparative study should be integrated with that by Cars and associates: before comparing, and possibly adapting practices and solutions, the comparative study of locally-based projects should be used to raise new questions, to see different dimensions and links, to look at each project differently.

Certainly, one can also learn new practices, organisational solutions, professional techniques and so forth. And the involvement of hundreds of researchers and practitioners in trans-national, as well as in multi-actors projects has contributed to create what we might define a European common social work culture. Yet this should not be over valued. It might even risk being inefficacious if it is simply the transferral of some techniques or some vocabulary, without understanding the specificity of each situation and without using it to problematise even one's own most cherished ideas and practices. Without this, one risk may also be that the most established practices and theoretical frameworks are superimposed on the less established or less organised ones: not because the former are more adequate and efficacious than the latter, but only because they have more powerful stakeholders and proponents. This, in turn, may cause the reverse reaction of heightened parochialism and over-stress on differences, with a loss in the capacity for mutual learning in both cases.

NOTES

1.   I am grateful to Chris Whelan for his comments at the conference and to Nicola Negri for his suggestions at different stages of rewriting this.
2.   I will rely mainly on the following projects among those funded under the TSER programme: 'Urban development and social polarisation in the city' (URSPIC) (project 3037 – coordinator F. Moulaert): a study on the impact of local development and urban renewal initiatives; 'New local policies against social exclusion in European cities' (project 3038, co-ordinator L. Matthies): an experiment and assessment of different patterns of developing social work initiatives in different local areas located within specific national cultures and welfare states patterns as well as within specific social work traditions; 'Evaluation of local socioeconomic strategies in disadvantaged urban areas' (ELSES) (project 3047, coordinators S. Weck and R. Zimmer Hegman): a study and evaluation of the impact of job insertion and other economic development projects; 'evaluation of income support policies at the local urban level' (ESOPO) (project 3001, coordinator C. Saraceno): a study (largely based on social assistance archives) of social assistance careers within different income support systems and welfare mixes. Material and insights are drawn also from two other projects: 'Border cities and towns: causes of social exclusion in peripheral Europe' (project 3048, coordinator L: Leontidou); 'The policies of social integration in Europe: systems of collective action' (project 3036, coordinator A. Evers).
3.   With regard to the relevance of social services see for example Taylor Gooby (1991); with regard to the role of the third sector see for example Evers and Svetlick (1993).

PROJECT REFERENCES

TSER projects documents:

For the project 'Urban development and social polarisation in the city' (URSPIC) (project 3037 – coordinator F. Moulaert):

Moulaert, F., and Swyngedouw, E. with the collaboration of Sekia, F. (1999). *Urban Redevelopment and Social Polarisation in the City, URSPIC, Final Report.*

Moulaert, F., and Swyngedouw, E. (2000) *Presentation of the Second Findings of the Research* (Year one report, 9. 3. 2000).

For the project 'New local policies against social exclusion in European cities' (project 3038, coordinator L. Matthies):

Matthies, A.L., Turunen, P., Albers, S., Boeck, T. and Närhi, K. (2000). 'Eco-Social Approach Against Social Exclusion in European Cities: A New Comparative Research Project in Progress', *The European Journal of Social Work 3*(1): pp. 43–52. Matthies, A.L., Järvelä, M., and Ward, D. (eds), (2000). *From Social Exclusion to Participation, Action Research in Community Work*, Jyväskylä: Jyväskylä Printing House.
Turunen, P. (1999) *Setting the Context*, Magdeburger: Magdeburger Reihe Schriften der Fachhochschule Magdeburg.

For the project 'Evaluation of local socio-economic strategies in disadvantaged urban areas' (ELSES) (project 3047, coordinators S. Weck and R. Zimmer Hegman):

ELSES (2000). *Routes into Jobs and the Society,* Abstract, 23. 3. 2000-04-25.
ELSES (2000). *Routes into Jobs and the Society: Good Practice Guide*, 29.2. 2000-04-25.

For the project 'Evaluation of Income support policies at the local urban level' (ESOPO) (project 3001, coordinator C. Saraceno).

Saraceno C. (ed.) (1998). *The Evaluation of Income Support Policies at the Local Urban Level – ESOPO, Final Report.*

For the project 'Border cities and towns: causes of social exclusion in peripheral Europe' (project 3048, coordinator L Leontidou): the project outline and:

Border Cities and Towns, Second Six-Monthly Scientific Report, May 1999.

For the project 'The policies of social integration in Europe: systems of collective action' (project 3036, coordinator A. Evers): the project outline and:

The Policies of Social Integration in Europe, Periodic Progress Report, January 1991 to December 1999.

OTHER REFERENCES

Allen, J., Cars, G. and Madanipour, A. (1998). 'Introduction', in A. Madanipour, G. Cars, J. Allen (eds), *Social Exclusion in European Cities*, London: Jessica Publishers, pp.7–24.
Bagnasco A. (1997). *Tre Italie*, Bologna: Il Mulino.
Becker S. (1997) *Responding to Poverty: The Politics of Cash and Care*, London: Longman.

Cars, G., Madanipou, A. and Allen, J. (1998) 'Social Exclusion in European Cities', in A. Madanipour, G. Cars and J. Allen (eds), (1998). *Social Exclusion in European Cities*, London: Jessica Publishers, pp. 279–88.

Giddens, A. (1983). *The Constitution of Society*, Cambridge: Polity Press.

Evers, A. and Svetlick, I. (eds), (1993). *Balancing Pluralism: New Welfare Mixes in the Care for the Elderly*, Aldershot: Avebury.

Glennerster, H., Lupton, R., Noden, P. and Power, A. (1999). *Poverty, Social Exclusion and Neighbourhood: Studying the Area Bases of Social Exclusion*, CASE Paper 22, ESRC, London: London School of Economics.

Kleinman, M. (1999). *Include Me Out? The New Politics of Place and Poverty*, CASE Paper 11, ESRC, London: London School of Economics.

Leisering, L. and Leibfried, S. (1999). *Time and Poverty in Western Welfare States*, Cambridge: Cambridge University Press.

Lipsky, S. (1980). *Street Level Bureaucracy*, New York: Russell Sage.

Madanipour, A., Cars, G. and Allen, J. (eds), (1998). *Social Exclusion in European Cities*, London: Jessica Publishers, pp. 75–94.

Paugam S. (ed.) (1996). *L'Exclusion. L'Etat des Savoirs*, Paris: La Decouverte.

Payne, M. (2000). 'Power Structures, Social Exclusion and The Local Welfare State: An Extended Hypothesis', in A.L. Matthies et al. (eds), *From Social Exclusion to Participation*, Jyväskylä: Jyväskylä Printing House, pp. 81–98.

Peyton Young, H. (1996). 'The Economics of Convention', *Journal of Economic Perspectives* 2: 105–22.

Roth, R., (2000). 'Chances of New Local Policies in European Cities – Time for Civil Society?', in A.L. Matthies et al. (eds), *From Social Exclusion to Participation*, Jyväskylä: Jyväskylä Printing House, pp. 19–40.

Putnam, D. (1993) *Making Democracy Work*, Princeton, NJ: Princeton Univ. Press.

Saraceno, C. (ed.), (forthcoming) *Social Assistance Dynamics: National and Local Poverty Regimes*, Bristol: Policy Press.

Sassen, S. (1994). *Cities in a World Economy*, Thousand Oaks, CA: Pine Forge Press.

Taylor Gooby P., (1991). 'Welfare State Regimes and Welfare Citizenship', *Journal of European Social Policy*, 1(2): 93–105.

Wilson, J. (1996). *When Work Disappears*, New York: Knopf.

14. Globalisation, social inequality and the role of country-specific institutions

Hans-Peter Blossfeld

14.1 INTRODUCTION

Globalisation as a process of increasing interdependence and exchange among national economies and nation states is by no means new (Tilly, 1984). However, since the end of the 1960s and, in particular, the breakdown of the political East-West divide, it appears that the pace of innovation is quickening considerably in all industrialised countries. Modern societies are moving towards a 'learning society' which is characterised by an acceleration of both knowledge creation and knowledge destruction (see Conceição, Heitor and Lundvall, Chapter One in this volume) and forces individuals, firms, regions, and national economies to rapid learning and forgetting (see the contributions of Carneiro, Chapter Eight in this volume). Established social divisions of class, gender, ethnicity and nation are fragmenting and re-forming in this process. Core institutions such as the family, education, work and welfare are becoming more diverse and complex. Economic and social change on this scale demands fresh theoretical, methodological, and policy perspectives. This chapter discusses possible effects of the growing pace of change in national systems of innovation on the life courses of people and addresses some open research and policy questions.

14.2 SOCIAL STRUCTURE IN EVOLUTION

Globalisation refers to: (1) the increasing dominance of a single, worldwide market with growing flows of capital, goods, services, labour and information across national borders; (2) the expanding global division of labour that makes national economies, nation states, and multiple cultural settings increasingly interdependent on each other; (3) the rising tendency to set up supranational organisations and the weakening of national ones in the economy and the political sphere; and (4) the enhancing of pressure on the national economy and the nation state to internally adjust to accelerating changes in the international environment. Globalisation is certainly not a coherent process and cannot be described as a single phenomenon. In socioeconomic terms, it entails rather a series of significant macroprocesses that are common to most modern societies: (1) the increasing significance of knowledge and information, as illustrated by educational expansion, highly qualified jobs and the growing importance of information and communication technologies (see Caraça, Introductory note to Part One in this volume); (2) the growing significance of the service sector in all modern societies as well as rising structural unemployment in many countries; (3) the growing need of flexibility, as illustrated by the growth in marginal work, part time employment, and short term labour contracts; (4) the increasing uncertainty of future developments and the instability of social relations, as illustrated by the pluralisation of private living arrangements and the decline in fertility; and (5) the intensified competition among nation states, as reflected in the stagnation and even erosion of the welfare state. The basic argument of this chapter is that these processes vary among different systems of innovation and, as a result, have different effects on the life courses of successive birth cohorts.

Of central importance for the evolutionary approach used in this chapter is the idea that macroprocesses are neither fully deterministic nor completely stochastic. Rather, they are considered as being moulded by country-specific logics and mechanisms (Lorenz, Introductory note Part Two in this volume) and exposed to a multitude of random factors. Thus, even if macroprocesses are clearly contingent and plural, they do have a path-dependent structure in each country. It is therefore to be expected that institutional settings and social structures, historically grown and country-specific, will have a certain inertial tendency to persist in the process of global innovation.

This persistence of country-specific differences might be explained by the fact that work organisations (see the contributions by Wickham, Chapter Five as well as Lundvall and Christensen, Chapter Seven in this volume), institutional systems and social structures in modern societies are mutually interdependent arrangements that have a high degree of internal complementarity. They are best understood as national 'packages' of innovation. For example, educational and employment systems in modern countries are closely interrelated (Blossfeld, 1985, 1989; Shavit and Müller, 1998). This is found in school curricula that are closely tailored to country-specific occupational needs; organisational forms of educational and labour market institutions; various functions of certificates as an entry requirement for particular jobs; particular relationships between vocational training systems and types of mobility regimes; forms of labour market segmentation, or intensity of downward mobility. Close interdependencies also exist between the educational and family systems (Blossfeld, 1995), between the labour markets and family structures or between the employment systems, the welfare states and the fertility patterns (Blossfeld and Hakim, 1997; Blossfeld and Drobnič, 2001). Thus, social institutions can only be properly analysed by taking into account their mutual interdependence within nations. With respect to the impact of global innovation on institutional change, the following four basic hypotheses should be studied:

1.   Although all institutions in modern societies have the property of changing and to some extent they always do, their mutual complementarity and interconnectedness lead to a certain rigidity that makes it difficult for these societies, or particular subsystems within them, to respond in a flexible manner to the new demands imposed by innovations at the global level. The first hypothesis is therefore that the process of innovation and competence building unfolds as a multidirectional and adaptive process which is constrained in the various countries by different social barriers, thus giving rise to strong path-dependence of national and/or regional systems of innovation.

2.   It may be true that the knowledge of the manifold existing institutional solutions and possible social organisational forms engendered in response to new technical, scientific or informational challenges is improving worldwide. However, the global innovation process will only very gradually, if at all, be able to wipe out the marked differences in social structures as well as economic, political and cultural institutions between modern societies. One reason might be that institutional solutions, which have proven to be successful in one country, are hardly ever directly exportable to other structural settings (see for example with regard to the problems of a transfer of vocational training systems: Blossfeld and Stockmann, 1998–99).

3.   This means that regions and nations which have been able to adapt successfully in a given historical period (for instance, as measured by high per capita income or low unemployment rate), may face considerable difficulties (such as rising youth unemployment and income inequality) if central components of this context are rapidly and all too durably changing as a result of global innovation. It is expected, and this is the third hypothesis, that these difficulties – depending on different national contexts – will manifest themselves across the generations in distinct patterns of opportunity and in various problems regarding specific life course transitions. For instance, as we can observe nowadays, the problem of unemployment is particularly severe among the youth in Spain, marginalises mainly unqualified

workers of all ages in Germany, promotes early retirement and part time work in the Netherlands, and creates a kind of flexible service proletariat in North America and Great Britain (DiPrete et al., 1997).

4.   Finally, it is very likely that, as a result of institutional barriers to innovation, some regions and/or nations will emerge as new economic leaders while others will loose their privileged position. In this context, Perez (1983) and Freeman (1991) claimed that most world regions have built their 'institutional packages' all too narrowly around some basic technologies. According to these authors, the increasing expansion of modern information and communication technologies since the 1980s poses problems in particular for Western industrial states that have led the way until today. They argue that these countries still have education and labour market institutions that are built around obsolete technologies. There is a huge strand of literature on this thesis and numerous empirical attempts to identify the relevant conditions for regions and/or nations to cope with innovation, or to develop scenarios about their relative fitness in the future. The author of this chapter, however, is sceptical of such endeavours because new technological developments and their diffusion are highly contingent processes. The fourth hypothesis of the evolutionary concept of social change is therefore that the (in)capacity of different institutional settings to adjust to rapidly changing technologies is generally quite uncertain and often paradoxical.

In sum, one has to assume that each national system of innovation follows its own logic of development. However, these systems are not seen here as isolated entities but as components of larger international systems that intensify their exchange relationships through a single, worldwide market, global technological diffusion processes, and increasing economic, social, and political networks as well as new means of information and communication systems. With regard to these processes, we agree with Breen's (1997) claim that global innovation reduces spatial uncertainties. That means that worldwide networks of information and communication make spatial distances increasingly less important. However, at the same time they enormously increase temporal uncertainties everywhere. This results especially from the accelerating pace of change on the worldwide interacting capital, product, and labour markets as well as from the rising speed with which technological innovations appear and diffuse into these markets globally. Thus, global innovation means first and foremost an acceleration of change and enhanced uncertainty with regard to social and economic outcomes. Modern societies move towards a 'learning society' (see Conceição, Heitor and Lundvall, Chapter One in this volume). This kind of society forces individuals, firms, regions, and national economies to rapid learning and forgetting. What matters in a globalised world is not just knowledge or information per se, but increasingly the ability to adjust the knowledge and information to new requirements. Global innovation is a self-reinforcing process because: (1) the rapid technological, economic and social changes force more and more actors to adjust and learn more quickly; and (2) those who do so represent at the same time a rapidly changing environment for others to adjust to. Accelerating global innovation is therefore also connected to a rising diversity of expert opinions on future developments (see the divers contributions and suggestions made by various authors in this volume), and a growing number of surprises as well as a declining trust in the technical predictability of social and economic processes. These trends also appear to have far reaching consequences for various social groups. For example, young people feel the consequences of growing uncertainty more directly (Mills and Blossfeld, 2001). On the one side, they are much more exposed to them because they are still unprotected by seniority and labour market experience (Blossfeld and Klijzing, forthcoming). On the other side, they are in a formative life course phase where they have to make various long term, self-binding commitments: young people have to opt for an educational track, a specific job, a career path, a particular partner, or having a child or not – decisions which once taken are often hard or even impossible to revise. Thus, in the learning society, for each successive younger generation these decisions are becoming more risky.

14.3   RATIONAL DECISION MAKING IN AN INCREASINGLY UNCERTAIN WORLD

An essential task for future research is therefore to reconstruct important structural changes of life course situations of specific social groups occurring in different national systems of innovation. In contrast to traditional rational choice approaches, which treat the decision situation as 'time-less', new research projects (see for example the GLOBALIFE project: http://alia.soziologie.uni-bielefeld.de/~globalife/) have to reconstruct the unfolding courses of action in their time-related sequence (Blossfeld and Rohwer, 1995; Blossfeld and Prein, 1998). This means they have to use longitudinal data. In this view it is, at first, important to identify the structural constraints within the life course which cut down the set of abstractly possible courses of action to a smaller subset of feasible actions at each point in time. Second, one has then to specify the mechanisms that single out which of these possible alternatives of actions are finally chosen. Third, because these decisions are made by individuals, the mechanisms must be conceptualised as based on the tastes, beliefs and expectations of individual agents. Of course, this research cannot try to model individual action as deterministic behaviour, but rather has to search for regularities among a larger number of actors (Blossfeld, 1996). Thus the explanations cannot be based on idiosyncratic motives of single actors but rather on the decisions of typical actors in typical situations. Modern choice models (see for instance Blossfeld and Prein, 1998) assume rational actors with limited time and knowledge (Gigerenzer, Todd and the ABC Research Group, 1999). Following Elster (1989), rational decision makers are characterised by trying to achieve three optimisations: 'finding the best action, for given beliefs and desires; forming the best-grounded belief, for given evidence; and collecting the right amount of evidence, for given desires and prior beliefs'. Therefore, the increasing temporal uncertainty and accelerating pace of change that come with global innovation should manifest themselves in the following three decision problems:

1.   Rising uncertainty about the behavioural alternatives themselves. This issue becomes more important, the more actors have to make rational choices among alternatives that become increasingly blurred. For instance, in the process of global innovation it becomes increasingly difficult for young adults to compare and rank the various future educational, professional or partnership careers, simply because they know less and less about future alternatives.

2.   Growing uncertainty about the probability of behavioural outcomes. This problem is especially acute when actors are less and less able to assign subjective probabilities in a reliable manner to the various outcomes of their future courses of action. In the process of global innovation this uncertainty becomes particularly severe when a decision requires beliefs about choices to be made by other people in the future.

3.   Increasing uncertainty about the amount of information to be collected for a particular decision. Collecting information is necessary, but costly and time consuming. In the process of global innovation, the question of how much information one should optimally collect before one is ready to form an opinion becomes more serious because the marginal costs and benefits of further information searches are increasingly unclear. One has therefore to assume that actors – whether consciously or not – will set themselves certain threshold limits which, once satisfied, stop the search for additional information (Simon, 1999).

Since growing uncertainties and indetermination increasingly prevent agents from maximising expected utilities, a hypothesis formulated by the economist Heiner (1983) is of particular interest for research on national systems of innovation. He claims that uncertainty requires actions to be governed by mechanisms that restrict the flexibility to choose potential courses of action, or which produce a selective alertness to information that might prompt particular courses of actions to be chosen. Heiner interprets cultural traditions, social institutions or norms as such rule mechanisms. They enable individuals to simplify behaviour to less complex patterns, which are easier to recognise and to predict by other actors (and by the social researcher). Thus, paradoxically, in the process of global innovation, local traditions, country-specific social institutions or national norms become effective decision 'heuristics' for individual and collective actors (Blossfeld and Prein, 1998). From this theoretical perspective, they are not seen as patterns that are being thoughtlessly repeated or imitated (as in the theoretical model of homo sociologicus) but as problem solving tools. In other words – contradictory as it may sound – as the complexity of decision situations increases in the process of global innovation, so does the predictability of what people will actually do. Lindenberg (1983) and Esser (1991) have called such mechanisms 'habits' and 'frames', which they understand as nation- or class-specific ways to interpret decision situations. With these analytical concepts at the individual actor's level we have not only an additional argument for the expected strong path-dependence at the macro level (see above) but also for the persisting differences in class-specific opportunities within each nation state.

The works of Heiner, Esser, and Lindenberg deal with complex and indeterminate choice situations, but they do not take into consideration further uncertainties of an actor's own future courses of action. Elster's (1979) concept of 'self-binding' appears helpful for this long term perspective. In order to reduce choice complexity of long term courses of action under uncertainty, individuals tend to constrain or bind their own future actions, in other words, they commit themselves to behave in a specific way in the future. Self-binding is an effective technique to make one's promises vis-à-vis significant others – be they partners for life or corporate actors in industrial relations – more credible. This technique is especially important in the process of global innovation because it makes communication about what one is going to do under still unknown future conditions more reliable. This credibility enhances the trust that actors will have in each other and enables them to interact and cooperate more effectively than without such self-binding commitments. This is particularly true for industrial relations.

14.4 RECOMMODIFICATION IN THE GLOBAL INNOVATION PROCESS

Self-binding, however, carries a paradoxical character in learning societies. A central problem is that rising uncertainties, brought about by global innovation, not only make it harder for individuals to plan their life, but in general reduce the appeal of long term, self-binding decisions for all kinds of (individual or collective) actors. In this respect, global innovation appears to gradually undermine social cohesion. It weakens the decommodifying functions of long term labour market institutions, stable family and kinship relationships and social security systems of modern welfare states. Global innovation seems to be connected with intensifying processes of recommodification, that is, increases in the degree to which individuals' life chances are becoming re-rooted in their position in the (labour) market (Breen, 1997). One of the open research questions is therefore whether (and if so, to what extent) such processes of recommodification within the labour market, family, and welfare state reinforce social inequalities in various countries.

In the labour market, it is expected that employers will increasingly attempt to use part time, fixed term or short term labour contracts as a reaction to rising uncertainties on globalising product markets (see also Blossfeld and Hakim, 1997). Thus, market risks tend to be shifted from the employers to the workers. A primary aim of future research will therefore be to analyse in each country whether these shifts are affecting particular social groups such as young people entering the labour force, the unemployed, the unskilled, or retired persons and married women who are seeking an additional income based on part time or marginal work. New research efforts will therefore have to pay special attention to changing patterns of marginal employment, part time work and fixed term contract arrangements as well as to their dynamics in various countries under conditions of globalisation.

With regard to class inequality, Breen's approach also highlights that rising economic risks in the process of global innovation are increasingly shifted towards the more disadvantaged and less powerful groups within the labour force. The line of division between these groups and the so-called 'service class' stems from differences in the labour contract and conditions of employment (see Erikson and Goldthorpe, 1993). Employment relationships regulated by a labour contract entail a relatively short term and specific exchange of money for effort. Wages are often calculated on a 'piece' or time basis. In contrast, employment relationships within a bureaucratic context involve a longer term and generally more diffuse exchange. Employees render service to their employing organisation in return for 'compensation' which takes the form not only of reward for work done, through a salary and various perquisites, but also includes important prospective elements (for example, salary increments on an established scale, assurances of security and well defined career opportunities). Thus, workers in the service class can get long-term contracts or tenure from companies and are thus shielded to a large extent from market uncertainties. However, employers will try to shift market risks increasingly back to those groups of workers who (as 'free riders') have profited from the general spread of long term labour contracts during the period of economic growth and strong labour unions – although the nature of their work does not really require such long term contracts. In Erikson and Goldthorpe's (1993) famous class schema, these are the 'routine non-manual employees' (class III) and 'lower grade technicians and supervisors of manual workers' (class V), in particular. Breen's thesis of the relative increase in social inequalities thus conflicts with claims that it is particularly the middle class that comes under growing downward pressure in the process of global innovation, or that social classes are simply disappearing as a result of an individualisation of inequalities. Future research has to explore these contrasting ideas from an international comparative perspective.

14.5   MECHANISMS OF JOB MOBILITY AND THE GLOBAL INNOVATION PROCESS

The growing global interdependence of markets and the accelerating worldwide diffusion of technological innovations (in the fields of media, telecommunications, computing, genetics or biotechnology) increase the pace of change in the distribution of jobs across the occupational or industrial spectrum of learning societies. Such structural change can be brought about by five fundamental types of mobility events (see DiPrete et al., 1997): (1) entry into the labour force by young workers or recent immigrants; (2) job mobility of those already in the labour force; (3) exit and reentry of mid-career workers because of unemployment or sickness; (4) exit and reentry into the labour force by women in connection with childbearing and/or rearing; and, (5) retirement or other long term exits from the labour force.

On balance, the global innovation process will lead to mobility flows out of obsolete and declining occupations and sectors as well as to mobility flows into the modern and expanding ones. However, workers leaving obsolete industries are not necessarily the same people who take jobs in the new and expanding ones. Workers may also move quickly to new jobs, or become unemployed for a short or longer period. Finally, the contraction of an obsolete industry achieved through early retirement of older workers hardly generates any job-to-job mobility. Thus, one and the same innovation process can induce quite diverse mobility patterns within various countries – with different effects on the life courses of subsequent birth cohorts (DiPrete et al., 1997). Future research has to investigate the claim that historically grown, nation-specific institutions not only enhance or restrain the rate of job creation and destruction in a country but also shape the direction and intensity of particular mobility flows in specific ways.

At the level of (individual or collective) actors, nationally distinct combinations of institutional structures will manifest themselves as incentives or disincentives for particular organisational (see Chapters Five to Seven in this volume) or individual adjustments (see Chapters Eight to Eleven). Three kinds of country-specific mechanisms that place restrictions on the freedom of action of employers or workers and clearly affect mobility flows need special attention: (1) the organisation of the educational systems; (2) industrial relations between employers and workers; and (3) the structure of the welfare state.

14.5.1   Consequences of Differences in Educational Systems

In modern societies, general and vocational training systems as well as institutions of higher education are organised in different ways with consequences for (1) the timing of entry into the labour force; (2) the way in which workers are matched to jobs at entry into the labour force and during their later career; and (3) the capacity of workers and organisations to adjust themselves in a flexible way to structural changes engendered by the global innovation process (Blossfeld, 1985, 1987; Erikson and Jonsson, 1996; Goldthorpe, 1996).

Vocational training systems in different countries can be compared with respect to the way in which they combine theoretical learning with practical work experience (see Blossfeld and Stockmann,op. cit.). Here it is important to make a distinction between countries which organise vocational training (1) mostly in vocational schools (for example, France, Luxembourg, the Netherlands, or Belgium); (2) mainly by on-the-job training at the workplace (for example, the United States, United Kingdom, or Italy); or (3) through the so-called dual system, a pragmatic combination of theoretical learning at school and job experience at the workplace (as, for example, in Germany, Austria, Switzerland, Denmark, or Spain).

Theoretical learning in vocational schools is likely to promote a broad theoretical understanding of occupational activities and foster general education – which is important in a globalising world. People in school learn to learn, in other words, to adjust themselves in a learning society. However, vocational schools also have the disadvantage that they do not confront people with real work situations and neglect the learning environments of firms and other working places. The acquiring of practical experience will therefore necessarily be shifted to the period after the phase of vocational training, with normally high youth unemployment rates during the transition from school to work (Blossfeld and Stockmann, op. cit.).

The German-type dual system has the comparative advantage of allowing a large number of young adults to make a smooth transition from the general educational school system to the employment system because this vocational training system feeds directly into the job system, with comparatively low youth unemployment (Blossfeld and Stockmann, op. cit.). In addition, the dual system is characterised by a highly standardised acquisition of job qualifications with recognised certificates. Employers can therefore use these certificates as an indication of particular employment possibilities for workers, and workers can use them as a reference point in defining their social status in collective and individual negotiations with employers. Thus the dual system fosters between-firm mobility, mainly among small and medium sized firms. The disadvantage of such a system in a world of growing change in the occupational structure is, however, that it leads to a too close coupling of vocational certificates and occupational opportunities, with a high degree of rigidity and a low level of job mobility in the labour force.

Uncontrolled on-the-job training, on the other hand, has the advantage that workers are not so much restricted to narrowly defined occupational fields in their later career and that new generations of entrants can be flexibly directed to new and future-oriented occupational fields. The disadvantage, however, is that the quality of training is normally very heterogeneous because training conditions are not controlled and standardised across firms. Furthermore, if workers move from one job to the next between firms, neither workers nor employers can rely on shared definitions and standards with respect to skills, income, and job requirements. This increases the risk for workers (in terms of income, job standards, and so on) in moving between firms and makes it more likely for employers to recruit the wrong person for a specific job. Thus, such a vocational training system fosters intra-firm mobility, mainly in large companies with great internal labour markets, and reduces between-firm mobility.

Finally, vocational training systems differ with regard to the extent to which they differentiate the workforce of unskilled or semi-skilled workers on the one hand and the occupationally trained on the other, and to which they give trained workers the opportunity to climb up the job ladder (Blossfeld and Mayer 1988). In the more or less 'open' system of on-the-job training there are only a few structural barriers in terms of recognised certificates between unskilled, semi-skilled and skilled workers. The career perspectives of the trained are also strongly dependent on the quality of on-the-job training in a specific company. In labour markets based on the dual system, however, there is a clear division of job opportunities in the labour force between the unskilled and the trained, and only the trained have a common basis for further qualifications as master craftsmen or technicians, and also often as technical college engineers.

14.5.2   Consequences of Different Industrial Relations Systems

Countries also differ with respect to the nature of their industrial relations between employers and workers (for example, types of work councils, collective bargaining systems, strength of unions versus employer organisations, labour legislation or administrative regulations). These differences produce distinct national variations of occupational structures and industries, patterns of labour-capital negotiations, strike frequencies and collective agreements on wages, job security, labour conditions, and work hours (Streeck, 1992; Soskice, 1993).

The United States of America (and after Margaret Thatcher also the United Kingdom) are often cited in the literature as examples of an industrial relations system that is decentralised, dualistic and based on free market forces, in short: as a system where so-called 'open' employment relationships dominate. That is, labour unions are quite weak so that workers are relatively unprotected against the uncertainties and flexibility demands of the global innovation process. The consequences of relatively unconstrained competition are that: (1) wages for most jobs are comparatively low; (2) entry into the labour force by young workers proceeds rather smoothly; (3) the rate of job mobility is relatively high; (4) unemployment is of short duration (principle of 'hire and fire'); and (5) precarious employment forms are more evenly spread among various social groups. It is characteristic of these 'individualistic' mobility regimes that an individual's resources (such as social origin, education, labour force experience, and so forth) play a dominant role in labour market outcomes over the life course (DiPrete et al., op. cit.).

Western European countries, on the other hand, are often classified as having labour markets with relatively 'closed' employment relationships and centralised mechanisms for negotiating wages (DiPrete et al., ibid.). Sweden and Germany are known as countries with particularly strong labour unions, while Southern European countries like Spain and Italy are taken as extreme cases of so-called 'insider-outsider' labour markets. In such 'closed' systems, most workers within companies are relatively shielded against the growing uncertainty and flexibility demands of the world market. Increasing economic and social risks are therefore largely channelled to groups that are outside the labour force (young workers who want to enter the labour force, women who want to reenter the labour force after a family-related employment interruption, or unemployed mid-career workers who are looking for work).

This means that the global innovation process in these countries tends to create a new kind of underclass of the socially excluded, while the employed have high levels of job security with relatively high wages (Esping-Andersen, 1999).

The main consequences of 'closed' employment systems are that: (1) entry into the labour force by young workers is problematic, particularly under conditions of high general unemployment; (2) the rate of job mobility is relatively low; (3) unemployment is usually of a long duration; and (4) precarious employment forms (fixed term contracts, part time work, seasonal labour) are highly concentrated among specific groups seeking access to the labour market. In these 'collective' employment systems, individual resources (such as social origin, education, labour force experience, and so on) of the already employed play a minor role for market outcomes such as income and career opportunities (DiPrete et al., op. cit.). Future research has to examine the degree to which differences between 'open' and 'closed' employment relationship systems make young adults more or less vulnerable to the forces of globalisation.

14.5.3   Consequences of National Welfare State Regimes

Modern countries have created different welfare states implying diverse national ideologies about social solidarity (Flora and Alber, 1981) as well as gender and social equality (Esping-Andersen, 1999). As far as job mobility is concerned, these differences between welfare states manifest themselves in the priority of: (1) active employment-sustaining labour market policies, in other words, the commitment to full employment; (2) welfare-sustaining employment exit policies, that is, welfare support for those who are outside of the labour market (such as the youth, unemployed, ill, poor, women taking care of the family, pensioners); and (3) the share of the public sector in the labour force.

The United States of America and, to a lesser extent, Canada as well as the United Kingdom are generally seen as 'liberal' welfare states characterised by passive labour market policies, moderate support for the underprivileged, and relatively small public sector employment.

Norway, Denmark and Sweden are in contrast often considered as examples of the so-called 'social democratic' welfare state model. Active labour market and taxation policies in these countries are aimed at full employment, gender equality at the workplace as well as at home, and a 'fair' income distribution with a high degree of wage compression. Achieving full employment is mostly attempted by a combination of Keynesian demand policies and mobility-stimulating measures such as retraining, mobility grants, and temporary jobs. The large participation of (married) women in full time employment in these welfare states rests on both: (1) the rapid expansion of job opportunities in the service and public sector, engendered in particular by the demands of social services (kindergartens, schools, hospitals, day care centres and homes for the elderly); and (2) the highly progressive individual income tax that makes a second household income necessary for most families if they want to enjoy the products of a technologically advanced service society.

Germany and the Netherlands are often cited in the literature as examples of 'conservative' welfare state regimes. Social policies in these countries are not so much designed to promote job mobility, employment opportunities and full employment by Keynesian demand policy measures, as to ensure that those workers who leave employment because of job loss, disability, or in some cases as part of an early retirement programme, are protected against serious declines in living standards. Countries like the Netherlands and Germany therefore support the unemployed for relatively long durations and in general have generous arrangements for early retirement. This type of welfare state is therefore strongly transfer-oriented, with decommodifying effects for those who are economically inactive. The conservative welfare state is also committed to the traditional division of labour in the family that makes wives economically dependent on their husbands. In particular, it supports wives and mothers who give priority to family activities (taking care of children and the elderly) and seek to work part time. Correspondingly, welfare state provisions (like kindergartens, day care centres, homes for the elderly, and the like) are far less developed than in the social democratic model and female economic activity rates are considerably lower and mostly restricted to part time jobs (see Blossfeld and Hakim, op. cit.).

With regard to welfare state institutions, Southern European countries like Italy, Greece and Spain also share common features. They have developed a welfare state model that might be called 'family-oriented' (Guerrero, 1995). In terms of labour market policy, support for the less privileged, and the importance of public sector employment, this welfare state is very similar to the 'liberal' one. Unlike the latter, however, it is characterised by a strong ideological and indeed practical involvement of family and kinship networks in protecting its members against economic and social risks. This model is based on the deeply rooted cultural view that family and kinship represent an important institution of reciprocal help and that family members should thus support each other. In everyday life, this support is, however, mostly provided by women, with two important results: (1) their labour force participation (including part-time work) is by international standards extremely low; and (2) especially if young women want to make their own career in the labour force, there is a particularly severe conflict between family tasks and (mostly full time) job requirements, leading to exorbitant-low fertility levels in Spain or Italy, for example. Thus, a paradoxical result of the process of globalisation in the family-oriented welfare state appears to be that the extended family is rapidly disappearing.

14.6   CHANGING SOCIAL INEQUALITY IN THE GLOBALISATION PROCESS

Based on specific combinations of labour market institutions and welfare state models, we expect that modern societies will differ in the extent to which the global innovation process changes social inequality. We formulate the following hypotheses about the changing class structure:

1.   In countries with 'liberal' welfare state and 'open' employment relationships, innovation should produce a growing 'service proletariat' because labour market and welfare state institutions do not shield individuals from the forces of rapid technical change. Three mechanisms of sectoral dynamics are important in this respect. First, new methods of production will lead to higher productivity growth in the industrial sector than in the service sector. This will lower the costs per unit in the production sector, make production workers increasingly redundant and increase the competition among workers seeking jobs in the service sector. Second, since a larger output of industrial goods can be sold at a lower price per unit, this will produce rising standards of living in modern societies and a shift of people's consumer demand from industrial goods towards services. Third, increasing competition for jobs in the expanding service sector will not only lead to decreasing prices for personal and social services but also to a deterioration of labour conditions and declining real wages for service workers. The results of these market processes are an increase in the number of low-skilled service workers with relatively poor working conditions and low incomes. The United States of America and, to a lesser extent, Canada and the United Kingdom are expected to be examples of societies with an increasing service proletariat. It remains to be seen, however, how far members of the middle class will also be affected by this structural downward pressure (see Breen, op. cit.). Another open policy question is for how long these societies can legitimately sustain a downward spiral in the service sector and, as a consequence, an increase in social inequalities in the process of global innovation.

2.   In countries with 'closed' employment relationships, innovation will lead to a division of society into a well protected and well paid service provider class and a growing marginalised class of 'outsiders'. Of course, also

in these societies the demand for goods will shift from the production sector towards the service sector as technology advances and real incomes in these countries rise. However, since workers of the service provider class are protected by labour market institutions against growing competition from redundant labour in the production sector, their labour conditions and wages do not come under severe pressure. Thus, as productivity in the manufacturing sector grows relative to the tertiary sector, service workers will become relatively expensive and may, ultimately, price themselves out of the market. As a result, the privately run part of the service sector can only grow moderately in these societies and a large part of the service work will have to be subsidised by the government. Depending on the welfare state regime, the following three scenarios are then conceivable:

(a)   In 'conservative' welfare states (like Germany, the Netherlands and partly also France) the government will be forced to reduce the provision of public services because the industrial relations system maintains relatively high ('male provider') wages of public service work which makes public services relatively expensive. At the same time this welfare state will also ensure that the workers who leave employment because of job loss, disability, or early retirement are protected against serious declines in living standards through generous transfer-oriented policy measures. Of course, this is costly and leads to tax increases, particularly during periods of high unemployment. Thus, an open policy question in this type of welfare state is how long the economically active population will accept cuts in public services and at the same time tax increases.

(b)   In 'social democratic' welfare states (like Sweden, Denmark or Norway), the government tries to achieve full employment through an expanding public service sector with relatively low wages for public employees and a high rate of female employment, in particular. It remains to be seen for how long these countries, under conditions of an increasingly compressed income distribution, will be able to integrate redundant workers in an expanding public sector.

(c)   In 'family-oriented' welfare states (like in Southern European countries), the government shifts the responsibility for the support of the unemployed and other vulnerable 'outsider' groups to families and kinship networks. Here the open policy question is for how long families will be able to fulfill this role, in particular if the extended family is declining rapidly through extremely low fertility rates.

14.7   CHANGING FAMILY AND FERTILITY IN THE GLOBAL INNOVATION PROCESS

The educational and employment systems as well as the various welfare state regimes are likewise closely connected to specific family systems (Blossfeld, 1995). Although a general trend towards pluralisation of private living arrangements can be discerned in most modern societies, it appears that the principal differences in family systems between modern societies persist. In Europe, there exists in particular a North-South divide in the pluralisation of private living arrangements (Blossfeld, ibid.). Scandinavian countries like Denmark or Sweden seem to have a pioneering role, while countries like Germany, France, the Netherlands, and the United Kingdom seem to follow this trend. Southern European countries are lagging even further behind.

One can anticipate that the close connection between the educational and employment system on the one hand and the family system on the other, will be particularly evident in the transition from youth to adulthood, when the parental home is being left to form an own household and/or family (with or without marriage). It is to be expected that educational expansion and the concomitant extension of educational participation of young people all over the world will make the period of economic dependence on parents and the welfare state in the life course everywhere longer (Blossfeld, ibid.). This clearly should lead to an increasing postponement of entry into a partnership and/or parenthood across cohorts (see Blossfeld and Huinink, 1991). The extent to which these processes go hand-in-hand with an increase in the age at leaving the parental home should essentially be a function of the different organisational forms of education and their financial safeguards. For example, in Northern European countries and the United States of America we observe a significant increase in the number of single households immediately after graduation.

Oppenheimer (1988) interprets the growing tendency among young adults in Northern European countries and the United States of America to live in non-marital unions before marriage as a result of increasing job uncertainty among young men and women in the process of globalisation:

Cohabitation gets young people out of high-cost search activities during a period of social immaturity but without incurring what are, for many, the penalties of either heterosexual isolation or promiscuity, and it often offers many of the benefits of marriage, including the pooling of resources and the economies of scale that living together provides.

Non-marital unions represent in this sense a 'rational' reply to growing uncertainty that surrounds the transition to adulthood in a globalising world.

These living arrangements permit the postponement of long term commitments and self-binding decisions such as marriage at least for some years. This applies in particular to historical periods of general economic uncertainty and rising unemployment, when the tendency to marry and have children appears to diminish. Although in various countries such as Sweden or the United States out-of-wedlock births no longer appear to be rare at all, pregnancies among non-marital couples still represent one of the most important reasons for them to get married in many countries, as in Germany, for example (Blossfeld et al., 1999). The strong institutionalisation of marriage in Southern Europe – contrary to Northern Europe and America – translates in the process of globalisation into small numbers of non-marital unions and one-person households among youth, low divorce and extra-marital birth rates as well as into an asymmetrical relationship between the sexes within the family.

> These features nurture the idea that the long stay of youngsters in the parental home in Southern Europe is closely associated with the high labour market risks and the lukewarm protection that the state provides against them. (Guerrero, op. cit.).

Future research has to investigate these changing patterns of family formation from an international comparative perspective and interpret them in the light of globalisation. In particular it has to seek answers to the question, in which ways the dynamics of leaving the parental home and the formation of a family are influenced by changes in other basic life course events (leaving the educational system, entry into the labour force, level of income, and so on). One has also to consider to what extent the service provider classes in the various countries reproduce themselves across the generations via the educational system, the entry into the labour market, and the process of assortative mating (Blossfeld and Timm, forthcoming). Finally, one has to assess the effects of the diffusion of one-parent families (especially in Sweden and the United States) on the individual chances of youth in education, labour and marriage markets.

14.8 DATA REQUIREMENTS

Based on this discussion, one of the central aims of future research should be to conduct comparative analyses of life course changes in different systems of innovation. The countries should offer a range of variation in important variables such as labour market structure, industrial relation, and political and educational systems. During the last two decades researchers in different countries have carried out life course and panel studies, gathering detailed data on work careers, educational careers, and marital and fertility histories. These datasets can form the basis for comparative research on global innovation processes, for cross-national collaboration among scientists interested in dynamic analysis, and for less culture-bound or country-specific research results. However, it is important to improve and further develop these databases and, in particular, to collect more cross-national comparable longitudinal data within Europe in the future. This would help to identify similarities and specific interdependencies between groups of European countries and, where necessary, allow for the study of regional differences within countries so as to trace global innovation processes at sub-national levels.

14.9 SUMMARY AND CONCLUSION

This contribution developed hypotheses on the influence of global innovation processes on life courses in OECD-type societies. Innovation on a global scale entails a series of significant macroprocesses that are common to all modern societies: (1) the increasing significance of knowledge and information; (2) the shift towards the service industry; (3) the growing need of flexibility; (4) the rising uncertainty of future developments; and (5) the intensified competition among individuals, firms, and nation states. These macroprocesses are closely linked with the rapid diffusion of new information and communication technologies, which reduce the importance of spatial distances for all kinds of interactions and make changes in economic and social life faster and less predictable everywhere.

Individuals, however, have to make long term binding commitments at various phases of their life course. For example, they have to opt for an educational track, a specific job, a career path, a particular partner, or having a child or not – decisions which once taken are normally hard to revise. Thus, in learning societies there is an increasing tension between growing uncertainty of future life course situations and individuals' natural needs to make self-binding decisions. A central question for future research is, therefore, how actors deal with this new kind of life course situation in various societies. A major hypothesis at the micro level is that greater uncertainty forces actors to simplify action situations to less complex patterns. It is assumed that actors generally tend to frame their courses of action in cultural terms and use national norms, regional traditions, or locally based social rules of thumb to make their (rational) decisions. Since these decision 'heuristics' vary by country, the expectation is that there are different reaction patterns in various national systems of innovation. In other words, the major question of future research is, to what extent do modern life courses develop in nation-specific, path-dependent ways in the process of global innovation? Or conversely: to what extent do specific life course patterns actually diffuse among modern societies, and, if they do, which ones are particularly successful models?

Of central importance for future research might be the idea that macroprocesses are neither fully deterministic nor completely stochastic. Rather, one would expect that they have a path-dependent structure in each country. This means that they would be moulded by country-specific institutions (in the educational, job market, welfare and family system) and shaped by social class and status groups with vast differences in terms of power and benefits received from society. Thus, rising uncertainty and economic and social risks are expected to shift towards the more disadvantaged and less powerful groups, which in turn increases social inequalities – with higher levels and different forms of group conflict. Research on national systems of innovation has to use a life course and longitudinal approach to deal with these changes. It needs more comparable longitudinal data on processes in different European countries over longer spans of historical time.

REFERENCES

Blossfeld, H.-P. (1985). *Bildungsexpansion und Berufschancen: Empirische Analysen zur Lage der Berufsanfänger in der Bundesrepublik*, Frankfurt a.M. et al.: Campus Verlag.

Blossfeld, H.-P. (1987). 'Labor Market Entry and the Sexual Segregation of Careers in the Federal Republic of Germany', *American Journal of Sociology* 93: 89–118.

Blossfeld, H.-P. (1989). *Kohortendifferenzierung und Karriereprozeß – Eine Längsschnittanalyse über die Veränderungen der Bildungs- und Berufschancen im Lebenslauf*, Frankfurt a.M. et al.: Campus Verlag.

Blossfeld, H.-P. (1995): *The New Role of Women. Family Formation in Modern Societies*, Boulder, CO: Westview Press.

Blossfeld, H.-P. (1996). 'Macrosociology, Rational Choice Theory and Time. A Theoretical Perspective on the Empirical Analysis of Social Processes', *European Sociological Review* 12: 181–206.

Blossfeld, H.-P. and Drobnič, S. (2001). *Careers of Couples in Contemporary Society: From Male Breadwinner to Dual-Earner Families*, Oxford: Oxford University Press.

Blossfeld, H.-P. and Hakim, C. (1997). *Between Equalization and Marginalization. Part-Time Working Women in Europe and the United States of America*, Oxford: Oxford University Press.

Blossfeld, H.-P. and Huinink, J. (1991). 'Human Capital Investments or Norms of Role Transition? How Women's Schooling and Career Affects the Process of Family Formation', *American Journal of Sociology* 97: 143–68.

Blossfeld, H.-P. and Klijzing, E. (forthcoming). *The transition to adulthood in a globalizing world: A comparison of fourteen countries*, Universität Bielefeld: Manuscript.

Blossfeld, H.-P., Klijzing, E., Pohl, K. and Rohwer, G. (1999). 'Why Do Cohabiting Couples Marry? An Example of a Causal Event History Approach to Inter-Dependent Systems', in: *Quality and Quantity* 33: 229–42.

Blossfeld, H.-P. and Mayer, K.U. (1988). 'Labor Market Segmentation in the Federal Republic of Germany: An Empirical Study of Segmentation Theories from a Life Course Perspective', *European Sociological Review* 4: 123–40.

Blossfeld, H,-P. and Prein, G. (1998). *Rational Choice Theory and Large-Scale Data Analysis,* Boulder, CO: Westview Press.

Blossfeld, H.-P. and Rohwer, G. (1995). *Techniques of Event History Modeling. New Approaches to Causal Analysis*, Mahwah, NJ: Erlbaum.

Blossfeld, H.-P. and Stockmann, R. (1998–99). *Globalization and Changes in Vocational Training Systems in Developing and Advanced Industrialized Societies, Vols I–III*, Armonk, NY: Sharpe (Vols 28 (4), 29 (1), and 29 (2) of the International Journal of Sociology).

Blossfeld, H.-P. and Timm, A. (forthcoming). *Who Marries Whom? Educational Systems as Marriage Markets in Modern Societies: A Comparison of Thirteen Countries*, Oxford: Oxford University Press.

Breen, R. (1997). 'Risk Recommodification and Stratification', *Sociology* 31: 473–89.

DiPrete, T., de Graaf, P., Luijkx, R., Tåhlin, M. and Blossfeld, H.-P. (1997). 'Structural Change and Career Mobility in the Netherlands, Germany, Sweden and the United States', *American Journal of Sociology* 103: 318–58.

Elster, J. (1979). *Ulysses and the Sirens,* Cambridge: Cambridge University Press.

Elster, J. (1989). Solomonic Judgements: Studies in the Limitations of Rationality, New York: New York University Press.

Erikson, R. and Goldthorpe, J.H. (1993). *The Constant Flux: a Study of Class Mobility in Industrial Societies*, Oxford: Clarendon Press.

Erikson, R. and Jonsson, J.O. (1996). *Can Education be Equalized?*, Boulder, CO: Westview Press.

Esping-Andersen, G. (1999). *Social Foundations of Postindustrial Societies*, Oxford: Oxford University Press.

Esser, H. (1991). *Alltagshandeln und Verstehen*, Tübingen: Mohr.

Flora, P. and Alber, J. (1981). 'The Development of Welfare States in Western Europe', in P. Flora and A.J. Heidenheimer (eds), *The Development of Welfare States in Europe and America*, New Brunswick, NJ and London: Transaction Books, pp. 37–80.

Freeman, C. (1991). 'The Nature of Innovation and the Evolution of the Productive System', in *Technology and Productivity*, Paris: OECD, pp. 303–14.

Gigerenzer, G., Todd, P.M. and the ABC Research Group (1999). *Simple Heuristics That Make Us Smart*, Oxford: Oxford University Press.

Goldthorpe, J.H. (1996). *Class Analysis and the Reorientation of Class Theory – the Case of Persisting Differentials in Educational Attainment*, Oxford: Nuffield College.

Guerrero, T.J. (1995). 'Legitimation durch Sozialpolitik? Die spanische Beschäftigungskrise und die Theorie des Wohlfahrtstaates', *Kölner Zeitschrift für Soziologie und Sozialpsychologie* 47: 727–52.

Heiner, R.A. (1983). 'The Origin of Predictable Behavior', *The American Economic Review* 73: 560–95.

Lindenberg, S. (1983). 'Utility and Morality', *Kyklos* 36: 450–68.

Mills, M. and Blossfeld, H.-P. (2001). 'Globalization and Changes in the Early Life Course', paper presented at the EURESCO conference on 'European Societies or European Society?', Kerkrade, The Netherlands, 5–10 October 2001.

Oppenheimer, V.K. (1988). 'A Theory of Marriage Timing', *American Journal of Sociology* 94: 563–91.

Perez, C. (1983). 'Structural Change and the Assimilation of New Technology in the Economic and Social System', *Futures* 15: 357–75.

Shavit, Y. and Müller, W. (1998). *From School to Work*, Oxford: Oxford University Press.

Simon, H.A. (1999). 'Invariants in Human Behavior', *Annual Review of Psychology* 41: 1–19.

Soskice, D. (1993). 'The Institutional Infrastructure for International Competitiveness: a Comparative Analysis of the UK and Germany', in A.B. Atkinson and R. Brunetta (eds), *The Economics of the New Europe*, Basingstoke: Macmillan, pp. 45–66.

Streeck, W. (1992). *Social Institutions and Economic Performance. Studies in Industrial Relations in Advance Capitalist Economies*, London: Sage.

Tilly, C. (1984). *Big Structures, Large Processes, Huge Comparisons*, New York: Russell Sage Foundation.

Name index

Subject index